Impact of Digitalization on Reporting, Tax Avoidance, Accounting, and Green Finance

Ahmad Alqatan
Arab Open University, Kuwait

Khaled Hussainey
University of Portsmouth, UK

Mounira Hamed
University of Tunis El Manar, Tunisia

Kameleddine Benameur
American University of Kuwait, Kuwait

IGI Global
PUBLISHER of TIMELY KNOWLEDGE

A volume in the Advances
in Finance, Accounting, and
Economics (AFAE) Book Series

Published in the United States of America by
IGI Global
Business Science Reference (an imprint of IGI Global)
701 E. Chocolate Avenue
Hershey PA, USA 17033
Tel: 717-533-8845
Fax: 717-533-8661
E-mail: cust@igi-global.com
Web site: http://www.igi-global.com

Library of Congress Cataloging-in-Publication Data

Names: Alqatan, Ahmad J., 1988- editor. | Hussainey, Khaled, 1972- editor. | Hamed, Mounira, 1973- editor. | Benameur, Kameleddine, 1962- editor.
Title: Impact of digitalization on reporting, tax avoidance, accounting, and green finance / edited by Ahmad Alqatan, Khaled Hussainey, Mounira Hamed, Kameleddine Benameur.
Description: Hershey, PA : Business Science Reference, 2024. | Includes bibliographical references. | Summary: "The objective of the book is to provide a comprehensive and insightful exploration of the impact of digitalization on four key areas: reporting, tax avoidance, accounting, and green finance"-- Provided by publisher.
Identifiers: LCCN 2023050883 (print) | LCCN 2023050884 (ebook) | ISBN 9798369316788 (hardcover) | ISBN 9798369316795 (ebook)
Subjects: LCSH: Accounting--Data processing. | Finance--Data processing. | Sustainable development--Data processing.
Classification: LCC HF5679 .I44 2024 (print) | LCC HF5679 (ebook) | DDC 657.0285--dc23/eng/20231213
LC record available at https://lccn.loc.gov/2023050883
LC ebook record available at https://lccn.loc.gov/2023050884

This book is published in the IGI Global book series Advances in Finance, Accounting, and Economics (AFAE) (ISSN: 2327-5677; eISSN: 2327-5685)

British Cataloguing in Publication Data
A Cataloguing in Publication record for this book is available from the British Library.

Advances in Finance, Accounting, and Economics (AFAE) Book Series

ISSN:2327-5677
EISSN:2327-5685

Editor-in-Chief: Ahmed Driouchi, Al Akhawayn University, Morocco

MISSION

In our changing economic and business environment, it is important to consider the financial changes occurring internationally as well as within individual organizations and business environments. Understanding these changes as well as the factors that influence them is crucial in preparing for our financial future and ensuring economic sustainability and growth.

The **Advances in Finance, Accounting, and Economics (AFAE)** book series aims to publish comprehensive and informative titles in all areas of economics and economic theory, finance, and accounting to assist in advancing the available knowledge and providing for further research development in these dynamic fields.

COVERAGE

- Finance
- Taxes
- Behavioral Economics
- E-Accounting
- Macroeconomics
- Economic Indices and Quantitative Economic Methods
- Applied Finance
- Internet Banking
- Wages and Employment
- Economic Policy

IGI Global is currently accepting manuscripts for publication within this series. To submit a proposal for a volume in this series, please contact our Acquisition Editors at Acquisitions@igi-global.com or visit: http://www.igi-global.com/publish/.

The Advances in Finance, Accounting, and Economics (AFAE) Book Series (ISSN 2327-5677) is published by IGI Global, 701 E. Chocolate Avenue, Hershey, PA 17033-1240, USA, www.igi-global.com. This series is composed of titles available for purchase individually; each title is edited to be contextually exclusive from any other title within the series. For pricing and ordering information please visit http://www.igi-global.com/book-series/advances-finance-accounting-economics/73685. Postmaster: Send all address changes to above address.

Titles in this Series

For a list of additional titles in this series, please visit:
http://www.igi-global.com/book-series/advances-finance-accounting-economics/73685

Financial Inclusion, Sustainability, and the Influence of Religion and Technology
Awais Ur Rehman (Faculty of Management Sciences, University of Central Punjab, Pakistan) and Arsalan Haneef Malik (College of Business Management, Department of Accounting and Finance, Institute of Business Management (IoBM), Karachi, Pakistan)
Business Science Reference • copyright 2024 • 324pp • H/C (ISBN: 9798369314753) • US $270.00 (our price)

Recent Developments in Financial Management and Economics
Abdelkader Mohamed Sghaier Derbali (Taibah University, Saudi Arabia)
Business Science Reference • copyright 2024 • 436pp • H/C (ISBN: 9798369326831) • US $325.00 (our price)

Issues of Sustainability in AI and New-Age Thematic Investing
Mohammad Irfan (NSB Academy, India) Khaled Hussainey (University of Portsmouth, UK) Syed Ahmad Chan Bukhari (St. John's University, USA) and Yunyoung Nam (Department of Computer Science and Engineering, Soonchunhyang University, South Korea)
Business Science Reference • copyright 2024 • 295pp • H/C (ISBN: 9798369332825) • US $325.00 (our price)

Exploring Central Bank Digital Currencies Concepts, Frameworks, Models, and Challenges
Guneet Kaur (University of Stirling, UK) Pooja Lekhi (University Canada West, Canada) and Simriti Popli (Kaplan International College, UK)
Business Science Reference • copyright 2024 • 359pp • H/C (ISBN: 9798369318829) • US $325.00 (our price)

Harnessing Blockchain-Digital Twin Fusion for Sustainable Investments
Syed Hasan Jafar (Woxsen University, India) Raul Villamarin Rodriguez (Woxsen University, India) Hemachandran Kannan (Woxsen University, India) Shakeb Akhtar (Woxsen University, India) and Philipp Plugmann (SRH Hochschule für Gesundheit Gera, Germany)
Business Science Reference • copyright 2024 • 441pp • H/C (ISBN: 9798369318782) • US $290.00 (our price)

For an entire list of titles in this series, please visit:
http://www.igi-global.com/book-series/advances-finance-accounting-economics/73685

IGI Global
PUBLISHER of TIMELY KNOWLEDGE

701 East Chocolate Avenue, Hershey, PA 17033, USA
Tel: 717-533-8845 x100 • Fax: 717-533-8661
E-Mail: cust@igi-global.com • www.igi-global.com

Table of Contents

Detailed Table of Contents

internet accounting, spreadsheets, and others. Accounting frameworks like the resource-event-agent (REA) system, triple-entry accounting (TEA), and blockchain have been developed to improve upon the traditional double-entry method. The study looks at and relies on the narrative investigation of the previous studies. This study proposes a novel framework that improves the effectiveness, openness, and safety of financial transactions using blockchain technology and makes a significant contribution to the developing area of blockchain-based accounting. Highlighted in this research are the REA structure's contributions to the TEA framework, a review of studies on the integration of REAs and TEAs with blockchain, and the advantages and potential framework for the implementation of TEA.

Morocco heavily relies on tax revenues; however, a persistent 6.7% GDP gap between potential and actual tax revenues (2013-2017) highlights the challenge of widespread tax fraud. With a growing taxpayer base and a limited number of tax inspectors, Morocco faces a structural deficit in tax control. In response, a comprehensive digital transformation of tax processes was initiated. This chapter delves into the profound impact of digitalization on tax control through lexicometric analysis on interviews conducted with tax inspectors, facilitated by the IRAMUTEQ software. The research findings reveal a substantial enhancement in the performance of tax control. Despite this positive shift, the study underscores potential impediments that require a coordinated effort from all stakeholders involved. Beyond offering practical insights for authorities, this research contributes valuable lessons for developing nations grappling with the multifaceted challenges of revenue collection in the digital age concerning the pivotal role of digitalization in modernizing tax control practices.

Oman holds a prominent location in the Middle East and North Africa (MENA) region. There were several structural reforms took place to enhance the adoption and implementation of smooth governance in Oman from the inception of the corporate governance structure. This study aims to review and document the digital reporting of accounting information of these Omani companies listed at the Muscat Stock Exchange (MSX) and registered with the Capital Market Authority (CMA). The purpose of the study is to highlight the adaptation of digital accounting reporting of listed companies at MSX and registered companies at CMA, its benefits, and the current challenges. From 2020, all the listed, licensed, and accredited companies by MSX and CMA were required to report their financial information digitally by using XBRL taxonomy. The research provides useful insight to regulators, decision-makers, businesses, and the academic world by filling the gap in the literature.

This chapter synthesises and critically reviews the existing research on digitalisation in accounting, particularly artificial intelligence (AI) and blockchain technology (BT). Drawing on a systematic literature review, the author of this chapter attempts to identify the risks and opportunities associated with the development and use of digitalisation in the accounting profession. In this chapter, the author used Google Scholar, Scopus, and Web of Science databases as sources for article collection. The author collected a sample of 160 articles from 2010 to 2023 through keyword searches. He employed a thematic analysis and identified six themes (i.e., creativity and openness; strategic partnership; smart contract; information governance, transparency, and trust; social, economic, and regulatory issues; and audit practices). The findings of this chapter are consistent with the theory of disruptive innovation. The findings reveal that AI and BT are disruptive technologies that will evolve over the years and, hence, disrupt and transform the business landscape.

This research aims to study the effect of the digitalisation of companies on audit quality and corporate governance in a sample of 150 Swedish companies from 2017-2022. The authors collected the data from the database of annual reports and reference documents available on the companies' websites. The results show that the digitalisation of companies has a positive and significant effect on audit quality. Similarly, the authors have demonstrated that the digitalisation of companies positively impacts corporate governance. In this sense, an effective digitalisation strategy will likely increase the quality of information and governance mechanisms.

Through the mechanics of contagion, bank failures not only cause economic agents to suffer financial losses but also cause the entire financial system to become unstable. As a result, the bank needs to safeguard itself against various threats. This study analyses the relationship between the diversification of banking activities and governance mechanisms while taking into account the concept of ownership structure in banking firms to explain the level of risk. The authors took the sample from 10 main Tunisian banks listed on the Tunis Stock Exchange for the period 2002 to 2020. The result of the FGLS regression showed that the separation between traditional and non-traditional activity has a favourable effect on banking stability because the diversification of activities allows banks to establish synergies between the different sectors, thus increasing the level of stability of banking firms by reducing the level of risk. The authors found that the financial strength of Tunisian banks is positively influenced by the degree of diversification of the banks' sources of income.

This chapter provides a comprehensive exploration of the intersection between digitalization and green finance, emphasizing its pivotal role in advancing environmental sustainability. Through a meticulous literature review, the authors identify the current state of digital green finance, highlighting both its transformative potential and the challenges it presents. The chapter offers a deeper understanding of the existing issues, controversies, and problems faced by practitioners and stakeholders in this domain. In response, the authors present well-reasoned solutions and recommendations, drawing from empirical evidence and innovative thinking. The chapter also ventures into future research directions, discussing emerging technologies and methodologies that promise to redefine the landscape of digital green finance. In conclusion, the authors reflect on the broader socio-economic and environmental implications of integrating digital tools in green finance, emphasizing the critical role they play in shaping a sustainable and resilient future.

This chapter delves into the Moroccan tax system's challenges, underscored by a significant tax shortfall as reported by the IMF. At its core, the study explores the nexus between digitalization in tax administration and taxpayer behavior, particularly focusing on tax avoidance. Conducted within the Moroccan reform context, the research utilizes qualitative insights from interviews with 30 tax administrators. The findings highlight that while digitalization and service facilitation promote tax compliance, a lack of trust and transparency can exacerbate tax avoidance. The study emphasizes the critical need for comprehensive tax reform in Morocco, targeting fairness and a robust relationship between tax authorities and taxpayers. Such reforms are essential to foster a business-friendly environment conducive to investment. This research contributes to the understanding of digital governance's role in tax administration and its potential to influence taxpayer behavior.

The use of digital financial technologies (DFTs) for green finance has been evolving and has created new risks and challenges for the environment and users. This chapter aims to explore the risks, challenges, and opportunities that are associated with the use of DFTs for green finance. In this chapter, authors used Google Scholar, Scopus, and Web of Science databases as sources for article collection. They initially collected over 245 articles for the period 2000 to 2023 through keyword searches, and their final sample consisted of 183 articles. They applied a thematic analysis and explored four themes (i.e., green innovation; green investment and sustainability; a data-driven approach; and the risks and challenges of using DFTs for green finance). In this chapter, the authors found that the DFTs offer several opportunities for green finance. However, the DFTs also pose several risks and challenges (such as cybercrime, fraud, scams, tax evasion, capital-intensive technologies, a lack of awareness, uncertain policies, and an absence of protection mechanisms) that need to be addressed.

Digitalization brings significant changes to the world, particularly in industries where information technology is essential. Accounting is one profession that has benefited from digital developments. The goal of this chapter is to synthesize recent academic studies on accounting digitalization and provide some suggestions for future research.

Preface

In the last few decades, the world has witnessed a technological revolution that has fundamentally transformed various aspects of our daily lives. This revolution, known as digitalization, has brought significant changes to multiple industries, including finance and accounting. As the digital world continues to evolve, it becomes crucial to understand and explore the impact of digitalization on reporting, tax avoidance, accounting, and green finance.

This book aims to delve into the intricate relationship between digitalization and these four pillars of the financial landscape. It is evident that digitalization has revolutionized reporting, provided real-time information, and enabled instant access to financial data. The advent of sophisticated accounting software and advanced data analytics has streamlined financial reporting processes, bringing about greater efficiency and accuracy. However, this transformation is not without its challenges, such as concerns surrounding data security, privacy, and the potential skewing of financial information.

Furthermore, the emergence of digitalization has not only influenced reporting but also altered the landscape of tax avoidance. With the rise of digital platforms and e-commerce, tax avoidance schemes have become more complex and pervasive. The ease of conducting international business transactions through digital channels has created both opportunities for tax planning and new challenges for taxing authorities. This book will explore the various forms and implications of digital tax avoidance, highlighting the need for international collaboration and regulatory responses.

Accounting practices have also been transformed by digitalization, as cloud-based systems and artificial intelligence are introduced into financial management. The automation of routine accounting tasks has not only increased efficiency but also raised concerns about job displacement and the evolving role of accountants. This book will explore the future of accounting in the digital age and the necessary skills and competencies required in this rapidly changing landscape.

Lastly, digitalization has had a profound impact on the concept of green finance, allowing for innovative and sustainable financial practices. The digitalization of financial services has facilitated the development of green investment products, enhanced transparency in environmental disclosure, and enabled more effective monitoring of green projects. In this book, we will explore the potential of digitalization in driving the transition to a greener and more sustainable economy.

The global relevance of International Financial Reporting Standards (IFRS) Taxonomy in the realm of digital corporate reporting is explored, providing insights into the expanded roles of auditors and compliance specialists. As the chapters unfold, readers will traverse the evolving expectations in worldwide accounting, delve into the complexities of tax control in nations like Morocco and Oman, and scrutinize the intersection of digitalization and green finance. Each contribution sheds light on the challenges, opportunities, and transformative potentials within the domains of reporting, tax avoidance, accounting, and green finance, offering a comprehensive overview of the digital frontier in the financial landscape.

Chapter 1 provides a comprehensive exploration of the significant changes witnessed in the auditing and compliance sectors due to the digital revolution. Technological advancements are scrutinized for their impact on financial reporting and regulatory compliance. The adoption of the International Financial Reporting Standards (IFRS) Taxonomy in digital corporate reporting takes center stage, shedding light on how auditors and compliance specialists have adapted to their expanded roles in managing digital financial data. The potential and challenges of the digital era are discussed, emphasizing the benefits of automation in data analysis, risk assessment, and compliance monitoring.

Delving beyond the early success stories of ERP accounting and internet accounting, Chapter 2 explores the evolving expectations for substantial value in accounting practices worldwide. Accounting frameworks such as the Resource-Event-Agent (REA) system, triple-entry accounting (TEA), and blockchain are introduced as transformative elements. The chapter employs a narrative investigation of previous studies and proposes a novel framework that enhances the effectiveness, openness, and safety of financial transactions through blockchain technology. The study unfolds the contributions of the REA structure to the TEA framework, reviews the integration of REAs and TEAs with blockchain, and outlines the advantages and potential implementation framework for TEA.

Focusing on Morocco's heavy reliance on tax revenues, Chapter 3 explores the structural changes initiated by a comprehensive digital transformation of tax processes. Using lexicometric analysis on interviews with tax inspectors facilitated by the IRAMUTEQ software, the study reveals a substantial enhancement in the performance of tax control. Despite positive shifts, potential impediments are underscored, necessitating coordinated efforts from stakeholders. The research offers practical insights for authorities and valuable lessons for developing nations grappling with the challenges of revenue collection in the digital age, emphasizing the pivotal role of digitalization in modernizing tax control practices.

Chapter 4 sheds light on Oman's prominence in the Middle East and North Africa region, focusing on structural reforms and the adoption of digital reporting in Omani companies listed at the Muscat Stock Exchange. The study reviews and documents the digital reporting of accounting information, highlighting the benefits and challenges faced by listed companies. The mandatory use of XBRL taxonomy for digital reporting is discussed, providing useful insights for regulators, decision-makers, businesses, and the academic world.

Chapter 5 synthesizes and critically reviews existing research on digitalization in accounting, with a specific focus on artificial intelligence (AI) and blockchain technology (BT). Through a systematic literature review, the author identifies risks and opportunities associated with digitalization, using thematic analysis to categorize findings. Six themes, including creativity and openness, strategic partnership, smart contract, information governance, transparency, trust, social, economic, and regulatory issues, and audit practices, are explored. The chapter aligns with the theory of disruptive innovation, emphasizing the evolving and disruptive nature of AI and BT in transforming the business landscape.

Chapter 6 explores the impact of digitalization on audit quality and corporate governance in a sample of 150 Swedish companies from 2017 to 2022. The research utilizes data from annual reports and reference documents available on the companies' websites, revealing a positive and significant effect of digitalization on both audit quality and corporate governance. The effective implementation of digitalization strategies is highlighted as a key factor in enhancing the quality of information and governance mechanisms.

Examining the relationship between diversification of banking activities, governance mechanisms, and the concept of ownership structure, Chapter 7 analyzes the level of risk in ten main Tunisian banks listed on the Tunis Stock Exchange from 2002 to 2020. The study employs FGLS regression to reveal that the separation between traditional and non-traditional activities has a favorable effect on banking stability. Diversification of activities allows banks to establish synergies between different sectors, reducing the level of risk and positively influencing the financial strength of Tunisian banks.

Chapter 8 provides a comprehensive exploration of the intersection between digitalization and green finance, emphasizing the pivotal role in advancing environmental sustainability. Through a meticulous literature review, the authors identify the current state of digital green finance, highlighting transformative potential and challenges. The chapter offers a deeper understanding of the existing issues and presents solutions and recommendations, drawing from empirical evidence and innovative thinking. Future research directions are discussed, exploring emerging technologies and methodologies that promise to redefine the landscape of digital green finance.

Chapter 9 delves into the challenges of the Moroccan tax system, exploring the nexus between digitalization in tax administration and taxpayer behavior, with a focus on tax avoidance. Utilizing qualitative insights from interviews with 30 tax administrators, the research highlights that digitalization and service facilitation promote tax compliance. However, a lack of trust and transparency can exacerbate tax avoidance. The study emphasizes the need for comprehensive tax reform in Morocco to foster a business-friendly environment and offers valuable lessons for developing nations grappling with revenue collection challenges in the digital age.

Exploring the use of digital financial technologies (DFTs) for green finance, Chapter 10 identifies the risks, challenges, and opportunities associated with their adoption. A thematic analysis of 183 articles from 2000 to 2023 is conducted, focusing on green innovation, green investment and sustainability, data-driven approaches, and risks and challenges. The findings reveal that while DFTs offer opportunities for green finance, they also pose risks such as cybercrime, fraud, scams, tax evasion, and uncertain policies, requiring careful consideration and mitigation.

Chapter 11 synthesizes recent academic studies on accounting digitalization, emphasizing the short and long-term effects of environmental factors on corporate and financial sectors. It underscores the necessity for business leaders and investors to measure and manage environmental risks in the context of digitalization, tax avoidance, reporting, accounting, and green finance. The chapter aims to contribute valuable insights to critical discussions on these topics.

Focusing on the implications of blockchain technology on financial auditing, Chapter 12 provides a thorough examination of its fundamentals, architecture, characteristics, and categorizations. The integration of blockchain into financial auditing is explored, highlighting benefits such as improved risk management, automated audit processes, fraud reduction, cost savings, and the emergence of a continuous audit model. The changing role of auditors in this technologically evolving landscape is discussed, offering an in-depth perspective on the transformative potential of blockchain to improve the efficiency and transparency of financial audits.

Each chapter in this edited reference book contributes to a nuanced understanding of the impact of digitalization on reporting, tax avoidance, accounting, and green finance. The diverse range of topics covered ensures that readers gain valuable insights into the challenges, opportunities, and transformations brought about by the digital era across various domains in the financial and business sectors.

Through a comprehensive analysis of these four domains, this book aims to provide an in-depth exploration of the impact of digitalization on reporting, tax avoidance, accounting, and green finance. By examining both the opportunities and challenges presented by digitalization, we hope to contribute to the ongoing dialogue surrounding these critical areas of financial transformation.

We would like to extend our gratitude to all the contributors whose research and expertise have made this book possible. Their insights and perspectives have enriched the discussions and analysis presented in these pages.

We hope that this book will serve as a valuable resource for researchers, practitioners, policymakers, and students who seek a deeper understanding of the impact of digitalization on reporting, tax avoidance, accounting, and green finance. May it provoke thoughtful discussions, inform decision-making processes, and inspire further exploration of this ever-evolving landscape.

Ahmad Alqatan
Arab Open University, Kuwait

Khaled Hussainey
University of Portsmouth, UK

Mounira Hamed
University of Tunis El Manar, Tunisia

Kameleddine Benameur
American University of Kuwait, Kuwait

Chapter 1
Opportunities and Challenges of Digital Audits and Compliance:
Adoption of International Financial Reporting Standards (IFRS) in the Digital Age

Siriyama Kanthi Herath
Clark Atlanta University, USA

Laksitha Maheshi Herath
New York University, USA

Jae Koo Yoo
Clark Atlanta University, USA

ABSTRACT

The auditing and compliance sectors have changed significantly with the digital revolution. Technology improvements are driving this change, which is altering how financial reporting and regulatory compliance are done. For digital corporate reporting, the international financial reporting standards (IFRS) taxonomy has been adopted, and auditors and compliance specialists have adapted to their enlarged roles in managing digital financial data. The introduction of new technology is examined in this chapter, along with the effects of digitization on auditing and compliance and the global relevance of IFRS. As the potential and problems of the digital era change, the benefits of automation in data analysis, risk assessment, and compliance monitoring are also highlighted.

DOI: 10.4018/979-8-3693-1678-8.ch001

1. INTRODUCTION

In the digital age, auditing and financial reporting are undergoing a digital revolution. This complex procedure known as "digital transformation," which has an impact on society, politics, and the economy, is driven by technology (Vial, 2019). In comparison to the previous era, society has gone through a revolutionary transformation brought-up by globalization, which is one of the greatest technological paradigms (Herath and Joshi, 2023). The economic revolution has been fueled by a number of reasons, which include enhanced information and communication technology, among others, as well as global markets. Globalization has also contributed to the opening of fresh opportunities for individuals to interact, collaborate and establish new partnerships. The traditional definition of digital transformation is a significant modification of the strategy, business structure, tactics, and operations of a company (Agarwal, 2020). According to Van de Wetering et al., (2022), the success of an organization depends on its ability to not only identify and capture new market opportunities and technological breakthroughs but, also simultaneously strengthen its internal capabilities in order to embrace new strategic objectives.

As more firms use digital technologies to manage their fiscal data and reporting processes, the job of auditors and compliance professionals is also expanding. The auditing industry will need to use unique managerial approaches and organizational frameworks to flourish in today's rapidly changing technological world (Al-Sabti, 2023). A key element of the electronic accounting system enabling international corporate reporting is the IFRS Taxonomy, an electronic representation of international accounting standards that corporations must use to create digital corporate reports (Troshani el al., (2018). For instance, starting in 2009, larger US-based listed corporations must produce digital corporate reports under the Structured Disclosure Standards (SEC, 2009). Beginning in 2020, the European Commission (2019) mandates that all EU-listed companies submit digital corporate reports using the IFRS taxonomy. Digital reporting, which changes the syntax as well as the meaning of the communication in annual reports, marks the shift from analog to digital expression under IFRS (Riaz et al., 2022: Rowbottom et al., 2021).

This book chapter focuses on the implementation of International Financial Reporting Standards (IFRS), and assesses the opportunities and difficulties brought by the computerization of auditing and compliance processes. The next section discusses the broad objectives of the chapter.

2. CHAPTER OBJECTIVES AND THE ROADMAP

In this part, we give a synthetic presentation of the goals and the argument line of the chapter. Our aim is to make a deep dive into digital transformation within the domains of auditing and compliance, related to the incorporation of modern technologies and relevant aspects of the process. We will next examine the consequences of digital transformation on auditing and compliance and present proposed measures. Then, we will give our own conclusions and recommendations for those organizations that are planning to start this undertaking. This chapter is guided by several goals. It starts by examining how digitalization is affecting auditing and compliance, how these procedures are changing fundamentally as a result, and just how well new technologies have been integrated into audit processes and compliance management. The importance of IFRS on a worldwide scale, as well as the benefits and drawbacks of implementing IFRS in the rapidly changing digital environment, are next covered in the chapter. This chapter has a focus on modern technologies and approaches used for auditing and compliance; the emphasis is on the use of automation for analysis of data, risk evaluation, and compliance monitoring. Zhang et al. (2020) reviewed modern advancements in big data and machine learning in accounting, presenting taxonomies of cognitive technologies applied today and noting the AI-based applications. Focusing on current issues like data security, privacy, and ethical issues, the chapter assesses the challenges that come along with the deployment of new technologies in audit. It evaluates digital training initiatives for auditors as well, recognizing changing skills demand and education needs for digital auditors in the technology age.

As the frameworks for those practices continue to evolve, the chapter explores the compliance standards, laws and regulations underpinning them in the wider context of digital practices as a way of understanding how well they could be adapted to the domain of digital monitoring and auditing. By anticipating future developments in these areas and analyzing the critical roles that new developments like artificial intelligence (AI), blockchain, and large amounts of data will play in affecting the future landscape of auditing and compliance, the chapter finally attempts to forecast future developments in digital auditing and compliance. The materials discussed in this section are outlined in Figure 1.

This chapter delves into the introduction of technology in the domains of auditing and compliance. It starts with the fields of digitalization, transforming the labor market, flexibility, and technological advancements; the age of information is upon us. The role of digital technologies in auditing is thus a key focus of this setting, with an emphasis on the benefits that these technologies provide through superior reporting, deeper data analytics, and live monitoring. The auditors' professional role in the digital environment is also constrained, particularly in the scope of the application of data

Figure 1. A roadmap of digital transformation in auditing and compliance

sciences and artificial intelligence to improve decision-making processes. Besides, the chapter is devoted to consulting strategies and ethics aspects, showing the shift to advisory positions and the moral quandaries that nowadays cybersecurity brings. Thus, it analyzes the digitalization of account and audit procedures in response to the use of various technological instruments, including blockchain technology, for the purposes of enhancing transparency and security. Finally, the chapter examines the regulatory landscape in the digital age with a view to generalizing the use of IFRS and how digital technology can be integrated into accounting reform. The section that comes after this one talks about the methodology of this chapter.

3. METHODOLOGY

The literature review and case studies form the methodology applied in the context of this chapter. This chapter aims to address the academic literature on digital auditing, compliance, and the use of International Financial Reporting Standards (IFRS) in the digital era so that it can satisfy all the chapter objectives. This literature review and theoretical foundations will help us integrate major findings and identify patterns, challenges and good practices in the haulage of cargo internationally. Besides the literature review, some real-life situations will be analyzed to provide examples of the principles mentioned. Businesses from diverse sectors and regions will be highlighted in these case studies to show how they used electronic devices for auditing and conformity while adhering to IFRS regulations. An analysis of the potentials and challenges regarding electronic auditing and compliance within the framework of implementing IFRS in the digital age will be presented, combining the insights gathered from literature and real-world evidence from the case studies. The next section discusses the nature of the digital revolution in auditing and compliance.

4. THE DIGITAL REVOLUTION IN AUDITING AND COMPLIANCE

These new paradigms that have been brought about by the growth of modern technology are discussed in this section, which covers the fields of auditing and compliance in an age of technological growth. Then we will review the way modern technologies revolutionize how organizations maintain integrity, validity, and multiple participants and can be held responsible. These technologies have also helped with compliance rules. We will witness the new world of auditing and compliance in the age of the Internet, where the law goes hand in hand with innovation and success depends on insights based on big data.

4.1 An Overview of the Digitalization Trends in Auditing and Compliance

In this section, we are going to analyze the process of digitalization in the fields of auditing and compliance, determining how quickly a recently emerged pattern is moving owing to technological innovations. The auditing and compliance sectors have also undergone substantial disruption as a result of improvements in digitization. As a result of automated modern day technologies, there is minimal use of human resources in auditing since modern day equipment includes aspects of automation, data analytics and artificial intelligence. The cost-efficient nature of big data analytic tools comes in, with auditors having a more revised risk assessment that has better accuracy in the identification of problems. The basic framework used in traditional auditing for this process is cyclical, which needs objective setting by humans, control objective evaluation and testing, undertaking the tests, and sampling only a few to ascertain the control efficiency or operational performance (KPMG, 2016). Due to progress in the field of digital technologies, auditors are now able to inspect all individual private operations, not just a portion of them, which allows for a higher level of research on a larger scale.

As firms resort to digital technologies as a means to manage the more complex regulatory milieu, compliance practices have transformed similarly. This chapter gives a comment on these digitalization trends and also provides a useful inspection of how technologies change audit and programming procedures to meet current requirements.

4.2 The Impact of Digital Technologies on Audit Procedures and Compliance Management

In this section, we will look at how automation, data analysis, and digital technology have altered the processes of trustworthy reporting, data analytics, and risk evaluation. It also looks at the direction that digital technologies are leading in relation to the effect they have on practices of auditing and monitoring compliance. Digital technologies have made it possible to negotiate compliance and auditing plans much better. Auditors utilize new data analytics methods more and more to make it possible to sort through huge volumes of datasets with far from unprecedented speed and accuracy and raise the discovery of financial anomalies and threats. This is due to the fact that previously complicated procedures have been automated, minimizing human error while enhancing the audit and auditor. Among the digital systems that provide real time reporting and monitoring, compliance management capabilities are also important (Chiu et al., 2014), enabling businesses to shift their operations to accommodate changes in the regulatory environment. Normally, digital technology has been efficient when it has led to increased audit effectiveness due to the fact that digital technologies allow companies to operate as rapidly and aggressively as possible in a complex regulatory environment that should be reasonably well contested and to defend their interests effectively.

4.3 The Evolving Role of Auditors in a Digital Environment

This section discusses how the emergence of digital media has redefined auditors' duties to protect data from security and confidentiality risks. We also uncover how using complex technologies could aid in developing the efficiency and productivity of the auditing process. Audit firms are using big data to change approaches from sample methods to in-depth global research in the form of higher standardization for effective and promising governance tools (Manita et al., 2020). Early on in their journey to digital AI enabled audits, auditors typically begin by automating activities and using analytics. AI will eliminate tedious operations, provide deeper insights, increase efficiency, and improve quality, similar to previous digital developments, enabling auditors to use their expertise, experience, and expert judgment more effectively (AICPA, 2020).

The new digital environment is significantly affecting the functions of auditors. Auditors are eschewing manual data gathering and verification as they become more analytically and technologically well-informed. Auditors rely substantially on technology and digital tools for effectively analyzing sizable datasets and spotting trends, abnormalities, and potential hazards. Additionally, in order to evaluate the safety of electronic systems and data, auditors must possess extensive knowledge of cybersecurity. Cybersecurity is one of the rapidly developing segments of risk in modern organizations (Valkenburg & Bongiovanni, 2024). Recent years have seen the digital landscape explode with cyber-breaches. Cyber-breaches are not only criminalized as huge outlays of wealth but also as offenses of stakeholders' trust, and this highlights the need for strong cybersecurity measures (Valkenburg & Bongiovanni, 2024). This new digital age has also ushered in new challenges, one of which is digital threats and vulnerabilities. Companies therefore need to invest in cybersecurity initiatives in order to shield themselves and, in fact, their stakeholders from such threats. Traditionally, cybersecurity interventions have focused more on technical controls such as the installation of firewalls, intrusion prevention and detection systems, and encryption mechanisms (Cremer et al., 2022; Haner & Knake, 2021). To protect the privacy, security, and availability of an organization's data against internal and external threats, cybersecurity employs a variety of technologies, processes, frameworks, and practices (Ursillo & Arnold, 2019). They must also address the ethical issues that modern data protection and processing raise. Auditors are becoming strategic consultants that help businesses use technology to improve their financial transparency, compliance with laws and regulations, and overall efficacy in today's changing corporate world.

Several studies look at the extent to which firms are adopting digital solutions today and what they plan to use in the future. Recent research on technological accounting improvements (Kroon et al., 2021) shows accounting and auditing issues for which potential technological solutions are still anticipated. Riaz et al. (2022) assessed whether the institutional shift made possible by global harmonization, standardization, and coordination of accounting has actually increased transparency through the use of IFRS's digital interface. The largest audit firms are mainly in charge of starting and carrying out these studies. Using new information technologies has been investigated by expert auditing and accounting firms like KPMG International (KPMG) and PricewaterhouseCoopers LLP (PwC). In a similar vein, studies on the novel roles and abilities of accountants have started to emerge, with most of them focusing on blockchain technology. Blockchain technology may demand a new generation of accounting and auditing experts who can work in the blockchain development framework (Munevar & Patatoukas, 2020). The electronic revolution has led to the introduction of new rules and guidelines that every accountant needs to be aware of and follow, such as the GDPR (General Data Protection Regulation) and the International Financial Reporting Standards (IFRS). The following part of the paper will address issues connected with IFRS in the digital age.

5. ADOPTION OF IFRS IN THE DIGITAL AGE

Adhering to International Financial Reporting Standards (IFRS) is essential for businesses everywhere in the digital age. Implementing IFRS not only provides financial transparency but also facilitates smooth cross-border financial reporting and analysis as businesses use digital technologies and grow globally. This section discusses how IFRS is operated in the digital era.

5.1 The Importance of IFRS as a Global Accounting Standard

The International Accounting Standards Committee's (IASC) major objective is to control and minimize variances in local accounting standards in order to ensure that financial information can be compared between countries (Gardi et al., 2023). IFRS is essential as a global standard for accounting because it improves global comparability and integrity in financial reporting, which makes it simpler for analysts, investors, and stakeholders to make informed decisions (Apochi & Musthapa, 2022). Transparency is improved by the rising use of sophisticated digital information technologies and universally accepted reporting standards for easy stakeholder comparison (Riaz et al., 2022). Through creating a common language for financial numbers, IFRS has a significant role in the promotion of confidence among the financial markets of the world, the global harmonization of accounting standards, and the avoidance of anxiety in the global economy. This is shown through the uptake of this by countries and organizations.

It is impossible to overestimate the importance of International Financial Reporting Standards (IFRS), leaving it outright as a global accounting standard. First, it is mainly the work of IFRS to standardize and facilitate the comparability of reported financial information in countries and industries and create confidence and transferability in financial accounting. As stated by Hashed and Almaqtari (2021), IFRS influences the transparency and comparability of financial statements by intensifying the unification of accounting principles and disclosure standards and, therefore, related directives prescribing this increased precision in financial reporting. Furthermore, by providing homogeneous fiscal language that can be used to rapidly understand and compare the fiscal performance of organizations from around the world, it fosters global investment and capital flows. Increases in international accounting standards as a basis for stakeholder comparability also increase transparency, as does a reliance on advanced digital information technologies (Riaz et al., 2021).

Additionally, IFRS improves the efficiency of cross-border corporate transactions by making it easier to balance a variety of accounting regulations. Individual IFRS competence can assist in maintaining the reliability and accuracy of financial records, identifying potential reporting issues, and adhering to rules and regulations (Song

& Trimble, 2022). Additionally, it promotes high standards of corporate governance by establishing stringent rules for financial reporting that ensure businesses behave honestly and morally on a worldwide basis. The ability of IFRS to adjust to new technological breakthroughs underscores the significance of this norm in a global economy that is constantly evolving.

5.2 Challenges and Opportunities Associated With Implementing IFRS in a Digital Environment

When applying IFRS in the digital age, organizations must face challenges like privacy, data security, and the need for a robust digital infrastructure, but they also benefit from developments like advancements in technology, instantaneous reporting, and improved precision. By incorporating IFRS into digital workflows, it is feasible to enhance financial reporting procedures, data accessibility, and comprehensive financial information quality. During this digital revolution, businesses must be aware of potential difficulties with information confidentiality and regulatory compliance. Digitalization poses the challenge of sustaining the adaptability of business reporting within generally recognized accounting practices, especially principles-based standards like those of the IASB, because it must be done to develop a uniform taxonomy to categorize and represent every one of the accounting disclosures while safeguarding the adaptability built-in to the principles-based approach (Rowbottom, et al., 2021).

International Financial Reporting Standards (IFRS) adoption in a digital setting offers both opportunities and challenges. On the one hand, the adoption of IFRS in the digital age presents the chance to streamline and automate the processes involved in financial reporting, improving both precision and efficiency. However, the current accounting systems have trouble integrating digital technologies and require substantial expenditures in technological infrastructure and personnel training. Troshani et al. (2018) claim that despite the taxonomy's ability to support IFRS-based reporting in the digital age, tensions and barriers require a realignment of the perspectives among taxonomy developers and accounting standard-setters, and this will have a significant impact on accounting practice and standard-setting.

To safeguard the confidentiality and reliability of financial information in the digital era, robust governance of data and security protocols are becoming more and more crucial as data quantities expand. Further, in the dynamic technical field, it may be challenging to ensure that there will be compliance, consistency, and uniformity during the IFRS implementation and interpretation. Organizations can embrace IFRS in a digital environment that has the benefits of financial transparency, allowing them to benefit from data analytics and have a better understanding of their financial performance.

5.3 Successful IFRS Adoption in Digitally Advanced Organizations

When applying IFRS in the digital age, organizations must face challenges like privacy, data security, and the need for a robust digital infrastructure, but they also benefit from developments like advancements in technology, instantaneous reporting, and improved precision. By incorporating IFRS into digital workflows, it is feasible to enhance financial reporting procedures, data accessibility, and comprehensive financial information quality. During this digital revolution, businesses must be aware of potential difficulties with information confidentiality and regulatory compliance. Digitalization poses the challenge of sustaining the adaptability of business reporting within generally recognized accounting practices, especially principles-based standards like those of the IASB, because it must be done to develop a uniform taxonomy to categorize and represent every one of the accounting disclosures while safeguarding the adaptability built-in to the principles-based approach (Rowbottom, et al., 2021).

International Financial Reporting Standards (IFRS) adoption in a digital setting offers both opportunities and challenges. On the one hand, the adoption of IFRS in the digital age presents the chance to streamline and automate the processes involved in financial reporting, improving both precision and efficiency. However, the current accounting systems have trouble integrating digital technologies and require substantial expenditures in technological infrastructure and personnel training. Troshani et al. (2018) claim that despite the taxonomy's ability to support IFRS-based reporting in the digital age, tensions and barriers require a realignment of the perspectives among taxonomy developers and accounting standard-setters, and this will have a significant impact on accounting practice and standard-setting.

To safeguard the confidentiality and reliability of financial information in the digital era, robust governance of data and security protocols are becoming more and more crucial as data quantities expand. Further, in the dynamic technical field, it may be challenging to ensure that there will be compliance, consistency, and uniformity during the IFRS implementation and interpretation. Organizations can embrace IFRS in a digital environment that has the benefits of financial transparency, allowing them to benefit from data analytics and have a better understanding of their financial performance.

6. DIGITAL TOOLS AND TECHNOLOGIES FOR AUDITING AND COMPLIANCE

Digital gadgets and technology are now vital tools in the conduct of auditing as well as conformity duties in today's fast changing business environment. In the present complex data-dominated environment where audit and financial reporting are data-driven, these developments saw the introduction of many types of automated tools as well as sophisticated data analytics, which completely revolutionized the way in which they were fulfilling financial and regulatory requirements. This has been achieved through enhanced efficiency, precision and speed in financial reporting and auditing processing. It has also made the organizations make better decisions, leading to high profitability.

6.1 Examination of Digital Tools and Software Used in Auditing and Compliance Activities

The application and implementation of computer programs and digital technologies as tools in the auditing and compliance functions will be the subject of study in this part, highlighting the strengths, weaknesses, and benefits. Thorough analysis will reveal that digital technology is changing auditing and compliance processes, increasing efficiency and, hence, bringing more precision to reflected information in the digital age. Creativity is exhibited in finance and regulation because auditing and compliance tools and software have been analyzed. The current data analytics solutions that auditors and compliance experts can utilize in software cover data analytics platforms, AI-powered risk assessment tools, and blockchain technology to gain more ideas. The advanced developments in technology, allowing detailed analysis of vast datasets in the shortest time possible, expose the source of financial performance and risks.

Automation of operations via these devices can significantly reduce tedious tasks and error rates while, at the same time, ensuring high productivity.

The simplicity of use and dissemination of real-time data also increases with the integration of cloud-based solutions, so auditors and compliance specialists can work internationally with no restrictions. In line with the developments in the digital environment, these sectors' professionals should follow these technologies, as they are strategic in assuring accuracy, openness and adherence to laws.

6.2 Benefits of Automation in Data Analysis, Assessment, and Compliance Monitoring

Automation drastically reduces human risk in processing information, assessing risks and monitoring compliance, which includes accuracy and reliability in accounting records and regulatory compliance. Also, companies benefit from the increased use of shared databases, email, video conferencing, IoT and workstations, which enables them to acquire more knowledge about their strategic operations in real time (De George et al., 2013; Liu et al., 2018). Automation enables live monitoring and faster reaction to newly emerged challenges, making auditing and compliance processes more effective and maneuverable.

Automation positively influences the processes of data analysis, risk assessment, and compliance monitoring. The first advantage of automation is that by identically processing large quantities of data, it shortens the time required for a human task. Automated systems enable a better risk assessment approach by revealing hazards and examining millions of data points, structures and anomalies. Fourthly, automation provides long-term regulatory compliance and hence reduces the chance of errors or violations in compliance monitoring. As well, automated solutions provide in-the-moment alerts and warnings, which enable companies to fix things on time before they become worse. Cost savings, increased accuracy and resources' efficient management are among these benefits. Learning machines are certainly the most effective on this list of benefits, since machine learning plays a critical role in modern businesses where there is a lot of data and is the best option for auditing (Dickey et al., 2019).

6.3 Real-World Examples of How Technology Is Enhancing the Efficiency and Accuracy of Audits

Using real - world examples, this section explains the impact of technological progress on the auditing process. These illustrations depict a considerable automation of auditing efficiency and accuracy through analytics, data and digital technology. By studying these case studies, the reader gains valuable lessons regarding the breakthrough possibilities of having advanced technologies in audit automation. This boils down to having less human involvement, more precise data, and better audit outcomes. Real-world examples presented below undeniably illustrate how technology is changing auditing across industries with regard to the efficiency and accuracy of audits across various industries.

Blockchain in Supply Chain Auditing: Retail giants like Walmart take advantage of blockchain technology in order to trace the origin of their products. Enabling auditors to use the blockchain platform enables an immutable record of transactions, which improves the credibility of supply chain auditing and reduces the risk of corruption or the sale of fake products.

Machine Learning in Financial Audits: Machine-learning methods are utilized by esteemed auditing firms such as KPMG to analyze financial data. Improvements in the performance of financial audits are achieved due to the capabilities of the algorithms to detect quickly and precisely deviations and inconsistencies in large data sets.

AI-Powered Compliance Monitoring: AI-driven compliance inspection tools, like R1 RCM's Revenue Integrity Solution, promote benefits to the healthcare sector. It checks medical data using natural language processing technology, which makes auditing more convenient by enabling them to identify billing errors, fraud, and compliance issues.

Predictive Analytics in Tax Audits: Tax evasion is identified by the United States IRS and other tax administrations by means of predictive analytics. Advanced algorithms work with economic information and rates to check returns that should be investigated further for having a high chance of being non-compliant.

Data Analytics in Energy Auditing: Energy companies such as ExxonMobil apply data analytics techniques to conduct energy audits. These assets serve the auditors in the identification of places where energy efficiency improvements could be made, like cutting costs and causing pollution. To achieve this, they look at patterns of energy consumption.

These actual instances give an impression of how technology can increase audit effectiveness and accuracy and thus equip auditors with the techniques and information necessary to handle complex data and regulatory demands. Section 3 is devoted to challenges related to digital auditing and compliance.

7. CHALLENGES IN DIGITAL AUDITING AND COMPLIANCE

Technology has enhanced auditing and compliance processes, but it has also created a new set of issues. In their pursuit of excellence in digital auditing and compliance, organizations now face a range of difficulties, from cybersecurity worries to the difficulties of managing huge amounts of information.

7.1 Potential Pitfalls and Challenges When Integrating Digital Technologies

This section explores in detail the risks and challenges for organizations when they embrace internet-based technology in their auditing systems, elaborating on such issues as data integrity, platform integration and resistance to technological change.

Figure 2. Challenges in digital auditing and compliance

Easy data access and a shortage of knowledge on how to apply data analytics in order to achieve the specified audit purpose are the problems that we have identified. Data analytics can be very practical. Nevertheless, data analytics will be useless if used separately, on an ad-hoc basis, and not integrated or connected with the audit plan of action and audit objectives (KPMG, 2016). A number of advantages are associated with including electronic devices in auditing and compliance procedures; however, such devices do have their own potential downsides and problems (Figure 2).

The prospects of Data Security Concerns increase with the escalating use of digital tools, thus making cyber-attacks and data breaches more likely, especially financial and regulatory information, entailing a high level of Security investment and proper management. Costs for resource allocation serve as challenges to organizations that they need to set aside a huge amount of capital to buy hardware, software and carry out training of staff to cope with new technology trends. Adoption of new digital tools and practices by employees can be hampered by aversion to changes, which can hinder the integration process and affect benefits that should be realized internally. Data Quality and Integrity is an essential element of automation, as operational outcomes heavily depend on precisely accurate and trustworthy data, therefore demanding strong quality assurance measures to prevent regulatory breaches or deceptive audit reports. Despite the fact that the Process of Making Sure Organizations Adhere to the Evolving Regulations is demanding and time-consuming, the organizations have to always ensure that they are adhering to the changing laws and regulations. Ethical challenges come from the dependency on sophisticated technologies such as AI and Big data, that bring along with them privacy, discrimination, and transparency issues that firms need to resolve if they are to uphold ethical prerequisites. While skills gap is a key reason, it is especially challenging to large enterprises with diverse technology landscape, which makes the existing problems such as data silos and interoperability even worse. Integration Complexity risks misuse of digital tools that might cause either the unthinking or analytical mindset needed for auditing and compliance. Relying on technology too much makes it possible for auditors to overlook anomalies within system programs and assumptions, thereby, resulting in the occurrence of expectancy or inappropriate judgments. Vendor Lock-In emerges as companies tend to depend too much on technology vendors, becoming susceptible to any changes in the price of their products and services and/ or other aspects that affect them. These risk can be mitigated by deploying complete plans, solid cybersecurity practices, regular employee trainings, and well-thought-out technology integration, with digital technologies bringing along the benefits and minimizing the risks.

7.2 Addressing Data Security and Privacy Concerns in a Digital Audit Environment

This chapter presents methods and recommended practices for securing confidential financial data, keeping personal customer information confidential, and abiding by data protection regulations. Data security and privacy issues management is crucially important in a digital audit environment. Data security and privacy must be added to the list of concerns in a digital audit environment to protect the confidentiality and integrity of highly confidential financial information. Based on the practitioners` and scholars` testimony, cybersecurity is not solely a technical issue but also an organizational and human one, as well as the governance process (Dalal et al., 2022; Savaş & Karataş, 2022; Uchendu et al., 2021). These include organizational policies, leadership commitment, and the security culture of an organization, which are vital components of the cyber resilience of an organization (Valkenburg & Bongiovanni, 2024). The aforementioned elements form the basis for a safe environment for any institution, since they help the institution shield its data and systems from adversaries. A strong cyber resilience meeting should have measures to enhance the security of these components. Below are key strategies to mitigate these risks (Figure 3):

Implementing strong encryption protocols for data both in transit and at rest is paramount to preventing unauthorized access to sensitive information. The access control measures need to be strictly and absolutely implemented using role-based permissions and multifactor authentication to restrict access to audit data. Security audits and vulnerability assessments on a periodic basis allow us to identify and rectify gaps in the digital audit environment. The application of data masking methods blocks the leakage of confidential data during testing and development. Employee training on data security best practices, including recognizing phishing attempts, is

Figure 3. Addressing data security and privacy concerns in a digital audit environment

- Data Encryption
- Access Control
- Regular Security Audits
- Data Masking
- Employee Training
- Secure Storage
- Privacy by Design
- Data Retention Policies
- Incident Response Plan
- Compliance with Regulations
- Data Minimization
- Third-party Assessment
- Secure Communication
- Regular Updates and Patch Management

a must. Using secure storage solutions, whether through compliant cloud storage or on-premises data centers with strong security features, increases security. Privacy considerations need to be embedded into the digital audit design to guarantee data protection. Developing data retention policies enables safe control of data and lessens the chance of breaches. A detailed incident response plan is indispensable to meeting security incidents' compliance with data protection legislation. Completely observing and complying with jurisdictional laws on data protection, such as GDPR and HIPAA (Health Insurance Portability and Accountability Act), is necessary. Data collection is minimized to what is required for auditing purposes, thereby reducing the risks. The security protocols and standards that third-party auditing software or services should comply with should be strictly observed. Both encrypted emails and Secure File Transfer Protocols (SFTPs) represent the secure medium that should be used for audit data transmission. Maintaining software and systems by updating them regularly and conducting patch management helps reduce known vulnerabilities. Applying these approaches in digital formats greatly minimizes breach susceptibility and privacy issues, producing trust among audit constituents in the security of their data. By applying these methods to the digital infrastructure, there will be a drastic drop in breaches and privacy issues; thus, auditors can fully trust that their data is secure.

7.3 Ethical Considerations in Digital Auditing and Compliance

We explore the morally challenging problems pertaining to tech use, i.e., transparency, conflicts of interest and ethical usage of AI. The ethics that underlie digital audits and compliance support trust, credibility, and accountability. The main ethical aspects have been shown in Figure 4.

Ensure data protection and consent by observing individuals' rights and getting their permission for data collection and processing activities carried out in accordance with standards such as GDPR or CCPA. Ensure data collection, analysis, and reporting are transparent, giving clear accounts to stakeholders. Minimize biases in automated processes, particularly in AI and machine learning algorithms, via periodic reviews and audits. Protect the confidentiality of sensitive financial and personal details by providing access only to authorized users and eliminating unauthorized disclosure. Undertake audits and compliance activities independently and objectively, free from conflict of interest, and ensure the training and competence of personnel. Protect whistleblowers and related ethical violation issues and compliance issues. Give accuracy and accountability priority when reporting audit findings of compliance, thinking of the long-term impacts and needs of society. Stay current with regulatory compliance and adapt practices accordingly. Communicate social responsibility and ethics in leadership throughout the organization. Such communication will include the current ethical review of digital auditing methods and compliance standards.

Figure 4. Ethical considerations in digital auditing and compliance

- Data Privacy and Consent
- Transparency
- Bias Mitigation
- Confidentiality
- Independence and Objectivity
- Competence and Training
- Whistleblower Protection
- Accuracy and Accountability
- Long-term Impact
- Regulatory Compliance
- Ethical Leadership
- Social Responsibility
- Continuous Ethical Review

It stems from the fact that ethical practice in digital auditing and compliance operations is one of the crucial factors for organizations that envision sustainable development and wish to hold stakeholder trust. The key principles that need to be upheld are data privacy rights, transparency, and independence, while at the same time avoiding biases. Therefore, preserving confidentiality, using training to build competence, and protecting whistleblowers encourage a culture of accountability and integrity. The long-term ethical thinking and compliance with the legislation are reflected in ethical management and corporate social responsibility. The continuous ethical review and adaptation of the norms are necessary in order to ensure that they are in alignment with the growing ethical norms. Organizations establish ethical standards when it comes to digital audits and compliance, and this protects their reputation and transcends to social development. The section that follows explores the necessary qualifications and education needed by auditors to work through the complexities of the digital era competently and morally.

For a successful long-term business, all organizations must safeguard their reputation, drive stakeholders' trust, and ethically practice digital auditability and compliance. The required competencies and education of auditors in the age of technology are provided in the forthcoming section.

8. SKILLS AND TRAINING FOR DIGITAL AUDITORS

In the age of technology, the role of the auditor changes and requires various skills of experts. To tackle the audit and compliance regulations of today's world, digital auditors must be trained on cybersecurity, emerging technologies, data analytics along with the classical auditing.

8.1 The Changing Skill Set Required for Auditors in the Digital Era

With the advancements in technology, in particular the ability to evaluate and audit complex digital systems and the knowledge of data analytics experts, it has become necessary for the auditors' skills. Technology literacy is perceived as a competitive edge as internal auditors start implementing new technologies, for instance, data analytics tools (Betti, 2021). The digital age has resulted in radical transformation in the skill set for auditors to keep up with efficiency and relevance. Below are the key changes in the skills auditors need in this digital landscape (Figure 5).

The data analytics know-how of auditors needs to be strong enough to draw insightful conclusions from extensive databases, entailing aptness in data visualization, data mining, and pattern recognition. Auditors need an understanding of digital

Figure 5. Strategies for training and upskilling auditors to meet digital demands

- Assessment of Current Skills
- Customized Training Programs
- Digital Skill Workshops
- Certifications and Accreditation
- Cross-Training
- Mentorship Programs
- Continuous Learning Culture
- Simulated Auditing Scenarios
- Guest Speakers and Subject Matter Experts
- On-the-Job Training
- Regular Skill Assessment
- Feedback and Improvement
- Collaboration with IT Teams
- Ethical Considerations Training
- Monitoring and Support
- Incentives and Recognition

technologies, e.g., cloud computing, data management systems, blockchain and AI, to properly evaluate their effect on financial processes. A sound understanding of cybersecurity concepts is indispensable for auditors of digital financial information to spot and remediate security risks and vulnerabilities. Familiarity with automation tools as well as AI technology empowers auditors to improve the automation of operations, increase efficiency and improve the quality of data analysis. Assessing the ethical ramifications of AI and machine learning algorithms is of paramount importance to guaranteeing fairness and transparency in automated operations. An up-to-date knowledge of the changing legal regulations is paramount in the digital age; therefore, audit procedures also require modification to be in line with the changing financial and data protection regulations. Indeed, auditors need outstanding communication abilities to convey the obscure digital data into valuable pieces of information for all concerned parties.

Developing critical thinking capacities empowers auditors to weigh the accuracy and credibility of technological information and delineate possible dangers and merits in ever-changing landscapes. Adaptability is critical in the dynamic digital environment, whereby auditors need to be engaged in life-long learning to match the constant change in auditing techniques and the development of technology.

Collaboration with IT professionals and skilled project managers is crucial for digital audits, enabling interdepartmental cooperation and timely audit engagements. Auditors require adequate problem-solving skills to satisfactorily address problems that pertain to data integration, quality issues, and regulatory compliance matters. The correctness and trust of digital auditing depend on the maintenance of integrity and compliance with confidentiality legislation and ethical standards. For auditors, continuous learning is unignorable to keep up to date with the digital world's constantly changing domain. The skill sets of auditors need to be revised when auditing becomes more technologically dependent and knowledge based. Meeting the requirements of the online working space builds auditors' competence in understanding the complex nature of the working environment in which they provide constructive information to organizations.

8.2 Strategies for Training and Upskilling Auditors to Meet Digital Demands

The upskilling section of audit professionals will cover practical training, mentoring initiatives and ongoing education to ensure they possess the skills needed in the digital age. Organizations can employ a number of upskilling and training techniques to provide auditors with the abilities they need to meet the requirements of the digital era:An effective method of soft skill development can be direct interaction with superiors and subordinates.

Improving the digital auditing capabilities is hinged on a detailed review of the audit team's current skills level, showing which fields with digital expertise need to be beefed up. Consequently, customized training programs should be designed to meet these particular needs. They should include, among others, workshops, practical training sessions, and access to external courses. The approach of providing motivation for auditors to gain appropriate certifications and accreditations in data analytics and cybersecurity would ascertain their expertise and willingness to expand learning. Through cross-training events and mentorship programs, auditors can share knowledge and develop skills, promoting a learning culture in the organization. Moreover, offering the opportunity to simulate audit cases, continuous feedback systems and resources for perpetual improvement guarantees that the auditors have the most up-to-date digital auditing techniques and best practices, hence improving their effectiveness in verifying the compliance and exactitude of the audit activities. Through such strategies organizations are able to develop a technically competent and adaptable audit team that can address the digital needs of the modern business world and maintain the consistency and effectiveness of their audits and compliance processes.

8.3 Certification and Professional Development Programs for Digital Auditors

The need for development programs arises, especially for digital auditors, to be knowledgeable of the latest developments in the auditing industry. The same is true for programs that deliver information and detail that are relevant for sound auditing practice in the digital arena. We will specifically focus on training on compliant products and test cases tuned specifically for digital auditors who will be able to cope with rapidly changing standards and thus get relevantly endorsed credentials.

The Certified Information Systems Security Professional (CISSP) certificate from the International Information System Security Qualification Consortium is ideal for auditors in data security and cybersecurity. The Certified Internal Auditor (CIA) program delivered by the Institute of Internal Auditors (IIA) covers extensive knowledge about auditing methodologies, including digital auditing. While the Certified Public Accountant (CPA) credential doesn't relate directly, it commands high honor in the auditing field. The Certified Fraud Examiner (CFE) program by the Association of Certified Fraud Examiners focuses on fraud prevention, detection, and recognition, crucial for digital audits. Additionally, certifications like Certified Data Analyst (CDA), Certification in Risk Management Assurance (CRMA), and Certified Blockchain Professional (CBP) are regarded as specializations in data analysis, risk-control methods, and blockchain technology. Continuous Professional Development (CPD) programs, online courses, vendor-specific training, ethical hacking courses and master's programs in related fields are among the ways digital auditors can stay current and sharpen their expertise.

Digital auditors need to evaluate their personal career goals, areas of specialization and role requirements to determine which certifications and professional development programs to pursue. One should move with the ever-changing industry in order to be successful. The next part looks at auditing frameworks and compliance standards.

9. REGULATORY FRAMEWORKS AND COMPLIANCE STANDARDS

A digital auditor should review his career goals, areas of specialization and role responsibilities to determine which certifications and professional development programs to follow. Moving in accordance with the constantly changing industry is the key to one's success. The next part deals with reviewing frameworks and compliance standards.

9.2 Examination of Evolving Regulatory Frameworks and Their Alignment With Digital Practices

In this section, we analyze the reforms of the frameworks concerning the dynamic needs in the digital space (data security, transparency, cross-border operations). It illustrates how the digitalization of audit and compliance revolutionizes the adjusting of regulation to digital operations, giving an idea of the transformational shift in the governance role and requesting the transformation of regulation to meet the new demands.

Sweeping privacy laws such as the General Data Protection Regulation (GDPR) in the European Union and the California Consumer Privacy Act (CCPA) in the US underscore the need for a high standard of treatment of private information in the digital sphere. Analogously, cybersecurity standards place major emphasis on defending digital assets and customers` data, which is regulated by international bodies to counteract cyber threats. The growth of cloud computing has paved the way for compliance frameworks like SOC 2 developed by the American Institute of Certified Public Accountants (AICPA) and ISO 27001 made by the International Organization for Standardization (ISO) to ensure compliance with legal requirements, while regulations governing the digital identity verification process have been designed to encourage safe digital transactions. Emerging technologies, among them blockchain, bring forth regulatory reform to achieve a balance between compliance preservation and innovation stimulation. In a way, banking and trading financial regulations, for example, Basel III developed by the Basel Committee on Banking Supervision (BCBS) and MiFID II developed by the European Union, redesign themselves to fit digital behaviors to increase transparency and investor protection. The cross-border data transfer laws, comprising tools like the EU-US Privacy Shield, seek to cover the complexities in the world of data flows. Moreover, e-commerce and consumer protection laws serve to protect against Internet fraud, while Reg Tech solutions help to make the compliance process more efficient. How issues of AI and automation ethics motivate regulatory policy and environmental laws is related to the ecological footprint of digital practices. International standards, which are influenced by the joint efforts of regulatory bodies, ensure efficient regulation of the digital economy on a global level.

Moving through this ever-changing regulatory terrain necessitates organizations to keep informed, make proactive compliance efforts, and adapt their digital practices to fit the evolving standards. The alignment of regulatory instruments with digital practices is a constant process of finding the equilibrium between innovation and accountability in the digital age.

9.3 How Compliance Standards Are Adapting to Digital Reporting and Auditing

In this section, we will review the ever-changing requirement for compliance with the rapid progress of new technologies, paying attention to the technologies' contribution to the change, which also refers to the reporting mechanism, risk assessment and accountability. Yet, the compliance standards are developing dynamically to fit the digital reporting and auditing approach. This is what they are getting accustomed to in the face of such a digital transformation.

With electronic document management systems on the rise, modern standards are in the process of transitioning to the "paperless" world, and businesses are adopting digital document management as the most reliable and effective measure for storing electronic documents instead of paper records. Electronic signatures are accepted as legally binding, making the electronic approval process easy. With blockchain and distributed ledgers, you can bring about some consistency and traceability in the records. Strict rules for data security and privacy, such as gdpr, ccpa and others, show how concerned people in cybersecurity are about security issues. Policies concerning retention and deletion of information refer to the management of sensitive data. Special attention is given to multifactor authentication and other strong authorization and authentication technologies. Data accuracy and integrity, including audit trails, should now be taken into account according to the law. Modern management systems are capable of lightning-fast responses to changes in regulations, and yet, the cross-border data transfer technologies maintain privacy and security. While ethical aspects, particularly their impact on machine learning and automation, are enshrined in compliance regulations, reg tech merchandise is also involved in streamlining procedures. Changes to the standards are made in time to keep up with the dynamism of the digital landscape, thus ensuring all the regulatory requirements are in force. Global compliance in digital cooperation and convergence achieves effective process integration, enhanced global trade and international collaboration. It is an effort to observe the relationship between digital entities and their systems on a global scale and find the right combinations of innovation, ethics and regulations. The next chapter will detail the new trends that are taking place in the digitalized audit market.

Enterprises that are evolving to a digital reporting and auditing environment should remain vigilant of changing compliance requirements and implement the required adaptations. Compliance is a continuous process; therefore, vigilance and a proactive approach to meeting reporting and auditing compliance requirements in a digital environment while upholding integrity and transparency are needed.

9.4 international Collaboration and Harmonization Efforts in Digital Compliance

We will examine how the need for conformity is changing to keep up with the most recent technological innovation by highlighting the function that cutting-edge technologies play in maintaining and modernizing reporting practices, risk assessment, and accountability. Auditor procedures on estimates must be performed due to the subjectivity of estimates and the fact that some financial statement components are sensitive to them. The value of judgment, supervision, and insight will rise even if the auditor's role in terms of validation is reduced. As a result, systemic review, risk assessment, predictive auditing, and fraud prevention will be the focus of audits in the context of contemporary technology. This issue could be resolved by involving auditors in the transaction validation process, whether on private or public blockchains (Bonyuet, 2020). International collaboration and harmonization efforts in digital compliance are essential to address the global nature of digital business and technology-driven practices. Here are key aspects of these collaborative efforts:

Among the bodies are the International Organization for Standardization (ISO) and the International Electrotechnical Commission (IEC), the international organizations that aim at unifying standards of digital compliance that include cybersecurity, data privacy and electronic signatures. The harmonization of data privacy rules among regions has led to the enactment of mutual recognition agreements, including the General Data Protection Regulation and the Asian-Pacific Economic Cooperation Cross-Border Privacy Rules (CBPR). In cases of cross-border human rights violations and/or cybercrime, international collaboration among law enforcement agencies like Interpol and Europol is of the utmost importance. Through the use of IFRS, there has been consistency in financial reporting on an international level. Digital business models pose challenges for taxation, and transfer pricing issues will be tackled through collaboration between tax authorities and organizations such as the Organization for Economic Co-operation and Development (OECD). The digital trade relevance section is included in agreements like the United States-Mexico-Canada Agreement (USMCA), the Comprehensive and Progressive Agreement for Trans-Pacific Partnership (CPTPP), and International Regulatory Cooperation for Herbal Medicines (IRCH), which is a forum that exposes harmonization in various sectors, such as pharmaceuticals. The interoperability standards provide uninterrupted connections between the digital systems. Example frameworks like the NIST Cybersecurity Framework provide guidance for cybersecurity compliance. Bilateral and multilateral accords define compatible digital compliance procedures for multinational transactions. The United Nations (UN) and the World Economic Forum (WEF) are some of the international organizations that have developed the ethical frameworks for AI and emerging technologies Digital ethics issues, for example, privacy and bias in digital technology use, are the focus of collaborations between states and organizations.

International collaboration and digital compliance standards increase process speed, promote international trade, and build up partnerships. The initiatives recognize the interconnectivity of global digital systems and aim at combining innovation with moral and compliance considerations. The latest part of the paper will focus on future trends in the digital auditing profession.

10. FUTURE TRENDS AND OUTLOOK

The section dealing with trends and projections is also included to analyze the application of IFRS (International Financial Reporting Standards) in the digital era. With technology taking the lead in changing the financial sector, both industries and government departments have to understand the principles behind IFRS adoption.

10.1 Anticipated Advancements in Digital Auditing and Compliance

One of the trends and future projections is compliance with the International Financial Reporting Standards. While the financial industry is concerned by the technology revolution, the most rapid phase is what results from it. But this needs education, as it is the necessary conditions that the basic motives of IFRS adoption must be grasped.

Technological developments have undoubtedly revolutionized auditing, and it's possible that the current auditing practices will be a thing of the past following the adoption of data analytics. Auditors are indeed beginning to take advantage of the capabilities of machine learning and artificial intelligence in the bid to unveil the mysteries of large and complex datasets, and predictive analytics is now a commonly accepted tool for risk management and anomaly detection. The transition from periodic audits to continuous ones, which is a result of automation and instant data analysis, is a new phase in the industry where auditors are able to detect risks in a timely fashion and ensure compliance adherence in real time. Furthermore, blockchain technology and smart contracts could help increase transparency and integrity in financial transactions, which would lead to the improvement of auditors' capability to store documents safely as well as verify blockchain assets. Robotic Process Automation (RPA) is not left behind either, as it simplifies auditing by automating rule-based tasks that heighten efficiency and accuracy as well. Moving with the changing times in auditing, cybersecurity is under the spotlight, as is scrutiny of the ethical concerns of AI algorithms and navigating through the complexities of the

Internet of Things (IoT) and environmental compliance. They acquire this expertise through training as well as international collaboration, thus having the capacity to successfully manage digital spaces and to ensure audit quality that is of a higher level, which is consistent across different industries and regulatory regimes. To avoid being left behind by these technological advancements in the future, organizations and auditors should always keep up with the latest developments in digital auditing and compliance. That way, they remain compliant, secure, and competitive in the digital-age.

10.2 The Role of Emerging Technologies Such as AI, Blockchain, and Big Data Analytics

The present-day technologies that can improve efficiency, transparency, and data-driven decision-making are blockchain, big data analytics, and machine learning (AI). Big Data analytics, blockchain technology, and artificial intelligence are among the key factors for encouraging innovation and competitive advantage in the current complex business environment, which is constantly evolving. In the digital age that is increasingly driving the world's dynamics, the traditional accounting and academic environment are being transformed, but not necessarily fast enough to accommodate the needs of blockchain-based accounting (Tiron-Tudor et al., 2021). Emerging technologies, including artificial intelligence (AI), blockchain, and big data analytics, are playing transformative roles in the fields of auditing and compliance, as revealed below:Emerging technologies, including artificial intelligence (AI), blockchain, and big data analytics, are playing transformative roles in the fields of auditing and compliance, as revealed below:

Automated Data Analysis is transforming auditing by relegating AI-powered tools to perform analytical tasks at a speed that is ten times faster than any human and with greater accuracy. With such tools, auditors manage to uncover sophisticated patterns and trends that would rarely be possible to discern by manual methods. With artificial intelligence (AI), predictive analytics provides auditors with forward-thinking capacities to identify and fix risks, fraud, and compliance problems, enabling effective decision-making through proactive actions. Other AI techniques, like Natural Language Processing (NLP) algorithms, also improve auditing functionality as they allow for inspecting unstructured data such as text documents and social media content for compliance and sentiment analysis. These algorithms are aware of many kinds of information, such as posts on forums, social networks, and news, with the result that they have a wider knowledge of the existing risks (Paltrinieri et al., 2019). Furthermore, automated execution of repetitive tasks automates the audit process, allowing AI platforms to do the manual work like data extraction and report generation while auditors perform the analytical review and create value. The trend in the fraud detection domain is characterized by advancements in artificial intelligence driven systems in the continuous effort of extracting fraudulent transactions and defrauding behavioral patterns from historical data to reinforce fraud mitigation in totality.

Through the use of a blockchain mechanism, it is ensured that an unalterable and secured registry is maintained, which supports financial transactions and data validity. Automating and improving the processes will be achieved by smart contracts by triggering defined actions immediately once conditions are met, thus reducing intermediaries and contract compliance. The transaction trace in the supply-chain is provided by auditing the blockchain of the supply chain, which facilitates good audit performance and the enforcement of regulations along the supply chain.

The key contributor to contemporary auditing practices is data integration, which happens in conjunction with big data analytics platforms that integrate information from different sources. This integration enables auditors to have access to detailed and instant information, resulting in higher accuracy and expediency in audits. Furthermore, sophisticated analytics assists in risk assessment by scrutinizing multiple datasets, such as historical data and market trends, which helps the auditors identify risks more precisely. The monitoring of compliance is enhanced through big data analytics, since these systems keep analyzing the large volumes of transaction data that they receive and give us ready-made reports of deviations or irregularities around the regulatory requirements. The scalability of big data solutions takes the audit utility a notch higher in auditing, particularly in the case of digital business data sets, which are often voluminous and complex, thus encouraging a more robust audit practice.

While modern technologies make auditing and compliance procedures more efficient and accurate, their deployment increases the risks of privacy breaches, ethical dilemmas, and issues with regulatory compliance. Auditors and organizations need to find a way to realize the potential offered by these technologies without violating moral and legal rules in the digital field. The security of data is one of the crucial aspects for which organizations should take proper measures to ensure its protection and be in line with existing regulations. Auditors are a critical part of the process of applying these technologies ethically and properly; regularly, audits are run to verify their correct usage.

10.3 Strategies for Staying Ahead of Digital Audit and Compliance Challenges

We will also see international collaboration and harmonization initiatives meant to push digital compliance processes to deal with the challenges of a globally interconnected digital realm. Initiatives that promote uniformity, the sharing of data, and global regulatory harmonization will receive special attention. It is possible to agree that the integrated effort of auditors is altered by blockchain technology, shifting away from the more conventional and time-consuming data entry and financial statement preparation towards the evaluation and verification of the pertinent documentary evidence as well as the rational thinking of smart contracts documented in the company ledger, which might also relegate the accountant's role in the accounting system to a historical footnote (Yu et al., 2018; Secinaro et al., 2021). Bonyuet (2020), who examined how blockchain might affect auditing, came to the conclusion that because blockchain makes all data instantly accessible, statistical sample methods might no longer be required. In that circumstance, auditors must be able to test the entire database using data analysis. Staying ahead of digital audit and compliance challenges requires proactive strategies to adapt to the rapidly evolving digital landscape. Here are key approaches:

Continuous execution of learning and training is required for auditors to build on their knowledge to understand the latest technologies and laws in digital auditing and compliance. Organizational performance is based on improving digital skills promotion and creating the right regulatory environment that allows compliance in business activities. The use of complex tools, working with IT and data teams, and sticking to ethical principles are some key undertakings for successful digital auditing. Standardization of risk assessment and mitigation, automation, and integration of AI are the pillars of successful audits, together with ensuring data privacy and security. The functional teams carry out regular audits of systems; system activities are kept on record, which serves as a foundation for transparency and accountability. Flexibility, sharing and receiving knowledge, and obtaining external help are core factors for the transformation and constant improvement of digital audit practices.

Companies may develop their competencies and have the belief that they will be able to overcome the complexities of the digital world by putting these techniques into action. The readers will have an overall comprehension of the positives and negatives concerning digitalizing auditing and compliance, with the transition to IFRS being a highlighted issue in this regard. Through the close analysis of actual cases, conventional processes, and the recent trends it provides, the chapter will be a valuable source of information for professionals, scholars and legislators who wish to gain insights into the dynamic cross-cutting of technology, finance and regulation in the digital age. In line with the work done by Lugli and Bertacchini (2023), corporate digitalization has amplified the quality gap between the big and small audit companies, with the big audit companies having a competitive advantage over the small companies because they have higher budgets for investment in new digital technologies.

11. CONCLUSION AND RECOMMENDATIONS

As with the dynamic world of auditing and compliance, the digitalization journey has become a crucial factor. The chapter, in the context of International Financial Reporting Standards (IFRS), has given a wide-ranging and proportionate examination of digitalization from different angles and has highlighted the prospects as well as the intricacies that come with the digitization of IFRS. We have outlined the ever-changing relationship between the internet, money, and regulation through a range of touching examples, elucidation of technological innovations and a close examination of regulatory issues. According to Lugli and Bertacchini (2023), the influence of corporate digitalization has had the effect of not only highlighting the importance of IFRS, but also highlighting the gap between large and small audit firms. The ability to take advantage of the potential of new digital technologies is what differentiates [one], ensuring the perennial superiority of those who have bigger budgets and resources.

To be successful in the digital era, it is essential that professionals and organizations put effort into the development of their skills; this entails creating a habit of life-long learning, which entails being invested in learning programs. Implementation of digital audit techniques and technologies as a tactical method that is in tune with organizational goals and safeguards sensitive data leads to more efficiency without compromising confidential information. The new technologies that evolve laws, as well as methods and tools used in practice, must be known just in time because it will help to achieve proactive actions for challenges and opportunities that appear. The process sets the stage for constructive cooperation between audit teams, IT departments, data specialists and lawyers, which becomes the basis for cross-functional groups to navigate the subtleties of digital audit compliance smoothly. Auditing the processing will place emphasis on data security and privacy, besides which ethical factors should also be a constant part and the assessment should take account of industry standards to strengthen transparency, fairness and accountability. The activity of accessing digital resources and international exchange promotes cross-border compliance with the practice, which preserves interoperability around the world. Based upon these advices, professionals and organizations can take advantage of digitalization besides the issues that come with it in order to strengthen auditing as well as compliance practices in this era.

We are in the epoch of digitalization, and digital literacy relevant educational investments are topical for everyone, including professionals and organizations. To make the professional development cycle complete, techniques such as continuous training and learning should be part of it to stay acquainted with the latest modern technologies. Digital tools should be used adequately; companies are supposed to settle for tools that suit their goals and security parameters. It is critical to be informed and adaptive in the midst of the dynamic digital space, as technology advancement brings the emergence of new technologies while the rules and regulations constantly shift. Tight collaboration between the audit teams, IT departments, lawyers and external consultants is the key to a successful digital audit. This should be accompanied by the strictest adherence to confidentiality and privacy-sensitive information. Besides this, innovation in the workplace should be considered part of the responsible use and openness of technology. Assessment against the best industry practices and, where necessary, the use of external expertise help in a viable response to digital issues. Implementation of the comprehensive audit trail and real-time reporting would contribute to transparency and accountability in the audit procedure. Promoting equitable access to digital resources and working in partnership at the global level create a conducive environment for harmonization and interoperability in the global digital sphere.

Through compliance with the regulations, experts, researchers, and policymakers can take advantage of digitalization while dealing with its shortcomings, thus making sure that auditing and reporting remain effective, transparent, and accountable in the digital era. The study has put forth the idea that AI has the power to turn the accounting and auditing domains upside down. Notwithstanding, other research is necessary to adequately identify the challenges and prospects presented by AI in accounting and auditing. Some of the main ideas discussed in this chapter are presented in Table 1.

Table 1.

AI in Risk Assessment	Application of AI algorithms for digital auditing involving risk assessment, prediction, and mitigation.
Automation	The systematic level of automation in data analysis, risk assessment, and monitoring of compliance.
Audit Trail	To what extent are digital actions and amendments followed up by audit trail mechanisms for accountability activities?
Case Studies	Practical cases depicting successful IFRS adoption in digitally developed enterprises.
Challenges and Opportunities	The special aspects of IFRS implementation in the digital environment of introducing.
Continuous Auditing	The degree to which continuous auditing procedures are applied facilitates monitoring and assessment in real time.
Cross-Border Data Transfer	Adherence to the legislative and contractual frameworks governing international digital data flows.
Data Governance	Data governance frameworks must have implementability and efficiency in place to ensure privacy, accuracy, and data quality.
Data Security and Privacy	The Elements of Data Security and Privacy in Digital Audit Environments.
Digital Reporting	The wide use of digital reporting methods and their efficiency and accuracy.
Digital Tools and Technologies	The categories of digital tools and technologies employed in auditing and compliance activities.
Digital Identity Verification	The approaches and tools for secure digital identification verification during audits The sentence is the link to a description of an audit with a document analyzer considering digital identities.
Digitalization Trends	Digital transformation in auditing and compliance practices—its direction and speed.
Environmental Compliance	These are digital activities that adhere to environmental laws while keeping in mind sustainability and carbon footprints.
Ethical AI Auditing	Study of fairness, bias, and transparency of AI systems.
Ethical Considerations	The ethical dimension of digital auditing and compliance.
Fraud Detection	AI and data analytics in fraud detection and prevention during digital audits.
Future Trends	The expansion of digital auditing and compliance is expected and new technologies such as AI, blockchain and big data will be included.
Global Collaboration	The international endeavors to harmonize the legal and regulatory standards for compliance online.
IFRS Adoption	The degree of IFRS implementation in a digital environment.
Interoperability Standards	Ensuring that digital technology is interoperable by the adoption of any compatible standards.
Regulatory compliance	The degree to which companies comply with the laws relating to technology, for instance, those that govern data protection, cyber-security and financial reporting, is of great interest.
Regulatory Frameworks	Development of the regulatory bodies for digital procedures that concern the changes in digital reporting and auditing.
Skills and Training Needs	All the training programs that may be used to meet modern auditors' changing educational requirements.
Smart Contracts	Smart Contracting as an Automated Tool for Aiding Agreement Implementation and Compliance.
Supply Chain Auditing	Blockchain technology and other digital technologies are applied in the auditing of supply chain processes and verification of compliance
Taxation in Digital Transactions	Transfer Pricing and Tax Law Compliance in the Digital Economy

REFERENCES

Agarwal, R. (2020). *Digital Transformation: A Path to Economic and Societal Value*. Retrieved from https://www.redalyc.org/journal/6381/638167728001/

AICPA. (2020). *The Data-Driven Audit: How Automation and AI are Changing the Audit and the Role of the Auditor*. Retrieved from https://us.aicpa.org/content/dam/aicpa/interestareas/frc/assuranceadvisoryservices/downloadabledocuments/the-data-driven-audit.pdf

Al-Sabti, A. A. W. H. (2023). Implications for Enhancing the Financial Reporting Quality Brought on by the Digital Revolution of Internal Control. *International Journal of Professional Business Review*, *8*(4), e01381. doi:10.26668/businessreview/2023.v8i4.1381

Apochi, J. G., & Mustapha, L. O. I. (2022). FRS Adoption Financial Reporting Quality in Nigeria: A Conceptual Approach. European Journal of Accounting. *Audit and Finance Research*, *10*, 9–18.

Arnold, V. (2018). The changing technological environment and the future of behavioural research in accounting. *Accounting and Finance*, *58*(2), 315–339. doi:10.1111/acfi.12218

Betti, N., & Sarens, G. (2021). Understanding the internal audit function in a digitalized business environment. *Journal of Accounting & Organizational Change*, *17*(2), 197–216. doi:10.1108/JAOC-11-2019-0114

Bonyuet, D. (2020). Overview and Impact of Blockchain on Auditing. *The International Journal of Digital Accounting Research*, *20*, 31–43. doi:10.4192/1577-8517-v20_2

Chiu, V., Liu, Q., & Vasarhelyi, M. A. (2014). The development and intellectual structure of continuous auditing research. *Journal of Accounting Literature*, *33*(1-2), 37–57. doi:10.1016/j.acclit.2014.08.001

Chu, M. K., & Yong, K. O. (2021). Big Data Analytics for Business Intelligence in Accounting and Audit. *Open Journal of Social Sciences*, *9*(9), 42–52. doi:10.4236/jss.2021.99004

Chukwuani, V. N., & Egiyi, M. A. (2020). Automation of Accounting Processes: Impact of Artificial Intelligence. *International Journal of Research and Innovation in Social Science*, *4*, 444–449. https://www.rsisinternational.org/journals/ijriss/Digital-Library/volume-4-issue-8/444-449.pdf

Cremer, F., Sheehan, B., Fortmann, M., Kia, A. N., Mullins, M., Murphy, F., & Materne, S. (2022). Cyber risk and cybersecurity: A systematic review of data availability. *The Geneva Papers on Risk and Insurance. Issues and Practice*, *47*(4), 698–736. doi:10.1057/s41288-022-00266-6 PMID:35194352

Cross-Border Privacy Rules (CBPR) System. (n.d.). *CBPR System*. Retrieved February 12, 2024, from https://cbprs.org/

Dalal, R. S., Howard, D. J., Bennett, R. J., Posey, C., Zaccaro, S. J., & Brummel, B. J. (2022). Organizational science and cybersecurity: Abundant opportunities for research at the interface. *Journal of Business and Psychology*, *37*(1), 1–29. doi:10.1007/s10869-021-09732-9 PMID:33564206

De George, E. T., Ferguson, C. B., & Spear, N. A. (2013). How Much Does IFRS Cost? IFRS Adoption and Audit Fees. *The Accounting Review*, *88*(2), 429–462. doi:10.2308/accr-50317

Dickey, G., Blanke, S., & Seaton, L. (2019). Machine Learning in Auditing: Current and Future Applications. *The CPA Journal*, *89*, 16–21.

European Commission. (2019). Commission delegated regulation 2018/815. *Official Journal of the European Union, 143*(2019), 1-792. https://eur-lex.europa.eu/legal-content/EN/TXT/PDF/?uri=CELEX:32019R0815&rid=1

Gardi, B., Aga, M., & Abdullah, N. N. (2023). Corporate Governance and Financial Reporting Quality: The Mediation Role of IFRS. *Sustainability (Basel)*, *15*(13), 9869. doi:10.3390/su15139869

Haner, J. K., & Knake, R. K. (2021). Breaking botnets: A quantitative analysis of individual, technical, isolationist, and multilateral approaches to cybersecurity. *Journal of Cybersecurity*, *7*(1), tyab003. Advance online publication. doi:10.1093/cybsec/tyab003

Hasan, A. R. (2022). Artificial Intelligence (AI) in Accounting & Auditing: A Literature Review. *Open Journal of Business and Management*, *10*(1), 440–465. doi:10.4236/ojbm.2022.101026

Hashed, A., & Almaqtari, F. (2021). The Impact of Corporate Governance Mechanisms and IFRS on Earning Management in Saudi Arabia. *Accounting*, *7*, 207–224. doi:10.5267/j.ac.2020.9.015

Herath, S. K., & Joshi. (2023). Audit Data Analytics: A Game Changer for Audit Firms. *International Journal of Auditing and Accounting Studies*, *5*(1), 29–48. doi:10.47509/IJAAS.2023.v05i01.02

IAASB (International Auditing and Assurance Standards Board). (2018). *Exploring the Growing Use of Technology in the Audit, with a Focus on Data Analytics*. International Auditing and Assurance Standards Board.

International Financial Reporting Standards (IFRS). (n.d.). In *Wikipedia*. Retrieved February 12, 2024, from https://en.wikipedia.org/wiki/International_Financial_Reporting_Standards

KPMG. (2016). *Leveraging data analytics and continuous auditing processes for improved audit planning, effectiveness, and efficiency*. https://assets.kpmg.com/content/dam/kpmg/pdf/2016/05/Leveraging-Data-Analytics.pdf

Kroon, N., Alves, M. C., & Martins, I. (2021). The Impacts of Emerging Technologies on Accountants' Role and Skills: Connecting to Open Innovation—A Systematic Literature Review. *Journal of Open Innovation*, *7*(3), 163. doi:10.3390/joitmc7030163

Lim, J. M., Lam, T., & Wang, Z. (2020). *Using Data Analytics in a Financial Statement Audit*. IS Chartered Accountant Journal.

Liu, M., Wu, K., & Xu, J. J. (2019). How Will Blockchain Technology Impact Auditing and Accounting: Permissionless versus Permissioned Blockchain. *Current Issues in Auditing*, *13*(2), A19–A29. doi:10.2308/ciia-52540

Lugli, E., & Bertacchini, F. (2023). Audit quality and digitalization: Some insights from the Italian context. *Meditari Accountancy Research*, *31*(4), 841–860. doi:10.1108/MEDAR-08-2021-1399

Manita, R., Elommal, N., Baudier, P., & Hikkerova, L. (2020). The digital transformation of external audit and its impact on corporate governance. *Technological Forecasting and Social Change*, *150*, 119751. doi:10.1016/j.techfore.2019.119751

MunevarK.PatatoukasP. N. (2020). The Blockchain Evolution and Revolution of Accounting. SSRN. doi:10.2139/ssrn.3681654

National Institute of Standards and Technology (NIST). (n.d.). *NIST Cybersecurity Framework*. Retrieved February 12, 2024, from https://www.nist.gov/itl/smallbusinesscyber/nist-cybersecurity-framework-0

Paltrinieri, N., Comfort, L., & Reniers, G. (2019). Learning about Risk: Machine Learning for Risk Assessment. *Safety Science*, *118*, 475–486. doi:10.1016/j.ssci.2019.06.001

Papagiannidis, E., Enholm, I. M., Dremel, C., Mikalef, P., & Krogstie, J. (2021). Deploying AI Governance Practices: A Revelatory Case Study. In Responsible AI and Analytics for an Ethical and Inclusive Digitized Society (pp. 208–219). Springer International Publishing. doi:10.1007/978-3-030-85447-8_19

Riaz, Z., Ray, P., & Ray, S. (2022). The impact of digitalisation on corporate governance in Australia. *Journal of Business Research*, *152*, 410–424. doi:10.1016/j.jbusres.2022.07.006

Rowbottom, N., Locke, J., & Troshani, I. (2021). When the tail wags the dog? Digitalisation and corporate reporting. *Accounting, Organizations and Society*, *92*, 101226. doi:10.1016/j.aos.2021.101226

Saleh, I., Marei, Y., Ayoush, M., & Abu Afifa, M. M. (2023). Big Data analytics and financial reporting quality: Qualitative evidence from Canada. *Journal of Financial Reporting and Accounting*, *21*(1), 83–104. doi:10.1108/JFRA-12-2021-0489

Savaş, S., & Karataş, S. (2022). Cyber governance studies in ensuring cybersecurity: An overview of cybersecurity governance. *International Cybersecurity Law Review*, *3*(1), 7–34. doi:10.1365/s43439-021-00045-4 PMID:37521508

SEC (Securities Exchange Commission). (2009). *Interactive data to improve financial reporting: Final rule SEC (2009) RIN 3235-AJ71*. https://www.sec.gov/rules/final/2009/33-9002.pdf

Song, X., & Trimble, M. (2022). The Historical and Current Status of Global IFRS Adoption: Obstacles and Opportunities for Researchers. *The International Journal of Accounting*, *57*(2), 2250. doi:10.1142/S1094406022500019

Taha, A. A. D., Ramo, W., & Alkhaffaf, H. H. K. (2021). Impact of external auditor–cloud specialist engagement on cloud auditing challenges. *Journal of Accounting & Organizational Change*, *17*(3), 309–331. doi:10.1108/JAOC-08-2020-0111

The International Electrotechnical Commission (IEC). (n.d.). In *Wikipedia*. Retrieved February 12, 2024, from https://en.wikipedia.org/wiki/International_Electrotechnical_Commission

Tiron-Tudor, A., Deliu, D., Farcane, N., & Dontu, A. (2021). Managing change with and through blockchain in accountancy organizations: A systematic literature review. *Journal of Organizational Change Management*, *34*(2), 477–506. doi:10.1108/JOCM-10-2020-0302

Troshani, I., Locke, J., & Rowbottom, N. (2018). Transformation of accounting through digital standardization: Tracing the construction of the IFRS Taxonomy. *Accounting, Auditing & Accountability Journal.* Advance online publication. doi:10.1108/AAAJ-11-2016-2794

Uchendu, B., Nurse, J. R., Bada, M., & Furnell, S. (2021, October). Developing a cyber security culture: Current practices and future needs. *Computers & Security, 109*, 102387. doi:10.1016/j.cose.2021.102387

Ursillo, S., & Arnold, C. (2019). *Cybersecurity Is Critical for all Organizations – Large and Small.* Retrieved from https://www.ifac.org/knowledge-gateway/preparing-future-ready-professionals/discussion/cybersecurity-critical-all-organizations-large-and-small

Valkenburg, B., & Bongiovanni, I. (2024). Unravelling the three lines model in cybersecurity: A systematic literature review. *Computers & Security, 139*, 103708. doi:10.1016/j.cose.2024.103708

Van de Wetering, R., Milakef, P., & Dennehy, D. (2022). Artificial Intelligence Ambidexterity, Adaptive Transformation Capability, and Their Impact on Performance Under Tumultuous Times. In The Role of Digital Technologies in Shaping the Post-Pandemic World (pp. 25–37). Springer International Publishing.

Vial, G. (2019). Understanding digital transformation: A review and a research agenda. *The Journal of Strategic Information Systems, 28*(2), 118–144. doi:10.1016/j.jsis.2019.01.003

Zemánková, A. (2019). Artificial Intelligence and Blockchain in Audit and Accounting: Literature Review. *WSEAS Transactions on Business and Economics, 16*, 568-581. https://www.wseas.org/multimedia/journals/economics/2019/b245107-089.pdf

Zhang, Y., Xiong, F., Xie, Y., Fan, X., & Gu, H. (2020). The Impact of Artificial Intelligence and Blockchain on the Accounting Profession. *IEEE Access : Practical Innovations, Open Solutions, 8*, 110461–110477. doi:10.1109/ACCESS.2020.3000505

Chapter 2
Assimilation of Triple Entry Accounting Framework Amidst Disruptive Technologies in Industrial Revolutions 5.0

Vyomkesh Bhatt
https://orcid.org/0000-0001-7456-4149
G.L. Bajaj Institute of Technology and Management, Greater Noida, India

Ram Singh
https://orcid.org/0000-0002-6565-3091
MM Institute of Management, Maharishi Markendshwar University, India

Vikas Tripathi
https://orcid.org/0000-0001-6103-1052
G.L. Bajaj Institute of Technology and Management, Greater Noida, India

ABSTRACT

Today's worldwide organizations' accounting expectations for substantial value go beyond the early success stories of implementing advanced levels of ERP accounting, internet accounting, spreadsheets, and others. Accounting frameworks like the resource-event-agent (REA) system, triple-entry accounting (TEA), and blockchain have been developed to improve upon the traditional double-entry method. The study looks at and relies on the narrative investigation of the previous studies. This study proposes a novel framework that improves the effectiveness, openness, and safety of financial transactions using blockchain technology and makes a significant contribution to the developing area of blockchain-based accounting. Highlighted in this research are the REA structure's contributions to the TEA framework, a review of studies on the integration of REAs and TEAs with blockchain, and the advantages and potential framework for the implementation of TEA.

DOI: 10.4018/979-8-3693-1678-8.ch002

1. INTRODUCTION

The field of accounting has matured and progressed alongside the development of business practises to better equip itself to solve the information asymmetry necessary to maintain confidence in the capital markets. (Manni, F., and Faccia, A., (2019). The International Accounting Standards Board recognises two primary aspects of financial reporting: To begin, most users, such as shareholders or lenders, do not have the capability of accessing information directly from the reporting company. This means they must consult general-purpose financial statements and other resources in order to get their hands on the data they need. Second, firm management has more knowledge at their disposal than the public does since they have access to proprietary data. The purpose of accounting is to rectify the information imbalance resulting from the aforementioned two criteria.

There are two primary types of accounting structures: the single-entry framework (also known as cash-based accounting) and the double-entry structure (also known as accrual-based accounting). The cash nature of all transactions is reflected in the Single-Entry Framework's ledger, as both cash inflows and outflows are recorded separately. (Gal, G., and McCarthy, W. E., 1986). The information asymmetry of cash-based transactions is reduced using this accounting system, but the resulting picture is still incomplete.

By recording both cash and credit transactions in the books of accounts, Lucas Pacioli's 14th-century Double Entry Framework helped alleviate the problem of information asymmetry and give stakeholders a clearer picture of a company's financial health. Since then, accounting practises have evolved, been fine-tuned, and integrated new technologies to guarantee that the imbalance no longer persists, and that accounting remains a vital part of each successive Industrial Revolution. (Manni, F., and Faccia, A., (2015). The double entry structure may have evolved, but accounting's fundamental premises remain the same. While accounting standards have helped shape the Double Entry Framework, it is still subject to the significant restriction of requiring auditing to guarantee the veracity of the data it presents.

However, auditing is a tedious, time-consuming procedure that is not foolproof. Even though several software integrations in record keeping have been deployed, they are not yet capable of providing the real-time insights into company operations required by IR 4.0 and the subsequent development towards IR 5.0. (Spanò, R., et al., 2022) As technology becomes increasingly integrated and disruptive technologies find a place in the global corporate environment, addressing the constraint of the double entry framework is of critical significance to satisfy the interests of stakeholders who value transparency and real-time information in IR 4.0 and IR 5.0.(Singh R., et al. 2023).

To keep accounting relevant in IR 4.0 and IR 5.0, it has been proposed that the industry move to a shared ledger system. The invention of distributed ledger technology dates to (McCarthy's 1982, 2001) Resource Event Agent concept. Subsequently, the REA framework was reworked to create the Triple Entry Accounting (TEA) framework, and the blockchain distributed ledger system (DLT) may serve as a crucial enabler for TEA to be fully equipped.

Historiographical voids have emerged because of the lack of scholarly analysis of these technical developments (Cai 2019). This is especially true for "triple-entry accounting" (TEA) designs with shared ledgers. (Gröblacher, M., and Mizdraković, V. 2019). It is widely recognized that the revolutionary cryptographic advancements that have occurred in shared ledger systems and TEA might have far-reaching ramifications for accounting (Rao 2020).

The article delves into the concept of triple entry accounting framework tracing its origin from REA and implementation of blockchain into accounting framework. The work carried out will provide a comprehensive literature and background over the development of accounting in the context of distributed ledger integration and probable methodology that can be incorporated in the implementation of triple entry accounting approach. In order to help the TEA system, provide real-time insights into corporate activities, this research seeks to sketch the fundamental architecture of a prospective triple-entry accounting system.

In the current study, the authors employ a unique method for financial management and reporting by using triple entry accounting with blockchain technology. This study contributes to the existing literature and proposes a novel framework that improves the effectiveness, openness, and safety of financial transactions using blockchain technology and makes a significant contribution to the developing area of blockchain based accounting.

The other sections include "Literature Review" in section 2, "Research Methodology" in section 3, "Progression of TEA from REA" in section 4.1, "TEA Framework" in section 4.2, "Blockchain Technology and TEA" in section 4.3, "Shifting Accounting Practices" in section 4.4, "Aspects to consider when adopting TEA" in section 4.5, "Conclusion" in Section 5, "Theoretical Implications in section 6, "Practical Implications" in section 7 and "Future Research" in section 8.

2. LITERATURE REVIEW

2.1 Accounting Practice Development

Authoritative Italian researchers in the twentieth century delved deeply into the study of the nature of accounting, allowing them to develop a straightforward, logical, and rigorous method for posting the accounts in the financial statement. The theoretical framework put forth by Gino Zappa (Dagnino, G.B., Quattrone, 2006), the "father of modern Italian business economics," defines the earnings system by drawing a line between the "original," numerical accounts, represented by the changes of money and its equivalents, and the "derived," referred to as economic measures, economic accounts, which are further subdivided into "economic accounts of capital" and "earnings economic accounts."

The capital and earnings system, as presented by modern academics (Melis, A., 2007), is the method currently used in Italy to determine the character of the accounts; it distinguishes between the original (financial) and derivative (economic) accounts. Numerical accounts (cash, operational receivables, and operating payables) and financial receivables and financial payables are all part of the financial accounting system. Cash in and cash out, as well as increases and decreases in receivables and payables, are the fundamental focus of financial statements. Equity is included in economic accounting with multi-annuals (which use up their value over several periods) and operational expenditures and revenues (which use up their value in a single period). Financial statements (their derivative nature enables one to trace the origins of every purchase, expense, and increase or decrease in equity)

Even if double-entry bookkeeping isn't an absolute system anymore, it may be rationally extended to triple-bookkeeping by adding a third axis of force (Yuji, I., 1982). Several initiatives have been launched to increase the openness of financial reports. Transparency in the financial markets is one way that the International Financial Reporting Standards (IFRS) hope to boost confidence, economic growth, and soundness throughout the world (IFRS, 2019).

To ensure that all three records are in agreement, the two books can be reconciled with a third public ledger (Unicorn, 2018). Triple-entry accounting combined with blockchain technology has the potential to revolutionise the accounting industry (Deloitte, 2016). Ijiri (1986) used the term "momentum" to describe "the rate at which income is being earned," with units of measurement being money earned per time period. To keep track of the variations in momentum, he also devised a third-level entry with a fresh set of trebit accounts. Yuji's innovation essentially included adding a third layer to the accounting equations, which coincided with the derivative/integration idea in mathematics.

$$\overset{\Delta}{\rightarrow} assets_{\mathrm{n}} = \text{Income} = \int_{T-t}^{T-t+n} \text{Momentum(n)}$$

where n is the time period

Grigg (2005) presented a significant conceptual improvement to the business recording system. At the time when the idea was first conceived, it was not known who would take on the role of a reliable and impartial third party to oversee the third shared ledger. The research conducted by Deloitte (2018) came to the conclusion that "momentum is shifting from a focus on learning and exploring the potential of the (blockchain) technology to identifying and building practical business applications." While the financial services industry is embracing blockchain technology and rethinking procedures and activities that haven't changed in decades, the accounting industry is lagging far behind.

The enormous potential of the triple-entry accounting system in accounting has resulted in a paucity of scholarly exploration of this issue. Schmitz and Leoni (2019) conducted a comprehensive literature evaluation of scholarly works published on blockchain technology in the field of accounting and auditing between 2008 and 2018. Twenty scholarly works have been published so far, and the vast majority of them focus on the theoretical aspects of blockchain advances in accounting and their potential practical consequences for the accounting and auditing industries.

2.2 Blockchain Applications in Accounting

The Big Four accounting firms, Deloitte, PwC, EY, and KPMG, innovate at a far higher rate than academic institutions (Karajovic et al., 2019). All of these organisations have conducted blockchain-related research and development. For instance, in 2016, Deloitte established a division dedicated to payments, rewards programmes, and digital banking known as Deloitte Rubix. PwC also introduced DeNovo the same year, a strategic consulting platform with a special emphasis on FinTech advancements. Pricing, digital contract integration, shared inventory data, invoices, and payments are all key components of EY Ops Chain, which was released in 2017 (EY, 2019). KPMG stated in February 2019 (KPMG LLP, 2019) that it has formed a strategic alliance with enterprise blockchain provider Guard Time to provide blockchain-based services to its clientele.

Low to moderate familiarity with blockchain-based accounting systems was found among Egyptian auditors when polled about their thoughts on the technology's potential benefits and drawbacks in the context of accounting and auditing. (Anis. A, 2023). It was also found that opinions on the advantages and disadvantages of blockchain-based accounting systems varied widely among major and medium-sized audit firms.

A systematic literature review (SLR) was conducted on 346 research products indexed in Scopus; these were mapped using bibliometric analyses and discussed critically in relation to three main themes: the effect of blockchain technology on accounting and auditing; crypto assets and finance; business models; and supply chain management. (Bellucci, M., et al., 2022). The widespread implementation of a distributed ledger and, most likely, a triple-entry accounting system is in its infancy.

This research aims to fill that void by providing a thorough examination of the triple entry accounting system and the first steps that may be taken in the aftermath of the fifth industrial revolution to implement the TEA framework.

3. RESEARCH METHODOLOGY

3.1 Research Problem

This study attempted to identify the framework and construct for Triple Entry Accounting framework.

3.2 Research Design

The study depends on narrative investigation. (Syed Moudud-Ul-Huq, et al., 2020) This research utilises a narrative investigative technique to uncover the complexities of the revolutionary financial framework of triple-entry accounting. This technique improves the comprehensiveness and contextualization of the study, offering a comprehensive grasp of the issue and enhancing the discussion on contemporary accounting procedures. In this examination the study focuses on the construct with a notional idea of triple entry framework adoption and its basic functionality. Findings were organized as follows:

- Progression of TEA from REA
- TEA framework
- Blockchain technology and TEA
- Shifting accounting practices.
- Aspects to consider when adopting TEA.

3.3 Research Model

The theoretical model of the exploration is introduced in Figure 1

4. ANALYSIS AND DISCUSSION

4.1. Progression of TEA From REA

McCarthy (1982) first proposed the Resource-Event-Agent (REA) paradigm for generalising the accounting of an enterprise information system's underlying software

Figure 1. Research model (Source: Author computation)

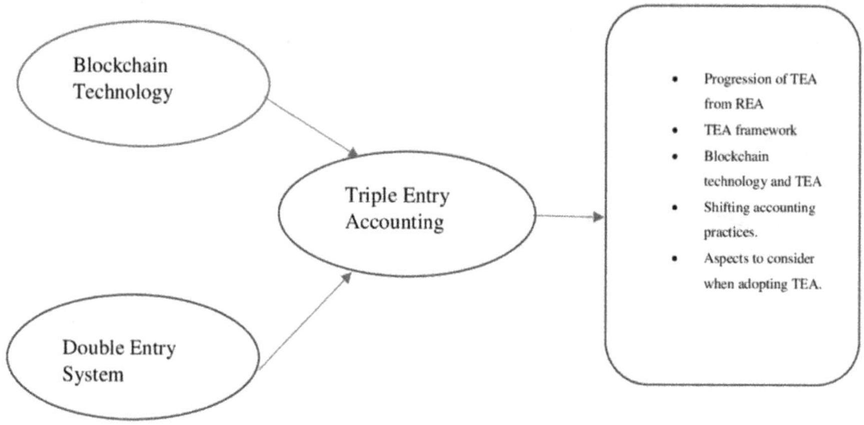

architecture (Haugen, 2000). The model's central tenet is an account of exchanges between company agents as business events. Existing accounting models have a number of limitations that may be solved with the help of REA, such as inaccurate categorization schemes, unrefined bookkeeping data, and a lack of connection between the accounting system and other corporate information systems (Geerts, et al., 2006).

McCarthy's Resource-Event-Agent (REA) structure for accounting provides a historical precedent for TEA. Despite the fact that many have pointed out the similarities between TEA and the REA framework (A. Gomaa et al. 2019; Grigg 2017c, 2017d, 2017e), the historical influence of the latter over the former is still largely unknown. This is due to a lack of recognition for the body of work that primarily traces the "missing link" between REA and TEA. (Boyle, T. 2000a, 2000b, 2000c).

While REA does support the reporting artefacts of double-entry accounting like balance sheets and income statements (McCarthy 1986, 2001), it aims to replace

Figure 2. REA role in development of TEA (Source: Authors computation)

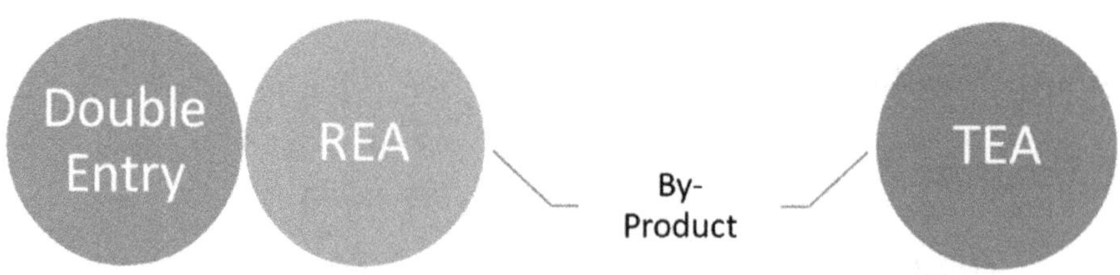

the traditional double-entry accounting system with an information system that is applicable across the board rather than being confined to accounting alone.

At first, McCarthy and his followers were developing a theoretical foundation for a company-wide information system. However, with the development of the Internet, the REA model has been used for inter-company accounting, often known as a shared ledger system, which involves several corporate organisations within a trading community. One example is the work of (McCarthy 2000), who built upon the REA model to provide a unified view of supply and demand based on an event-driven, generalised depiction of material flows.

Intercompany transactions are normally documented twice, once from the viewpoint of each company involved and once from the viewpoint of the third party (ISO/IEC 2015, 3). For instance, when a vendor records a sale in accounts receivable, the purchaser will do the same in accounts payable (Boyle, 2000d). As a result, books of accounts are biassed. McCarthy, on the other hand, recommended representing actual business events from the perspective of many companies.

In contrast to TEA, which may be thought of as an implementation of REA, REA is a more abstract framework for building an ontology. However, REA provides a notion that is functionally comparable to TEA when it is applied to inter-entity transactions: the Open-edi16 Distributed Business Transaction Repository (OeDBTR) (ISO/IEC 2015; McCarthy and Holman 2019).

A system that uses the open-EDI standard for electronic data interchange described in ISO/IEC 15944-21 (Holman 2019) and an independent view of the transaction as a single source of truth to track the immutable history of events triggering changes of state in multiple business entities is called an OeDBTR within the REA ontology (OeDBTR). As such, TEA and OeDBTR are similar in that they both maintain a view-point-independent record of transactions that is shared by two or more parties and allows for alternative "views" of the transactions to be maintained at the local level.

Specifically, database design, trust, and consensus are three different facets of a shared ledger system that REA, TEA, and the blockchain address (Gröblacher M. and Mizdrakovic, V.2019). Each model requires a different number of verification steps before the community can trust it. For instance, an OeDBTR record must adhere to REA database specifications in order to achieve semantic expressiveness, whereas a TEA transaction record requires three signatures. However, they are complementary since they each target unique aspects of the record. In addition, the two sets of records are equivalent; there are no significant differences between them.

4.2. TEA Framework

Triple Entry Accounting (TEA) is a record-keeping method that uses digitally signed messages and a shared transaction repository (STR) structure to ensure all parties

Figure 3. TEA basic framework (Source: Author computation)

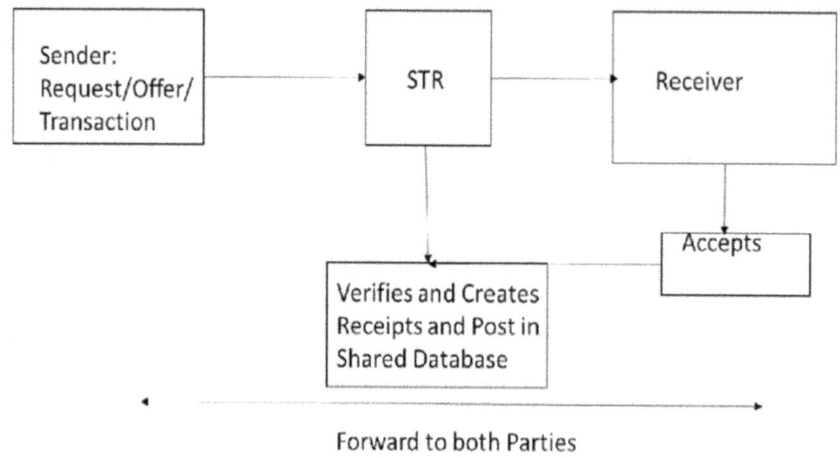

involved can agree on the details of the transaction. Thus, the record is built on the accumulated signed receipts.

A new transaction may only be added to the STR when it has been initiated by one party sending a "request," "offer," or "transaction draught" to the other party. (Inghirami 2019). A receipt is generated, the transaction is confirmed, and the information is stored in a central database before being sent to the relevant parties. It is important to remember that in the case of a system interruption recovery, the STR reads back the database's log and re-forwards the receipt; therefore, it is conceivable for transaction counterparties to get several copies of a receipt. (Pacio 2018)

After the other party approves the entry and the server verifies it (this may occur asynchronously if the system is used just for making payments), the transaction is complete. This process may be seen as gathering signatures for a document: one party signs a draught of the transaction entry, and the other party confirms their acceptance by countersigning the document. Only then does the STR (which may be a middleware server or a distributed ledger) process the entry.

The STR is responsible for verifying the authenticity of the signatures, and then, if everything is in order, the STR will sign off on the entry as well (Boyle 2001). All participants will have access to the same, immutable data since this system creates a digitally signed receipt; this entry will then serve as the verifiable truth for all participants.

In a nutshell, TEA is all about constructing a shared transaction record involving at least three participants through the use of signed messages. The shared record is built on top of the accumulated signed copies of these receipts. The best example of this is the triple-signed receipts that Odom uses: the offer is signed once, the acceptance is signed twice, and the server validates the transaction in a third signed message, resulting in a triple-signed receipt.

Depending on the implementation of TEA, the sequence of the three signed messages may change. Boyle's joint accounting suites and Grigg and Odom's payment systems are the two most fundamental possibilities for TEA architectures. Digital check systems and digital cash systems are two further categories of payment systems. All aspects of a transaction are recorded in a joint accounting system since business deals are recorded as payment and consideration given by both parties. Therefore, agreement from both parties (offer and acceptance messages) is required to establish the record.

Payment systems only keep track of the cash exchanged for goods or services. As a result, digital check systems are the only ones that necessitate a message from the recipient (as payees need to cash the check), while digital cash systems are the only ones that don't. But even with electronic cash systems, the recipient confirms the exchange by spending the money they were given. To put it another way, the placement of the second signature occurs in an asynchronous manner. At the very least, three parties must work together to reach agreement on a single transaction record using signed messages for any TEA implementation to work.

4.3. Blockchain Technology and TEA

There is a common misconception that blockchain and TEA are related, when in fact they are completely separate. It's a popular misperception that blockchain is the third entry; however, this is definitely not the case. Incredibly useful is the blockchain's capacity to keep track of several parties' information in real time throughout a transaction. Automation of corporate operations, in particular those involving payments and controls, has virtually infinite potential. In the last several years, blockchain technology has become increasingly common in a wide variety of practical contexts across virtually all industries. The blockchain is a decentralised digital ledger that is stored in a number of different places for maximum security and convenience.

Whether or not a blockchain uses a triple-entry model depends on the type of state machine it is (Fowler, 2010). Depending on the application, state machines can be one of two types. (Grigg 2016b, 2017b):

- Machines of state, such as machines that keep the user's balance and update it based on messages

- Message processing devices, such as those that keep a user's transaction history and determine their balance by reading them in order.

If a blockchain is based on the messaging paradigm, only then will it use a triple-entry approach. Accounting data in the case of double entry accounting practises might be readily manipulated by human entities, but in the case of triple entry accounting practises, all accounting data is encrypted, which may entirely preclude the possibility of manipulation. As a result, triple-entry accounting eliminates the possibility of monetary fraud and accounting data tampering caused by a weak human connection.

Furthermore, blockchain technology will enable fully automated and decentralised accounting procedures. That's because it was unable to change or delete previously recorded transactions in the books of account. In addition, the immutability of blockchain data means that every recorded transaction can be trusted to be genuine. This is particularly useful for the rigorous record-keeping required by accounting systems.

Let's take a look at how blockchain technology can simplify the current double entry accounting process. The triple-entry accounting system will allow for the automated recording of transactions onto the blockchain once either of the two accountants has created double-entry transaction records. In addition, the second accountant may instantly access, examine, and record the aforementioned accounting transaction data in its own books of accounting thanks to blockchain technology.

Let's use a basic transaction to practise triple-entry accounting. Let's pretend X lends Y 10,000 Indian rupees. Figure 3 depicts the results of the aforesaid transaction using double entry accounting principles. However, X and Y are not always equal and may have recorded different amounts due to their independence. What if Y has nefarious intentions, only accounts for INR 5,000, and optimistically passes the audit procedure as well? If Y continues to understate its liabilities book for an extended period, the current situation will deteriorate further.

The current framework lacks the wherewithal to provide satisfactory resolutions to this problem. Rather, auditors in the current system are seen as guardians tasked with preventing any such inconsistencies from occurring. Triple-entry bookkeeping has been proposed as a possible answer to this problem. In order to eliminate the need for auditor oversight, the problem is addressed by introducing a public ledger (blockchain) into the accounting system, which triple entry accounting does. Fig. 4 shows a diagram showing how TEA works and helps illustrate this concept.

Figure 4. Double entry bookkeeping limitation (Source: Author computation)

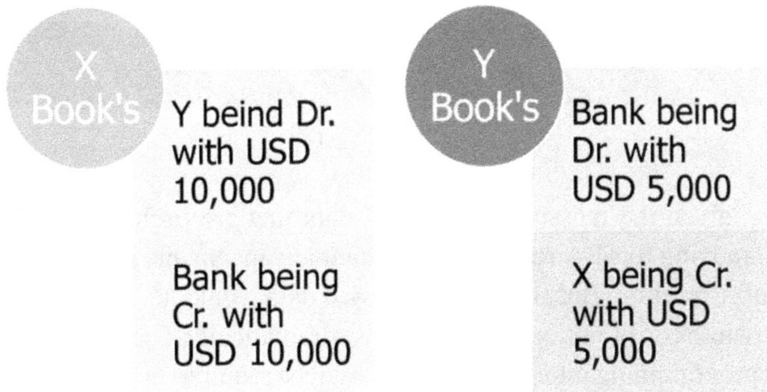

Figure 5. TEA bookkeeping system (Source: Author computation)

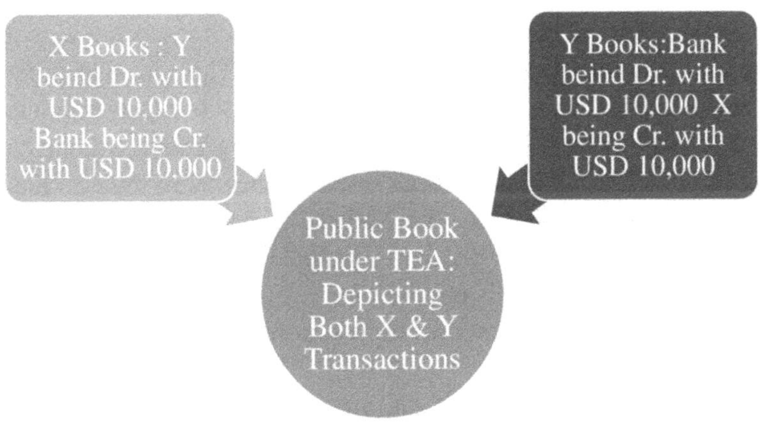

4.4. Shifting Accounting Practices

While many businesses now use high-end accounting software, most of these solutions are built on the DEA concept and hence lack the nimbleness to provide real-time insights into corporate processes. Because of the growing need for openness and real-time data about a company's projected financial health, these restrictions have assumed greater significance. The development of blockchain technology, which functions as a third ledger, enables TEA. As a result of this, many companies are considering making the switch from DEA to TEA.

Figure 6. Basic architecture to deliver real-time insights of the business operations (Source: Maiti et al., 2021)

However, given the massive amounts of data that are exchanged daily across enterprises, moving to TEA requires significant advancements in cloud server and computer infrastructure. Because less processed data would need to go to the cloud server, bandwidth consumption would decrease dramatically. The implementation of application programming interfaces, or APIs, will be required in order to circumvent this barrier. The pool layer of APIs includes a wide range of API programmes for various tasks (such as invoicing, transaction processing, account administration, fraud prevention, and financial reporting).

The transaction pool is another crucial component of TEA's rollout. All of the transactions make up the transaction pool layer. The transaction pool receives all incoming transactions and processes all outgoing transactions. A message structure may be created using the Transactions data structure. This message structure can include many elements, such as the version number, a list of inputs and outputs, the lock time, and other fields. All of the miners working together as a group constitute the miner pool layer. The blockchain's hash links are generated by miners. Blockchains are decentralised public ledgers that are updated in real time when miners verify and record transactions by solving a mathematical problem using a cryptographic hash algorithm. The final layer is part of a larger collection of blocks known as a blockchain. One way to think of a block is as a hash tree or Merkle tree containing data about several transactions.

The APIs of both parties are the starting point for the transaction. "X lends USD 10,000 to Y." The APIs of X and Y communicate with one another to share financial data. In this case, X and Y might have utilised any one of three types of APIs—external, internal, or shared—to exchange transactional data with one another. If X and Y engage in transactions often, then an external API may be the best option; otherwise, an internal API or a shared API may be more appropriate. After the API has been validated, X and Y will share transaction details with each other. After consensus is reached amongst the parties involved in a transaction, the transactions are verified and validated by the relevant miners in the mining pool.

Mining is the process by which new tokens (such as utility, security, reward, and others) are created and distributed. The completed transaction data would then be saved in the cloud using API gateways. Through their cloud computing systems, banks

Figure 7. TEA framework real time insights (Source: adapted from Maiti et al., 2021)

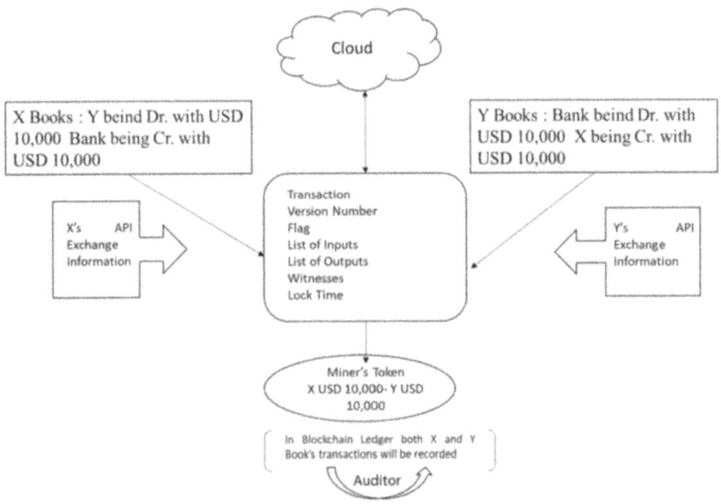

would have access to these transaction details. Access to the blockchain or shared ledger can be requested by auditors using one of the many API apps now available.

An auditor might check the legitimacy of a transaction after it has been approved by the API application by using the hash recorded in the blockchains at the time each original transaction is generated or by contacting each intended recipient directly. Organisations may be able to employ real-time analytics of data held on the edge nodes or servers of various parties to predict their future financial standing.

4.5 Aspects to Consider When Adopting TEA

Adopting blockchain-based accounting introduces an unprecedented way of handling and protecting financial data, but doing so successfully requires careful consideration of a number of factors. The inviolability of stored information is an important feature. A high degree of confidence and transparency in monetary records is fostered by the distributed ledger technology of blockchain, since once data is published on the chain, it can no longer be altered or deleted.

However, as mistakes or fraudulent inputs might be maintained indefinitely, immutability features need precise data entry and validation methods. In order to reduce the likelihood that incorrect data will be entered into the system, businesses must implement stringent standards for data verification and input correctness.

Protecting one's personal information and assets should also be a top priority. Blockchain's openness is a virtue, but it may create problems when trying to protect private information, especially when it comes to finances. Finding a happy medium between openness and privacy is crucial. Permissioned blockchains and other forms of advanced encryption can be used to control who has access to what data while still taking advantage of the blockchain's immutability. To prevent the misuse of private financial information, businesses should have stringent encryption policies and control procedures.

5. CONCLUSION

The Industrial Revolution 5.0 has altered the corporate landscape in profound ways. Triple-entry accounting, which uses blockchain technology, is a significant development in modern times. By using a distributed ledger, this innovative accounting method boosts trust in financial statements by making them more transparent and accountable to all parties involved. This innovative method of accounting has the potential to boost confidence in financial reporting as well as its dependability and accuracy, simplify audits, increase regulatory compliance, save costs, and boost efficiency. As such, it is an exciting development with enormous potential to revolutionise both the accounting industry and the global financial system.

Beyond the early success tales of implementing cutting-edge ERP accounting, online accounting, spreadsheets, and others, today's multinational organisations want much more from their accounting systems. In terms of technological advancement, distributed ledgers represent a watershed moment. They are not a silver bullet since they cannot replace the work of human accountants and they cannot stop fraud, money laundering, etc. on their own. However, in the Internet era, accounting apps may now be more efficient and transparent thanks to shared ledger systems. In particular, TEA is one of the ground-breaking ideas for accounting in shared-data environments; it provides numerous advantages such as the ability to perform or facilitate external integration, instant reconciliation, reduced redundancy, cost-effective real-time auditing, financial reporting, automated invoicing, dispute resolution, etc.

Research into the feasibility of making the transition from DEA to TEA in future accounting practises is presented. To that end, the research delves into potential scenarios for the future of accounting. Transitioning to the TEA system is difficult, and at present it is merely a mentally stimulating activity. However, in the last year or two, blockchain technology has become increasingly commonplace in many practical contexts, including accounting. The advent of rapidly evolving technologies like blockchain necessitates a deliberate shift towards the so-called TEA.

Experts feel that the advantages of the TEA far outweigh the difficulties of transforming accounting practises generally. There is a growing discussion over whether or not it is worthwhile to embrace alternative accounting practises like triple entry accounting (TEA), which is presently not employed in any meaningful way. Entities interested in entering the TEA industry should be aware of this trend and be prepared to adopt TEA procedures when the time comes. In addition to blockchain and TEA, these studies also consider the possibility of incorporating other disruptive technologies into future accounting.

However, switching from double-entry accounting (DEA) to triple-entry accounting (TEA) will require more than just using blockchain technology. Which indicates, without a doubt, that in spite of the tremendous promise offered by blockchain-based TEA, it would require further deliberations and a robust framework. The lack of appropriate legal frameworks, the possibly high cost of implementation, and the technological and organisational inadequacies mean that it is not yet suitable for immediate use by businesses.

In order to help the TEA system provide real-time insights into corporate activities, this research seeks to sketch the fundamental architecture of a prospective triple-entry accounting system. There are five parts to this system, including an API pool, an edge computing pool, and a transaction pool. Both miners and blockchains share resources. There are certain caveats to the current research, such as the fact that the anticipated TEA system to provide real-time insights on the business operations has yet to be implemented.

5.1. Theoretical Implications

In the context of the upcoming Industrial Revolution 5.0, the widespread adoption of blockchain-based triple entry accounting will theoretically have a significant impact on the financial reporting process. The use of blockchain-based triple-entry accounting has far-reaching effects on the credibility and precision of financial reports. Because each participant has their own copy of the ledger, every transaction can't be altered after it's been recorded. This adds a new level of scrutiny and responsibility, decreasing the possibility of mistakes, fraud, and manipulation. Stakeholder trust in the financial reporting process is bolstered as a consequence of increased dependability and accuracy in financial statements.

Adopting blockchain technology for triple-entry accounting might change how government agencies oversee financial statements. Compliance with rules may be monitored and enforced more efficiently with the use of a distributed ledger that provides authorities with near-real-time access to financial data. In addition to lowering the potential for financial misdeeds, this can also increase the reliability of financial reporting.

The use of blockchain-based triple-entry accounting has ramifications for the credibility of financial reports. In order to make educated decisions, stakeholders must have faith in the accuracy and transparency of financial reports. Distributed ledgers are useful for lowering the chances of fraudulent or manipulative behaviour by providing an immutable and verifiable log of all transactions. This has the potential to boost the trust that investors have in companies and the financial system as a whole through more accurate financial reporting.

5.2 Practical Implications

Businesses can benefit from more transparency and control over their financial activities with the implementation of blockchain technology and the use of triple entry accounting. Distributed ledger technology allows organisations to keep tabs on their financial activities in real time, improving their ability to make educated choices regarding their money management. This has the potential to improve the quality of financial management while decreasing the likelihood of mistakes, fraud, and mismanagement.

Financial reporting may be streamlined by the application of blockchain technology, saving time and money in record-keeping and reconciliation. Transactions may be recorded and reconciled in real-time using a distributed ledger, which greatly reduces the need for human intervention and speeds up the accounting process. This has the potential to reduce expenses, making firms more competitive. When used in bookkeeping, blockchain technology can boost confidence in monetary dealings. Distributed ledger technology allows for the immutable recording of transactions, making them resistant to forgery and other forms of tampering.

This has the potential to improve the safety of monetary transactions, saving companies money and protecting their good name. Businesses functioning in the framework of Industrial Revolution 5.0 will have profound management consequences as a result of the widespread implementation of triple entry accounting utilising blockchain technology. Increased financial transaction visibility and control, streamlined financial reporting, increased credibility and transparency in financial reporting, improved security and integrity in financial transactions, and improved regulatory compliance are all possible outcomes of this new accounting paradigm.

8. FUTURE RESEARCH

Future research can zero in on the following to put the TEA framework to the test:

a) Future research can compare TEA's results to those of conventional double-entry accounting to empirically assess TEA's efficacy. To achieve this, we need to compare the time and effort needed to complete accounting activities using TEA versus those completed using more conventional approaches.
b) The Resource Event Agent (REA) database requirements are widely used in the field of accounting information systems, and future research might investigate whether or not TEA is compatible with these standards. This can be useful for figuring out if the current accounting systems are compatible with TEA or if adjustments need to be made.
c) Future research can assess TEA's effectiveness in the context of inter-firm accounting transactions, expanding the scope of accounting research beyond the firm's walls. This may be used to gauge how well TEA is able to capture the value generated by these exchanges.

REFERENCES

Anis, A. (2023). Blockchain in accounting and auditing: Unveiling challenges and unleashing opportunities for digital transformation in Egypt. *Journal of Humanties and Applied Sciences*, *5*(4), 359–380. doi:10.1108/JHASS-06-2023-0072

Bellucci, M., Cesa Bianchi, D., & Manetti, G. (2022). Blockchain in accounting practice and research: Systematic literature review. *Meditari Accountancy Research*, *30*(7), 121–146. doi:10.1108/MEDAR-10-2021-1477

Boyle, T. (2000a). *CDEA General Ledger Schema*. Ledgerism. Available online: https://web.archive.org/web/20071001201740/http://www.ledgerism.net/GLSchema1.txt

Boyle, T. (2000b). *Draft Schema for General Ledger*. Ledgerism. Available online: http://web.archive.org/web/20051003224536 /http://ledgerism.net/GLSchemaDraft1.txt

Boyle, T. (2000c). *Re: Company Centric View Ends. Data Goes to the Net*. Available online: http://linas.org/mirrors/www.gldialtone.com/2001.07.14/ToddREAPost.htm

Boyle, T. (2000d). *The Public Transaction Repository (PTR) Project*. GL Dialtone. Available online: http://web.archive.org/web/20000622133330/http://www.gldialtone.com/PTR.htm

Boyle, T. (2001). *The Shared Transaction Repository (STR) ver. 0.60 spec*. Available at: http://linas.org/mirrors/www.gldialtone.com/2001.07.14/STR.htm

Boyle, T. (2003a). *The Argument to Abolish Double-Entry Accounting and Abolish the Assets=Liabilities + Owner's Equity Equation*. Available at http://web.archive.org/web/20031208235246/http://ledgerism.net/GLSchema2.txt

Boyle, T. (2003b). *Accounting Hypercubes on the Internet*. Available at http://web.archive.org/web/20060102014117/http://www.ledgerism.net/hypercub.htm

Boyle, T. (2003c). *File-Based Commerce (FBC) Architecture ver. 0.31 spec. Business Requirements Viewpoint*. Available at http://web.archive.org/web/20050211111755/http://ledgerism.net/fbc.htm

Boyle, T. (2003d). *General Ledgerism*. Available at http://web.archive.org/web/20060425114848/http://ledgerism.net/

Boyle, T. (2003e). *Shared Transaction Repository (STR) A High Level Software Specification*. Available at http://web.archive.org/web/20060102052824/http://www.ledgerism.net/STR.htm

Cai, C. W. (2019). Triple-entry Accounting with Blockchain: How far Have we Come? *Accounting and Finance*, *61*(2), 71–93. doi:10.1111/acfi.12556

Dagnino, G. B., & Quattrone, P. (2006). Comparing institutionalisms: Gino Zappa and John R. Commons' accounts of "institution" as a groundwork for a constructivist view. *Journal of Management History*, *12*(1), 36–52. doi:10.1108/13552520610638265

Deloitte. (2018). *Breaking blockchain open: Deloitte's 2018 global blockchain survey*. Available at: https://www2.deloitte.com/content/dam/Deloitte/cz/Documents/financial-services/cz-2018-deloitte-global-blockchain-survey.pdf

EY. (2019). *EY Ops Chain industrializes the blockchain at scale for enterprises*. Available at: https://www.ey.com/en_gl/news/2019/04/ey-ops-chain-industrializes-the-blockchain-at-scale-for-enterprises

Fowler, M. (2005). *Event Sourcing*. Available at: https://martinfowler.com/eaaDev/EventSourcing.html

Gal, G., & McCarthy, W. E. (1986). Operation of a Relational Accounting System. *Advances in Accounting*, *3*, 83–112.

Geerts, G. L., & McCarthy, W. E. (2006). Policy-Level Specifications in REA Enterprise Information Systems. *Journal of Information Systems*, *20*(2), 37–63. doi:10.2308/jis.2006.20.2.37

GomaaA.GomaaM.FaragM. (2019), The Creation of One Truth: Single-Ledger Entries for Multiple Stakeholders Using Blockchain Technology to Address the Reconciliation Problem. *Social Science Research Network (*SSRN*).* Available at https://papers.ssrn.com/sol3/papers.cfm?abstract_id=3397684 doi:10.2139/ssrn.3397684

Grigg, I. (2005). *Triple Entry Accounting. Systemics.* Available at https://iang.org/papers/triple_entry.html

Grigg, I. (2016). *The Message is the Medium.* Available at https://steemit.com/eos/@iang/the-message-is-the-medium

Grigg, I. (2017a). *But it's not modelled there, it's only modelled up in the cloud. That's triple entry accounting at the triple A.* Twitter Post. Available at https://twitter.com/iang_fc/status/939243253060329475

Grigg, I. (2017b). *My thanks to Todd Boyle, originator of the concept of triple entry, for pointing out this video by Bill McCarthy* https://t.co/rwGAZZaHfo. Twitter Post. Available at https://twitter.com/iang_fc/status/939258799654924288

Grigg, I. (2017c). *Wildest dream: REA (triple entry accounting) is the Golden Spike that brings the conventional industry together with wild-eyed blockchain.* Twitter Post. Available at https://twitter.com/iang_fc/status/939256814314622976

Grigg, I. (2017d). *EOS – An Introduction.* EOS Whitepaper. Available at https://www.iang.org/papers/EOS_An_Introduction-BLACK-EDITION.pdf

Gröblacher, M., & Mizdraković, V. (2019). *Triple-entry Bookkeeping: History and Benefits of the Concept.* Digitisation and Smart Financial Reporting.

Holman, G. K. (2019). *Blockchain and eBusiness.* LinkedIn. Available at https://www.linkedin.com/pulse/blockchain-ebusiness-ken-holman/

IFRS. (2019). *IFRS Foundation publishes IFRS taxonomy 2019.* Available at: https://www.ifrs.org/news-and-events/2019/03/ifrs-foundation-publishes-ifrs-taxonomy-2019/

Ijiri, Y. (1986). A framework for triple-entry bookkeeping. *The Accounting Review, 61*(4), 745–759.

Inghirami, I. E. (2019). *Accounting Information Systems: the Scope of Blockchain Accounting.* Conference paper. ITAIS and MCIS 2019: 13th Mediterranean Conference on Information Systems and 16th Conference of the Italian Chapter of AIS (Pavia).

ISO. (2019). *ISO/IEC CD 15944-21*. ISO. Available at https://www.iso.org/standard/78924.html

ISO/IEC. (2015). Information Technology — Business Operational View — Part 4: Business Transaction Scenarios — Accounting and Economic Ontolog. ISO/IEC International Standard 15944-4. Second edition 2015-04-01.

Karajovic, M., Kim, H., & Laskowski, M. (2019). Thinking outside the block: Projected phases of blockchain integration in the accounting industry. *Australian Accounting Review*, *29*(2), 319–330. doi:10.1111/auar.12280

KPMG LLP. (2019). *KPMG forms strategic alliance with Guard time*. Available at: https://www.prnewswire.com/news-releases/kpmg-forms-strategic-alliance-with-guardtime-300798827.html

Manni, F., & Faccia, A. (2015). *Introduction to accounting*. Aracne Editrice.

Manni, F., & Faccia, A. (2019). *Financial Accounting - Text and cases*. doi:10.1016/j.bcra.2021.100037

McCarthy, W. E. (1982). The REA Accounting Model: A Generalised Framework for Accounting Systems in a Shared Data Environment. *The Accounting Review*, *57*(3), 54–78.

McCarthy, W. E. (2001). *Re: Company centric view ends. Data goes to the Net.* Available at http://linas.org/mirrors/www.gldialtone.com/2001.07.14/McCarthyPost.htm

McCarthy, W. E., & Holman, G. K. (2019). *Blockchain and eBusiness. The Open-edi Distributed Business Transaction Repository*. ISO/IEC 15944-21 OeDBTR.

Melis, A. (2007). Financial statements and positive accounting theory: The early contribution of Aldo Amaduzzi. *Accounting Business & Financial History*, *17*(1), 53–62. doi:10.1080/09585200601127640

Pacio. (2018). *Pacio Technology*. Pacio Whitepaper Extract. Available at https://www.pacio.io/docs/Pacio_Technology.pdf

Rao, V. S. (2020). Blockchain Accounting in A Triple Entry System – Its Implications on the Firm. *Our Heritage*, *68*(1), 10499–10512.

Schmitz, J., & Leoni, G. (2019). Accounting and auditing at the time of blockchain technology: A research agenda. *Australian Accounting Review*, *29*(2), 331–342. doi:10.1111/auar.12286

Singh, R., Bhatt, V., & Bansal, R. (2023). Accounting in the demesne of big data, data analytics and artificial intelligence in industrial revolution 5.0: Applications, challenges and opportunities. Big Data: A Road-Map for Successful Digital Marketing, 49–63.

Spanò, R., Massaro, M., Ferri, L., Dumay, J., & Schmitz, J. (2022). Blockchain in accounting, accountability and assurance: An overview. *Accounting, Auditing & Accountability Journal*, *35*(7), 1493–1506. doi:10.1108/AAAJ-06-2022-5850

Syed Moudud-Ul-Huq, M. (2020). Role of cloud computing in global accounting information systems. *The Bottom Line (New York, N.Y.)*, *33*(3), 231–250. doi:10.1108/BL-01-2020-0010

Unicorn. (2018). *Can blockchain truly disrupt the accounting industry?* https://blockchain.wtf/2018/08/industry-impacts/finance/accounting/

Yuji, I. (1982). *Triple-Entry Bookkeeping and Income Momentum*. American Accounting Association.

Chapter 3
Contribution of Dematerialization to Tax Control Performance:
A Focus on Morocco

El Houssain Attak
https://orcid.org/0009-0007-4228-1057
Cadi Ayyad University, Morocco

ABSTRACT

Morocco heavily relies on tax revenues; however, a persistent 6.7% GDP gap between potential and actual tax revenues (2013-2017) highlights the challenge of widespread tax fraud. With a growing taxpayer base and a limited number of tax inspectors, Morocco faces a structural deficit in tax control. In response, a comprehensive digital transformation of tax processes was initiated. This chapter delves into the profound impact of digitalization on tax control through lexicometric analysis on interviews conducted with tax inspectors, facilitated by the IRAMUTEQ software. The research findings reveal a substantial enhancement in the performance of tax control. Despite this positive shift, the study underscores potential impediments that require a coordinated effort from all stakeholders involved. Beyond offering practical insights for authorities, this research contributes valuable lessons for developing nations grappling with the multifaceted challenges of revenue collection in the digital age concerning the pivotal role of digitalization in modernizing tax control practices.

DOI: 10.4018/979-8-3693-1678-8.ch003

INTRODUCTION

In the contemporary landscape, it is increasingly evident that the revolution brought about by new information and communication technologies (NICT) and data digitization has touched every field of activity. The transformative impact of global digital transformations has permeated various sectors, compelling governments to embark on the digitization of public finances for the creation of more efficient frameworks in revenue generation and expenditure management.

While the level of maturity varies significantly among states, tax administrations are no exception, actively seeking to elevate their performance and implement automated solutions to enhance the effectiveness of their interventions. The imperatives are unequivocal: administrations must respond in real-time, or at least within progressively shorter timeframes, to safeguard and ensure tax revenue (Wolf & Dale, 2019).

In the domain of national tax systems, the convergence of Big Data, advanced analytics, and an intensified digital presence represents a substantial opportunity. This shift has not only facilitated significant cost savings but has also aligned with fiscal policy objectives. The opportunity extends to the transition to a real-time tax system and the exploration of innovative approaches to tax management, fraud prevention, and addressing the shadow economy (OECD, 2016). The ongoing digital transformation signifies a fundamental shift from outdated infrastructures to cutting-edge technologies, fostering cost-saving initiatives for both tax administrators and taxpayers. The adoption of streamlined digital workflows not only improves operational efficiency but also markedly reduces the need for extensive interactions between taxpayers and tax collectors (Jacquemot & Raffinot, 2019).

Digital transformation is reshaping the dynamics between taxpayers and tax authorities by harnessing vast data and enhancing processing efficiency. The incorporation of technologies like blockchain and AI enriches data collection, facilitating tax collection and fraud detection (Attias Assouline & Glon, 2018).

These objectives are crucial for states heavily reliant on tax revenues, and Morocco is no exception. In Morocco, the role of taxation is particularly pivotal as the country grapples with a social deficit and depends solely on tax resources to fund its budget (OXFAM, 2021).

The majority of the Moroccan state's expenditures are funded by tax revenues, averaging 87% of the general budget's ordinary income between 2015 and 2022. However, Morocco has yet to fully exploit its tax potential. In 2022, the International Monetary Fund (IMF) observed that tax revenues as a percentage of GDP remained relatively low in Morocco, at 21.6%, compared to a potential of 33.8%. This 12% disparity between actual and potential tax collections within the Moroccan GDP deprives the country of vital additional tax revenue needed for improving growth prospects and social inclusion (Verdier et al., 2022).

The deficiency in tax revenues is attributed to factors such as a restricted tax base, a tax system marked by low efficiency, and particularly, a tax base eroded by tax fraud, resulting in an estimated 1% loss of GDP (Tax Justice Network, 2023).

Hence, there is a pressing need to fortify tax control mechanisms. However, faced with a growing taxpayer population and a limited number of tax inspectors, the tax administration confronts a structural deficiency in tax control. In this context and drawing inspiration from successful global experiences, Morocco initiated the digitization of its tax administration in 2010. The administration has undertaken an extensive dematerialization initiative to digitize all processes related to tax returns and settlements for various taxes.

The anticipated goal of this digitization of tax collection is to broaden the tax base and effectively combat tax fraud by consolidating electronic systems for tax compliance. Leveraging digital technologies for tax compliance involves the immediate and inclusive utilization of electronically available data from various aspects of taxpayers' routine business activities.

Studies conducted by Bellon et al. (2022), Fan et al. (2018), and Kitsios et al. (2020) illuminate the impact of digitization on tax control performance. Fiscal digitalization provides information on taxpayers' compliance with fiscal obligations and enables, to some extent, precise revenue forecasts and immediate electronic collection of certain tax obligations. The effective use of various electronic records inherent to taxpayers streamlines compliance processes and directs tax controls towards situations with a high probability of fiscal irregularities.

Therefore, the central research inquiry is: to what extent has the digitization of the Moroccan tax administration contributed to the performance of tax control?

This study aims to investigate two key subsidiary questions:

To what extent has the digitization of the Moroccan tax administration improved the effectiveness of tax controls, gauged by the number of verified cases and corresponding revenue figures?

How do tax inspectors perceive the effectiveness of the controls enacted subsequent to the digitization process within the Moroccan tax administration?

The main aim of this chapter is to assess the influence of digital transformation, particularly the digitization of tax procedures, on tax control performance in Morocco. It delves into how the transition to digital processes has improved the efficiency and effectiveness of tax control initiatives within the country. Moreover, it aims to elucidate the consequences of this digital transformation for Moroccan authorities and other developing nations grappling with revenue collection challenges.

In light of the limited research conducted in the Moroccan context, this chapter endeavors to enrich existing knowledge through an in-depth qualitative study. By placing a specific focus on examining how the digitization process influences the efficiency of tax control, this research aims to provide nuanced insights. These insights will not only help in assessing the current state of fiscal digitization in Morocco but also in identifying potential shortcomings within the existing system. The ultimate goal is to inform and guide future reforms in the ongoing digitization process of tax administration.

Additionally, this study seeks to shed light on the perspectives and viewpoints of tax auditors concerning the digitization initiatives within their administration. Understanding their perceptions is crucial for developing effective strategies and measures to bolster the efficiency of fiscal management practices in Morocco.

The outcomes of this research are anticipated to offer valuable insights to policymakers, tax authorities, and various stakeholders. These insights will empower decision-makers to make well-informed choices and devise policies that create an environment conducive to the advancement of e-tax administration in Morocco.

The organizational structure of this paper unfolds systematically. The initial section presents a literature review, exploring the impact of digitization on the efficiency of tax control. Subsequently, the paper details the methods employed in the study, the results obtained, and engages in subsequent discussions. Finally, the concluding section not only summarizes the key findings but also critically examines the implications and limitations inherent in this research.

LITERATURE REVIEW

Before exploring studies on digitization's impact on tax control, it's crucial to highlight key scholarly contributions related to tax control and tax digitization.

Tax Control

Allingham and Sandmo (1972) contend that deterring tax evasion can be effectively achieved through two distinct avenues. The first involves escalating the penalties associated with noncompliance with tax obligations, while the second entails amplifying the frequency and rigor of tax controls.

In a predominantly declarative tax framework, the presence of tax control authority, is essential to ensure accurate fulfillment of tax obligations by the taxpayer (Ricou, 2022). Tax control serves three primary objectives (Table 1):

OECD (2016) defines tax control as a meticulous examination and assessment by tax authorities to ascertain whether a taxpayer has accurately calculated and disclosed their tax obligations. This process ensures compliance with tax laws and regulations, aiming to maintain tax fairness and uphold the rule of law. Tax controls

Table 1. Tax control's objectives

Objective	Description
Ensuring equality in taxation	This involves upholding equality among individuals in taxation to prevent the transfer of their contribution to public expenses onto other taxpayers, emphasizing equitable distribution of the tax burden.
Fulfilling budgetary requirements	Tax control plays a vital fiscal role in facilitating the prompt and effective retrieval of evaded taxes.
Dissuasion and punitive functions	Tax control, coupled with substantial sanctions, aims to dissuade taxpayers from attempting to elude the establishment and payment of taxes, reinforcing fiscal responsibility.

Source: Ricou (2022)

Note. The table illustrates the tripartite objectives of tax control, ensuring equality in taxation, addressing budgetary needs, and serving dissuasive and punitive functions

involve a thorough examination of financial records, documents, and relevant information to validate the accuracy of the taxpayer's reported tax liability and identify any discrepancies.

Tax control comprises two primary methods: document reviews and external tax audits. Document reviews rely on information provided by taxpayers and documents from external sources to rectify non-submissions and address errors in filed declarations. Taxpayers are notified if additional information is needed or if a reminder is issued. In contrast, external tax audits, applicable to both businesses and individuals, adhere to rigorous procedures. Business audits may involve on-site visits, while individual audits are typically conducted at tax authority premises. These verifications cover all aspects of income, assets, and relevant taxes, ensuring a thorough examination of business affairs (The General Tax Administration, 2023).

According to George & Diavastis (2015), the significance of tax controls is pronounced due to an escalating demand for audit services. Tax controls constitute rigorous investigative procedures by tax authorities to identify potential instances of underreporting in tax declarations. The focus extends to assessing the accuracy of financial statements and verifying the correct amount of tax owed.

For Enofe et al. (2019), tax controls are crucial for ensuring tax reporting integrity, preventing evasion, and safeguarding government revenues. This involves a complete audit of financial records, documentation, and data to validate tax report accuracy. Similar to a financial audit, tax controls gather information to confirm legal compliance, aiming to affirm the reliability and accuracy of reported financial information for a definitive opinion on the fairness of financial statements.

Kircher (2008) defines tax controls as examinations of a taxpayer's financial records to assess compliance with applicable tax laws, procedures, and state standards. These audits ensure that taxpayers meet their compliance obligations and involve a thorough examination of a company's profits and returns in accordance with tax laws.

The primary objective of tax controls is to instill trust in the integrity of the tax system and promote voluntary compliance by identifying and rectifying instances of noncompliance. This serves as an effective strategy for preventing tax evasion and bolstering government revenue (Teszner, 2020). Tax controls can manifest in various forms, such as desk audits, field audits, or back duty audits. Desk audits, conducted within the offices of tax officials, involve administrative checks on submitted returns to verify compliance with tax laws.

Field audits, initiated subsequent to desk audits, involve on-site examinations of financial records and business operations. This meticulous scrutiny allows auditors to gain deeper insights into the intricacies of an entity's financial transactions and compliance practices. (Olaoye & Ogundipe, 2018).

The European Commission (2019) defines tax control as the process by which relevant tax authorities examine tax reports to ensure compliance with state tax laws. The significance of tax controls is multifaceted, playing a pivotal role in collecting necessary tax revenue, maintaining economic and financial stability, ensuring accurate returns, and mitigating tax avoidance.

Niu's (2011) study found a positive association between audits and voluntary compliance, emphasizing the impact of audits on compliance. The findings offer incentives to strengthen audit capabilities for additional revenue generation. Tax controls are categorized into random, cut-off, and conditional schemes.

Tax authorities implement an extensive system of control measures within the framework of tax administration, playing a pivotal role in safeguarding state interests against tax evasion. Tax controls serve the fundamental purpose of verifying taxpayers' compliance with tax legislation (Dečman et al., 2019).

In summary, tax controls encompass various methods and objectives, aiming to ensure compliance, maintain fairness, and enhance government revenue. The multifaceted nature of tax controls makes them indispensable in contemporary tax administration.

Tax Digitization

Digitalization, commonly defined as the use of electronic systems with advanced technology, has transformed various sectors, offering rapid access to information while reducing manual labor dependency (Bayrak, 2022). The COVID-19 pandemic has accelerated this digital transformation, making it a crucial agenda for governments. The journey towards this endpoint varies across countries, with unique strategies, timelines, and technology adoption (Ernst & Young, 2017).

In the realm of taxation, the surge in digitalized economic activities necessitates a reevaluation of tax inspection methods. The transition from paper-based record checks to e-applications like e-ledger and e-invoice, coupled with big data utilization, exemplifies the evolving nature of tax examinations (Üyümez & Hacıköylü, 2023).

Digitalizing accounting processes is crucial, but equally important is the digitalization of the tax system, going beyond the mere conversion of paper-based returns to PDFs (ICAEW, 2019). This transformation envisions changes in how taxpayers complete filings and what is subject to taxation, allowing tax authorities to utilize tough data pipelines for efficient audits.

Critical elements for the successful digital transformation of tax administration encompass a robust compliance strategy, legislative framework development, operational framework design, tax technology and infrastructure planning, change management, training, and education structuring, and performance measurement (Baisalbayeva et al., 2017).

Advantages of tax digitalization include streamlined compliance, combating tax fraud through automated data entry, enhanced access to relevant data for informed decision-making, accelerated refund processes, improved transparency, and enhanced risk management and audit efficiency (ICAEW, 2019; Üyümez & Hacıköylü, 2023).

The digitalization framework described by Ernst & Young (2017) provides a structured approach to upgrading tax administration systems. Starting with E-filing and progressing through e-accounting, e-match, e-audit, and finally e-access (table 2)

Table 2. Tax administration digitalization levels

Level (N°)	Description
E-filing (1)	At this foundational level, tax administrations introduce standardized electronic forms for filing tax returns. E-filing simplifies the data collection process and can lead to significant time and cost savings. It sets the stage for further digitalization.
E-accounting (2)	Level 2 builds upon e-filing by incorporating electronic accounting systems. These systems support the filing process and further streamline data collection. Taxpayers can submit data in electronic formats, reducing manual data entry.
E-match (3)	This level represents a crucial step in data validation. Tax authorities match data across various tax forms, potentially across different taxpayers and jurisdictions. This helps verify the accuracy of the data and reduces errors and fraud.
E-audit (4)	With real-time data analysis and review, level 4 enables more efficient tax audits. The availability of up-to-date data simplifies the auditing process, making it faster and more accurate.
E-access (5)	The highest level of digitalization eliminates the need for traditional tax forms. Instead, data collected can be used to compute taxes directly. Taxpayers receive electronic audit assessments, and they have a limited time to respond.

Source: Ernst & Young (2017)

Note. The table illustrates the progression of tax administration digitalization through five distinct levels: E-filing, E-accounting, E-match, E-audit, and E-access. Each level represents a significant advancement in leveraging technology for tax-related processes

These progressive levels, demonstrating the increasing sophistication of digital tools, highlight their profound impact on current tax systems. This transformative journey enables governments to effectively leverage technology, leading to enhanced tax compliance, minimized fraud, and streamlined tax processes. The positive outcomes of adopting digital tools in tax administration, such as simplified reporting procedures and more efficient audit processes, extend benefits to taxpayers, emphasizing the significant advantages associated with this technological evolution (Krieger, 2021).

Tax authorities are grappling with escalating demands, and the advent of digitalization provides an avenue to streamline resource allocation by minimizing human involvement and harnessing automation, as indicated by the OECD (2021). This digital shift mirrors a broader trend focused on enhancing efficiency within tax collection and enforcement mechanisms. The OECD (2021) emphasizes the transformative potential of digitalization for tax administrations, offering opportunities for improved revenue collection, heightened efficiency, reduced administrative burdens, and overarching societal changes. Successful digitalization initiatives typically involve context analysis, strategy development, and effective project delivery.

Digitalization in taxation, as noted by the ICAEW (2022), transcends the mere conversion of forms to online submissions; it signifies a revolutionary shift in how taxes are managed. Addressing digital exclusion is underscored as pivotal for establishing a modern and equitable tax system. Furthermore, Chernousova (2021) highlights the global transformative impact of digitalization on tax administration, enhancing the quality of tax processes through desk tax audits and monitoring. This ongoing digital transformation is anticipated to yield more transparent, secure, and efficient tax control processes. The Asian Development Bank (2022) echoes this sentiment, emphasizing a shift toward a fully automated tax system driven by the need for enhanced revenue collection and improved taxpayer services.

Insights from Baisalbayeva et al. (2017) highlight fundamental components crucial for a successful digital transformation in tax administration. This involves developing a comprehensive compliance strategy, updating tax and procedural laws, and aligning governance models with the chosen strategy. Achieving this transformation requires strategic change management, targeted training, and education for well-defined roles and transparent decision-making processes. Emphasizing the importance of restructuring units based on taxpayer segments and fostering a clear vision to prevent and detect tax fraud, they underscore the implementation of key performance indicators tied to the compliance strategy. This facilitates ongoing monitoring of progress, capacity-building efforts, and objectives, enhancing overall transparency and accountability throughout the digitalization process.

Transitioning from foundational tax control principles and exploring the influence of digitalization on tax administration, the focus now narrows to examine how digitization specifically impacts tax control processes. This section delves into the intricate dynamics of digitization influencing the landscape of tax control.

Digitization and Tax Control

The pivotal role of digitalization in tax control is underscored by Zhutiaeva (2021), emphasizing electronic services for taxpayers and extensive data analysis for risk assessment. Ouyang et al.'s (2023) research explores the impact of digital finance on small business tax compliance, revealing how digitalization influences compliance dynamics. Chen et al.'s (2023) study in China correlates tax policy reform with digitalization, acting as a catalyst for enhancing digital capabilities and innovation within enterprises.

Bellon et al. (2022) investigate e-invoicing adoption, showing substantial increases in reported firm sales and VAT liabilities. Milosavljević et al.'s (2023) use of machine learning assesses tax administration efficiency, offering a nuanced understanding of digital technology challenges. Ofori et al. (2022) envision digital platforms transforming tax compliance across African countries, addressing informality and fostering business growth. He & Yi's (2023) examination of the China Tax Administration Information System sheds light on digitalization's impact on tax burdens.

A broad analysis by Durán Cabré & Esteller Moré (2020) acknowledges digitalization challenges but underscores enhanced data access advantages. Uyar et al.'s (2021) exploration emphasizes well-implemented digitalization in government services as a key factor in mitigating tax evasion. Chen (2017) underscores digitalization's role in enhancing tax enforcement capabilities, reducing tax evasion.

Various studies highlight how digital technology streamlines tax compliance procedures, fosters innovative tax policies, and transforms tax administration and policy development. Changing dynamics between taxpayers and tax authorities in the digital era, improved data management, and real-time monitoring through technologies like blockchain and smart contracts contribute to the multifaceted impact of digitalization on tax control. The imperative of digital transformation is echoed by Hamid et al. (2023), emphasizing a whole overhaul of tax authorities' operations. Mascagni et al. (2021) suggest that electronic Sales Registration Machines (SRMs) enhance tax control and compliance, Okunogbe & Pouliquen's (2022) evidence from Tajikistan indicates the positive impact of electronic filing (e-filing) on tax compliance and payments, and Okunogbe (2021) highlights technology's pivotal role in enhancing property tax collection in Liberia.

Studies from Bellon et al. (2022) and Fan et al. (2018) demonstrate the significant impact of digitization, especially through e-invoicing, on tax compliance. Research on e-filing in developing countries by Yılmaz & Coolidge (2013) emphasizes effective policy implementation and a learning curve's role in shaping the multifaceted impact of digitalization on tax control. Vishnevsky & Chekina (2018) argue that digitalization, particularly through technologies like blockchain and smart contracts, enables real-time monitoring, reducing opportunities for tax evasion. Kitsios et al. (2020) stress the crucial role of digitalization in enhancing tax control by improving information collection and processing, reducing trade fraud, and increasing revenue gains. Tiantian et al. (2023) advocate for governments to invest in dynamic information disclosure platforms and integrated supervision systems, leveraging digitalization to promote tax compliance. Grigorieva et al. (2020) acknowledge the dual impact of digitalization on tax evasion, enhancing tax authorities' capabilities while also presenting new challenges that necessitate adaptive strategies.

In essence, the literature reviewed underscores the transformative impact of digitalization on tax control, emphasizing its multifaceted implications for compliance, enforcement, and policy development. The integration of automated techniques, data-driven methodologies, and innovative digital platforms emerges as a common thread, offering new possibilities for effective tax governance in the evolving landscape of the digital era.

Tax auditing, a cornerstone of governance, is undergoing a profound digital transformation. Traditional manual examination methods are yielding to innovative automated techniques, leveraging data mining and predictive analysis for faster, more extensive, and objective assessments. This shift is evident in income tax and social benefit declarations, with integrated solutions like pre-filled declarations benefiting smaller entities, while larger enterprises identify critical areas within their accounting systems through digital approaches.

After summarizing various scholarly studies and theoretical models on digitalization's impact on tax control, the next section will explore the employed empirical framework.

METHODOLOGY

In this section, the research methodology used to explore the effects of digitalization on tax control in Morocco is clarified. The study adopts a qualitative, deductive, and exploratory approach.

Sample Selection

To ensure a significant sample size, the principles of empirical saturation were meticulously applied during the participant selection phase. As elucidated by Paillé & Mucchielli (2021), empirical saturation represents the stage in qualitative research where the collection and analysis of additional data are unlikely to yield significantly novel insights. This indicates that researchers have achieved a thorough understanding of the phenomenon under investigation, and supplementary data are improbable to substantially alter or significantly enhance their findings.

The attainment of empirical saturation holds paramount importance, especially in upholding academic rigor and credibility, as it signifies an exhaustive and thorough exploration of the data. In alignment with this principle, a total of twenty (20) highly experienced tax inspectors were deliberately selected to participate in this study. Participant selection was conducted with careful consideration, leveraging their substantial expertise in tax control. This approach ensures a multi-dimensional perspective from tax auditors well-versed in the intricate operations of tax control, thereby enhancing the depth and authenticity of the research outcomes.

Epistemological Stance

The study is grounded in the epistemological foundation of critical realism, a theoretical approach dedicated to elucidating social phenomena by identifying underlying causal mechanisms (Bhaskar, 2020). This paradigm recognizes that the intricate mechanisms shaping the impact of digitalization on tax control are concealed from direct observation. Consequently, the study seeks to delve into these hidden realities, bringing to light the intricate interplay of factors and decoding the causal pathways at play.

Critical realism operates within a stratified ontology that encompasses the realms of the "real," the "actual," and the "empirical," allowing for the examination of interactions within these layers (Bhaskar, 2020). Embracing a critical realist perspective empowers researchers to transcend superficial observations and comprehend the deep-rooted causal mechanisms that give rise to social practices (Fletcher, 2017). This holistic approach provides a nuanced understanding of the complexities of social phenomena by considering causal mechanisms, different layers of reality, and specific contextual influences.

The adoption of the critical realist framework is motivated by the aspiration to unveil the intricate dynamics linking digitalization and tax control. Through unraveling these multifaceted connections, the study aims to yield valuable insights into the profound repercussions of digitalization on tax control.

In the pursuit of data collection, an inductive and qualitative methodology is employed, with interviews serving as the primary means of gathering information. The study endeavors to capture valuable insights and perspectives from tax inspectors, facilitating an in-depth exploration of their experiences and perceptions regarding the intricate interplay between digitalization and tax control.

Data Collection

The primary data for this research was acquired through a series of methodically planned semi-structured interviews, utilizing an interview guide (Appendix). This guide aimed to explore the nuanced dimensions of the impact of digitalization on tax control, specifically within the Moroccan context.

The thematic areas covered by the guide included descriptive aspects, where essential demographic variables like age, and the commencement date of professional activity were systematically gathered to offer indispensable contextual insights. Furthermore, the guide extensively investigated the influence of digitalization on both taxpayers and tax administration. It delved into participants' evaluations of taxpayers' engagement, the objectives pursued by the tax administration through digitalization, and the ensuing effects on work organization and relationships with other state administrations.

Additionally, the study scrutinized the impact of digitalization on tax controls, considering aspects such as the quality of taxpayers' declaration verification, the efficiency of tax controls, and the potential contributions to expanding the tax base and revenue.

The semi-structured nature of the interviews was deliberately designed to allow flexibility, providing participants with the freedom to express their thoughts openly.

The interviews spanned over a four-month period from April to mid-August 2023, with each individual session lasting between 25 and 40 minutes, ensuring a thorough and diverse dataset for analysis.

Data Analysis

The collected data underwent transcription and subsequent automated lexical analysis using the IRaMuTeQ software (Ratinaud, 2009). This software systematically scrutinized the textual data to unveil discernible patterns, thematic elements, and insights relevant to the impact of digitalization on tax control. Employing IRaMuTeQ ensured a uniform analytical process, thereby minimizing potential biases in data interpretation. The software's automated algorithm facilitated the precise identification of linguistic attributes and their interconnections, expediting the exploration of the dataset. This approach revealed recurrent terms, semantic clusters, and patterns of co-occurrence, providing a thorough exploration of the textual corpus and establishing a robust foundation for deriving empirically substantiated conclusions.

FINDING

Before presenting the study findings, an overview of tax control in Morocco is provided.

Overview of Digitalization and Tax Control in Morocco

Since the early 2000s, Morocco has embarked on an extensive program aimed at modernizing its public administration. This progress is manifested through the gradual and widespread digitization of financial transactions and government services, signifying a significant leap towards a more technologically integrated administrative landscape. Concurrently, the ambitious modernization strategy has actively propelled the dematerialization of the tax administration, representing a strategic pursuit aligned with broader national objectives.

As an integral component of the overarching strategy dedicated to simplifying tax procedures and fostering greater compliance, the General Tax Administration (GTA) has consistently and ardently embraced digitalization in recent years. This unwavering commitment is manifest in the successful implementation of diverse online tax services, ushering in a new era of convenience and accessibility for taxpayers. The wide-ranging digitization of essential taxpayer records, encompassing declarations, payments, certificates, and more, stands as a cornerstone of the GTA's approach. Through this embrace of digital transformation, the GTA aims to optimize the taxation process and enhance operational efficiency and service quality on a full scale.

The tangible outcomes of this digitalization effort are evident in the escalating number of digitized operations and the heightened intensity of tax controls, coupled with the resultant increase in associated revenues. This transformative impact is elucidated in the table provided below, underscoring the positive correlation between digitalization initiatives and the operational and fiscal advancements achieved within the Moroccan tax administration.

Digitized Operations. The consistent growth in digitized operations is evident, ascending from 6.88 million in 2017 to 21.2 million in 2022, reflecting a remarkable 208% increase. This expansion underscores the tax administration's commitment to digital transformation, likely enhancing operational efficiency and responsiveness.

Number of tax controls. The number of tax controls experienced a significant surge, escalating from 13,853 in 2017 to 52,589 in 2022, marking a substantial 280% increase. This noteworthy growth reflects a strategic emphasis on tax enforcement, likely facilitated by the adoption of digital technologies.

Revenue from tax controls. Despite fluctuations, the revenue from tax controls exhibited an overall positive trajectory. Revenue increased from 7.8 billion MAD

Table 3. Evolution of digitized operations, tax controls, and revenue (2017-2022)

	Digitized Operations (Million)	Number of Tax Control	Revenue From Tax Controls (in Billions MAD)
2017	6,88	13 853	7,8
2018	9,98	31 106	12,1
2019	14,71	52 702	12,1
2020	14,25	32 569	5,8
2021	18,82	54 852	7,9
2022	21,2	52 589	10,4

Source: General Tax Administration (2023)

Note. The table illustrates the dynamic evolution of digitized operations, tax controls and revenue generation, within the Moroccan tax administration from 2017 to 2022.

in 2017 to 10.4 billion MAD in 2022, indicating a commendable 33% growth. The positive correlation with the rise in tax controls suggests that digitalization contributes to improved fiscal outcomes.

In summary, the interplay between increased tax controls, revenue growth, and the continuous expansion of digitized operations highlights the transformative impact of digitalization within the Moroccan tax administration. These trends underscore the positive outcomes and efficiency gains resulting from the integration of digital technologies in tax control processes.

Following this overview, the study findings are introduced with an initial analysis of the profiles of the interviewees.

Characteristics of the Participants

The sample comprises 20 interviewees, providing a balanced representation of sex, with 55% male and 45% female participants. Age distribution indicates a diverse range, with a concentration in the 30-50 age group (35% to 45%). Professionally, the interviewees are characterized by a mix of experience levels, with 50% having over 15 years of experience. This diversity suggests a complete spectrum of perspectives, from seasoned professionals to those in the early stages of their careers, potentially enriching the insights gathered from the study.

The next section analyzes the textual corpus from conducted interviews, providing valuable insights into the intricate relationship between digitalization and tax control.

Table 4. Summary of interviewees' data

Interviewees	Category	Frequency	%
Sex	Female	9	45%
	Male	11	55%
Age	under 30	1	5%
	30-40 years	7	35%
	41-50 years	9	45%
	51-60 years	3	15%
Working experience	6 – 9 years	5	25%
	10 – 15 years	5	25%
	> 15 years	10	50%

Source: The author

Note. The presented data underscores the balanced sex distribution, diverse age demographics, and varied professional experience within the surveyed cohort.

Descriptive Analyses

To analyze the textual corpus derived from the conducted interviews, two main methods of lexicometric analysis are employed using IRaMuTeQ: Similarity Analysis and the Reinert Method.

Similarity Analysis. The Similarity Analysis, based on graph theory, allows for the identification of frequently associated word communities within a textual corpus and their representation as a network graph of grouped lexical forms.

Utilizing Similarity Analysis methodologically reveals latent patterns and interconnections within the compiled textual dataset. This technique identifies themes, evolving trends, and divergences in viewpoints. It visually demonstrates word interconnections and co-occurrence patterns, aiding in detecting key concepts and themes within the corpus. This facilitates in-depth exploration of subject intricacies (Ratinaud & Marchand, 2012).

Initial exploration involves similarities using frequent terms and their corresponding "universe of words" in a figure visually represents linguistic relationships, offering insight into thematic undercurrents in the interview corpus.

The figure (Figure.1) below presents the results of this analysis of the corpus.

The examination initiates with a comparative scrutiny of prevailing terms and their respective "word universes," encapsulating the central themes of interviews across three pivotal clusters.

Embarking on the first thematic cluster, "Digitalization and taxpayers," the focus intensifies on participants' evaluations of taxpayers' involvement in the

Figure 1. Similarity analysis carried out at IRaMuTeQ
Source: The author
Note. This figure depicts the patterns of co-occurrence and associations among words identified through the utilization of the Similarity Analysis methodology.

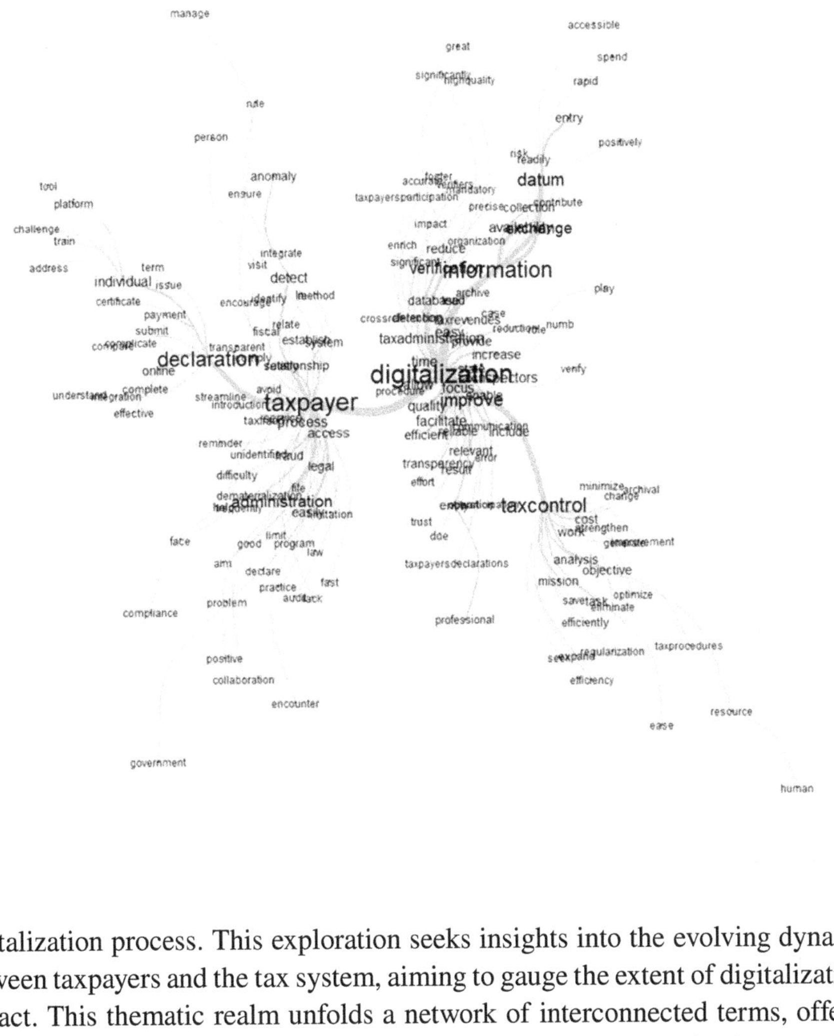

digitalization process. This exploration seeks insights into the evolving dynamics between taxpayers and the tax system, aiming to gauge the extent of digitalization's impact. This thematic realm unfolds a network of interconnected terms, offering illumination on the challenges and changes introduced by digitalization.

Transitioning to the second thematic cluster, "Digitalization and tax administration," the analysis delves into the objectives pursued by the tax administration through digitalization. Simultaneously, it investigates the repercussions of digitalization on the organization of work within the tax department and its relationships with other state administrations.

As the analysis progresses, the third thematic cluster, "Digitalization and tax control," resonates with participants' perspectives on the effects of digitalization on the quality of taxpayers' declaration verification. It explores how digitalization has influenced the efficiency of tax controls and investigates potential contributions to expanding the tax base and revenue.

Reinert Method

Two analyses were employed:

- Descending Hierarchical Classification (DHC)
- Correspondence factor analysis(CFA)

DHC is a methodological framework employed to systematically categorize linguistic forms or units based on shared linguistic traits or thematic content. Through iterative grouping and division, DHC facilitates the organization of textual segments into hierarchical clusters, often visualized as dendrograms. This classification process enhances the identification of patterns, relationships, and overarching themes present within the corpus, thereby offering insights into its underlying structure and thematic composition (Ratinaud & Marchand, 2012).

CFA explore relationships between categorical linguistic variables within a corpus. By transforming these variables into a lower-dimensional space, CFA facilitates the visualization and interpretation of patterns, associations, and dependencies among linguistic categories. This method provides insights into the intricate interplay and thematic connections among categorical variables present in the corpus, contributing to a thorough understanding of its thematic nuances and underlying relationships. CFA performs a two-dimensional projection of the textual corpus, where lexical classes are projected onto a two-dimensional graph based on the similarity or dissimilarity of their constituent terms (Ratinaud & Marchand, 2012).

The DHC generated tree classes (Figure.2).

In analyzing the distinctive linguistic patterns within each class, the outcomes provide nuanced insights.

Class 1 (28%) sheds light on the diverse dimensions of tax digitalization-related challenges, encompassing issues such as compliance difficulties, limitations in available tools, and the need for effective training programs. It underscores the importance of addressing these challenges to enhance understanding and facilitate efficient tax filing procedures.

Class 2 (36%) highlights the significance of digitalization in addressing challenges faced by taxpayers. It emphasizes the role of technology in providing easy access to services, improving transparency, and detecting anomalies and potential fraud

Figure 2. Descending hierarchical classification generated by IRaMuTeQ
Source: The Author
Note. This figure categorizes terms into separate clusters, delineating their similarities and differences.

Figure 3. Correspondence factor analysis carried out at IRaMuTeQ
Source: The author
Note. The figure illustrates the arrangement of terms in a multidimensional space, emphasizing the closeness or separation between them.

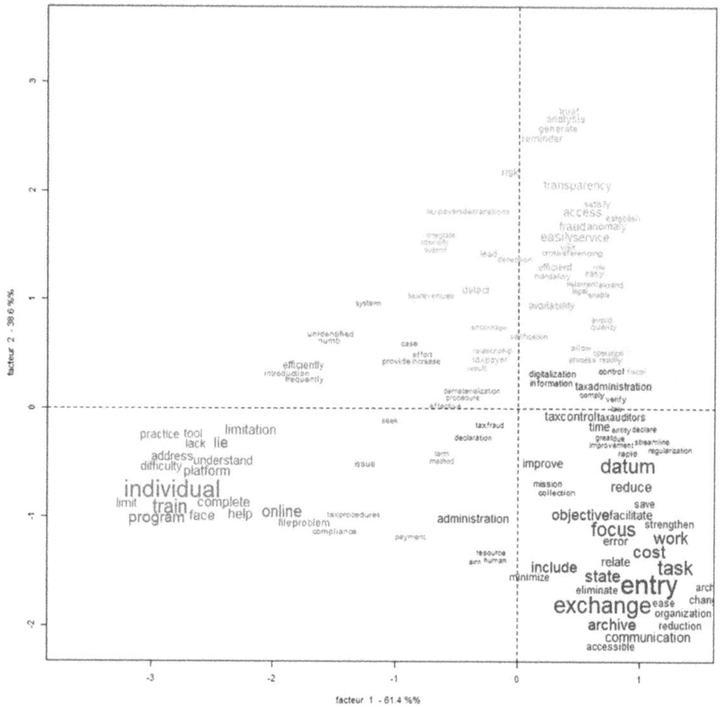

risks. The class emphasizes the need for a robust digital infrastructure to enhance taxpayer trust and satisfaction.

Class 3 (36%) focuses on the administrative aspects of tax control and digitalization. It addresses tasks related to data entry, archival processes, and communication within tax administration. The recommendations include reducing costs, improving efficiency, and strengthening tax audit processes through effective digitalization strategies.

These three classes collectively contribute to in-depth understanding of the challenges and opportunities in the context of tax control and digitalization, with Class 1 serving as a pivotal branch in the dendrogram, and Classes 2 and 3 forming the second branch.

In order to study the proximity of the classes defined in the DHC, a CFA was then performed (Figure.3).

The findings extracted from the CFA unveil a significant association between Classes 1 and 3 in the context of tax digitalization challenges, particularly concerning the influence of digitalization on tax control. These classes jointly illuminate diverse dimensions within the challenges posed by tax digitalization, offering insights into the multifaceted aspects of the digital transformation in taxation, with a specific focus on its impact on tax control mechanisms. While Class 2 places specific emphasis on the significance of digitalization in addressing challenges faced by taxpayers, it maintains its distinct characteristics. However, a nuanced and subtle connection between Class 2 and the broader themes of Classes 1 and 3 emerges, suggesting an interplay between tax inspectors' perceptions of the impact of digitalization on tax control.

In the "Discussion" section, lexicometric analysis findings explore the impact of digitalization on tax control. The discussion centers on three identified classes from the data analysis, examined in detail using IRaMuTeQ.

DISCUSSION

The automated lexical analysis of the semantic universe, complemented by an examination of verbatim responses, provides valuable insights into the tax inspectors' perceptions of the influence of digitalization on tax control. This analysis delves into the direct implications of digitalization on tax auditing and its indirect effects, mediated through its influence on both taxpayers and the tax administration. Additionally, this analysis has identified factors that may constrain or limit the influence of digitalization on tax control, providing a nuanced understanding of the complex dynamics at play

Digitalization and Taxpayers

Assessing taxpayer participation in the fiscal digitalization process reveals a nuanced perspective. The acceptance and engagement levels vary among different taxpayer segments. Initially, individual taxpayers exhibited resistance and hesitancy, facing challenges in adapting to digital platforms and navigating new online systems. However, with increased familiarity, many individuals have gradually embraced digitalization, leading to improvements in their participation and compliance.

In contrast, businesses and corporate entities demonstrated a higher degree of readiness to adopt digital tax processes. Their preparedness is often facilitated by dedicated financial personnel or accountants, making the transition relatively smoother. Transparency and accessibility, integral components of digitalization, have positively influenced taxpayer participation. The convenience of filing taxes, checking records, and making payments online, without the need for physical visits to tax offices, has fostered collaboration and compliance. This shift is particularly noteworthy as it aligns with the advantages of accurate, easily accessible, and real-time financial information.

Furthermore, the digitalization process has significantly empowered tax administrations in detecting anomalies and discrepancies in taxpayer declarations efficiently. This enhanced capability contributes substantially to fostering taxpayer compliance, as awareness grows regarding the increased likelihood of detecting tax evasion and fraud in a digitalized environment.

Examining the impact of digitalization on the relationship between taxpayers and tax administrations reveals profound changes. Transparency and convenience have substantially increased, allowing taxpayers to seamlessly engage in tax-related activities, verify financial records, and build trust. The digitization process has led to enhanced efficiency by reducing bureaucratic complexities, streamlining interactions with tax authorities, and making processes more time-efficient.

Moreover, digitalization plays a pivotal role in encouraging compliance. The ease of detecting irregularities and potential fraud acts as a strong incentive for taxpayers to adhere strictly to tax regulations. The use of digital platforms facilitates improved communication not only between taxpayers and tax authorities but also between tax authorities and other government agencies, reinforcing overall compliance efforts. However, it is crucial to acknowledge that specific groups, particularly those less proficient in technology, face challenges, necessitating tailored support and training for inclusivity.

This overview underscores the multifaceted impact of digitalization on both taxpayers and tax administrations, emphasizing the need for continued support and adaptation to ensure effective and inclusive outcomes.

Digitalization and Tax Administration

Examining the objectives pursued by tax administrations through digitalization reveals a multifaceted set of goals. Primarily, these initiatives aim to rationalize and simplify operational processes by reducing costs associated with manual tasks like data entry, storage, and archival of physical records. The consequence is a notable upswing in operational efficiency.

A pivotal goal is to elevate the quality and efficacy of tax control mechanisms. The digitization paradigm equips tax authorities with expeditious and precise data analysis tools, bolstering their capability to discern inconsistencies and potential instances of tax evasion or fraud. These initiatives are underpinned by the desire to gain a more profound understanding of taxpayer activities, fostering transparency. Leveraging digitalization, tax authorities can access holistic, real-time insights into taxpayers' businesses affairs, cultivating well-informed decision-making and transparency within the taxation sphere.

Simultaneously, digitalization aims to save time for both taxpayers and tax officials by mitigating manual data entry and processing tasks. This shift involves moving away from mundane paperwork tasks towards engaging tax personnel in more substantive facets of tax control. An overarching objective is to facilitate collaboration and the seamless exchange of information between tax administration and other government agencies. Establishing an integrated system for sharing taxpayer data among governmental entities aspires to ensure uniformity and conformity across different governmental sectors.

Regarding the effects of digitalization on the organization of work within tax administration, the impact has been significant. Digitalization has catalyzed a profound reconfiguration of work processes, streamlining traditionally paper-intensive tasks such as data entry, record archiving, and document retrieval. The shift from manual record-keeping to automated digital systems has liberated considerable resources channeled into more value-driven activities.

Additionally, the transition to digital systems has resulted in a greater degree of specialization and a shift in the focus of tax personnel. With routine data entry tasks mitigated, tax officials can concentrate more on the substantive mission of tax control, enhancing productivity and efficiency. The temporal dimension of tax-related work has transformed, providing 24/7 accessibility to taxpayers, enabling them to file declarations, make payments, and access records at their convenience. This real-time accessibility has redefined work hours within the tax administration, transcending traditional temporal constraints.

The digitalization drive has also engendered improvements in internal communication and teamwork. Digital platforms for data sharing and collaborative work enable more seamless interactions among tax officials, enhancing the overall flow of information and communication within the administration.

Examining the effect of digitalization on the relationship between tax administration and other state administrations reveals significant impacts. This transformation is characterized by increased efficiency, transparency, and collaboration in the exchange of information between various government entities.

First and foremost, digitalization has streamlined the process of collecting and sharing data between the tax administration and other government agencies. The availability of digital records and real-time information access has greatly facilitated this exchange, reduced administrative burdens and minimized errors associated with manual data entry and retrieval.

Furthermore, the digitalization of tax administration has fostered a culture of transparency and accountability in interactions with other state bodies. The availability of accurate and easily accessible data enables more rigorous oversight and scrutiny, promoting integrity and adherence to established legal and regulatory frameworks.

Collaboration between different state administrations has been significantly enhanced by digitalization. Sharing data and coordinating efforts, such as identifying discrepancies or anomalies in financial reporting, is now more efficient and effective. The ability to quickly cross-reference information has expedited interagency communication and cooperation, enabling a more synchronized approach to governance.

Digitalization and Tax Control

Assessing the impact of digitalization on taxpayers' compliance reveals its potential to significantly influence adherence to tax regulations. Key observations include the empowerment of tax authorities through digital formats, enabling swift detection of discrepancies in taxpayers' declarations. This heightened scrutiny acts as a deterrent, fostering conscientious compliance. The ease of digital record-keeping reduces manual entry errors, enhancing submission accuracy and encouraging timely compliance. The transparency of digital systems minimizes room for tax evasion, promoting adherence to tax laws. Digitalization also fosters greater engagement and communication between tax authorities and taxpayers, leading to higher compliance rates.

Examining the effect of fiscal digitalization on the quality of verification of taxpayers' declarations shows substantial positive impacts. Digitalization facilitates real-time access to inclusive information crucial for accurate verification. The use of digital platforms expedites the verification process by eliminating manual data entry and allowing swift cross-referencing of declarations. The reduction in human errors associated with manual processing enhances the reliability of verification outcomes, minimizing disputes and errors in tax assessments.

Analyzing the influence of digitalization on the efficiency of tax control highlights substantial positive impacts. Digitalization significantly improves the accuracy of tax control activities by reducing the margin for human error. The adoption of digital platforms and automated data exchange systems streamlines the entire process, enabling rapid access and cross-referencing of taxpayer information. This efficiency not only expedites the control process but also optimizes resource allocation, allowing focus on more complex cases and strategic analyses.

Exploring the contribution of digitalization to expanding the tax base and revenue underscores its transformative potential. Firstly, digitalization enables more complete and automated procedures for cross-referencing taxpayer data, enhancing the identification of irregularities and non-compliance. Secondly, it equips tax authorities with streamlined and efficient verification and auditing processes, revealing unreported income and instances of tax evasion. Additionally, the convenience and accessibility of digital platforms incentivize a larger number of taxpayers to participate actively. Moreover, digitalization facilitates data sharing among government entities, bringing previously unregistered entities into the formal tax system and accelerating the tax collection process. These facets collectively contribute to a broader tax base and heightened revenue collection.

Factors Influencing the Impact of Digitalization on Tax Control

The influence of digitalization on tax control, whether through direct or indirect means, is intricately shaped by a range of factors, as highlighted in the insights gleaned from interview responses.

Navigating the complexities of digitalization in the realm of tax controls poses substantial challenges, particularly for individual taxpayers who grapple with technological barriers. The pervasive nature of digitalization has not only transformed tax processes but has also heightened anxieties surrounding data security. To assuage these concerns, thorough measures must be implemented.

Universal access to digital tax services faces hindrances, especially in remote areas with limited internet connectivity. This gives rise to accessibility challenges that demand innovative solutions to ensure inclusivity in the digitalization process.

Resistance to the adoption of digital systems may manifest due to unfamiliarity or concerns about job displacement. Overcoming such resistance requires targeted initiatives aimed at familiarizing individuals with the benefits and opportunities afforded by digitalization.

The considerable initial investments required for modernization carry significant cost implications, necessitating meticulous financial planning for long-term sustainability. Legal and regulatory frameworks often lag behind technological advancements, emphasizing the need for collaborative efforts to adapt and modernize tax laws effectively.

Interoperability challenges in seamless data exchange add complexity to digitalization efforts, demanding the development of standardized protocols and integration mechanisms. Adapting human resources to the shift toward digital platforms requires a widespread reevaluation of skills and roles within tax administration.

The lack of awareness among taxpayers emerges as a potential hurdle to adoption, highlighting the challenge of strategic investments in public awareness campaigns. Crucially, the establishment of effective channels for taxpayer feedback is paramount for the iterative refinement and enhancement of digital systems in tax control.

In summary, addressing these multifaceted challenges requires a holistic understanding of the obstacles posed by technological, accessibility, resistance, financial, legal, and interoperability issues in the context of transitioning to digital tax processes.

CONCLUSION AND RECOMMENDATIONS

This chapter delves into the impact of digitalization on tax control, employing a lexicometric analysis of interviews with tax inspectors to unveil its effects on efficiency and effectiveness. The research discloses that digitalization enables tax inspectors to concentrate on their core mission, fostering relationships with taxpayers and stakeholders through enhanced data exchange. Consequently, this leads to an uptick in verified cases and associated tax revenues, showcasing both qualitative and quantitative improvements in the tax administration's efficiency.

Examining the influence of digitalization within the Moroccan tax administration, the study delineates direct effects on tax control, indirect implications through interactions with taxpayers, and a restructuring within the tax administration. It underscores various factors that either facilitate or impede this influence. The transformation of tax control mechanisms is emphasized, resulting in heightened efficiency, accuracy, and transparency across operational processes, from data entry to verification. The positive impact on taxpayers is evident, promoting compliance through improved transparency, accessibility, and communication.

Furthermore, the study uncovers a noteworthy enhancement in operational efficiency and overall performance of tax control in Morocco, attributed to the digital transformation of tax processes. The digitization of tax procedures introduces precision in data collection, facilitating unprecedented traceability and cross-referencing of information from diverse sources, thereby elevating the accuracy and reliability of tax control mechanisms.

Additionally, the strategic reallocation of human resources within the tax administration contributes to operational efficiencies. Optimizing staff allocation from routine tasks to high-value tax control functions reduces costs associated with administrative management and archiving, enhancing financial sustainability. In essence, the integration of digital technologies not only refines data accuracy and collection processes but also unlocks the potential for value within the tax administration. These findings underscore the multifaceted benefits of digitalization in the realm of tax control.

The findings regarding the multifaceted impact of digitalization on tax control align with the conclusions drawn by Hamid et al. (2023). This alignment underscores the crucial need for modernizing the tax system in developing countries, emphasizing heightened efficiency and reshaped dynamics between tax authorities and taxpayers. In addition, the study resonates with Niu's (2010) insights, revealing a positive correlation between audits and voluntary compliance. This highlights the imperative for tax professionals and authorities to fortify audit capabilities for enhanced revenue generation.

Furthermore, the observations of Tiantian et al. (2023) reinforce the transformative influence of digital technologies on tax control. Their emphasis on inhibiting tax avoidance and improving information transparency through dynamic platforms aligns seamlessly with the overarching theme of the research. Lastly, the research aligns with Krieger's (2021) acknowledgment of challenges faced by tax authorities and underscores the potential of minimizing human involvement and harnessing automation for optimal resource allocation amidst financial constraints. The expanding reservoir of data emerges as a strategic asset in fortifying tax administration performance.

However, challenges such as technological barriers, data security concerns, and resistance to change necessitate strategic interventions. The nuanced impact of digitalization on tax control, both direct and indirect, is influenced by various factors revealed in interview responses. Challenges and opportunities emerge, especially for those encountering technological barriers, requiring extensive outreach programs for user-friendly interfaces and digital literacy training. Addressing data security concerns demands substantial investments and transparent communication. Proactive measures are imperative for accessibility issues, including exploring offline alternatives and deploying mobile tax units. Resistance to digital systems can be mitigated through targeted training initiatives, emphasizing the advantages of digitalization.

Financial considerations, including substantial upfront investments, underscore the importance of long-term financial planning for sustainable modernization. Collaborative efforts with legislative bodies are essential to align legal and regulatory frameworks with technological advances. Interoperability challenges in data exchange mandate standardized protocols and integration mechanisms. The shift to digital platforms necessitates a transformation in the skills of tax administration staff, justifying human resource development programs.

Public awareness poses a challenge, potentially hindering widespread adoption, emphasizing the need for strategic investments in awareness campaigns and user-friendly educational materials. Establishing effective feedback mechanisms is crucial for the continuous development and improvement of digital tax control systems. These recommendations, crucial for successful implementation, are thoughtfully considered in the comprehensive conclusion, ensuring the adaptability and improvement of the digitalization program within the Moroccan tax administration.

Overcoming these challenges, Moroccan tax authorities should progressively embrace the pre-population of tax returns, a measure highlighted by J. Chen et al. (2017). This strategy holds the potential to enhance the efficiency of tax control in Morocco, effectively combating tax fraud. Transitioning towards pre-population offers a promising avenue to reduce compliance costs for taxpayers, minimize errors and omissions, and streamline the overall tax filing process. Additionally, it aligns with the global trend of leveraging digital innovations to modernize tax systems, ensuring a more seamless interaction between tax authorities and taxpayers. As emphasized by Chen et al., the associated benefits, including time savings for revenue agencies, are readily discernible, making pre-population a viable and impactful step in optimizing tax processes in Morocco.

IMPLICATIONS AND LIMITATIONS

This study has implications for future research and acknowledges certain limitations, providing avenues for further inquiry and contributing to a comprehensive understanding of its scope and findings.

Implications for Future Research

Policy intervention. The study's outcomes provide valuable insights for policymakers seeking to optimize tax control mechanisms through digitalization. Implementing recommended digital reforms could establish a more agile and efficient fiscal environment, enhancing tax compliance and revenue generation.

Cross-jurisdictional comparative studies. Future research endeavors could conduct cross-jurisdictional analyses to assess how varied tax control digitalization strategies impact overall tax administration. Such comparative studies would contribute to identifying best practices and offering evidence-based recommendations applicable in diverse contexts.

User behavioral dynamics. Delving into the behavioral dynamics of tax professionals and taxpayers within the digital realm is crucial for understanding how digitalization influences decision-making, perceptions, and overall compliance. Future studies in this area can guide the design of targeted interventions and user-friendly digital systems.

Long-term impact assessments. To gauge the sustained effects of digitalization on tax control, longitudinal studies are recommended. Tracking the evolution of tax control practices over an extended period will offer insights into the endurance and lasting impact of digital reforms.

Limitations

Sample specificity. Caution is advised when generalizing findings, as the study's insights are derived from a specific sample of tax inspectors. The unique characteristics of this sample may limit the broader applicability of the results to diverse tax administration settings.

Methodological considerations. Given the qualitative nature of this study, potential biases and subjective interpretations may be present. Future research could enhance methodological rigor by incorporating quantitative elements or employing diverse research methods.

Scope and focus. While the study concentrates on the influence of digitalization on tax control, it acknowledges the broader context of factors affecting tax administration. Future research might explore the interconnectedness of digitalization with other facets of tax administration for a broader understanding.

Note

A single study may serve multiple research objectives.

REFERENCES

Allingham, M. G., & Sandmo, A. (1972). Income tax evasion: A theoretical analysis. *Journal of Public Economics*, *1*(3-4), 323–338. doi:10.1016/0047-2727(72)90010-2

Asian Development Bank. (2022). *Launching A Digital Tax Administration Transformation : What You Need to Know*. Asian Development Bank. doi:10.22617/TCS210343

Attias Assouline, A.-V., & Glon, G. (2018). Fiscalité du digital, digitalisation de la fiscalité. *Revue d'Economie Financiere*, *131*(3), 217–232. doi:10.3917/ecofi.131.0217

Baisalbayeva, K., Enden, E., Ion, V., & Tsavdaris, H. (2017). *Digital Transformation of Tax Administrators*. Microsoft and PwC.

Bayrak, T. (2021). *Digital Future*. Peter Lang Verlag. doi:10.3726/b18869

Bellon, M., Dabla-Norris, E., Khalid, S., & Lima, F. (2022). Digitalization to improve tax compliance : Evidence from VAT e-Invoicing in Peru. *Journal of Public Economics*, *210*, 104661. doi:10.1016/j.jpubeco.2022.104661 PMID:35711616

Bhaskar, R. (2020). Critical realism and the ontology of persons. *Journal of Critical Realism*, *19*(2), 113–120. doi:10.1080/14767430.2020.1734736

Chen, J. (2017). Testing and Implementing Digital Tax Administration. In *Digital Revolutions in Public Finance*. International Monetary Fund. doi:10.5089/9781484315224.071.ch005

Chen, Z., Xiao, Y., & Jiang, K. (2023). The impact of tax reform on firms' digitalization in China. *Technological Forecasting and Social Change, 187*, 122196. doi:10.1016/j.techfore.2022.122196

Chernousova, K. S. (2021). *Digital Transformation Of Tax Administration As A Function Of State Administration*. doi:10.15405/epsbs.2021.04.02.158

Dečman, N., Sever Mališ, S., & Mamić Sačer, I. (2019). Digitalization of Accounting and Tax Processes-Challenges and Opportunities for Accountants and Tax Administrators. *Proceedings of FEB Zagreb International Odyssey Conference on Economics and Business, 1*(1), 30-40.

Durán Cabré, J. M., & Esteller Moré, A. (2020). Los retos de la Administración tributaria en la era de la digitalización. ICE. *Información Comercial Española, 917*(917). Advance online publication. doi:10.32796/ice.2020.917.7130

Enofe, A., Embele, K., & Obazee, E. P. (2019). Tax audit, investigation, and tax evasion. *Journal of Accounting and Financial Management, 5*(4), 47–66.

Ernst & Young. (2017). *Tax technology and transformation*. https://assets.ey.com/content/dam/ey-sites/ey-com/en_gl/topics/digital/ey-tax-technology-transformation.pdf

Ernst and Young. (2017). *Tax Technology and Transformation: Tax Functions "Go Digital"*. Ernst & Young LLP.

European Commission, Directorate-General for Taxation and Customs Union. (2019). *TaxCompEU: EU tax competency framework: role descriptions – tax audit*. Publications Office. https://data.europa.eu/doi/10.2778/603542

Fan, H., Liu, Y., Qian, N., & Wen, J. (2018). *Computerizing VAT Invoices in China* (w24414). National Bureau of Economic Research. doi:10.3386/w24414

Fletcher, A. J. (2017). Applying critical realism in qualitative research: Methodology meets method. *International Journal of Social Research Methodology, 20*(2), 181–194. doi:10.1080/13645579.2016.1144401

George, D. S., & Diavastis, I. (2015). Tax audit effectiveness in Greek firms : Tax auditors perceptions. *Journal of Accounting and Taxation, 7*(7), 123–130. doi:10.5897/JAT2015.0186

Grigorieva, E. M., Chernyaev, M. V., & Kirichenko, O. S. (2020). Impact of Digitalisation on the Fiscal and Regulatory Functions of the Tax System. *Digital Finance 2020 (DF2020)*, 93.

Hamid, N., Saruji, S., Shamsuddin, R., & Othman, R. (2023). Determining the Factors of Tax Agents' Readiness Towards the Digitalisation of Tax Administration. *Revue d'Economie Financiere, 21*, 32–42. doi:10.55365/1923.x2023.21.4

He, Y., & Yi, Y. (2023). Digitalization of tax administration and corporate performance : Evidence from China. *International Review of Financial Analysis, 90*, 102859. doi:10.1016/j.irfa.2023.102859

ICAEW. (2019). *Digitalisation of tax : International perspectives*. https://www.icaew.com/-/media/corporate/files/technical/technology/thought-leadership/digital-tax.ashx

ICAEW. (2022). *Digitalisation of tax : International perspectives*. https://www.icaew.com/-/media/corporate/files/technical/technology/thought-leadership/digital-tax.ashx

Jacquemot, P., & Raffinot, M. (2019). La mobilisation fiscale en Afrique. *Revue d'économie financière, 131*(3), 243-263. doi:10.3917/ecofi.131.0243

Kircher, E. E. (2008). Enforced versus voluntary tax compliance : The slippery framework. *Journal of Economic Psychology, 29*(2), 210–225. doi:10.1016/j.joep.2007.05.004

Kitsios, E., Jalles, J., & Vedier, G. (2020). *Tax Evasion from Cross-Border Fraud Does Digitalization Make a Difference?* International Monetary Fund.

Krieger, T. (2021). A model-theoretical analysis for digital tax administrations. *International Journal of Innovative Technologies in Economy*, *2*(34). Advance online publication. doi:10.31435/rsglobal_ijite/30062021/7543

Mascagni, G., Mengistu, A. T., & Woldeyes, F. B. (2021). Can ICTs increase tax compliance? Evidence on taxpayer responses to technological innovation in Ethiopia. *Journal of Economic Behavior & Organization, 189*, 172–193. doi:10.1016/j.jebo.2021.06.007

Milosavljević, M., Radovanović, S., & Delibašić, B. (2023). What drives the performance of tax administrations? Evidence from selected european countries. *Economic Modelling, 121*, 106217. doi:10.1016/j.econmod.2023.106217

Niu, Y. (2011). Tax audit impact on voluntary compliance. *Journal of Economic and Social Measurement, 36*(4), 237–251. doi:10.3233/JEM-2011-0346

OECD. (2016). *Technologies for Better Tax Administration : A Practical Guide for Revenue Bodies*. OECD. doi:10.1787/9789264256439-

OECD. (2021). *Supporting the Digitalisation of Developing Country Tax Administrations*. www.oecd.org/tax/forum-on-tax-administration/publications-and-products/supporting-the-digitalisation-of-developing-country-taxadministrations.htm

Ofori, P. E., Ofori, I. K., & Asongu, S. A. (2022). Towards efforts to enhance tax revenue mobilisation in Africa : Exploring the interaction between industrialisation and digital infrastructure. *Telematics and Informatics*, *72*, 101857. doi:10.1016/j.tele.2022.101857

Okunogbe, O. (2021). *Becoming Legible to the State : The Role of Detection and Enforcement Capacity in Tax Compliance*. The World Bank. doi:10.1596/1813-9450-9852

Okunogbe, O., & Pouliquen, V. (2022). Technology, Taxation, and Corruption : Evidence from the Introduction of Electronic Tax Filing. *American Economic Journal. Economic Policy*, *14*(1), 341–372. doi:10.1257/pol.20200123

Olaoye, C. O., & Ogundipe, A. A. (2018). Application of tax audit and investigation on tax evasion control in Nigeria. *Journal of Accounting Finance and Auditing Studies*, *4*(1), 79–92.

Ouyang, J., Liu, S., & Li, H. (2023). How does the development of digital finance affect small business tax compliance? Empirical evidence from China. *China Economic Review*, *80*, 101971. doi:10.1016/j.chieco.2023.101971

OXFAM. (2021). *Fair Tax Monitor : Analyse du système fiscal marocain*. Oxfam International. https://www.oxfam.org/fr/publications/fair-tax-monitor-analyse-du-systeme-fiscal-marocain

Paillé, P., & Mucchielli, A. (2012). L'analyse qualitative en sciences humaines et sociales (3e éd.). Paris: Armand Colin.

Ratinaud, P. (2009). *IRaMuTeQ: Interface de R pour les Analyses Multidimensionnelles de TExtes et de Questionnaires*. http://www.iramuteq.org

Ratinaud, P., & Marchand, P. (2012). L'analyse de similitude appliquée aux corpus textuels: Les primaires socialistes pour l'élection présidentielle française (septembre-octobre 2011). In A. Dister, D. Longrée, & G. Purnelle (Éds.), *11èmes Journées internationales d'Analyse statistique des Données Textuelles*. http://lexicometrica.univ-paris3.fr/jadt/jadt2012/Communications/Marchand,%20Pascal%20et%20al.%20-%20L'analyse%20de%20similitude%20appliquee%20aux%20corpus%20textuels.pdf

Ricou, B. (2022). *Droit des procédures fiscales*. Ellipses. doi:10.14375/NP.9782340064386

Tax Justice Network. (2023). *The state of Tax Justice 2023*. https://taxjustice.net/wp-content/uploads/SOTJ/SOTJ23/English/State%20of%20Tax%20Justice%20 2023%20-%20Tax%20Justice%20Network%20-%20English.pdf

Teszner, K. (2020). Country Note : Customs And Fiscal Control In Poland As A Radical Measure To Eliminate Tax Evasion. *Intertax*, *48*(10), 922–928. doi:10.54648/TAXI2020090

The General Tax Administration. (2023). *General Tax Code*. https://www.finances.gov.ma/Publication/dgi/2023/CGI2023FR.pdf

Tiantian, G., Hailin, C., Zhou, X., Ai, S., & Siyao, W. (2023). Does corporate digital transformation affect the level of corporate tax avoidance? Empirical evidence from Chinese listed tourism companies. *Finance Research Letters*, *57*, 104271. doi:10.1016/j.frl.2023.104271

Uyar, A., Nimer, K., Kuzey, C., Shahbaz, M., & Schneider, F. (2021). Can e-government initiatives alleviate tax evasion? The moderation effect of ICT. *Technological Forecasting and Social Change*, *166*, 120597. doi:10.1016/j.techfore.2021.120597

Üyümez, M. E., & Hacıköylü, C. (Eds.). (2023). *Current debates on public finance : Theory and practice*. Peter Lang. doi:10.3726/b20820

Verdier, M. G., Rayner, B., Muthoora, M. P. S., Vellutini, C., Zhu, L., Koukpaizan, V. de P., Marahel, A., Harb, M., Benmohamed, I., Hebous, M. S., Okello, A., Reyes, N., Benninger, T., & Sanya, B. (2022). *Mobilisation des recettes pour une reprise résiliente et inclusive au Moyen-Orient et en Asie centrale : Executive Summary*. International Monetary Fund. doi:10.5089/9798400215346.087

Vishnevsky, V. P., & Chekina, V. D. (2018). Robot vs. tax inspector or how the fourth industrial revolution will change the tax system : A review of problems and solutions. *Journal of Tax Reform*, *4*(1), 6–26. doi:10.15826/jtr.2018.4.1.042

Wolf, M., & Dale, S. (2019). Les technologies numériques au service de l'administration de l'impôt. *ERA Forum, 19*(3), 457-464. 10.1007/s12027-018-0540-5

Yılmaz, F., & Coolidge, J. (2013). *Can E-Filing Reduce Tax Compliance Costs in Developing Countries?* The World Bank. doi:10.1596/1813-9450-6647

Zhutiaeva, S. A. (2021). *Digitalization Of Tax Control In The Russian Federation : Analysis And Trends*. doi:10.15405/epsbs.2021.03.56

KEY TERMS AND DEFINITIONS

Lexicometric Analysis: Quantitative approach for examining and analyzing textual data, using statistical techniques and computational tools to reveal patterns, word frequencies, and semantic associations.

Tax Administration: Framework of procedures, protocols, and activities by government authorities for tax assessment, collection, and management, ensuring compliance.

Tax Control: Regulatory oversight and managerial procedures ensuring adherence to tax laws, fostering compliance and optimizing fiscal outcomes.

Tax Digitalization: Integration of digital technologies in tax processes, enhancing efficiency through electronic filing, data automation, and technological solutions.

Taxpayers: Individuals or entities subject to taxation, primary contributors to public revenue by fulfilling tax obligations.

APPENDIX

Interview questions:

1. How do you assess taxpayers' adoption of the digital tax process?
2. In your opinion, to what extent has digitalization impacted the relationship between the taxpayer and the tax administration?
3. According to you, how could digital tax transformation influence taxpayers' compliance level?
4. In your opinion, what are the objectives pursued by the tax administration through this digitalization initiative?
5. According to you, what are the effects of digitalization on the organization of work within your department?
6. Based on your experience, and in the context of its missions, to what extent has the digitalization of the tax administration impacted its relationship with other state administrations?
7. In your opinion, what are the effects of digital tax transformation on the quality of verifying taxpayers' declarations?
8. In your opinion, to what extent has digital tax transformation influenced the efficiency of tax control?
9. According to you, how could digital tax transformation contribute to expanding the tax base and revenues?
10. In your opinion, what are the limitations of the tax administration modernization program, and what are the avenues for improvement?

Chapter 4
Digital Reporting of Accounting Information and AIS in Oman

Afshan Younas
https://orcid.org/0000-0001-7481-4953
Arab Open University, Oman

ABSTRACT

Oman holds a prominent location in the Middle East and North Africa (MENA) region. There were several structural reforms took place to enhance the adoption and implementation of smooth governance in Oman from the inception of the corporate governance structure. This study aims to review and document the digital reporting of accounting information of these Omani companies listed at the Muscat Stock Exchange (MSX) and registered with the Capital Market Authority (CMA). The purpose of the study is to highlight the adaptation of digital accounting reporting of listed companies at MSX and registered companies at CMA, its benefits, and the current challenges. From 2020, all the listed, licensed, and accredited companies by MSX and CMA were required to report their financial information digitally by using XBRL taxonomy. The research provides useful insight to regulators, decision-makers, businesses, and the academic world by filling the gap in the literature.

INTRODUCTION

The business world has seen rapid growth as a result of the increasing degree of complexity, market openness, and intense competition, rationale businesses are required to pay focused attention to the various data and information that are used

DOI: 10.4018/979-8-3693-1678-8.ch004

by external and internal users (Kyeremeh et al., 2022). Digital transformation has made structural transformation in various fields of life including business. Digital transformation refers to the complete development of a new organization that responds to changes that occur in the environment (Ivanov et al., 2019).

Digital transformation is a critical element of the industrial revolution. The first industrial revolution started at the end of the 18th century to the beginning of the 19th century. The biggest transformation came in the form of mechanization which accelerated the economy (Meraghni et al., 2021). The second industrial revolution started at the end of the 19th century with massive technological developments through a new source of energy (electricity, gas, and oil). The Second Industrial Revolution's greatest inventions are the automobile and plane due to which the Second Industrial Revolution is considered more critical. Almost a century later, a third industrial revolution began in the second of the twentieth century (Chan & Zary, 2019). Another transformational change occurred in the economy due to the inventions of computers, nuclear energy, the advancement of telecommunications, and robotics which introduced an era of high level of automation. The fourth industrial revolution which is denoted as Industrial Revolution 4.0 (IR4.0) was started in 2011. All four industrial revolutions shaped the world economies. The main outcome of Industrial Revolution 4.0 is digitalization and other outcomes are yet to appear (Ivanov et al., 2019).

Industry 4.0 brings significant advantages to organizations including real-time data availability, analysis, autonomous monitoring, competitiveness, and enhanced productivity. The key characteristics of Industry 4.0 are collaboration and integration both vertical and horizontal (Lawal et al., 2022).

History records that initially the use of computers in the business world was limited to processing transactions. The concept of a Management Information System (MIS) was introduced in the 1960s and was a broad system that seeks to provide information to managers for suggesting solutions to problems. But initially, the system did not work well, later the Decision Support System (DSS) was introduced with the aim of supporting managers in the decision-making process. Later, a decision support system was combined with artificial intelligence (AI) (Saad, 2023). Artificial intelligence refers to actions performed by computers with the ability to display behavior that is considered intelligent of the ability displayed by humans. AI is the most advanced application of computers because it copies the way humans think and responds. AI is now widely applied in more of the business world in the form of expert systems, artificial neural networks, genetic algorithms, and intelligent agents (Sobb et al., 2020). An expert system is a computer program that aims to represent human knowledge and expertise through heuristics. Heuristics are rules that serve as benchmarks or guidelines for making educated guesses. While heuristics may not always be as reliable as algorithms used in mathematical models, they typically provide specific and useful results (Pebrina et al., 2022). By utilizing heuristics, expert systems can mimic human expertise and offer guidance in problem-solving. The process of using this program is referred to as consulting, as users seek advice from the expert system. Expert systems are developed by information specialists, often referred to as knowledge engineers, who possess specialized knowledge in the field of artificial intelligence. Whereas, neural networks imitate the functioning of the human brain and possess the ability to identify and differentiate patterns (Sukoharsono, 2020). This quality makes them highly valuable in industries such as speech recognition and optical character recognition. Genetic Algorithms (GAs) utilize the concept of "survival of the fittest" to help problem solvers generate improved solutions to problems. Intelligent agents are commonly employed to carry out repetitive tasks in the realm of computers (Ping, 2021). For instance, they play a crucial role in data aggregation, enabling data warehouse systems to uncover previously unidentified connections between data (Pebrina et al., 2022).

Accounting

Accounting is a basic term used by businesses to show their performance. Thus, accounting is the process of consolidating financial information into understandable and readable form. Accounting is the process of recording and classifying a company's financial events, and then summarizing, analyzing, and reporting these to communicate with interested parties. Digital transformation deeply shapes the future of accounting by reforming the main functions of storing, processing, and communicating accounting data (Meraghni et al., 2021). In the past accountants primarily focused on preparing financial statements, working as stewards, and being accountable to auditing processes. Rapid changes in technology lead to changes in the role of accountants (Baker El-Ebiary & Alawi, 2020). The role of accountants has become more complex now, accountants work as business analysts because they have a complete picture of business financial resources. Accountants also help businesses optimize their processes in order to achieve and sustain competitive advantage (Nguyen & Nguyen, 2020). In addition, accountants are also assumed to be accountable for maximizing shareholder value. Accountants work to support evidence-based decision making which includes strategic planning, process improvement, and compliance management (Mat et al., 2020).

Under stewardship and reporting requirements, accountants are responsible for regulatory compliance, tax returns, stakeholder assurance, investor relations, raising capital and loans, board reports, and any type of statutory reports (Lombardi et al., 2021). In IR4.0 along with stewardship and reporting, accountants are responsible for various other business support functions which cover a wide range of management functions such as planning budgeting, forecasting, performance measurement, risk management, investment appraisal, and supply chain management (Al-dmour et al., 2017; Lutfi, Alkelani, et al., 2022).

Information asymmetry is the main concern of several stakeholders in recording, preparing, and communicating accounting data, whereas digital transformation of accounting function seems to address this issue by enhancing the authenticity, completeness, and effectiveness of accounting data (Ni, 2022). With digitalization, accounting data becomes more accessible to investors and transparency of data significantly improves with digital reporting.

Accounting Information System

An accounting information system is a source to report accounting information digitally. It is crucial to discuss the accounting information system before discussing the digital reporting of accounting information (Kareem et al., 2021). An accounting information system is a system that gathers, stores, and handles financial and business data. It then shares this data with authorized users who can utilize it for conducting a company's operations (Lutfi, Alkelani, et al., 2022). An accounting information system tracks all accounting and business activity for an organization (Mardi et al., 2020). It is composed of six primary components: people, procedures, data, software, technology infrastructure, and internal controls. People refer to those professionals or groups of professionals that are involved with the use of AIS. These are the professionals who work in a business and use an organization's AIS (Soudani, 2012). These professionals may include accountants, business analysts, consultants, managers, auditors, and financial officers. Another component of AIS is procedures which relates to the methods it uses to collect, store, process, retrieve, and report information in meaningful form (Teru et al., 2017). This information can be internal or external.

One more critical component of AIS is data. An AIS stores its information in a database (Monteiro et al., 2021). A commonly used database is called Structured Query Language (SQL), which allows the manipulation and retrieval of information for reporting purposes. Software is the fourth component of AIS which is related to the computer programs used to store, retrieve, process, and analyze business financial data (Kareem et al., 2021). The key aspects of AIS software are quality, reliability, and security because various stakeholders rely on the information which is produced by this software. Whereas, AIS software can be customized to fulfill the unique needs of different types of firms (Meraghni et al., 2021).

Another notable AIS component is technology infrastructure which covers a wide range of tools such as computers, mobiles, tablets, servers, routers, and backup power supply. These factors also highly depend on speed, storage capacity, and capacity to be upgraded and expanded. In addition, servicing, replacing, and upgrading is one of the critical aspects which is linked to the technology infrastructure (Soudani, 2012). The last AIS component is internal control which is the security measure to protect sensitive data. This can be protected through passwords, biometrics, or complex identification. Internal controls limit access to authorized users only (Meraghni et al., 2021).

Is it reported that Oman is also experiencing deployment of strong AIS to reap the full benefits of digitalization reporting. Oil and gas and manufacturing industries have enjoyed many advancement opportunities but at the same time, various challenges stand in keeping their growth tendency and high profitability (Stalin & Manayseh, 2023). One of the biggest challenges is identified as a lack of digitalization in accounting data due to which the quality of accounting data is compromised (Alsulmani et al., 2021). Thus, it is suggested to use SAP (System Application Products) software to enhance financial reporting. Similarly, the need for highly transparent information and data has required the industry to adopt well-developed and integrated ERP (Enterprise Resource Planning) tools. Tally is another accounting package which is heavily used by Omani companies to meet the need of industry but still many companies reported end to end processes issues which can be sorted out by digital transformation of basic business functions (Teresa & Matriano, 2022).

Digital reporting of Accounting Information

Compared to accounting information systems, digital reporting of accounting information is to report digitally financial information of the business through a coded language (Vlahovic, 2023). During the last two decades the internet revolution as a source of digital transformation has transformed the way financial information was traditionally reported to stakeholders. Several researchers and experts have documented the benefits of "Internet Financial Reporting" (IFR) (Mohamed et al., 2009). It is evident that IFR potentially increases the understanding of financial information by using modern data presentation methodology which includes videos, audio, and graphics (Mulyani et al., 2019). The greater benefit of IFR is to provide users with an opportunity to access real-time financial information (Olsen, 2023). Digital reporting accounting information leads to a revolution in the firm's voluntary disclosure and creates important implications for the accounting and auditing profession.

As discussed in the previous section Oman is witnessed to use various accounting software to digitalize their accounting information but reporting is still a concern that needs uniform financial reporting (AL-Masharfi & Matriano, 2022). To uniform with international taxonomy and follow the general standard in the accounting and finance field, CMA Oman offers various initiatives to report business information digitally.

Digital reporting of accounting is of great importance in influencing accounting information and the quality of financial reports, as a result, increases the effectiveness of strategic decisions (Meraghni et al., 2021). Various technologies are used to record data digitally. However, for accounting purposes, XBRL (Xtensible Business Reporting Language) is the international standard for digital reporting of financial data (Shapovalova et al., 2023).

XBRL Background

Due to the changes in the economy and business sector, there is a need for education to align with these developments. This includes the digitalization process, which impacts both business and education (Meraghni et al., 2021). In order to meet the standards of accounting education, professional accountants must be able to adapt to changing systems and continuously enhance their skills. The use of different programs for data input in businesses creates difficulties when comparing the data. As a result, there is a need for a universal accounting reporting language to address these differences (Srinath & Swathi, 2022). Charles Hoffman developed a project called XBRL, which is an encoding language for data. He presented this project to the AICPA, who supported and funded it, leading to the creation of a board of directors (Isbil et al., 2021). The SEC also supported the project, and the XBRL commission published the first draft of the taxonomy in 2001 (Ping, 2021). Over time, taxonomies in various languages have been developed. XBRL is a standardized and platform-independent digital data coding language used by financial information producers and users for data exchange (Spilnyk et al., 2020).

XBRL, an international standard for digital business reporting, is managed by XBRL International, a global not-for-profit consortium (Cormier et al., 2019). The goal of XBRL is to enhance reporting in the public interest (Debreceny & Farewell, 2010). It is widely used in over 50 countries, with millions of XBRL documents created annually. These digital versions replace outdated paper-based reports, offering more usefulness, effectiveness, and accuracy (Hoitash & Hoitash, 2018).

In essence, XBRL provides a language to define reporting terms authoritatively. These terms are then utilized to represent the contents of financial statements and various compliance, performance, and business reports (Bajaher, 2023). XBRL facilitates the rapid, accurate, and digital transfer of reporting information between organizations.

XBRL International serves as a central hub for the study of XBRL, a language that has revolutionized commercial reporting worldwide (Ping, 2021). Developed by a non-profit consortium, XBRL is an open standard that does not require any license fees. Its use is widespread, with countries in America, Europe, and Asia already implementing or preparing to implement XBRL (Isbil et al., 2021). Various stakeholders, including regulators, companies, governments, data providers, analysts, investors, and accountants, utilize XBRL (Alkayed et al., 2023).

The main components of XBRL are XML, specifications, taxonomies, and sample documents. XML, which stands for eXtensible Markup Language, serves as the foundation for many internet-based services and is also used by XBRL (Isbil et al., 2021). Taxonomies, on the other hand, classify and organize financial information provided by businesses in a hierarchical manner. This standardized system allows for the establishment of mathematical relationships between elements and the creation of human-readable labels and tags (Wulandari & Ali, 2019). Taxonomy providers have the flexibility to expand taxonomies based on their specific needs, making XBRL a highly adaptable reporting language that promotes standardization and automation (Debreceny & Farewell, 2010).

XBRL International has established two main specifications, namely XBRL FR and XBRL GL. XBRL FR focuses on standardizing reporting in the financial reporting system, allowing for data analysis, transfer, and comparison (Isbil et al., 2021). On the other hand, XBRL GL serves as the taxonomy for general journal and ledger preparation in electronic ledger applications. The tagged data, following the taxonomy, forms the basis of sample documents (Alkayed et al., 2023). These sample documents are created once and can be used to generate reports in various formats and contents (Mosteanu & Faccia, 2020).

Benefits of Reporting Accounting Information Digitally

Digital reporting of accounting information refers to the use of digital technology, software, or XBRL to collect, analyze, and present financial data digitally (Vlahovic, 2023). It involves the transformation of traditional paper-based accounting reports into digital formats, making them more accessible, efficient, and accurate for all stakeholders (Meraghni et al., 2021).

There are several benefits that various stakeholders can gain from digital reporting of accounting information. One of the main advantages of digital reporting is the ability to automate the process of collecting and analyzing financial data (Olsen, 2023). With the use of accounting software and XBRL, transactions can be recorded and classified automatically, reducing the risk of errors, mistakes, and fraud as well as saving time (Isbil et al., 2021).

The use of XBRL enhances the trustworthiness and transparency of financial and business data produced by experts (Tawiah & Borgi, 2022). XBRL has empowered financial reporting users, including governments, financial analysts, investors, and others, to efficiently extract, utilize, and assess a company's financial information in minimum time and make the right decisions (Pustylnick et al., 2017).

The adoption of XBRL language in financial reports is currently seen as a crucial matter. It is considered one of the most important programming languages in the accounting industry today (Tawiah & Borgi, 2022). XBRL and other search-facilitating technologies have a significant impact on the ability of financial statement users to access and integrate relevant financial information (Vysochan et al., 2023). When companies assign comparable data tags to related financial information items, search-facilitating technology can retrieve these items from anywhere in the financial report (Alkayed et al., 2023). Additionally, the use of similar tags indicates to users that these items are connected and helps facilitate decision-making by allowing for transparent cross-company comparisons and highlighting differences in choices (Pustylnick et al., 2017). Therefore, XBRL has the potential to empower users of financial statements to make more informed decisions based on the information presented in the reports, regardless of its location. However, the importance of improving corporate and financial information transparency and achieving efficiency gains in information gathering, analysis, and dissemination has not been adequately addressed by researchers (Bai et al., 2018).

XBRL is a vital standard for electronic communication of business and financial data. Its purpose is to simplify the exchange and analysis of financial information, such as financial statements, for both public and private companies (Tawiah & Borgi, 2022). One of the main advantages of XBRL is its ability to automate data collection and analysis, streamlining the reporting process for companies and enabling investors and stakeholders to analyze the information more efficiently. By utilizing XBRL, companies can save time and resources in preparing financial reports while enhancing the accuracy and consistency of their data (Saragih et al., 2021). Additionally, XBRL plays a crucial role in promoting transparency and standardization in financial reporting. Through the use of standardized tags and definitions, XBRL ensures that financial data is uniform and comparable across different companies and jurisdictions, facilitating understanding and comparison for investors and stakeholders. The adoption of XBRL can have various effects on firms, both positive and negative (Hoitash & Hoitash, 2018).

The automation of accounting information and financial data allows for real-time reporting, providing up-to-date information for decision-making. There are several benefits of real-time reporting for internal and external users (Dai & Vasarhelyi, 2017). Real-time accounting information allows firms to make updated and timely decisions. With up-to-date accounting information, firms can quickly identify trends, mark potential risks, and make necessary adjustments to their operations (Sukoharsono, 2020). In addition, with real-time financial information businesses are in a position to understand their financial position at any given time. This allows firms to monitor and control cash flows and manage budgets more effectively, leading to improved financial control and stability (Wang et al., 2021).

In addition, XBRL simplifies the analysis of financial data and facilitates comparisons between companies and jurisdictions, benefiting investors, analysts, and other stakeholders (Tawiah & Borgi, 2022). This, in turn, helps companies attract and retain investors. Moreover, XBRL aids in meeting regulatory requirements, minimizing the likelihood of non-compliance and associated penalties. Consequently, having precise and standardized financial data available enables companies to make more informed decisions and enhance their overall financial performance (Ping, 2021).

Digital reporting through XBRL also enables the integration of data from various sources, such as bank statements, invoices, and receipts (Tawiah & Borgi, 2022). This integration improves data accuracy and reduces the need for manual data entry. It also allows for better data analysis and forecasting, as trends and patterns can be identified more easily (Saragih et al., 2021).

Another benefit of digital reporting is the increased accessibility of financial information. With digital platforms, accounting reports can be accessed remotely and shared with stakeholders in real time. This improves communication and collaboration between different departments and stakeholders, facilitating better decision-making and transparency (Sukoharsono, 2020).

There are various successful examples of digital interactive business reports that are Zendesk, dice, Contentoo, European Investment Fund, WorkingNation, and Financial Annual Report, which is the digital reporting of accounting information. A successful financial organization, the European Investment Fund (EIF) created a colorful report filled with interactive statistics and eye-catching illustrations to showcase how EIF performed in 2021 and 2022.

Furthermore, digital reporting enhances data security and compliance. Digital platforms often have built-in security measures, such as encryption and access controls, to protect sensitive financial information (Nguyen & Nguyen, 2020). Additionally, digital reporting can help organizations comply with regulatory requirements by providing accurate and auditable records.

Digital Reporting of Accounting Information in Oman

Oman is a progressing country and many developments have been taking place since 1998 after the restructuring of the stock market. In alignment with progressive measures in 2020, CMA adopted IFRS Taxonomy which aligns with Oman Vision 2040 for digital transformation of reporting of company's financial data. Currently, all listed and licensed companies in Oman are required to report their financial data digitally (Stalin & Manayseh, 2023).

Accounting software plays a crucial role in the digital reporting of accounting information. With a wide range of options available, it can be challenging to choose the right and most suitable accounting software for business. One of the famous cloud-based accounting software that caters to most of the needs of businesses is Elate Accounting. It offers various features which enable businesses to streamline their financial processes efficiently. Another renowned accounting software in Oman is Tally Prime, it provides robust accounting functionalities and seamless integration options.

QuickBooks is another leading accounting software trusted by many businesses in Oman. SAP Business One is business-level accounting software that features complex financial requirements. Zoho Books is also cloud-based accounting software that integrates accounting functions with holistic business management functions. Finally, ERPNext accounting software caters to the needs of various industries in Oman from accounting functions to inventory management, human resource management and payroll, and comprehensive business solutions.

In Oman, the Capital Market Authority (CMA) and Muscat Stock Exchange (MSX) launched an analytical portal named "Bayanat" in 2021, to prepare and report accounting information digitally. Various training sessions have been provided to prospective users to prepare and submit XBRL fillings using the portal. The portal contains significant historical data on the financial results of businesses. The main aim of launching this portal is to make sure that data will be available to a large number of users for analysis and comparison. Users will be able to perform various types of data analysis including ratio analysis across companies by sectors which assist them in their decision-making processes (CMA, 2020).

In 2009, there were 142 companies listed on the Muscat Stock Exchange (previously called Muscat Securities Market) and it was evident that only 84 of the listed companies had their websites, and only 31 companies reported their information digitally (Mohamed et al., 2009). CMA joined XBRL in 2020 and oriented companies to report their accounting information digitally through XBRL. It is worth noting that currently according to data available on CMA Oman and MSX, all companies are reporting their information digitally through XBRL. Information regarding companies is listed below based on sectors and markets (CMA, 2020).

CMA has adopted the IFRS Taxonomy 2020, under which all listed and licensed companies are required to report data using the "Bayanat" platform. The taxonomy contains the Arabic translation for labels and documentation for all concepts. The reporting firms are classified as SAOG, SAOC (LLC or Branch of MNC), and investment funds. These firms are required to report annually and quarterly their financial statements including notes and reports of auditors (XBRL, 2023).

Several research studies have provided evidence in favor of implementing XBRL, yielding favorable outcomes (Alkayed et al., 2023; Debreceny & Farewell, 2010;

Table 1. List of companies listed on the Muscat Stock Exchange that follow XBRL

Sectors	Regular Market	Parallel Market	Under-Monitoring Market	Bonds Market	Right-Issue Market	Book Building Market	Public Offering Market	Total
Financial Sector	11	21	0	0	0	0	0	**32**
Mutual Funds	0	3	0	0	0	0	0	**3**
Industrial Sector	4	24	10	0	0	0	0	**38**
Bond Sukuk	0	0	0	0	0	0	0	**0**
Services Sector	8	27	5	0	0	0	0	**40**
Total	**23**	**75**	**15**	**0**	**0**	**0**	**0**	**113**

Pustylnick et al., 2017; Shapovalova et al., 2023; Tawiah & Borgi, 2022; Vysochan et al., 2023). In alignment with IFRS Taxonomy 2020, CMA Oman designed the taxonomies for the different industries where all listed and licensed companies are required to report their information on the new platform. The scope of the taxonomy will cover SAOG (Public Joint Stock Corporation - Société anonyme Omanaise general), SAOC (Closed Join Stock Corporation - Société anonyme Omanaise close) (LLC, Branches of Foreign Entities), and investment funds. These entities are required to submit their financial statements annually and quarterly (IFRS, 2020).

CMA uses the latest IFRS (International Financial Reporting Standard) 2020 taxonomy for developing CMA Oman Taxonomy. This taxonomy is bilingual and contains Arabic translation for labels and key concepts. This allows entities to submit their fillings through XBRL which is available as an Offline tool, Online tool, and integrated XBRL system (third-party tool). Oman XBRL is regulated by CMA and MSX whereas filers are the entities listed on MSX and licensed with CMA (CMA, 2020).

There are currently 113 companies listed on MSX under 7 classifications of market (based on data available in December 2023). Similarly, 343 CMA-licensed and accredited companies are classified under 12 categories. All these listed, licensed, and accredited companies are required to use XBRL to report their financial as well as non-financial information digitally. The details of entities listed on MSX are given in below table 1.1 and the details of CMA-licensed companies are given in Table 1.2.

Table 1 shows the total number of companies listed at MSX with the classification of sectors and markets. Services is the most dominant sector in Oman with 40 firms out of 27 listed on the parallel market and only 8 are listed on the regular market.

Table 2. List of companies licensed by Capital Market Authority Oman that follows XBRL

CMA Licensed & Accredited Companies	No of Companies
Insurance Companies	16
Insurance Brokers	32
Insurance Agents	147
Re-Insurance Companies	1
Health Insurance Third Party	4
Companies working in the field of security	40
Investment funds	24
External Funds	17
Internal Funds	13
Capital market Institution	2
Legal Advisor	37
Valuation Companies	10
Total	343

Followed by the industrial sector with 38 and the financial sector with 32 companies (based on data available in December 2023). All the listed companies are advised by CMA to report their financial reporting digitally through the new IFRS 2020 Taxonomy. Their digitally reported accounting and financial information is available publicly on the MSX website.

Table 2 shows the list of companies that are licensed and accredited by CMA Oman under 12 classifications. These companies are also required to report their financial and non-financial information through XBRL. Insurance agents are one of the dominant sectors in Oman's economy licensed by CMA, followed by Companies working in the field of security, legal advisor insurance brokers, and the remaining companies as the details are given in Table 2.

It can be seen that from 2020 Oman has started to follow XBRL and all companies on MSX and CMA are required to report their information digitally. According to the information available, it can be stated that all the companies are reporting their information digitally, as reporting through XBRL is assumed to be mandatory in Oman.

Challenges of Reporting Accounting Information Digitally

There are several benefits of reporting accounting information digitally through XBRL but there are a few challenges that need to be addressed for smooth digital reporting One of the main challenges of using XBRL is ensuring error-free XBRL filing, to achieve this companies have to attempt multiple times and make revisions (Lombardi et al., 2021). Most of the staff are not XBRL professionals and as a result, they are not experts in proper XBRL taxonomy. This is the reason a business needs to spend high costs on hiring XBRL experts or outsource for the short term (Srinath & Swathi, 2022).

The entire process of reporting financial and non-financial information digitally is time-consuming. Additionally, the financial statements include several taxonomy compliances that require more attention, and as a result, the whole process takes a long time to complete. Furthermore, complex taxonomies in financial reports require companies to perform manual entries to convert into the correct XBRL format (Lutfi, Al-Khasawneh, et al., 2022).

Budget is another critical challenge that affects the business's decisions on adopting and implementing accounting information digitally. The initial and set-up cost is higher and usually requires a number of specialists from technology backgrounds to plan, develop, tailor, and implement digital reporting of accounting information. In addition, work culture and fear of change usually stand in the successful implementation of digital accounting reporting.

Future Scope and Limitations

Digital reporting of accounting information is the future of all companies. The world is moving to digitalization and reporting financial and non-financial information digitally is mandatory to achieve and sustain competitive position and advantage. Advancement in artificial intelligence leads to automation in accounting processes to a greater extent. This will cover automated financial analysis and reconciliation. Artificial intelligence will be strongly used in identifying patterns and help to improve fraud detection. Similarly, real-time information allows various stakeholders to access the latest information and make relevant decisions faster and reliably. AIS can be integrated with other business systems to improve efficiency and accuracy in the digital reporting of financial information. Future studies may discuss the challenges and opportunities faced by the listed, licensed, and accredited companies in following XBR in Oman and suggest improvements.

From the discussion, it is evident that there are numerous benefits of digital reporting of accounting information. This paper has a few limitations, the study highlighted the digital reporting of accounting information and presented data in content of Oman only. The study can be extended and can apply comparative study among GCC countries. Similarly, the study discusses the benefits and challenges of digital reporting of accounting information in general, not from the perspective of a particular industry or company. Thus, future studies may consider adding these limitations to the study and fill the gap of the current study.

CONCLUSION

Digital transformation has had a significant impact on the business world, particularly in the field of accounting. The four industrial revolutions have shaped the global economy and paved the way for the digitalization of various industries. Industry 4.0, in particular, has brought numerous advantages to organizations, including real-time data availability, analysis, autonomous monitoring, competitiveness, and enhanced productivity. In the accounting field, digital transformation has reformed the main functions of storing, processing and communicating accounting data. Accountants now play a more complex role as business analysts, optimizing processes and supporting evidence-based decision-making. The digitalization of accounting data has also addressed concerns regarding information asymmetry, enhancing the authenticity, completeness, and transparency of financial information. The accounting information system, composed of people, procedures, data, software, technology infrastructure, and internal controls, plays a crucial role in reporting accounting information digitally. Digital reporting of accounting information, facilitated by technologies such as XBRL, has revolutionized the way financial information is presented and accessed, leading to more effective strategic decision-making. Overall, digital transformation has transformed the accounting profession and continues to shape its future.

The adoption of XBRL and digital reporting in accounting has numerous benefits for various stakeholders. XBRL simplifies the exchange and analysis of financial information, enhances transparency and standardization, and enables real-time reporting and data integration. It automates data collection and analysis, saving time and resources for companies while improving accuracy and consistency. Digital reporting also improves accessibility, communication, and collaboration, as well as data security and compliance. Overall, XBRL and digital reporting have revolutionized the accounting industry, providing a more efficient and effective way to collect, analyze, and present financial data.

The launch of the "Bayanat" analytical portal by the Capital Market Authority (CMA) and Muscat Stock Exchange (MSX) in Oman has significantly improved the digital reporting of accounting information. The portal has provided users with access to historical financial data and the ability to perform data analysis and comparison.

The adoption of XBRL and the IFRS Taxonomy 2020 has ensured that all listed and licensed companies report their information digitally. Despite the benefits of digital reporting, there are challenges such as ensuring error-free filing and the need for XBRL expertise. However, the future scope of digital reporting is promising, with advancements in artificial intelligence and automation improving efficiency and accuracy. While this study focused on Oman, future research could explore comparative studies among GCC countries and industry-specific perspectives to further enhance our understanding of digital reporting of accounting information.

REFERENCES

Al-dmour, A., Al-Fawaz, K. M., Al-dmour, R., & Allozi, N. M. (2017). Accounting Information System and Its Role on Business Performance: A Theoretical Study. *Journal of Management and Strategy*, *8*(4), 79. doi:10.5430/jms.v8n4p79

Al-Masharfi, M. H. R., & Matriano, M. T. (2022). The Role of Electronic Accounting Information System in Measuring Credit Risk in National Bank of Oman. *GSJ*, *10*(1), 1789–1800. https://www.researchgate.net/profile/Maria-Teresa-Matriano/publication/358273351_The_Role_of_Electronic_Accounting_Information_System_in_Measuring_Credit_Risk_in_National_Bank_of_Oman/links/61f9dc3111a1090a79c9216e/The-Role-of-Electronic-Accounting-Inform

Alkayed, H., Zighan, S., Qabajeh, M., & Almaharmeh, M. I. (2023). The role of XBRL adoption on enhancing transparency of information disclosure: A case study of Jordanian financial companies. *Cogent Business and Management*, *10*(3), 2265082. Advance online publication. doi:10.1080/23311975.2023.2265082

Alsulmani, A. H., Alkindi, S. S., & Ahmed, E. R. (2021). Customer Accounting Information and Omani Service Companies' Performance. *International Journal of Finance & Banking Studies*, *10*(2), 79–88. doi:10.20525/ijfbs.v10i2.1245

Bai, L., Koveos, P., & Liu, M. (2018). Applying an ontology-augmenting XBRL model to accounting information system for business integration. *Asia-Pacific Journal of Accounting & Economics*, *25*(1–2), 75–97. Advance online publication. doi:10.1080/16081625.2016.1170616

Bajaher, M. S. (2023). Exploring user perception of XBRL adoption and its impact on accounting data in the Saudi context. *Electronic Journal of University of Aden for Humanity and Social Sciences*, *4*(1), 184–192. Advance online publication. doi:10.47372/ejua-hs.2023.1.242

Baker El-Ebiary, Y. A., & Alawi, N. A. M. (2020). The risks of accounting information systems. *International Journal of Engineering Trends and Technology*, *1*, 120–127. Advance online publication. doi:10.14445/22315381/CATI3P220

Chan, K. S., & Zary, N. (2019). Applications and Challenges of Implementing Artificial Intelligence in Medical Education: Integrative Review. *JMIR Medical Education*, *5*(1), e13930. Advance online publication. doi:10.2196/13930 PMID:31199295

CMA. (2020). *Capital Market Authority, Sultanate of Oman - XBRL*. https://cma.gov.om/Home/XBRL/aboutxbrl

Cormier, D., Dufour, D., Luu, P., Teller, P., & Teller, R. (2019). The Relevance of XBRL Voluntary Disclosure for Stock Market Valuation: The Role of Corporate Governance. *Canadian Journal of Administrative Sciences*, *36*(1), 113–127. Advance online publication. doi:10.1002/cjas.1483

Dai, J., & Vasarhelyi, M. A. (2017). Toward blockchain-based accounting and assurance. *Journal of Information Systems*, *31*(3), 5–21. Advance online publication. doi:10.2308/isys-51804

Debreceny, R., & Farewell, S. (2010). XBRL in the accounting curriculum. *Issues in Accounting Education*, *25*(3), 379–403. Advance online publication. doi:10.2308/iace.2010.25.3.379

Hoitash, R., & Hoitash, U. (2018). Measuring accounting reporting complexity with XBRL. *The Accounting Review*, *93*(1), 259–287. Advance online publication. doi:10.2308/accr-51762

IFRS. (2020). *IFRS - IFRS Taxonomy 2020*. https://www.ifrs.org/issued-standards/ifrs-taxonomy/ifrs-taxonomy-2020/

Isbil, N., Koroglu, A. G. N., & Zaif, F. (2021). Digital reporting in accounting: XBRL and integration to accounting department curriculum. *Gazi Journal of Economics and Business*, *7*(3), 188–202. doi:10.30855/gjeb.2021.7.3.001

Ivanov, D., Dolgui, A., & Sokolov, B. (2019). The impact of digital technology and Industry 4.0 on the ripple effect and supply chain risk analytics. *International Journal of Production Research*, *57*(3), 829–846. Advance online publication. doi:10.1080/00207543.2018.1488086

Kareem, H. M., Dauwed, M., Meri, A., Jarrar, M., Al-Bsheish, M., & Aldujaili, A. A. (2021). The role of accounting information system and knowledge management to enhancing organizational performance in Iraqi SMEs. *Sustainability (Basel)*, *13*(22), 12706. Advance online publication. doi:10.3390/su132212706

Kyeremeh, K., Kyeremeh, B. B., & Forson, M. A. (2022). Role of Accounting Information Systems In Organizational Decision Making: Evidence From Banking Sector In Ghana. *Journal of Accounting and Taxation*, *2*(3), 123–144. doi:10.47747/jat.v2i3.912

Lawal, A., Mohamed, R., Abdalla, H., Elkelish, W. W., & Lasyoud, A. A. (2022). the Role of Accounting Information Systems in Firms' Performance During the Covid-19 Pandemic. *Journal of Governance and Regulation*, *11*(1), 45–54. doi:10.22495/jgrv11i1art5

Lombardi, R., de Villiers, C., Moscariello, N., & Pizzo, M. (2021). The disruption of blockchain in auditing – a systematic literature review and an agenda for future research. *Accounting, Auditing & Accountability Journal*. Advance online publication. doi:10.1108/AAAJ-10-2020-4992

Lutfi, A., Al-Khasawneh, A. L., Almaiah, M. A., Alsyouf, A., & Alrawad, M. (2022). Business Sustainability of Small and Medium Enterprises during the COVID-19 Pandemic: The Role of AIS Implementation. *Sustainability (Basel)*, *14*(9), 5362. Advance online publication. doi:10.3390/su14095362

Lutfi, A., Alkelani, S. N., Alqudah, H., Alshira'h, A. F., Alshirah, M. H., Almaiah, M. A., Alsyouf, A., Alrawad, M., Montash, A., & Abdelmaksoud, O. (2022). The Role of E-Accounting Adoption on Business Performance: The Moderating Role of COVID-19. *Journal of Risk and Financial Management*, *15*(12), 617. Advance online publication. doi:10.3390/jrfm15120617

Mardi, M., Perdana, P. N., Suparno, S., & Munandar, I. A. (2020). Effect of Accounting Information Systems, Teamwork, and Internal Control on Financial Reporting Timeliness. *Journal of Asian Finance. Economics and Business*, *7*(12), 809–818. Advance online publication. doi:10.13106/jafeb.2020.vol7.no12.809

Mat, Z., Meiryani, S. L., & Tsudrajat, J. (2020). *Accounting information systems as a critical success factor for increased quality of accounting information* [Los sistemas de información contable como factor crítico de éxito para mejorar la calidad de la información contable]. Academic Press.

Meraghni, O., Bekkouche, L., & Demdoum, Z. (2021). Impact of Digital Transformation on Accounting Information Systems – Evidence from Algerian Firms. *Economics and Business*, *35*(1), 249–264. doi:10.2478/eb-2021-0017

Mohamed, E. K. A., Oyelere, P., & Al-Busaidi, M. (2009). A survey of Internet financial reporting in Oman. *International Journal of Emerging Markets*, *4*(1), 56–71. doi:10.1108/17468800910931670

Monteiro, A. P., Vale, J., Silva, A., & Pereira, C. (2021). Impact of the internal control and accounting systems on the financial information usefulness: The role of the financial information quality. *Academy of Strategic Management Journal, 20*(3).

Mosteanu, N. R., & Faccia, A. (2020). Digital systems and new challenges of financial management – fintech, XBRL, blockchain, and cryptocurrencies. *Quality - Access to Success, 21*(174).

Mulyani, S., Kasim, E., Yadiati, W., & Umar, H. (2019). Influence of accounting information systems and internal audit on fraudulent financial reporting. *Opcion, 35*(21).

Nguyen, H. T., & Nguyen, A. H. (2020). Determinants of accounting information systems quality: Empirical evidence from Vietnam. *Accounting, 6*(2), 185–198. Advance online publication. doi:10.5267/j.ac.2019.10.004

Ni, X. (2022). The Impact of Enterprise Digital Transformation on Innovation Performance. In *Proceedings - 2022 8th International Conference on Information Management, ICIM 2022*. Atlantis Press International BV. 10.1109/ICIM56520.2022.00046

Olsen, C. (2023). Toward a Digital Sustainability Reporting Framework in Organizations in the Industry 5.0 Era: An Accounting Perspective. *Lecture Notes in Networks and Systems, 557*, 463–473. Advance online publication. doi:10.1007/978-3-031-17746-0_37

Pebrina, E. T., Novitasari, D., Sukriyah, S., Firmawati, Y., & Tsoraya, N. D. (2022). The Role of Accounting Information Systems in the Industrial Revolution 4.0 Era. *Edumaspul: Jurnal Pendidikan, 6*(2), 2409–2412. doi:10.33487/edumaspul.v6i2.4571

Ping, W. (2021). Data mining and XBRL integration in management accounting information based on artificial intelligence. *Journal of Intelligent & Fuzzy Systems, 40*(4), 6755–6766. Advance online publication. doi:10.3233/JIFS-189509

Pustylnick, I., Temchenko, O., & Gubarkov, S. (2017). Analysis of the use of XBRL-based accounting data in financial research. *WSEAS Transactions on Business and Economics, 14*.

Saad, M. (2023). The influence of accounting information system adoption on business performance amid COVID-19. *Computers in Human Behavior Reports, 10*(March), 100286. doi:10.1016/j.chbr.2023.100286 PMID:37122822

Saragih, A. H., Soraya, A., & Hendrawan, A. (2021). A Decade of XBRL Research in Accounting in Indonesia: A Literature Study. *The Indonesian Journal of Accounting Research*, *24*(02). Advance online publication. doi:10.33312/ijar.522

Shapovalova, A., Kuzmenko, O., Polishchuk, O., Larikova, T., & Myronchuk, Z. (2023). Modernization of the national accounting and auditing system using digital transformation tools. *Financial and Credit Activity: Problems of Theory and Practice*, *4*(51). Advance online publication. doi:10.55643/fcaptp.4.51.2023.4102

Sobb, T., Turnbull, B., & Moustafa, N. (2020). Supply chain 4.0: A survey of cyber security challenges, solutions, and future directions. *Electronics (Basel)*, *9*(11), 1864. Advance online publication. doi:10.3390/electronics9111864

Soudani, S. N. (2012). The Usefulness of an Accounting Information System for Effective Organizational Performance. *International Journal of Economics and Finance*, *4*(5), 136–145. doi:10.5539/ijef.v4n5p136

Spilnyk, I., Brukhanskyi, R., & Yaroshchuk, O. (2020). Accounting and Financial Reporting System in the Digital Economy. *2020 10th International Conference on Advanced Computer Information Technologies, ACIT 2020 - Proceedings*. 10.1109/ACIT49673.2020.9208976

Srinath & Swathi. (2022). Trends in Accounting Information System: Opportunities and Challenges in MSMEs. *Journal of Contemporary Issues in Business and Government, 28*(3).

Stalin, D., & Manayseh, M. (2023). Accounting Software Analysis of the Oman Organizations' Accounting Information System. *Shanlax International Journal of Management*, *11*(1), 11–16. doi:10.34293/management.v11i1.6377

Sukoharsono, E. G. (2020). Industrial Revolution 4.0 and the development of accounting information system: An imaginary dialogue. *IACSIT International Journal of Engineering and Technology*, *9*(2), 474–479. www.sciencepubco.com/index.php/IJET

Tawiah, V., & Borgi, H. (2022). Impact of XBRL adoption on financial reporting quality: A global evidence. *Accounting Research Journal*, *35*(6), 815–833. Advance online publication. doi:10.1108/ARJ-01-2022-0002

Teresa, M., & Matriano, D. G. (2022). *The Impact of Accounting Information on the Managerial Decision Making Process : Case of Oman Integrated Logistics Services Company, SAOG The Impact of Accounting Information on the Managerial Decision Making Process : Case of Oman Integrated Logistics*. Academic Press.

Teru, S. P., Idoku, I., & Ndeyati, J. T. (2017). A Review of the Impact of Accounting Information Systems for Effective Internal Control on Firm Performance. *Indian Journal of Finance and Banking*, *1*(2), 52–59. doi:10.46281/ijfb.v1i2.89

Vlahovic, N. (2023). E-Accounting System as a Service (E-ASaaS): A Conceptual Overview. *2023 46th ICT and Electronics Convention, MIPRO 2023 - Proceedings*. 10.23919/MIPRO57284.2023.10159833

Vysochan, O. S., Hyk, V., Mykytyuk, N., & Vysochan, O. O. (2023). Taxonomy of Financial Reporting in the Context of Digitalization of the Economy: Domestic and International Analysis Scientific Research. *Studia Universitatis Vasile Goldis Arad. Economics Series*, *33*(2), 49–70. Advance online publication. doi:10.2478/sues-2023-0008

Wang, J., Wei, B., Zhang, J., Yu, X., & Sharma, P. K. (2021). An optimized transaction verification method for trustworthy blockchain-enabled IIoT. *Ad Hoc Networks*, *119*, 102526. Advance online publication. doi:10.1016/j.adhoc.2021.102526

Wulandari, S. S., & Ali, S. (2019). Incorporating XBRL topics into the accounting curriculum: Empirical evidence from Indonesia. *Accounting Education*, *28*(6), 597–620. Advance online publication. doi:10.1080/09639284.2019.1679205

XBRL. (2023). *Oman launches Bayanat data portal | XBRL*. https://www.xbrl.org/news/oman-launches-bayanat-data-portal/#

Chapter 5
Digitalisation in Accounting:
Is It a Risk or an Opportunity?

Muhammad Arslan
https://orcid.org/0000-0001-5046-7627
Open Polytechnic, New Zealand

ABSTRACT

This chapter synthesises and critically reviews the existing research on digitalisation in accounting, particularly artificial intelligence (AI) and blockchain technology (BT). Drawing on a systematic literature review, the author of this chapter attempts to identify the risks and opportunities associated with the development and use of digitalisation in the accounting profession. In this chapter, the author used Google Scholar, Scopus, and Web of Science databases as sources for article collection. The author collected a sample of 160 articles from 2010 to 2023 through keyword searches. He employed a thematic analysis and identified six themes (i.e., creativity and openness; strategic partnership; smart contract; information governance, transparency, and trust; social, economic, and regulatory issues; and audit practices). The findings of this chapter are consistent with the theory of disruptive innovation. The findings reveal that AI and BT are disruptive technologies that will evolve over the years and, hence, disrupt and transform the business landscape.

1. INTRODUCTION

In recent years, business fields have transformed rapidly, and technology has become a critical success factor in most professions (Alam & Hossain, 2021; Tu & Akhter, 2023). Globalisation and the digital revolution have changed several aspects of the functioning of enterprises and organisations around the globe. Digitalisation

DOI: 10.4018/979-8-3693-1678-8.ch005

is a wide concept, and several classifications fall under this umbrella, such as machine learning (ML), artificial intelligence (AI), blockchain technology (BT), and big data (BD) (Redlein & Höhenberger, 2020). Artificial intelligence, or AI, has gained evolving development and importance and is being integrated into all types of industries (Rospigliosi, 2023). Based on market demands, a need arises to redefine business processes. AI development has enabled information collection and sharing through automated tools that draw information from huge volumes of data. AI has also become one of the hot topics in policy debates and has received increased attention in education (Miao, Holmes, Huang, & Zhang, 2021). The Institute of Management Accountants reported that about two percent of large firms have already implemented artificial intelligence, or machine learning, on the one hand. On the other hand, about one in five firms has indicated that they are planning to start implementing AI. Though AI implementations are used to address labour shortages, automate labour-intensive tasks, and deliver more insightful data, it is a rapidly evolving technology for which the speed of deployment and the reasons for adoption are hard to track in real-time. AI has become widespread in our daily lives, finding its way into everyday activities (Prentice, 2023); however, awareness about the potential of AI is very limited (Cummings, 2021; Suchman, 2023), and this has directly impacted the adaptation and success of AI on a wider scale. Prasad and Green (2015) argued that technology is dynamic and highlighted the need for more research on technology's impact on accounting. In addition, scholars also highlighted the need for more research exploring the nexus between accounting and digitalisation (Payne, 2014). This provides an opportunity to explore the risks and opportunities of AI and BT in the area of accounting.

Management accountants can use AI and automation, which implies that businesses benefit from them at an inter- and intra-organisational level by creating value and providing a competitive advantage (Korhonen, Selos, Laine, & Suomala, 2021). AI can provide useful and actionable insights into information that can help in driving novel business decision strategies (Arslan, 2022; Quattrone, 2016), creating operational efficiencies, and reducing employee supervision (Brown, Ly, Pham, & Sivabalan, 2020). However, it is essential to know how to make sense of the information and how to use it for fruitful business decisions (Al-Htaybat & von Alberti-Alhtaybat, 2017; Arslan, 2023). AI tends to replicate human biases from the available data without compromising the quality of reports. Humans and artificial technology both have distinct sets of strengths and weaknesses. One of the most obvious limitations of AI is its inability to interpret data and make informed decisions. In addition, AI still relies on reliable data and any misleading data may impact its effectiveness.

Using AI information, management accountants can develop their controlling and monitoring techniques while identifying areas for improvement and opportunities in the business (Lamboglia, Lavorato, Scornavacca, & Za, 2021). Nonetheless, AI is underdeveloped within management accounting in its current state and lacks an understanding of its maturity within the field. Besides these, the intensification of analysis does not essentially lead to effective management control (Liew, 2015). In contrast, accountants can face certain challenges, such as data veracity and an overload of information, leading to intertemporal choice problems (Abernethy, Bouwens, & Van Lent, 2013), and a lack of resources in terms of the unavailability of people with proper knowledge of AI and automation. The existing literature on artificial intelligence, blockchain technology, and management accounting is limited (Norén & Alldén, 2023). The standard A5 of AACSB 2018 accounting accreditation expects the integration of information technologies in accounting graduate programmes through the development of related knowledge and skills. It states, *"the ability of both faculty and students to adapt to emerging technologies as well as the mastery of current technology"* (AACSB, 2018, p. 27). Accordingly, the need and development of technologies (such as ML, AI, BT, and BD) put educators at the centre of these developments, and teachers and administrators are expected to adopt the ground-breaking technologies in their practice (Chiu, Liu, Muehlmann, & Baldwin, 2019). In addition, Knudsen (2020) argued that technology such as AI is evolving and has a dynamic impact on management control; thus, more research is needed. The existing literature reveals diverse views on the use of AI and BT in accounting. Therefore, it is critical to explore the use of digitalisation in accounting, particularly artificial intelligence (AI) and blockchain technology (BT). This chapter provides an in-depth review of existing studies and perspectives on digitalisation in accounting. The rest of the chapter is structured as follows: Section 2 provides background information and discusses the theory of innovation disruption and Gartner's AI maturity model. Section 3 presents the methodology of this chapter, while Section 4 presents the thematic analysis. At the end, Section 5 presents the conclusions, recommendations, and future research directions.

2. BACKGROUND INFORMATION

In the contemporary era, digitalisation has become one of the key success factors of new business models for all sizes, and it will continue disrupting the current business landscape (Vitale, Cupertino, & Riccaboni, 2020). People often confuse digitalisation with digitisation and use these terms as synonyms (Knudsen, 2020); nonetheless, these terminologies expound on distinctive aspects of a firm's environment (Schallmo, Williams, Schallmo, & Williams, 2018). Digitisation refers to the technical process of encoding analogue information into a digital format, thus making the digitised content programmable, transmissible, and traceable (Fähndrich, 2023). It is a less comprehensive change (Knudsen, 2020), and firms should not turn analogue things into digital artefacts to meet contemporary developments and demands (Schallmo et al., 2018). On the other hand, digital transformation or digitalisation is linked with pivotal changes to the sociotechnical structure within an organisation (Reis, Amorim, Melão, Cohen, & Rodrigues, 2020; Yoo, Lyytinen, Boland, & Berente, 2010) and involves a key organisational change that is motivated by digital technologies along with reforms in business strategy and management (Knudsen, 2020). Schallmo et al. (2018) defined the digitalisation as *"use of digital technologies and data (digitised and natively digital) to create revenue, improve business, replace/transform business processes (not simply digitising them) and create an environment for digital business, whereby digital information is at the core" (p. 6).*

The digital revolution has affected several professions, presenting challenges, and the accounting profession is no different (Arnold, 2018; Belfo & Trigo, 2013; dos Santos, Suave, Ferreira, & Altoé, 2020; Taipaleenmäki & Ikäheimo, 2013). Due to automation, accountants will need to develop different skill sets to interpret and analyse AI-generated data for developing a business strategy. Schmitz and Leoni (2019) argued that accountants and auditors need new skill sets for the effective use of blockchain technology. Similarly, George and Patatoukas (2021) argued that accountants need to learn blockchain technology to understand its opportunities and limitations. Secinaro, Calandra, and Biancone (2021) argued that blockchain technology can complement trust and provide novel features for enhancing trust in accounting systems.

Similarly, the digital revolution can expand the opportunities an organisation gets in terms of visibility and predicting consumption patterns (with help from statistical models and AI) of users of services and products provided by the organisation (Vitale et al., 2020). However, the digital revolution also brings uncertainty as these models are complex (Knudsen, 2020) and not goofproof to ponder deviations. Thus, these models can sometimes work unwarily and show false correlations while working with high volumes of data and choices (Fullana & Ruiz, 2021). Several researchers argued that blockchain can increase the trustworthiness of accounting and auditing information (Arslan & Alqatan, 2020; Coyne & McMickle, 2017; Kokina, Mancha, & Pachamanova, 2017). AI and automation have shown huge potential for solving various everyday tasks and assisting humans in several ways (Korhonen et al., 2021). AI and automation have far exceeded the expectations of humans than originally anticipated. As such, there is no shortage of rumours that "AI is going after our job," but is it really? What is the impact of artificial intelligence on the accounting profession, and the management accounting profession in particular? Management accounting is a vast concept that covers numerous vital aspects by integrating the essential skills of an accountant and a management professional. Management accounting is crucial not only at the operational level but also at the strategic level.

Moreover, management accountants play an imperative role in risk management, taking measures against negative impacts on the organisation.

In this chapter, the author took a broader approach to digitalisation (such as machine learning (ML), artificial intelligence (AI), blockchain technology (BT), and big data (BD)) that can add value to a business. Platov, Kalemulloev, and Zikirova (2021) documented three phases of digitalisation of management accounting, i.e., the introduction of the computer, internet availability, and technological advancements such as machine learning, blockchain, and artificial intelligence. The third phase is still evolving. AI is a process of simulating human intelligence with the development of machines capable of doing human-like tasks (Bharadiya, 2023). Some scholars agree that digital technologies have a moderate positive effect on firm performance (Oduro, De Nisco, & Mainolfi, 2023) while AI has the largest effect on firm performance (Oduro et al., 2023). Similarly, Chen (2019) argued that artificial intelligence technology and its ability to address issues have been thoroughly established. Big data deals with large complex data volume, data velocity, and variety (Al-Htaybat & von Alberti-Alhtaybat, 2017). Similarly, blockchain technology or distributed ledger technology is a system that records and stores the transactions in a block across a network of several peer-to-peer computers and verifies through it (Alkafaji, Dashtbayaz, & Salehi, 2023; Coyne & McMickle, 2017; Dai & Vasarhelyi, 2017; Han, Shiwakoti, Jarvis, Mordi, & Botchie, 2023; Kokina et al., 2017). In recent years, bitcoin cryptocurrency which is considered one of the impactful technologies and a disruptive innovation, has been run on blockchain technology (Peters & Panayi, 2016; Schlatt, Guggenberger, Schmid, & Urbach, 2023; Tan & Low, 2017). Scholars (e.g., Deloitte (2016); Vigna and Casey (2019)) argued that BT is a game changer for many industries (such as financial services (Tan & Low, 2017), agriculture, trade, corporate governance (Yermack, 2017), healthcare, transportation as well as government (Ølnes, Ubacht, & Janssen, 2017)) and it will transform the market structure and contemporary business models. Similarly, scholars argued that BT will strongly affect the accounting and auditing profession in the future (Coyne & McMickle, 2017; Dai & Vasarhelyi, 2017; Ostern, 2017) and will develop a new accounting ecosystem (Dai & Vasarhelyi, 2017). However, decision-makers are already abandoning digitalisation (Arnaboldi, Busco, & Cuganesan, 2017) due to a lack of relevant training and knowledge (Strohm, Hehakaya, Ranschaert, Boon, & Moors, 2020). This chapter tries to synthesise and critically review the existing research on digitalisation in accounting and artificial intelligence (AI) and blockchain technology (BT) in particular. The findings will aid in understanding how digitalisation affects accounting in new ways and, thus, provide future research opportunities and directions.

2.1 Theory of Disruption

In today's dynamic environment, firms aim to be competitive and tend to adapt to continuous innovation. Therefore, firms produce more and more sophisticated products for the markets (Christensen, Raynor, & McDonald, 2015; Christensen, Raynor, Dyer, & Gregersen, 2011). The term disruption was first introduced in 1995 by Christensen et al. (2015) and has proved to be a powerful way of thinking about innovation-driven growth. However, the term has become virtually ubiquitous from Wall Street to Silicon Valley. Disruption is a process of continuous evolvement rather than a product or service at one point in time. Christensen et al. (2015) defined the term disruption as "a process whereby a smaller company with fewer resources can successfully challenge established incumbent businesses" (p.3).

Figure 1 shows the Disruption Innovation Model. It reveals the product performance improvement over time and shows a red line. On the other side, the blue lines show the customers' demands and their willingness to pay for the performance. The upper red line shows that the incumbent firms satisfy the high-end and more profitable market by introducing higher-quality products or services. Hence, these incumbent firms overlook the needs of the low-end-low-profit market and mainstream customers and thus leave room for entrants. The lower red line shows that entrants follow a disruptive trajectory to satisfy the needs of overlooked customers, improve their services and products, and move up the market while challenging the dominance of incumbents.

This theory is helpful for all sizes of firms and signifies the disruptive impact of new technologies. However, this theory will only apply to those firms that offer their products and services first to low-end customers and then to mainstream

Figure 1. Disruptive innovation model
(Christensen et al., 2015)

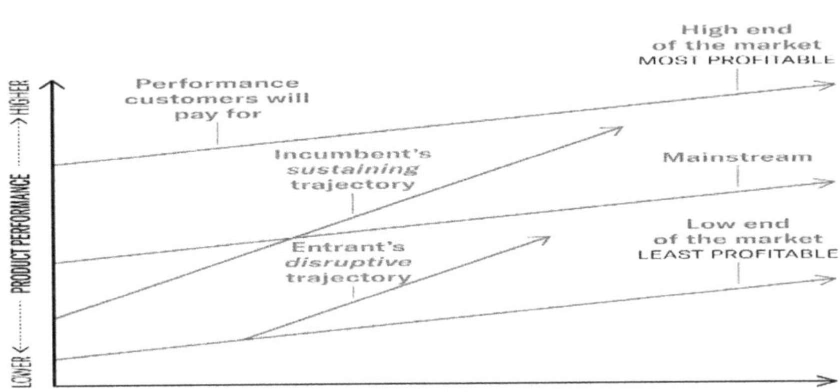

customers (those overlooked by incumbents). In some cases, the disrupters create a new market and convert non-consumers into consumers. Scholars also referred AI to theory of disruptive innovation (Păvăloaia & Necula, 2023). Păvăloaia and Necula (2023) argued that AI is a disruptive technology, and it will transform the business landscape through disruption. Consequently, investments have increased in AI technology due to its proven success and further development potential (Khamis, Li, Prestes, & Haidegger, 2019). The theory predicts that incumbents will accelerate their innovations to defend their businesses after being challenged by entrants. Disruption theory does not, and will never, expound everything about business success or innovation.

2.2 Gartner's AI Maturity Model

AI has received increased attention and has become critical for many businesses. The advancement in AI is influential and firms need to use AI to meet the market needs and remain competitive (L'Hours et al., 2022). On the contrary, Hofmann, Jöhnk, Protschky, and Urbach (2020) found that organisations are not well aware of AI and its potential which leads to misunderstanding and exaggerated expectations when implementing AI. In a similar vein, scholars argued that organisations are reluctant to implement digitalisation (Arnaboldi et al., 2017) because the decision-makers don't have relevant knowledge and training. AI can be used in several ways within a firm (Lichtenthaler, 2020). Figure 2 reveals the Gartner (2019) five levels AI maturity model. Johnson (2020) found that most firms are at the lower levels of AI implementation. Similarly, Panetta (2019) also argued that the majority of firms are at an awareness level. The Gartner five levels of AI's maturity model are awareness; active; operational; systematic; and transformational. Firms may be on any level of AI maturity level; however, it depends on the industry and resources of the firms.

Gartner's AI maturity model has five levels. The first level is awareness where firms show an early interest in AI, and it may lead to overhyping (Johnson, 2020). At this stage, firms haven't implemented the AI in their business processes. It may be due to a lack of resources and/or knowledge. The second level is active where firms start to integrate AI experimentally and informally. The maturity is rising, however, AI is still used as a pilot project (Panetta, 2019). In the Gartner AI maturity model, the third level is operational. AI is used for creating value and maturity has further raised. Firms have implemented more ML techniques to optimise the processes and product developments (Johnson, 2020) and budgets are approved for AI implementation (Panetta, 2019). At this level, the focus is on optimisation and tasks are performed at a faster speed. Hofmann et al. (2020) argued that artificial intelligence is a by-product of machine learning which finds distinctive patterns in larger databases. The fourth level is systematic where AI is used in a novel way to

Figure 2. Gartner AI maturity model
(Gartner, 2019)

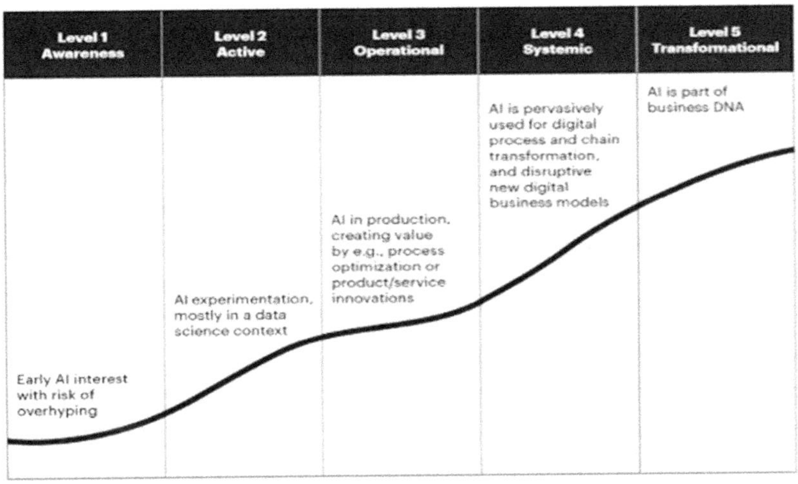

disrupt the existing business models (Panetta, 2019) to create value and productivity. At this level, AI removes a lot of manual tasks (such as correct data gathering and reporting) and reduces labour requirements. The last level is transformational where AI is part of business DNA and firms rely heavily on AI for value offering towards their customers. Therefore, machine learning is regularly used to run algorithms and develop product offerings (Johnson, 2020). This is the most disruptive level and firms remove all manual labour, and repetitive and basic tasks are performed with AI. The last three levels can significantly affect the accounting profession. The next section expounds the methodology used in this chapter.

3. METHODOLOGY

The purpose of this chapter was to synthesise and critically review the existing research on digitalisation in accounting, particularly artificial intelligence (AI) and blockchain technology (BT). In this chapter, the author attempts to explore the risks and opportunities of AI and BT through thematic analysis. Thematic analysis is a qualitative research methodology which is used to develop a grounded theory. Thematic analysis identifies, analyses and reports the patterns within data (Braun & Clarke, 2006). This technique is relevant here because the author attempts to synthesise and critically review the existing literature to explore themes from published papers. Braun and Clarke (2006) presented the following six steps to perform a thematic analysis:

i. Familiarize with data.
ii. Create open codes.
iii. Identify themes.
iv. Revisit identified themes.
v. Define and give new names to themes and
vi. generate report.

It is challenging to gather a representative sample from the existing literature on digitalisation in accounting, particularly artificial intelligence and blockchain technology. In this chapter, the author searched the phrase digitalisation in accounting on Google Scholar without any restrictions. Based on the abstract and/or the full text, the 70 sample articles were selected. The author of this chapter then applied the rank order approach and stopped looking for new articles when three sequential articles were found irrelevant. In this chapter, the author also puts further restrictions and limits on the articles published in or after 2010. In this way, the author found 120 articles to give him a total of 190 articles for this chapter. Arslan (2020) emphasised that the rank-order approach may exclude some relevant articles, therefore, the author searched again with close synonyms such as emerging technologies, artificial intelligence, blockchain, machine learning, and big data in accounting. This method helped in adding a further 40 articles. The author of this chapter then repeated the same search criteria on Scopus and Web of Science databases and selected 130 articles. The author noticed that some articles appeared in all three databases, therefore duplicate articles were removed and that brings a total sample of 160 articles. Due to the rank order approach, the chapter author believes that his sample was saturated enough to explore the themes and adding further articles would not bring any more themes. Additionally, this chapter aims to explore the existing themes rather than finding gaps in existing literature. Therefore, the sample acquired from Google Scholar, Scopus, and Web of Science was quite satisfactory in capturing diversity and exploring themes related to digitalisation in accounting. The author of this chapter applied three types of coding methods (i.e., open coding, axial coding, and selective coding) for thematic analysis which is consistent with Arslan (2020). Open coding was the first stage in this chapter, where the author went through the articles to abridge the raw data into codes based on research inspiration. This stage created several codes. Axial coding was the next phase in this chapter, where the author found common and repeating ideas by looking for the relationships and links among the codes and creating the subcategories. This stage created fundamental categories from the previous stage codes. Selective coding was the final stage in the coding of data where the author of this chapter discovered the aggregate themes by looking into all the categories and subcategories. The following six themes were obtained from the thematic analysis:

i. Creativity and Openness
ii. Strategic Partnership
iii. Smart Contract
iv. Information Governance, Transparency, and Trust
v. Social, Economic, and Regulatory Issues
vi. Audit Practices

These themes are discussed in the next section.

4. THEMATIC ANALYSIS

4.1 Creativity and Openness

Scholars argued that accountants have always been very open to new technologies (Arnold, 2018; Belfo & Trigo, 2013; dos Santos et al., 2020) and existing studies have presented future technological challenges for accountants. Similarly, several studies have been conducted that highlighted the need for new skills and roles of accountants (Schmitz & Leoni, 2019), especially in the area of blockchain and artificial intelligence (Han et al., 2023; Secinaro et al., 2021). Moll and Yigitbasioglu (2019) argued that emerging technologies have the potential to change and disrupt the work of accountants. This is consistent with the theory of disruption. In a similar vein, Marrone and Hazelton (2019) highlighted the need for new paradigms for understanding the data. Professional bodies have tried to address this issue. Therefore, the AACSB 2018 accounting accreditation expects the integration of information technologies in accounting graduate programs through the development of related knowledge and skills. Demirkan, Demirkan, and McKee (2020) argued that future technological advancement will disrupt the accounting profession and may open new avenues. Scholars argued that integrated technological advancement provides more time for to accountants for decision-making (Chapman & Kihn, 2009), enabling the decentralization of decisions (Dechow & Mouritsen, 2005), and extending the accountants' role (Caglio, 2003; Järvenpää, 2007; Suddaby, Saxton, & Gunz, 2015).

4.2 Strategic Partnership

Several accounting profession studies have focused on big data analytics. Scholars have indicated how accountants can retain a strategic place in the world of big data (Richins, Stapleton, Stratopoulos, & Wong, 2017), exploring the prospects and challenges that this technology can pose for the accounting profession. Al-Htaybat and von Alberti-Alhtaybat (2017) explored the relationship between big data and corporate reporting and found three categories. They also argued that dual communication flows of corporate reporting with BD are pivotal. In a similar vein, Nielsen (2018) highlighted the increasing need for data scientists in the accounting profession.

4.3 Smart Contract

Currently, the involvement of human elements in the accounting and auditing profession is high, however, scholars argued that it could change with the introduction of blockchain technology (Coyne & McMickle, 2017; Ølnes et al., 2017). BT can execute the smart contract to reduce the risk of error or manipulation (Yermack, 2017) when certain conditions are met (Hileman & Rauchs, 2017; Rozario & Vasarhelyi, 2018). Scholars also suggested a holistic hybrid audit model comprising blockchain smart audit procedures inside and outside of BT (Rozario & Vasarhelyi, 2018). In a similar vein, Dai and Vasarhelyi (2017) and Marshall and Lambert (2018) reported that artificial intelligence can also be used for smart contracts and can detect damage to the inventory. Kozlowski (2018) also highlighted the need to embed accounting standards into the blockchain and encode them into smart contracts.

4.4 Information Governance, Transparency, and Trust

Digital technologies, particularly blockchain can be used for voluntary information disclosure (Yu, Lin, & Tang, 2018), reducing information asymmetry, errors in disclosure, and earnings management. Thus, it provides data security and immutability (Piazza, 2017). In a similar vein, Casey and Vigna (2018) referred to blockchain as a truth machine. Scholars (see Rooney, Aiken, and Rooney (2017); Yermack (2017)) also argued that BT and AI can push accountants and auditors towards more transparent behaviour. Additionally, Scholars argued that shareholders and stakeholders can have immediate access to relevant accounting information with BT (Atzori, 2015) and hence increase transparency (Tapscott & Tapscott, 2017), and trustworthiness (Hileman & Rauchs, 2017). On the other hand, physical verification of transactions may be a challenge (Coyne & McMickle, 2017). The digital recording of a transaction doesn't necessarily mean that the transaction happened in the real world (Dai & Vasarhelyi, 2017). Therefore, a cautious approach is needed.

4.5 Social, Economic, and Regulatory Issues

Kokina et al. (2017) argued that the need for human accountants will not go away, nevertheless, accountants need different skill sets to perform the tasks. On the other side, Gardner and Bryson (2022) argued that innovation concurrently destroys and creates tasks/jobs and thus innovation always has a darker side. Similarly, Goretzki and Messner (2019) found that the management accountants' identity is rooted in wider organisational beliefs. Consequently, the need arises to understand the collaboration among different groups involving management accountant roles within an organization (Järvenpää, 2007). In existing literature, Abbott (2014) argued that professional occupations rest on more or less abstract knowledge and also highlighted the need to represent competition over authority in terms of explicit conflicts (Suddaby et al., 2015) and dedicated to how professions can assert specialised knowledge to form monopolies (Cooper & Robson, 2006) at a macro level. Still, digital technologies can cause individuals to see their roles as disconnected from their identity and appear as nightmares due to automation. Nevertheless, scholars (see Abbott (2014); Goretzki and Messner (2019); Suddaby et al. (2015)) have identified the accountants' role as an underdeveloped area of research.

4.6 Audit Practices

The current audit practices are labour-intensive and lengthy processes in which auditors need to review several electronic and physical documents alongside a lot of entries and spreadsheet files. Conversely, this costs efficiency and effectiveness of auditing (Rückeshäuser, 2017). BT and AI can solve this issue, can record validated transactions (real-time auditing), and provide confidentiality (Rooney et al., 2017; Wang & Kogan, 2018). BT and AI can enhance the efficiencies significantly through automatic processing, recording, and reconciling of transactions, and removing the need for statistical sampling (Bonyuet, 2020). However, there is a need for auditors to embrace these technologies by conducting risk management and advising on solutions and assurance for internal control (Liu, Wu, & Xu, 2019). Liu et al. (2019) argued that auditors should gain competence both in the governance of blockchain and blockchain technology.

4.7 Discussion

Several existing studies also highlighted the need for uplifting skills or accountants to utilise the potential of blockchain and artificial intelligence. However, accountants need to be creative and open to embrace new technologies. Organisations are already at different levels of the Gartner AI maturity model and more and more organisations are adopting AI technology. It may be difficult for accountants to embrace these changes in the short run; however, it will provide more benefits in the long run. The understanding and adaptation of digital technologies will provide accountants with an opportunity to work as strategic partners, especially in the area of big data. Digital technologies can reduce the manual workload and it provides more time for accountants to focus on strategic decision making. Digital technologies such as BT and AI are indeed disruptive in nature, however, these can enhance transparency and trust among stakeholders.

5. CONCLUSION, LIMITATIONS, AND FUTURE RESEARCH DIRECTIONS

No doubt, digitalisation has transformed the way accountants work, and it will have an immense impact on the management of businesses and decision-making aspects. This chapter synthesises and critically reviews the existing literature on digitalisation in accounting, particularly artificial intelligence (AI) and blockchain technology (BT). In this chapter, the author applied a thematic analysis and explored six themes i.e., (1) creativity and openness; (2) strategic partnership; (3) smart contract; (4) information governance, transparency, and trust; (5) social, economic, and regulatory issues; and (6) audit practices. The author of this chapter found that AI and BT are disruptive technologies which will evolve over the years, and these will change the business landscape through disruption and transformation. This is consistent with the theory of disruptive innovation (Christensen et al., 2015). The author of this chapter also concludes that several tasks can be substituted using AI and BT, but they cannot replace the need for human accountants. Nevertheless, accountants need to uplift their skills and embrace these technologies for their effective use. The effective use of these technologies will provide accountants time and energy to focus on more important aspects of business, thus adding value to their firms. It is pivotal for management accountants to manage and monitor these advanced technologies (i.e., AI and BT) and capitalise on opportunities while avoiding pitfalls. In this chapter, the author found that digital technologies, particularly blockchain and artificial intelligence can enhance information disclosure and trust while reducing information asymmetry, errors, and earnings management. There is no doubt that digital technologies can automate several tasks and record transactions in real time. However, there are several areas where a physical verification of transactions needs to be done. Therefore, accountants need to develop high cognitive abilities, such as data science and analytics skills, leveraging the power of large data sets and solving strategic tasks, which will become increasingly important in the near future.

This chapter contributes to the existing literature on digitalisation in accounting and has several practical implications for scholars and policymakers. The educational institutes can use these findings to change their curriculum to equip the students with much-needed skills in accounting. The regulators and professionals may also use these findings for reforms and change the rules, standards, and relevant laws to tackle technological innovations. This chapter also has several limitations. In this chapter, the author only searched the articles from 2010 to 2023 and it is possible that the author couldn't incorporate some earlier studies. Therefore, future research can be conducted over a longer period. The author of this chapter only conducted the thematic analysis due to cost and time constraints. Future studies may be conducted by collecting primary data through surveys or interviews for a better understanding of the current dynamics in the business environment.

REFERENCES

AACSB. (2018). *Eligibility Procedures and Accreditation Standards for Accounting Accreditation*. The Association to Advance Collegiate Schools of Business.

Abbott, A. (2014). *The system of professions: An essay on the division of expert labor*. University of Chicago Press.

Abernethy, M. A., Bouwens, J., & Van Lent, L. (2013). The role of performance measures in the intertemporal decisions of business unit managers. *Contemporary Accounting Research, 30*(3), 925–961. doi:10.1111/j.1911-3846.2012.01178.x

Al-Htaybat, K., & von Alberti-Alhtaybat, L. (2017). Big Data and corporate reporting: Impacts and paradoxes. *Accounting, Auditing & Accountability Journal, 30*(4), 850–873. doi:10.1108/AAAJ-07-2015-2139

Alam, M. S., & Hossain, D. M. (2021). Management Accounting in the Era of Digitalization. *The Journal of Industrial Distribution & Business, 12*(11), 1–8.

Alkafaji, B. K. A., Dashtbayaz, M. L., & Salehi, M. (2023). The Impact of Blockchain on the Quality of Accounting Information: An Iraqi Case Study. *Risks, 11*(3), 58. doi:10.3390/risks11030058

Arnaboldi, M., Busco, C., & Cuganesan, S. (2017). Accounting, accountability, social media and big data: Revolution or hype? *Accounting, Auditing & Accountability Journal, 30*(4), 762–776. doi:10.1108/AAAJ-03-2017-2880

Arnold, V. (2018). The changing technological environment and the future of behavioural research in accounting. *Accounting and Finance, 58*(2), 315–339. doi:10.1111/acfi.12218

Arslan, M. (2020). Corporate social sustainability in supply chain management: A literature review. *Journal of Global Responsibility, 11*(3), 233–255. doi:10.1108/JGR-11-2019-0108

Arslan, M. (2022). Succession Planning in Family-Owned Business Evidence From an Emerging Economy. In *Research Anthology on Strategies for Maintaining Successful Family Firms* (pp. 504–528). IGI Global. doi:10.4018/978-1-6684-3550-2.ch022

Arslan, M. (2023). CEO Compensation and Say on Pay: Does CEO-to-Employee Pay Ratio Matters? *Proceedings - Academy of Management*, *2023*(1), 11035. doi:10.5465/AMPROC.2023.11035abstract

Arslan, M., & Alqatan, A. (2020). Role of institutions in shaping corporate governance system: Evidence from emerging economy. *Heliyon*, *6*(3), e03520. doi:10.1016/j.heliyon.2020.e03520 PMID:32181393

AtzoriM. (2015). Blockchain technology and decentralized governance: Is the state still necessary? *Available at* SSRN 2709713. doi:10.2139/ssrn.2709713

Belfo, F., & Trigo, A. (2013). Accounting information systems: Tradition and future directions. *Procedia Technology*, *9*, 536–546. doi:10.1016/j.protcy.2013.12.060

Bharadiya, J. P. (2023). A Comparative Study of Business Intelligence and Artificial Intelligence with Big Data Analytics. *American Journal of Artificial Intelligence*, *7*(1), 24.

Bonyuet, D. (2020). Overview and impact of blockchain on auditing. *The International Journal of Digital Accounting Research*, *20*, 31–43. doi:10.4192/1577-8517-v20_2

Braun, V., & Clarke, V. (2006). Using thematic analysis in psychology. *Qualitative Research in Psychology*, *3*(2), 77–101. doi:10.1191/1478088706qp063oa

Brown, P., Ly, T., Pham, H., & Sivabalan, P. (2020). Automation and management control in dynamic environments: Managing organisational flexibility and energy efficiency in service sectors. *The British Accounting Review*, *52*(2), 100840. doi:10.1016/j.bar.2019.100840

Caglio, A. (2003). Enterprise resource planning systems and accountants: Towards hybridization? *European Accounting Review*, *12*(1), 123–153. doi:10.1080/0963818031000087853

Casey, M. J., & Vigna, P. (2018). *The Truth Machine: The Blockchain and the Future of Everything*. St. Martin's Press.

Chapman, C. S., & Kihn, L.-A. (2009). Information system integration, enabling control and performance. *Accounting, Organizations and Society*, *34*(2), 151–169. doi:10.1016/j.aos.2008.07.003

Chen, H. (2019). *Success factors impacting artificial intelligence adoption: Perspective from the Telecom Industry in China*. Old Dominion University.

Chiu, V., Liu, Q., Muehlmann, B., & Baldwin, A. A. (2019). A bibliometric analysis of accounting information systems journals and their emerging technologies contributions. *International Journal of Accounting Information Systems*, *32*, 24–43. doi:10.1016/j.accinf.2018.11.003

Christensen, C., Raynor, M. E., & McDonald, R. (2015). *Disruptive innovation*. Harvard Business Review. Retrieved from https://hbr.org/2015/12/what-is-disruptive-innovation

Christensen, C. M., Raynor, M. E., Dyer, J., & Gregersen, H. (2011). *Disruptive Innovation: The Christensen Collection (The Innovator's Dilemma, The Innovator's Solution, The Innovator's DNA, and Harvard Business Review article" How Will You Measure Your Life?")(4 Items)*. Harvard Business Press.

Cooper, D. J., & Robson, K. (2006). Accounting, professions and regulation: Locating the sites of professionalization. *Accounting, Organizations and Society*, *31*(4-5), 415–444. doi:10.1016/j.aos.2006.03.003

Coyne, J. G., & McMickle, P. L. (2017). Can blockchains serve an accounting purpose? *Journal of Emerging Technologies in Accounting*, *14*(2), 101–111. doi:10.2308/jeta-51910

Cummings, M. (2021). Rethinking the maturity of artificial intelligence in safety-critical settings. *AI Magazine*, *42*(1), 6–15. doi:10.1002/j.2371-9621.2021.tb00005.x

Dai, J., & Vasarhelyi, M. A. (2017). Toward blockchain-based accounting and assurance. *Journal of Information Systems*, *31*(3), 5–21. doi:10.2308/isys-51804

Dechow, N., & Mouritsen, J. (2005). Enterprise resource planning systems, management control and the quest for integration. *Accounting, Organizations and Society*, *30*(7-8), 691–733. doi:10.1016/j.aos.2004.11.004

Deloitte. (2016). *Blockchain Technology–A Game-Changer in Accounting*. White paper.

Demirkan, S., Demirkan, I., & McKee, A. (2020). Blockchain technology in the future of business cyber security and accounting. *Journal of Management Analytics*, *7*(2), 189–208. doi:10.1080/23270012.2020.1731721

dos Santos, B. L., Suave, R., Ferreira, M. M., & Altoé, S. M. L. (2020). Profissão contábil em tempos de mudança: Implicações do avanço tecnológico nas atividades em um escritório de contabilidade. *Revista de Contabilidade e Controladoria*, *11*(3).

Fähndrich, J. (2023). A literature review on the impact of digitalisation on management control. *Journal of Management Control, 34*(1), 9–65. doi:10.1007/s00187-022-00349-4

Fullana, O., & Ruiz, J. (2021). Accounting information systems in the blockchain era. *International Journal of Intellectual Property Management, 11*(1), 63–80. doi:10.1504/IJIPM.2021.113357

Gardner, E. C., & Bryson, J. R. (2022). The dark side of the industrialisation of accountancy: Innovation, commoditization, colonization and competitiveness. In *The Dark Side of Innovation* (pp. 56–71). Routledge.

Gartner. (2019). *Gartner AI Maturity Model.* Retrieved from https://www.gartner.com/smarterwithgartner/the-cios-guide-to-artificial-intelligence

George, K., & Patatoukas, P. N. (2021). The blockchain evolution and revolution of accounting. In Information for Efficient Decision Making: Big Data, Blockchain and Relevance (pp. 157-172). World Scientific.

Goretzki, L., & Messner, M. (2019). Backstage and frontstage interactions in management accountants' identity work. *Accounting, Organizations and Society, 74*, 1–20. doi:10.1016/j.aos.2018.09.001

Han, H., Shiwakoti, R. K., Jarvis, R., Mordi, C., & Botchie, D. (2023). Accounting and auditing with blockchain technology and artificial Intelligence: A literature review. *International Journal of Accounting Information Systems, 48*, 100598. doi:10.1016/j.accinf.2022.100598

HilemanG.RauchsM. (2017). 2017 global blockchain benchmarking study. *Available at* SSRN 3040224.

Hofmann, P., Jöhnk, J., Protschky, D., & Urbach, N. (2020). *Developing Purposeful AI Use Cases-A Structured Method and Its Application in Project Management.* Symposium conducted at the meeting of the Wirtschaftsinformatik (Zentrale Tracks).

Järvenpää, M. (2007). Making business partners: A case study on how management accounting culture was changed. *European Accounting Review, 16*(1), 99–142. doi:10.1080/09638180701265903

Johnson, J. (2020). Gartner's AI Maturity Model: How AI Can Work for You. *BMC.* Retrieved from https://www.bmc.com/blogs/ai-maturity-models/

Khamis, A., Li, H., Prestes, E., & Haidegger, T. (2019). AI: A key enabler of sustainable development goals, part 1. *IEEE Robotics & Automation Magazine, 26*(3), 95–102. doi:10.1109/MRA.2019.2928738

Knudsen, D.-R. (2020). Elusive boundaries, power relations, and knowledge production: A systematic review of the literature on digitalization in accounting. *International Journal of Accounting Information Systems*, *36*, 100441. doi:10.1016/j.accinf.2019.100441

Kokina, J., Mancha, R., & Pachamanova, D. (2017). Blockchain: Emergent industry adoption and implications for accounting. *Journal of Emerging Technologies in Accounting*, *14*(2), 91–100. doi:10.2308/jeta-51911

Korhonen, T., Selos, E., Laine, T., & Suomala, P. (2021). Exploring the programmability of management accounting work for increasing automation: An interventionist case study. *Accounting, Auditing & Accountability Journal*, *34*(2), 253–280. doi:10.1108/AAAJ-12-2016-2809

Kozlowski, S. (2018). An audit ecosystem to support blockchain-based accounting and assurance. In *Continuous Auditing* (pp. 299–313). Emerald Publishing Limited. doi:10.1108/978-1-78743-413-420181015

L'Hours, H., Verburg, M., de Vries, J., Cepinskas, L., von Stein, I., Huber, R., . . . Mathers, B. J. (2022). *D4. 6 Report on a maturity model towards FAIR data in FAIR repositories*. Academic Press.

Lamboglia, R., Lavorato, D., Scornavacca, E., & Za, S. (2021). Exploring the relationship between audit and technology. A bibliometric analysis. *Meditari Accountancy Research*, *29*(5), 1233–1260. doi:10.1108/MEDAR-03-2020-0836

Lichtenthaler, U. (2020). Five maturity levels of managing AI: From isolated ignorance to integrated intelligence. *Journal of Innovation Management*, *8*(1), 39–50. doi:10.24840/2183-0606_008.001_0005

Liew, A. (2015). The use of technology-structured management controls: Changes in senior management's decision-making behaviours. *International Journal of Accounting Information Systems*, *17*, 37–64. doi:10.1016/j.accinf.2014.05.001

Liu, M., Wu, K., & Xu, J. J. (2019). How will blockchain technology impact auditing and accounting: Permissionless versus permissioned blockchain. *Current Issues in Auditing*, *13*(2), A19–A29. doi:10.2308/ciia-52540

Marrone, M., & Hazelton, J. (2019). The disruptive and transformative potential of new technologies for accounting, accountants and accountability: A review of current literature and call for further research. *Meditari Accountancy Research*, *27*(5), 677–694. doi:10.1108/MEDAR-06-2019-0508

Marshall, T. E., & Lambert, S. L. (2018). Cloud-based intelligent accounting applications: Accounting task automation using IBM watson cognitive computing. *Journal of Emerging Technologies in Accounting, 15*(1), 199–215. doi:10.2308/jeta-52095

Miao, F., Holmes, W., Huang, R., & Zhang, H. (2021). *AI and education: A guidance for policymakers*. UNESCO Publishing.

Moll, J., & Yigitbasioglu, O. (2019). The role of internet-related technologies in shaping the work of accountants: New directions for accounting research. *The British Accounting Review, 51*(6), 100833. doi:10.1016/j.bar.2019.04.002

Nielsen, S. (2018). Reflections on the applicability of business analytics for management accounting–and future perspectives for the accountant. *Journal of Accounting & Organizational Change, 14*(2), 167–187. doi:10.1108/JAOC-11-2014-0056

Norén, G., & Alldén, S. (2023). *The development of artificial intelligence (AI) within the management accounting and control profession*. Umea University.

Oduro, S., De Nisco, A., & Mainolfi, G. (2023). Do digital technologies pay off? A meta-analytic review of the digital technologies/firm performance nexus. *Technovation, 128*, 102836. doi:10.1016/j.technovation.2023.102836

Ølnes, S., Ubacht, J., & Janssen, M. (2017). *Blockchain in government: Benefits and implications of distributed ledger technology for information sharing*. Elsevier.

Ostern, N. (2017). Do we really want Blockchain-based accounting? Decentralized consensus as enabler of management override of internal controls. Darmstadt Technical University.

Panetta, K. (2019). The CIO's guide to Artificial Intelligence. *Gartner*.

Păvăloaia, V.-D., & Necula, S.-C. (2023). Artificial intelligence as a disruptive technology—A systematic literature review. *Electronics (Basel), 12*(5), 1102. doi:10.3390/electronics12051102

Payne, R. (2014). Discussion of 'Digitisation,' Big Data' and the transformation of accounting information' by Alnoor Bhimani and Leslie Willcocks (2014). *Accounting and Business Research, 44*(4), 491–495. doi:10.1080/00014788.2014.910053

Peters, G. W., & Panayi, E. (2016). *Understanding modern banking ledgers through blockchain technologies: Future of transaction processing and smart contracts on the internet of money*. Springer.

Piazza, F. S. (2017). Bitcoin and the blockchain as possible corporate governance tools: Strengths and weaknesses. *Bocconi Legal Papers*, *9*, 125.

Platov, A., Kalemulloev, M., & Zikirova, S. (2021). Management accounting in the context of digitalization. *SHS Web Conf.*, *106*. 10.1051/shsconf/202110601037

Prasad, A., & Green, P. (2015). Governing cloud computing services: Reconsideration of IT governance structures. *International Journal of Accounting Information Systems*, *19*, 45–58. doi:10.1016/j.accinf.2015.11.004

Prentice, C. (2023). Leveraging Emotional and Artificial Intelligences for Employees and Customers. In *Leveraging Emotional and Artificial Intelligence for Organisational Performance* (pp. 157–176). Springer. doi:10.1007/978-981-99-1865-2_11

Quattrone, P. (2016). Management accounting goes digital: Will the move make it wiser? *Management Accounting Research*, *31*, 118–122. doi:10.1016/j.mar.2016.01.003

Redlein, A., & Höhenberger, C. (2020). Digitalisation. *Modern Facility and Workplace Management: Processes, Implementation and Digitalisation*, 139-175.

Reis, J., Amorim, M., Melão, N., Cohen, Y., & Rodrigues, M. (2020). Digitalization: A literature review and research agenda. *Springer.*

Richins, G., Stapleton, A., Stratopoulos, T. C., & Wong, C. (2017). Big data analytics: Opportunity or threat for the accounting profession? *Journal of Information Systems*, *31*(3), 63–79. doi:10.2308/isys-51805

Rooney, H., Aiken, B., & Rooney, M. (2017). Q. Is internal audit ready for blockchain? *Technology Innovation Management Review*, *7*(10), 41–44. doi:10.22215/timreview/1113

Rospigliosi, P. a. (2023). *Artificial intelligence in teaching and learning: what questions should we ask of ChatGPT?* Taylor & Francis.

Rozario, A. M., & Vasarhelyi, M. A. (2018). Auditing with Smart Contracts. *The International Journal of Digital Accounting Research*, *18*, 1–27. doi:10.4192/1577-8517-v18_1

Rückeshäuser, N. (2017). *Do we really want blockchain-based accounting? Decentralized consensus as enabler of management override of internal controls.* Academic Press.

Schallmo, D. R., Williams, C. A., Schallmo, D. R., & Williams, C. A. (2018). History of digital transformation. *Digital Transformation Now! Guiding the Successful Digitalization of Your Business Model*, 3-8.

Schlatt, V., Guggenberger, T., Schmid, J., & Urbach, N. (2023). Attacking the trust machine: Developing an information systems research agenda for blockchain cybersecurity. *International Journal of Information Management*, *68*, 102470. doi:10.1016/j.ijinfomgt.2022.102470

Schmitz, J., & Leoni, G. (2019). Accounting and auditing at the time of blockchain technology: A research agenda. *Australian Accounting Review*, *29*(2), 331–342. doi:10.1111/auar.12286

Secinaro, S., Calandra, D., & Biancone, P. (2021). Blockchain, trust, and trust accounting: Can blockchain technology substitute trust created by intermediaries in trust accounting? A theoretical examination. *International Journal of Management Practice*, *14*(2), 129–145. doi:10.1504/IJMP.2021.113824

Strohm, L., Hehakaya, C., Ranschaert, E. R., Boon, W. P., & Moors, E. H. (2020). Implementation of artificial intelligence (AI) applications in radiology: Hindering and facilitating factors. *European Radiology*, *30*(10), 5525–5532. doi:10.1007/s00330-020-06946-y PMID:32458173

Suchman, L. (2023). The uncontroversial 'thingness' of AI. *Big Data & Society*, *10*(2). doi:10.1177/20539517231206794

Suddaby, R., Saxton, G. D., & Gunz, S. (2015). Twittering change: The institutional work of domain change in accounting expertise. *Accounting, Organizations and Society*, *45*, 52–68. doi:10.1016/j.aos.2015.07.002

Taipaleenmäki, J., & Ikäheimo, S. (2013). On the convergence of management accounting and financial accounting–the role of information technology in accounting change. *International Journal of Accounting Information Systems*, *14*(4), 321–348. doi:10.1016/j.accinf.2013.09.003

Tan, B. S., & Low, K. Y. (2017). Bitcoin–its economics for financial reporting. *Australian Accounting Review*, *27*(2), 220–227. doi:10.1111/auar.12167

Tapscott, D., & Tapscott, A. (2017). How blockchain will change organizations. *MIT Sloan Management Review*, *58*(2), 10.

Tu, J. J., & Akhter, S. (2023). Exploring the role of entrepreneurial education, technology and teachers' creativity in excelling sustainable business competencies. *Ekonomska Istrazivanja*, *36*(1), 2119429. doi:10.1080/1331677X.2022.2119429

Vigna, P., & Casey, M. J. (2019). *The truth machine: the blockchain and the future of everything*. Picador.

Vitale, G., Cupertino, S., & Riccaboni, A. (2020). Big data and management control systems change: The case of an agricultural SME. *Journal of Management Control*, *31*(1-2), 123–152. doi:10.1007/s00187-020-00298-w

Wang, Y., & Kogan, A. (2018). Designing confidentiality-preserving Blockchain-based transaction processing systems. *International Journal of Accounting Information Systems*, *30*, 1–18. doi:10.1016/j.accinf.2018.06.001

Yermack, D. (2017). Corporate governance and blockchains. *Review of Finance*, *21*(1), 7–31.

YooY.LyytinenK.J.BolandR.J.BerenteN. (2010). *The next wave of digital innovation: Opportunities and challenges*. doi:10.2139/ssrn.1622170

Yu, T., Lin, Z., & Tang, Q. (2018). Blockchain: The introduction and its application in financial accounting. *Journal of Corporate Accounting & Finance*, *29*(4), 37–47. doi:10.1002/jcaf.22365

KEY TERMS AND DEFINITIONS

Accounting: Refers to the process of recording financial transactions and preparing reports on assets, liabilities and operations of a business.

Artificial Intelligence: Is the process of simulating human intelligence through machines and computer systems.

Blockchain: Refers to an advanced database mechanism that allows secure and transparent information sharing within a network.

Digitalisation: Refers to the ongoing integration of digitised data and technologies across the economy and society.

Disruptive Innovation: Is the idea of simplifying and making more affordable products and services to undesirable or ignored markets.

Smart Contract: Is a process of coding and executing the terms of an agreement or contract through blockchain.

Thematic Analysis: Is a method of analysing qualitative data to identify themes through coding.

Chapter 6
Digitalisation, Audit Quality, and Corporate Governance in the Swedish Context

Hichri Abir
University of Sfax, Tunisia

ABSTRACT

This research aims to study the effect of the digitalisation of companies on audit quality and corporate governance in a sample of 150 Swedish companies from 2017-2022. The authors collected the data from the database of annual reports and reference documents available on the companies' websites. The results show that the digitalisation of companies has a positive and significant effect on audit quality. Similarly, the authors have demonstrated that the digitalisation of companies positively impacts corporate governance. In this sense, an effective digitalisation strategy will likely increase the quality of information and governance mechanisms.

1. INTRODUCTION

Today's society is constantly evolving, and digitalisation is one of the main trends. Companies are affected by these technological waves and must continuously adapt to remain competitive in the market and respond as effectively as possible to the needs of increasingly demanding customers (Lugli et al., 2023). Audit quality is an essential function within these organisations more than ever, and we can, therefore, ask ourselves about the various impacts that this digitalisation of the environment is having on this function.

DOI: 10.4018/979-8-3693-1678-8.ch006

Indeed, artificial intelligence, robotics, data analysis, the Internet of Things, and blockchain are emerging technologies revolutionising the world (Seethamraju and Hecimovic, 2023). Businesses continue to invest heavily in new technologies to harness this connectivity, and many are now leveraging large-scale digital transformation to radically change traditional business models (Lascău, 2022). Part of this evolution and disruption involves prioritising investment in new data analysis systems and technologies that enable them better to understand their businesses and the needs of the mark

Auditors are at the forefront of this large-scale transformation. They are themselves directly impacted by changes in their clients' operating environments, 'disruptions' in economic cycles, their consequences in terms of impact on operational and financial organisation models, and the digitalisation of processes (D'Onza and De Santis, 2020).

Similarly, the role of an audit professional is changing in response to the digital transformation of businesses. Using automation and analytics to process increasing volumes of data contributes to high-quality audits and allows auditors to focus more on identifying risks and understanding organisations (Cipek, 2021). This auditing evolution leads to more excellent connectivity, increased transparency and, consequently, greater trust from all stakeholders, which brings us to our investigation.

However, although digitisation in auditing brings significant benefits, it is essential to consider these criticisms and challenges to ensure successful implementation and guarantee digital audit processes' quality, security, and ethics. Consequently, the increasing use of technologies such as artificial intelligence and automation makes auditors dependent on these tools, which can compromise audit quality.

Therefore, digitisation significantly impacts corporate governance, affecting how companies are directed, supervised and managed. Digitalisation enables more efficient data analysis, collection, and presentation, promoting transparency by providing users with easier access to financial, operational, and compliance information. Increased transparency is, therefore, essential to improve stakeholder confidence and facilitate the effectiveness of governance mechanisms. Similarly, digitisation offers advanced means of communication, such as corporate social networks, online platforms and collaboration tools. These tools facilitate communication between managers and stakeholders, contributing to more transparent governance. Thus, digitalisation transforms corporate governance by improving disclosure, enhancing communication, facilitating data-driven decision-making, promoting organisational agility, and requiring stakeholders to upgrade their skills. In this respect, effective corporate governance in a digital context is essential to ensure a company's sustainability and business continuity.

In this respect, we will study the association between digitalisation and audit quality in the Swedish context. We will test our problem on a sample of 150 Swedish companies to do this. The hypotheses likely to identify the effect of digitalisation on audit quality are based on contributions from organisation theory.

Sweden is renowned for its highly innovative technology sector. Digitalisation is, therefore, essential to strengthen and maintain the competitiveness of Swedish companies. Similarly, corporate governance must encourage innovation while ensuring that the risks associated with digitisation are appropriately managed, and high audit quality helps to guarantee the relevance of information in this context. Therefore, understanding the interaction between digitisation, corporate governance, and audit quality is essential, given the specific business environment and governance culture that characterises the country.

There is little literature on the impact of digitalisation on audit quality and corporate governance in the Swedish context during the period 2015-2022. This manuscript attempts to fill this research gap by addressing the following research question: What is the impact of digitalisation on audit quality and corporate governance in the Swedish context? Our study explains the interaction between digitisation, audit quality and corporate governance in Sweden. It is crucial for meeting the specific requirements of the Swedish context, strengthening transparency, supporting innovation, and maintaining trust between the company and its stakeholders in a constantly changing business environment.

The empirical results of our study show a positive and significant association between digitisation and audit quality and a positive and significant relationship between digitisation and corporate governance. For the control variables, the regression results show that company size does not affect audit quality and corporate governance. Thus, company performance has a positive and significant effect on audit quality and corporate governance, which explains why company performance is a determining factor in digitalisation. On the other hand, the legal system positively affects audit quality and corporate governance.

This article is organised as follows: first, a review of the literature and the research hypotheses developed. Second, the research methodology adopted. Finally, the results will be presented and discussed.

2. LITERATURE REVIEW AND RESEARCH HYPOTHESES

2.1. Theoretical Framework

Several theories can explain the relationship between digitalisation and audit quality. The agency and stakeholder theories remain the most widely used in the literature on the subject. Indeed, managers and shareholders, whose interests are assumed to converge, will use the audit, particularly the external auditor's report, to maximise the value of their shares and increase the credibility of the financial statements they have drawn up. Jensen and Meckling (1979) argue that, given the preparation by management of this information for other users, the company will have every interest in preparing the financial statements and having them certified by an independent auditor (D'Onza and De Santis, 2020). As for creditors, particularly bankers, the audit is a perfect means of ensuring that the financial statements drawn up by management are reliable and fair and that management complies with the restrictive contractual clauses that have been drawn up for the capital. The financial audit forms part of the agency relationship around the company as a process of checking the accounts drawn up to remove the asymmetry of information between the directors and the other parties involved.

In addition, stakeholder theory aims to refocus theories of the firm around all the actors who influence the company. It defines stakeholders as "any group or individual who can influence or be affected by achieving the organisation's objectives". Therefore, Stakeholders include all of the company's internal and external partners who have directly or indirectly contributed a specific resource to the achievement of the company's objectives and who can expect to receive repercussions in return and bear a share of the risk (Lascău 2022). The relevance of this theory here stems from the fact that as soon as the company is seen as an organisation influenced by formal and informal institutions, the governance process can no longer ensure total control (Lugli et al., 2023). Taking stakeholders into account becomes a signal that should enable disciplinary mechanisms to be improved and strengthened, promote collaboration between all partners and create value. So, what about previous work on the subject?

2.2. Digitalisation and Audit Quality

New digital technologies are revolutionising how companies are organised, forcing them to change their internal processes and rethink their businesses (Lugli et al., 2023). This is particularly true of audit firms, which are having to contend with the arrival on the market of specialists in digital technology and extensive data analysis who could eventually come to compete with them.

Today's audit firms must evolve their offerings by proposing cutting-edge technological solutions. They need to automate their internal processes and upgrade their information systems, ultimately transforming the audit profession by redirecting it towards higher value-added tasks. Similarly, shareholders and managers often perceive auditing as a necessary and compulsory cost that adds little or no value to the company (D'Onza and De Santis, 2020). To increase the relevance of the audit, it is necessary to add value for clients. New digital tools offer the opportunity to improve the relevance of the audit by providing clients with new, high-value-added services.

Thanks to data analytics, the auditor can, for example, make recommendations and propose benchmarks (observation of the practices of other players in the market) using indicators and statistics (Cipek, 2021). Making the figures speak for themselves and explaining to customers the various stages through which the data passes in internal processes is a source of value for the customer. In addition, with new digital technologies, the auditor can collect previously untapped data from social media, television or the Internet and determine whether this information impacts the audit. All these elements allow audit firms to evolve their audit offer and make it more relevant.

As a result, the audit profession needs new talent with expertise in data analysis and processing who can develop new audit tools and bring added value to clients. In the past, auditing was seen as a repetitive, highly demanding job that required many hours of work, which explains the high staff turnover in the sector. With the introduction of new technologies (Cloud, analytics, robotics, etc.), audit firms can improve their attractiveness by offering new, high-value-added functions to their future auditors.

In addition to their technical digital skills, tomorrow's auditors will need to have skills in critical thinking, innovation and creativity (Lascău, 2022). These skills are required in order to constantly improve the monitoring and analysis of data and, consequently, to develop the quality of the audit.

More broadly, the development of audit firms today depends more than ever on introducing a culture of innovation at all levels and in all business lines to constantly develop their offerings and adapt to new market needs (Lugli et al., 2023). However, as auditing remains a regulated activity, standard-setters and regulators must keep up with the times by developing auditing standards that better integrate new technologies.

Several researchers have attempted to understand the effects of new technologies on companies in terms of data analysis (Warren et al., 2015) and external reporting (Al-Htaybat and Von Alberti Alhtaybat, 2017). However, research on audit quality is still limited (Issa et al., 2016). In this respect, some authors have studied the impact of digitalisation on the performance or risk analysis of audit firms (Krahel and Titera, 2015; Cao et al., 2015). Similarly, Appelbaum et al. (2018) point out that there is some research analysing the influence of digitalisation on the transformation of audit firms and audit processes. Several studies have shown that digitisation has many positive effects on the audit sector in the European context (Tiberius and Hirth, 2019; Manita et al., 2020). Lugli and Bertacchini (2023) found a positive and significant relationship between numeration and big4 in the Italian context.

Nambisan et al. (2017) state that digital management based on implementing processes, tools, and uses... improves audit quality. Indeed, the use of Big Data and social media is changing the way companies can access information with the availability of new key performance indicators. Thus, several authors have examined the impact of technology on audit quality (Brown-Liburd et al., 2015). Vasarhelyi et al. (2015) identified that adopting digitalisation increases and improves internal audits more than external audits. Gepp et al. (2018) argue that big data analytics is not widespread, and more studies must recognise the opportunity to use such technology. Furthermore, a reinventing audit is not something new, according to (Manita et al., 2020a). Hence, audit firms must evolve their business model and services by acquiring innovative technologies to offer digital solutions that help improve audit quality and maintain relevance in their market.

In this sense, some studies focus on the impact of data analysis on the auditor's ability to detect fraud and errors. Indeed, one of the main objectives of the digitalisation of audit firms is to detect fraud and understand and quantify information quality risk (Nigrini, 2018; Richins et al., 2017). Lombardi et al. (2014, 2015) conclude that digitalisation is changing the auditor's strategy and will revolutionise audit services. Furthermore, Krahel and Titera (2015) show that auditors see digitisation as a tool to improve the relevance of audit functions, data collection and reconciliation. In addition, Dines and Juvanna (2017) highlight that companies must consider software to ensure corporate security and privacy and minimise risk. Indeed, Zhang et al. (2015) find that Big Data analytics will enable auditors to manage data gaps. Kimmetal (2016) determines that specific tools can be used to analyse Big Data collected by classifying, identifying and securely eliminating redundant data. We propose to test the following hypothesis:

H1: Digitalisation affects audit quality.

2.3. Digitalisation and Corporate Governance

Consistent corporate governance aims to ensure the long-term viability of a company. Nowadays, corporate governance has become an essential element in the management of organisations, particularly for investors seeking visibility over the management of the companies in which they are shareholders (Cipek, 2021). In particular, corporate governance aims to increase corporate transparency, promote best practices, identify risks and minimise them appropriately. Corporate governance also seeks to define a framework for effective risk management within a company while protecting the interests of shareholders through an appropriate division of powers within the Board of directors.

In other words, this set of processes focuses the company's decisions on its responsibilities, rights and obligations. These policies directly affect the Board of directors, management, shareholders and other stakeholders. In today's environment, corporate governance needs to strike the right balance between appropriate technology, knowledge and processes to promote organisational transparency and enable companies to respond effectively to market movements (Cipek, 2021). À cet égard, les outils informatiques utilisés par les sociétés jouent un rôle crucial pour les conseils d'administration dans leurs prises de décision, car ces outils permettent de fluidifier les communications, tout en les sécurisant, partout dans le monde et instantanément.

Digitalisation is changing the rules of the game in which companies operate. Board members must have a clear and precise understanding of the consequences of digitalisation for their company, their sector and the environment surrounding their business (Lugli et al., 2023). Companies must ensure they have the right skills in-house for digital transformation to keep pace with this transition. The role of the Board of Directors has evolved from a formal advisory body to one that plays a much more active role in the management of the business. As a result, the Board's processes must evolve in line with its new role in the organisation's life (Seethamraju and Hecimovic, 2023). By ensuring that information is shared effectively internally, companies are bound to gain agility, enabling them to react quickly and effectively to the changes they face.

Several studies have found that digitisation affects corporate governance in the European context (Monica et al., 2022; Ivaninskiy et al., 2021; Kohtamäki et al., 2020).

Gepp et al. (2018) argue that big data analytics is not yet widespread, and more studies must recognise the opportunity of using such technology. Furthermore, reinventing governance is not something new, according to (Manita et al., 2020a). Hence, boards need to evolve their business model and services by acquiring innovative technologies to offer digital solutions that help improve the quality of information and maintain relevance in their market. Indeed, digitalisation significantly impacts governance mechanisms (Dengler and Matthes, 2018) and has changed how businesses are done in all areas. Therefore, digitalisation is expected to change how directors manage the company's business by providing additional information to meet customer needs. We propose to test the following hypothesis:

H2: Digitalisation affects corporate governance.

3. RESEARCH METHODOLOGY

3.1. Sample Selection and Data Collection Method

The main objective of this work is to study the effect of digitalisation on audit quality in the Swedish context during the period 2017-2022. Sweden aims to be one of the best countries in the world in its use of digital technology, which is seen as one of the critical factors in global societal change. For the Swedish government, "digital technology permeates all activities, so everyone should have the opportunity to take part in digitisation and make the most of the benefits it brings for sustainable growth, a high level of employment and a cohesive society". This commitment is reflected in the major strategies that have been put in place since 2017, such as the digital strategy "For sustainable digital transformation in Sweden - A digital strategy", the national cybersecurity strategy and the national approach to artificial intelligence. A new administrative authority governs this, the Digital Management Authority (Myndigheten för Digital Förvaltning). As a result, our sample includes 150 Swedish companies.

We collected the data from the ASSET4 database of annual reports and reference documents available on the companies' websites.

3.2. Measurement of Variables

Table 1. Measurement of the research variables of the model

The Variables	Code	Operationalisation of Variables
Audit quality	$AQ_{i,t}$	Experian logarithm of the audit fees
Digitalisation of businesses	$DB_{i,t}$	binary variable, which takes the value one if the company uses digitalisation and 0 otherwise
Corporate governance	$GOV_{i,t}$	A score was determined and calculated by the rating agency ASSET4.
Firme size	$F\_SIZE_{i,t}$	Ln (total assets at year-end N).
ROE	$CODI_{I,t}$	the equity ratio (ROE).
Legal system	$LEG\_SYS_{i,t}$	The legal system is a binary variable that takes the value 1 if the company belongs to a country that applies civil law and 0 otherwise.
Fixed effects years	$YEARS_{i,t}$	Six variables equal 1 or 0 for each year from 2017 to 2022.

3.3. Search Model

Our study's objective is to investigate the effect of digitalisation on audit quality and corporate governance. The models introduced in this study involve panel data least squares methodology.

Model 1:

$$AQ_{i,t} = \beta_0 + \beta_1 DB_{i,t} + \beta_2 F\_ZISE_{i,t} + \beta_3 ROE_{i,t} + \beta_4 LEG\_SYS_{i,t} + \sum_{i=10}^{19} \beta_i YEARS_{i,t} + \varepsilon_{i,t}$$

Model 2:

$$GOV_{i,t} = \beta_0 + \beta_1 DB_{i,t} + \beta_2 F\_ZISE_{i,t} + \beta_3 ROE_{i,t} + \beta_4 LEG\_SYS_{i,t} + \sum_{i=10}^{19} \beta_i YEARS_{i,t} + \varepsilon_{i,t}$$

With:

- DB: Digitalization of businesses;
- AQ: Audit quality;
- GOV: Corporate governance;
- FSIZE: Firme size;
- ROE: Performance;
- LEG_SYS: Legal system;
- $\beta 0_{\rightarrow}\beta 5$: Parameters to be estimated.
- YEARS: years Fixed effect;
- $\varepsilon i_{,t:}$ Error term.

4. ANALYSIS OF RESULTS

4.1. Descriptive Analyses, Correlations Between Explanatory Variables, and the VIF Test

The table below shows the descriptive statistics and correlations of the variables in our research model. The mean value of digitisation (DB) is 0.774. And its standard deviation is 0.621. The mean value of the audit quality variable (AQ) is 0.752. The mean value for corporate governance is 0.832, with a standard deviation of 0.712. The average value of the (FSIZE) for the control variables is 0.711. In addition, the ROE variable has a mean of 0.541. Finally, for the variable LEG_SYS, the mean is 0.602. In addition, the Pearson correlation matrix test between the different variables allows us to study the null hypothesis of no correlation between two variables. As Table 2 shows, all the coefficients were significantly lower than 0.8, according to the limit suggested by Kennedy (1985). The VIF test shows that all the values are below 2.54 and below 10, which is the limit Myers drew (1990). This confirms that there is no multi-colinearity problem.

Table 2. Descriptive analyses, correlations between variables, and the VIF Test

Variable	Mean	SD	1	2	3	4	5
DB	0.774	0.621	1				
AQ	0.752	0.652	0.222*	1			
GOV	0.832	0.7 12	0.501***	0.140 *	1		
FSIZE	0.711	0.655	-0.142 **	-0.147**	0.457 **	1	
ROE	0.541	0.689	0.012 *	0.225	0.743 ***	0.415 *	1
LEG_SYS	0.602	0.555	0.147**	0.325 *	0.325*	-0.365	1
VIF			2.14	2.33	2.54	1.14	1.48

Note: For a description of variables, see Table 1, * Significant at $p < 0.05$; ** significant at $p < 0.01$; *** significant at $p < 0.001$.

4.2. Multivariate Analysis

The results of the multivariate regression of the two models show the following Fisher statistic (F) measuring the overall significance of the model, which is equal to 325.452 (Model 1) and 355.175 (Model 2). This confirms the excellent quality of the model at the 1% significance level.

Similarly, the statistical results show a significant Fisher statistic at the 1% level. In this respect, the two models are significant overall and explain the phenomenon studied. Similarly, the models show an explanatory power equal to 0.652 and 0.699, respectively.

The regression results in Table 3 show that DB has a positive and significant impact on QA (β =0.354, p <0.023). These results justify that digitalisation is an essential factor for improving audit quality. As a result, new digital technologies are disrupting how companies are organised, leading them to change their internal processes and rethink their businesses. This is particularly true of audit firms, which are having to contend with the arrival on the market of specialists in digital technology and extensive data analysis who could eventually come to compete with them. Likewise, audit firms today need to evolve their audit offering by proposing solutions at the cutting edge of technology. They must automate their internal processes and develop their information systems (HR applications, charge sheets, safes, etc.), ultimately transforming the audit profession towards higher value-added tasks.

Our results confirm that digital technologies will significantly impact the future profile of auditors and will create a culture of innovation for all sectors of audit firms' activity. Indeed, artificial intelligence, robotics, data analysis, the Internet of Things, and blockchain are emerging technologies revolutionising the world. Of this non-exhaustive list, this analysis will focus on RPA tools, blockchain and data

Table 3. Multivariate regression analysis

Variables	Model 1 (AQ)		Model 2 (COV)	
	β	t- stat	β	t- stat
Constant	0.214***	3.457	0.325**	2.415
DB	0.354**	3.254	0.355**	4.215
FSIZE	0.255	1.222	0.145	1.321
ROE	1.254**	4.157	0.444***	2.847
LEG_SYS	0.125**	2.214	0.222***	3.253
YEARS	YES		YES	
R2	0.652		0.699	
R2 adjusted	0.599		0.601	
F (p-value)	325.452 ***		355.175***	

Note: For a description of variables, see Table 1, * Significant at $p < 0.05$; ** significant at $p < 0.01$; *** significant at $p < 0.001$.

analytics. Furthermore, through the use of technological tools, the internal audit function can take advantage of these new technologies to deliver an audit of superior quality thanks to broader coverage, reduced risk of human error, and the elimination of redundant tasks, allowing the auditor to concentrate on those that require more excellent judgement and professional scepticism. Thus, our results are in line with the contribution of stakeholder theory. Digitalisation can improve communication between the company and its stakeholders by facilitating the rapid and transparent dissemination of audit results. Similarly, our findings confirm that digitalisation can significantly affect audit quality by improving data analysis, process efficiency and communication with stakeholders.

These innovations, such as cognitive technology (artificial intelligence, blockchain, predictive data analytics and smart contracts), have the potential to improve audit quality and generate significant benefits for clients, auditors, investors and financial markets. In this evolving context, today's auditors face the challenge of keeping their professional skills and knowledge up to date to adapt to the digital age.

Similarly, according to Table 3, corporate digitisation is positively and significantly correlated with corporate governance ($\beta = 0.355$, $p < 0.023$). This result shows that corporate digitisation can be crucial in improving governance mechanisms. Our results show a positive and statistically significant relationship between corporate digitisation and corporate governance. This means that when technological progress is contributing to the rapid development of organisations, companies need to be agile and responsive to respond rapidly to market changes. The digital environment in which businesses operate is constantly changing. Managing their digital transformation is, therefore, becoming a critical competitive factor. On top of this, globalisation is becoming more and more restrictive due to the regulatory complexities that arise when companies expand internationally.

As a result, this changing environment poses several challenges for boards of directors and senior executives responsible for managing corporate governance, who must deal with the risks and opportunities that arise daily.

Our empirical results confirm that digitisation offers several advantages. In particular, this revolution means that a large amount of information can be archived in a small space, that it can be accessed from anywhere in the world, and that information can be shared with any partner in real time. The digital age has revolutionised society: administrative tasks that used to take days or weeks can now be completed in minutes. Our results also confirm the contribution of agency theory, which suggests that digitisation can help reduce information asymmetry between shareholders and managers. Consequently, digitalisation can play an essential role in improving corporate governance by aligning the interests of managers and shareholders, increasing information transparency and providing more effective means for monitoring in line with the principles of agency theory.

In this sense, digitisation enables managers to work more efficiently, thanks to more effective processes and immediate access to crucial business information. This technological support can be an undeniable competitive advantage. This effective use of new technologies is the driving force behind effective corporate governance.

For the control variables, the regression results show that company size does not affect audit quality and corporate governance. Thus, company performance has a positive and significant effect on audit quality and corporate governance, which explains why company performance is a determining factor in the context of digitalisation. On the other hand, the legal system positively affects audit quality and corporate governance.

5. CONCLUSION

This work aims to analyse the effect of digitalisation on audit quality and corporate governance in the Swedish context during the period 2017-2022. Digitalisation is using digital technologies to improve business and social operations within an organisation. It aims to transform how a company interacts with its customers and maximise its return on investment. Indeed, digitalisation has long since become an integral part of our daily routine outside the workplace. Most of us use smartphones to communicate, shop or listen to music online, and digitalisation has become a natural part of our habits. But as far as companies and their governance are concerned, it's not that simple. A significant business challenge for companies must be to improve their operational performance. Digitalisation is an opportunity to gain efficiency, evolve in-depth, align ourselves, and put ourselves at the service of customer expectations. This improvement involves working on the agilitý of the organisation and overhauling internal processes and functions. This research gives rise to several critical empirical contributions. Companies must adopt strategies such as digitalisation to win and increase their value.

Our study also enables company managers to create strategies based on more effective and informed numbering. In this way, we contribute to the literature on the relationship between digitalisation, audit quality and corporate governance. Our results show that, to some extent, digitalisation improves audit quality and corporate governance. Thus, our study provides practical recommendations for companies and managers to adjust their practices to reap the benefits of digitisation. Similarly, the results can provide information on how corporate governance and the quality of a digital context affect stakeholder trust. This can help to identify the factors that strengthen trust in digitised companies. Therefore, our research can be applied to improve audit approaches to ensure they are adapted to digital realities. This can incorporate recommendations on the skills needed by auditors and the technologies to be integrated. Finally, the results of this study provide practical implications that may also affect regulators, with recommendations for adapting regulatory policies to maintain financial stability and public confidence and to better respond to the challenges of digitisation.

However, despite these contributions, this study suffers from limitations that must be addressed in future research. Indeed, the sample adopted in our analysis refers to a sample from a single country. Future studies could consider other countries to produce homogeneous results. Future research could also explore the ethical implications of using digital technologies in the audit process.

REFERENCES

Al-Htaybat, K., & von Alberti-Alhtaybat, L. (2017). Big data and corporate reporting: Impacts and paradoxes. *Accounting, Auditing & Accountability Journal, 30*(4), 850–873. doi:10.1108/AAAJ-07-2015-2139

Appelbaum, M., Cooper, H., Kline, R. B., Mayo-Wilson, E., Nezu, A. M., & Rao, S. M. (2018). Journal article reporting standards for quantitative research in psychology: The APA Publications and Communications Board task force report. *The American Psychologist, 73*(1), 3–25. doi:10.1037/amp0000191 PMID:29345484

Brown-Liburd, H., Issa, H., & Lombardi, D. (2015). The behavioural implications of Big Data's impact on audit judgment, decision making, and future research directions. *Accounting Horizons*, *29*(2), 451–468. doi:10.2308/acch-51023

Cao, X., Li, X., Zhu, Y., & Zhang, Z. (2015). A comparative study of environmental performance between prefabricated and traditional residential buildings in China. *Journal of Cleaner Production*, *109*, 131–143. doi:10.1016/j.jclepro.2015.04.120

Cipek, K. (2021). The Impact of Digitalisation on Tax Audit. *WCLF Tax und IP Gesprächsband 2019: Immaterielle Werte als zentrale Komponente internationaler Steuerstrategien*, 59-73.

D'Onza, G., & De Santis, F. (2020). Professional impact of digital audit-thinking beyond the realm of audit standards. *JOURNAL*, (1), 141–144.

Dengler, K., & Matthes, B. (2018). The impacts of digital transformation on the labour market: Substitution potentials of occupations in Germany. *Technological Forecasting and Social Change*, *137*, 304–316. doi:10.1016/j.techfore.2018.09.024

Dinesh, N., & Juvanna, I. (2017). Dynamic auditing and deduplication with secure data deletion in the Cloud. *Artificial Intelligence and Evolutionary Computations in Engineering Systems Proceedings of ICAIECES, 2016*, 305–313.

Gepp, A., Linnenluecke, M. K., O'Neill, T. J., & Smith, T. (2018). Big data techniques in auditing research and practice: Current trends and future opportunities. *Journal of Accounting Literature*, *40*(1), 102–115. doi:10.1016/j.acclit.2017.05.003

Kennedy, D. W. (1985). Functional endoscopic sinus surgery: Technique. *Archives of Otolaryngology*, *111*(10), 643–649. doi:10.1001/archotol.1985.00800120037003 PMID:4038136

Kimm, T., Cen, R., Rosdahl, J., & Sukyoung, K. Y. (2016). Formation of globular clusters in atomic-cooling halos via rapid gas condensation and fragmentation during the epoch of reionisation. *The Astrophysical Journal*, *823*(1), 52. doi:10.3847/0004-637X/823/1/52

Krahel, J. P., & Titera, W. R. (2015). Consequences of big data and formalisation on accounting and auditing standards. *Accounting Horizons*, *29*(2), 409–422. doi:10.2308/acch-51065

Lascău, A. (2022). The benefits of audit digitalisation and the effects on the work of auditors. *Annals of University of Craiova-Economic Sciences Series*, *1*(50), 68–75.

Lugli, E., & Bertacchini, F. (2023). Audit quality and digitalisation: Some insights from the Italian context. *Meditari Accountancy Research, 31*(4), 841–860. doi:10.1108/MEDAR-08-2021-1399

Manita, R., Elommal, N., Baudier, P., & Hikkerova, L. (2020). The digital transformation of external audit and its impact on corporate governance. *Technological Forecasting and Social Change, 150*, 119751. doi:10.1016/j.techfore.2019.119751

Myers, N. (1990). The biodiversity challenge: Expanded hot-spots analysis. *The Environmentalist, 10*(4), 243–256. doi:10.1007/BF02239720 PMID:12322583

Nambisan, S., Lyytinen, K., Majchrzak, A., & Song, M. (2017). Digital innovation management. *Management Information Systems Quarterly, 41*(1), 223–238. doi:10.25300/MISQ/2017/41:1.03

Negrini, S., Donzelli, S., Aulisa, A. G., Czaprowski, D., Schreiber, S., de Mauroy, J. C., Diers, H., Grivas, T. B., Knott, P., Kotwicki, T., Lebel, A., Marti, C., Maruyama, T., O'Brien, J., Price, N., Parent, E., Rigo, M., Romano, M., Stikeleather, L., ... Zaina, F. (2018). 2016 SOSORT guidelines: Orthopaedic and rehabilitation treatment of idiopathic scoliosis during growth. *Scoliosis and Spinal Disorders, 13*(1), 1–48. doi:10.1186/s13013-017-0145-8 PMID:29435499

Richins, G., Stapleton, A., Stratopoulos, T. C., & Wong, C. (2017). Big data analytics: Opportunity or threat for the accounting profession? *Journal of Information Systems, 31*(3), 63–79. doi:10.2308/isys-51805

Seethamraju, R., & Hecimovic, A. (2023). Adoption of artificial intelligence in auditing: An exploratory study. *Australian Journal of Management, 48*(4), 780–800. doi:10.1177/03128962221108440

Vasarhelyi, M. A., Kogan, A., & Tuttle, B. M. (2015). Big data in accounting: An overview. *Accounting Horizons, 29*(2), 381–396. doi:10.2308/acch-51071

Warren, D., Peytcheva, M., & Gaspar, J. (2015). When ethical tones are at the top of conflict: Adapting priority rules to reconcile conflicting tones. *Business Ethics Quarterly, 25*(4), 559582. doi:10.1017/beq.2015.40

Zhang, J. C., Yao, W., Dong, C., Yang, C., Ren, Q., Ma, M., Han, M., & Hashimoto, K. (2015). Comparison of ketamine, 7, 8-dihydroxyflavone, and ANA-12 antidepressant effects in the social defeat stress model of depression. *Psychopharmacology, 232*(23), 4325–4335. doi:10.1007/s00213-015-4062-3 PMID:26337614

Chapter 7
Diversification, Ownership Structure, and Solidity of Banks in Era of Digitalisation

Ahmad Alqatan
Arab Open University, Kuwait

Raoudha Dhouibi
https://orcid.org/0009-0001-4737-4080
University of Sousse, Tunisia

Najoua Talbi
https://orcid.org/0000-0002-6399-5848
University of Sousse, Tunisia

Muhammad Arslan
https://orcid.org/0000-0001-5046-7627
Open Polytechnic, New Zealand

ABSTRACT

Through the mechanics of contagion, bank failures not only cause economic agents to suffer financial losses but also cause the entire financial system to become unstable. As a result, the bank needs to safeguard itself against various threats. This study analyses the relationship between the diversification of banking activities and governance mechanisms while taking into account the concept of ownership structure in banking firms to explain the level of risk. The authors took the sample from 10 main Tunisian banks listed on the Tunis Stock Exchange for the period 2002 to 2020. The result of the FGLS regression showed that the separation between traditional and non-traditional activity has a favourable effect on banking stability because the diversification of activities allows banks to establish synergies between the different

DOI: 10.4018/979-8-3693-1678-8.ch007

sectors, thus increasing the level of stability of banking firms by reducing the level of risk. The authors found that the financial strength of Tunisian banks is positively influenced by the degree of diversification of the banks' sources of income.

1. INTRODUCTION

The financial context has seen various fluctuations in recent years, which have disrupted and shaken the banking sector. Banking firms play a key role in economic development in all countries. As a result, the major challenge facing banks remains the level of risk, given that "preserving financial stability is a public good" (Scialom, 2011). In financial theory, it is recognised that diversification of the financial asset portfolio is necessary to reduce the level of risk. Banks then choose to diversify their operations to offer a full range of services and products to their customers. In this way, they hope to attract more customers in order to increase their market share, which will reduce the level of risk. In addition, the concept of corporate governance could be defined as the set of processes that are put in place to reduce conflicts of interest between managers and shareholders through a good governance structure to mitigate these conflicts and consequently increase the level of banking strength. In particular, according to Choi (2000), it is usually agreed that one of the root causes of a financial crisis is a deficient governance system. Governance mechanisms are therefore seen as factors in mitigating economic shocks. Under this umbrella, an increase in control techniques is necessary to ensure the stability of large financial institutions around the world. Poor control of banking firms and insufficient risk management are the main causes of financial crises. In addition, research analysing the relationship between the governance system and the level of banking stability has not paid much attention to the African context, particularly in Tunisia. It appears that the study concerned with banking risks is not complete if the impact of the ownership structure on the level of risk is not taken into account. In this research work, we try to identify and analyse the diversification of banking activities and governance mechanisms while taking into account the concept of ownership structure in banking firms and analysing their functions in explaining the level of risk. Using a sample composed of the 10 main Tunisian banks listed on the Tunis Stock Exchange over the period from 2002 to 2020 (19 years), we will therefore empirically analyse the relationship between the diversification of banking activities, the structure of properties, and the level of Tunisian banking risk. This raises the question: what is the impact of trading activity and governance mechanisms, specifically the ownership structure, on the level of risk of Tunisian banks? Therefore, this study aims to examine the effects of diversification of banking activity, ownership structure (concentration of ownership, public ownership, institutional ownership, and foreign ownership), and bank characteristics (capital, size, liquidity, profitability, GDP, and inflation rate) on the risk profile of Tunisian banks.

2. LITERATURE AND HYPOTHESIS DEVELOPMENT

In today's dynamic environment, diversification is pivotal for reducing unsystematic risks. Similarly, portfolio theory highlights the ways of managing portfolios while reducing the risks. Mulier (2018) argued that banks' risk levels decrease with their sector competence and increase both with industrial differentiation and their exposure to the stability level. De Jonghe (2010) used the data on European banking from 1992 to 2007 and found that an increase in income excluding interest leads to an increase in banking risk. Given the structure of the banking market in countries during its valuation, Moshirian (2011) indicates that trading activity only increases the risk profile of banks in a highly concentrated market; it also states that the increase in transaction turnover has resulted in banks only facing risk in low-concentration markets. Kamani (2018) analyses the impact of European banks' trading activity on their exposure to the risk profile. She found that non-traditional banking, particularly commercial banking, only increases the risk exposure of small banks. However, many scholars argue that diversification does not reduce bank risk but can increase it. In this context, De Jonghe (2010) found that banks that focus on profitable lending activities are better than diversified banks and are less risky. Correspondingly, Stiroh (2002) noted that from the late 1970s to 2001, a greater dependence of US banks on non-interest income was linked with lower risk-adjusted earnings and higher risk at the individual bank level. Lastly, Huizinga (2010) took a global sample of banks for the period 1995–2007 and found risk diversification benefits which arise from an expansion of non-interest income-generating activities. This leads to the first hypothesis of this chapter.

H1: There is a positive relationship between the diversification of a bank's activities and its risk.

Moreover, the various government structures are considered to be the fundamental ones responsible for controlling the level of banking risks. Within the same framework, Lobez (2010) considers that banking governance is the main instrument for increasing the stability and soundness of banking institutions. The governance mechanism plays a much more important and effective role, including the shareholding structure, in the minimisation and control of bank risks than external mechanisms. In this case, Boussaada (2015) indicates that the ownership structure must help to determine the level of acceptable risk because it aims to reduce the opportunistic behaviour of managers. Good management also helps to reduce risks and, therefore, achieve organisational objectives. Berle (1932) and Jensen (1976) were the first to take an interest in the unclear relationship between the ownership structure and stability of banking firms. The findings are mixed with the existing literature. Some studies have found an adverse impact of the ownership concentration on the risk profile; others have concluded that there was a neutral impact; and some have highlighted that the concentration of ownership has a positive impact on risk.

Scholars (e.g., Saunders (1990); Levine (2009); and Haw (2010)) noted that the concentration of ownership is related to a significant risk on the one hand, while on the other hand, scholars (e.g., Burkart (1997); Iannotta (2007); and García-Marco (2008)) argued that the concentration of ownership is accompanied by a lower risk. In a similar context, Allen (2008) and Dickstein (2008) have found that the impact of concentration is not significant in the presence of strict regulations. In addition, Adnan (2011) and Sironi (2006) argued that concentrated ownership leads to an improvement in the quality of loans granted, and low-risk assets, and thus increases the level of stability. In simple words, it is the rules that discipline leaders. Under different institutional conditions, Caprio (2006) has found that concentrated ownership and banking risk vary proportionately.

In addition, the study of Haw (2010) found a positive relationship between ownership concentration and level of risk. On the other hand, for a low level of regulatory control, concentrated ownership can reduce the level of banking risk, Nouha (2016) indicates that the ownership concentration variable has a detrimental but not significant effect on executive fraud. Shehzad (2010) and Bratanovic (2004) highlighted a significant negative link between capital concentration and risk level, this is because majority shareholders want to control managers.

On the other hand, if shareholder oversight is weak, conflicts between organizations and moral risk may coexist. Two situations must be considered, if the directors take more risks than is optimally compatible with the interests of the shareholders, then increasing the risk resulting from agency problems. Alternatively, managers want to protect their investments in human capital, so they exhibit unfavourable risk-taking behaviours and increase their level of financial stability. In this regard, Agrawal (1990) has shown that dispersed ownership weakens management oversight and, as a result, administrators can choose an inefficient organization, increasing the level of risk. On the other hand, in most previous research, industrial government is defined as a conflict between shareholders and managers (referred to as type I), Charreaux (1997). Yet, global ownership concentration has led to the emergence of a new conflict between majority and minority shareholders (Porta, 1999) (known as Type II). Claessens (2006) found that the majority of shareholders can defend their interests by encouraging managers to take risks to make their investments as profitable as possible. Laeven (2009) has demonstrated that the higher the majority ownership percentage, the greater the risk tolerance.

Indeed, a key position in controlling voting rights allows him to appoint a majority of directors, who will govern general meetings and have a strong influence on all decisions of the company (Daniels, 1996). These shareholders thus have an informational advantage over minority shareholders, which makes it easier for them to profit from private profits to the detriment of minority shareholders and thus an increased incentive to manipulate the accounting and financial information provided to conceal their opportunistic actions (Chau, 2002; Doidge, 2009; Laidroo, 2009; Zhang, 2012). Empirically, Ali (2013) found that low-quality financial publishing companies are characterized by a failure of their governance mechanisms. Similarly, Klai (2011) pointed out the concentration of ownership in the Tunisian context and found a negative impact on the quality of accounting information. However, Salhi (2012) found that concentrated ownership has an adverse effect on the risk level of banking firms. Similarly, Boussaada (2015) argued that ownership concentration increases bank counterparty risk because the majority of owners can push their managers towards a less prudent credit policy.

Similarly, Bouaziz (2012) shows that concentrated ownership has a negative effect on the risk level of Tunisian banks. If the hypothesis of the moral risk of the majority shareholders has been validated at the theoretical level, the debate is not decided at the empirical level. The few studies on the relationship between shareholder concentration and bank risk remain controversial. During our research, We put forward the following hypothesis:

H2: Ownership concentration has a positive impact on the risk of Tunisian banks.

Moreover, in the banking sector, the heads of public banks are appointed by the state, provided that they comply with the State's commitments and directives, they will not be punished in case of poor performance or will accept excessive risks. Where the bank is characterised by greater state ownership, this stimulates risk reduction as public ownership should ensure the financial soundness of banks and increase good governance (Talwar, 2001), in this spirit, it makes it possible to monitor bank managers and regulate their behaviour (La Porta, 2002). Also, Houcine (2017) argued that the credibility of the information published in the financial statements as to its impact on economic decision-making. Second, managers decrease their level of risk, thus, public ownership seems to be associated with a higher level of stability, On the other hand, the existing studies (e.g., Berger, 2005; Iannotta, 2007; Cornett, 2010; Angkinand, 2010; and Lassoued, 2016) demonstrate that public ownership encourages managers to take risks.

In this regard, Zheng (2017) views public ownership as a source of administrative inefficiency caused by government bureaucracy and leaders do not have sufficient control over their counterparts in the private sector. In this context, Dicko (2016) and Dicko (2017) highlight the fragility and failure of governance systems of political banking firms.

Another explanation for this is that public banks can take more risks that result in excessive costs, which the government must always assume. (Demirgüç-Kunt, 2002), and can protect banks through explicit financial and regulatory support (Faccio, 2006). In this sense, banks with political connections are likely to exhibit poor governance practices (Borisova, 2012), and (Shen, 2015). From an empirical perspective, Iannotta, Sironi, and Nocera (2012) examine the impact of public ownership on the level of risk, these results have shown that risk increases significantly over election years, and this is consistent with the idea that governments use their bank participation to achieve their political goals. Chaney (2011) claims that the reported earnings quality of politically connected companies is significantly lower than that of similar companies not connected. Also, Hasnan (2017) shows that the political link is positively associated with financial statement fraud. In this context, Patti (2006) has detected a favourable result between the state's participation in capital and the level of risk and that public banking firms have lower results than private banks, whether local or foreign, still they finance riskier projects and grant more credits to companies to increase their economic development (Salas, 2002). In the same context, Panizza (2004) shows that state-owned banks play a significant role in facilitating credit policies, as loans are more resilient to macroeconomic shocks than private institutions.

Of course, the State representative can facilitate the flow of information between the regulatory authorities and the management of the bank (Schaede, 1995). This helps to reduce the risks incurred by the bank.

Therefore, we expect to find the following hypothesis:

H3: Public ownership has a positive impact on the level of risk of Tunisian banks.

The role of institutional ownership in governance has been studied in particular for non-financial enterprises, but relatively neglected for banking institutions. Advocates of activist theory are based on knowledge of agency theory and consideration of institutional investors as influential partners for the bank (Zahra, 1992). It has better access to information (Jensen, 1993) and exercises very active control over the management team (Whidbee, 1997). It can be seen that the control exercised by institutional investors is probably less important in the case of banks than in the case of companies because of the regulation, It seems to replace the control of institutional shareholders (Elyasiani, 2008). To our knowledge, the only studies that have dealt with the relationship between institutional investors and bank risk-taking from an empirical perspective are those of Jia (2008) in the American context, a favourable effect of institutional existence on risk and banking institutions is examined. Guo (2012) indicated that the institutional shareholder is the main governance mechanism that positively influences the banks' return and risk. In contrast, Nu Nu Htay (2012) reported a negative link between institutional ownership and bank risk level. Conversely, Levine (2009) analyzes the effect of ownership structure on the level of banking stability, they have highlighted the existence of a positive link between. In this context, Ellul (2010) found a statistically positive relationship between institutional investors and the level of risk.

Several researchers have examined the importance of institutional investor control and its impact on bank risk-taking. It follows that this type of shareholding may discourage the use of optional effects. The following hypothesis is put forward:

H4: Institutional ownership has a negative impact on the risk-taking of Tunisian banks.

The presence of foreign investors in banks offers microeconomic and macroeconomic advantages. As regards the characteristics of each bank, foreign participation in developing countries improves equity and can lead to more diversified products and better use of technology and knowledge transfer. At the national level, foreign presence can increase control in host countries (Claessens, 2013). It also lobbies governments to accelerate internal reforms by improving regulation and control (Levine, 1996). Foreign ownership thus stimulates a good governance regime and also strengthens control processes to protect foreigners and reduce financial statement fraud (Höglund and Sundvik 2016). Thus, foreign ownership plays an important supervisory role and pushes management to publish reliable and fair information.

In this regard, Ben-Hassoun (2018) report a positive relationship between the quality of external audits and foreign ownership, so this seems to increase risk management. Aydogan (2002) found that studying the involvement of foreign investors in the bank is associated with a reduction in banking risk. We can therefore conclude that these investors provide sufficient capital to reduce the risk of insolvency and they also provide adequate tools to detect the solvency of the borrower by reducing the level of risk in this way.

However, Guédhami, Pittman and Saffar (2009) ensure that foreign owners have an interest in demanding transparency, reducing the asymmetry of information and the incentive to expropriate depends on the governance of a country. For Porta, Lopez-de-silanes, and Shleifer 1999, foreign ownership is seen as an incentive to take risks, as they can experience asymmetric information problems that are mainly explained by linguistic and cultural differences. In addition, foreign banks may also suffer from distance problems, and large banks are at a disadvantage in the qualitative analysis of information (Stein, 2002). Bouaziz and Bouri (2012) have confirmed this result through research on the effects of ownership structure on risk-taking. Similarly, Lassoued, Sassi, and Attia (2016) prove that foreign ownership can have a negative effect on the level of risk. We therefore envisage the following hypothesis:

H 5: Foreign ownership positively associated with Tunisian banking risk.

3. METHODOLOGY

3.1. Data

The sample of the study included 10 Tunisian banks listed on the Tunis Stock Exchange which are characterized by respect for the principles of good governance and accountability. Due to the small number of listed banks, the sample consists of (10 * 19) = 190 observations, Since the study period is 19 years from 2002 to 2020, it includes the following banks (see Table 1).

The information used comes from several data sources. First, we use the unconsolidated financial statements published on the Tunis Stock Exchange website[1]. We have received information on the characteristics of the board of directors and the structure of shares from the inventory guide of the Tunis Stock Exchange. Finally, we use the annual performance reports of different banks to calculate and also to collect missing information for other variables that banks cannot provide.

Table 1. Sample specification

	Name of the Bank
BIAT	Banque internationale arabe de Tunisie
ATB	Arab Tunisian Bank
BT	Banque de Tunisie
BNA	Banque Nationale Agricole
AB	Amen Bank
STB	Société tunisienne de banque
ATTIJARI BANK	Attijari Bank
BH	Banque de l'habitat
UIB	Union internationale de banques
UBCI	Union bancaire pour le commerce et l'industrie

3.2. Measurement of Variables

3.2.1. The Dependent Variable

The first challenge of this research is to measure the level of risk-taking of banks. Following the existing literature (e.g., Bhagat, 2015), we apply as an independent variable the Z-score, which has also been used in various empirical studies to express the insolvency risk of a bank (Huizinga, 2010; Köhler, 2015; Laeven, 2009). The Z-Score is a common indicator used as part of a bank bankruptcy risk analysis (Boyd, 1993; Maechler, 2005), It has often been used as an indicator of bank robustness, the higher the Z-Score is, the better the stability and the lower the risk of insolvency. This measure is defined as the number of standard deviations where a bank's return on assets must be below average for the bank to become insolvent (Delis, 2011). The Z-Score is considered to be a better measure of bank risk than the NPL, as non-performing loans are traditionally retrograde and highly pro-cyclical (Bikker, 2005; Laeven, 2003). This is a criticism that is not as relevant to the Z-Score because the variance component of this index takes into account changes in banking risk (Delis, 2011).

This is a widely used measure, based on accounting information and is specified as follows:

$$Z_{i,t}= \frac{ROA_{i,t+(E/A)_{i,t}}}{\hat{\partial}(ROA_{i,t})}$$

ROA: refers to the return on assets calculated as the bank's net income divided by the total assets.

E/A: is the capital ratio to total assets

$\hat{\partial}$ **(ROAi,t):** is the standard deviation of the return on assets, calculated over a previous three-year period for each observation in the banking year.

Z score is inversely linked to the probability of insolvency. Insolvency is a higher magnitude of the Z score consequently indicates a safer bank and a lower level of risk-taking. Since the Z score is highly asymmetric, we took a natural logarithm of the score in the analysis. Natural logarithm of the score in our empirical application, according to the literature for example, (Levine, 2009).

3.2.2. Independent Variable

Diversification of activity: The first explanatory variable of the model measures the level of diversification of a credit institution. These are revenues generated by so-called non-traditional activities. They cover all other transactions carried out by banks, whether they are financial trading, stock exchange orders, insurance products, brokerage, off-balance sheets, financial engineering, or advice to clients. We call the net income from these activities "Interest-Free Revenue". The ratio of income excluding interest to total assets has been used in the majority of empirical studies devoted to identifying the link between the diversification of the business portfolio and the performance of credit institutions. Thus, we use this same ratio as the second explanatory variable. Where non-interest income is the composition of commission income plus other net non-interest income while operating income is the sum of net interest income and non-interest income (Majumder and Uddin, 2017).

Concentration of Ownership (CONC): The threshold of control of the majority shareholder varies according to the legislation of the countries. In Tunisia, as regards credit institutions, any shareholder who holds a share equal to or greater than 5% of the capital is considered to be a principal shareholder. In our case study, we followed Pichard-Stamford (2000) and Iannotta (2007), and the concentration of ownership is measured by the percentage of capital held by the main shareholder.

Institutional Ownership (PINST): In the banking sector, institutional investors play an important role in monitoring, which reduces bank risk. This finding has been studied by several researchers. As part of this work, we are trying to enrich the discussion by focusing on the Tunisian banking sector, PINST is the percentage of institutional ownership in the capital of the bank that has been taken into account in some research numbers (Knopf, 2006; Jia, 2008; and Hadley, 2012).

Public Ownership (PPUB): By referring to Yasuda (2004), we took into account the variable PPUB to measure the effect of public ownership on the level of risk of Tunisian banks. We measure it by the percentage of shares held by the state. Such a measure was used by Barry (2009) and Berger (2006).

Foreign Ownership (PETR): The participation of foreign investors in a bank's funds is considered an indicator of good governance (Guerreiro, 2009). Indeed, in recent years, foreign ownership has increased significantly in the banking systems of many countries around the world. Several studies have shown that this variable is associated with a low level of risk compared to other types of banks (Claessens, 2001; Bonin, 2005; Micco, 2007). We determine this variable based on the percentage of capital held by foreign investors, which is also used by Bonin (2005).

3.3.3. Control Variables

Bank Size: Measured by the logarithm of the bank's total assets at the end of the accounting year. This measure was also used by Pathan (2007); Pathan (2009); and Azofra (2011).

Capital: Understood as the ratio of equity to the bank's total assets (Iannotta, 2007).

Profitability: ROA (Return On Assets) = operating income/total assets.

This ratio measures the bank's economic profitability relative to the size of its operations and does not take into account exceptional items. This ratio is most commonly used to measure bank profitability (Goddard, 2004).

Liquidity: LIQ is the level of liquidity of bank i for year t. This variable is measured as current assets divided by current liabilities (Bourkhis, 2013).

Credit: Is the ratio of loan provisions to total loans (Ahmed, 2011), (Iqbal, 2012), (Munteanu, 2012).

Table 2. Presentation of the explanatory variables bank risk and the expected signs

Variables	Definition of Variables	Signs
Dependent Variable		
z-score	The level of risk in Tunisian banks.	
Independent Variables		
DIV	The ratio of income excluding interest to total assets was used.	+
Governance Mechanisms: Property Structure		
CONC	The proportion of the total number of shares owned by the major shareholders holding more than 5% of the total capital.	+
PINST	The proportion of the total number of shares owned by institutional investors.	+
PPUB	The proportion of the total number of shares owned by the state	-
PETR	The proportion of the total number of shares owned by foreigners.	-
The control variables		
TAILLB	Natural logarithm of the active total.	-
CAR	equal to the ratio of equity to total assets.	-
CRD	the ratio of loan provisions to all loans.	-
ROA	Return on Assets (ROA) = net income after tax divided by total asset amount	+
LIQ	current assets divided by current liabilities	+
PIB	Economic growth measured by the consumer price index	+
INF	It is inflation as measured by the consumer price index.	+

Rate of inflation: We measure the effect of inflation on bank profitability using the average annual rate of change of the Consumer Price Index (CPI). the effect of inflation on profitability and, ultimately, stability should be positive (Männasoo, 2009).

Annual Growth Rate of Domestic Product: We use the annual growth rate of the country's real gross domestic product (GDP) to explore the association between economic growth and banking risk (Uhde, 2009).

3.4. Model Specification

In order to measure the variables that have an impact on the stability of banking firms, we have constructed an econometric model that regresses the dependent variable z-score on the explanatory variables that characterize banks. The regression model then looks like this:

$$Z\text{-}SCORE_{it} = \beta_0 + \beta_1 DIV_{it} + \beta_2 CONC_{it} + \beta_3 PROPINST_{it+} \beta_4 PROPPUB_{it} + \beta_5 PROPETRA_{it} + \beta_6 SIZE_{it} + \beta_7 CAR_{it} + \beta_8 CRD_{it} + \beta_9 LIQ_{it} + \beta_{10} ROA_{it} + \beta_{11} PIB_{it} + \beta_{112} L'INFL_{it} + u_{it}$$

Where:
Z-SCORE: Bank Risk Level
DIV: Bank Diversification
CONC: Ownership Concentration
PINST: Institutional Ownership
PPUB: Public Property
TAILLB: Size of the bank
CAR: Capital
CRD: Credit
LIQ: Liquidity
ROA: Profitability
GDP: Economic growth
The consumer price index.i= 1,…,10
t= 2002,…., 2020
β_0 = The constant of the model
β_i= Variable coefficients (i=1,…,12)
u_{it}= The error term

4. DISCUSSION OF THE RESULTS

4.1. Descriptive Statistics

Descriptive statistics are presented for the entire sample for each variable. The mean, standard deviation and minimum and maximum values of the sample selected will be determined.

Table 3 provides descriptive statistics of the variables used to explain the level of insolvency risk of Tunisian banks. This table shows the overall mean, standard deviation, minimum and maximum values for each variable. First, We note that the level of financial stability of Tunisian banks that is measured by the variable z-score is, during the period 2002-2020, around 4.50 in Tunisia with a minimum of -3.71 and a maximum of 13.49 which means that Tunisian banks are characterized by an increased diversity of their risk level. This finding further demonstrates the value of examining the factors that may explain the level of risk in the Tunisian banking sector. Especially since the latter finances the Tunisian economy by 90%.

Secondly, according to the results presented in this table, we note that the DIV variable, which captures the non-traditional activity of banking firms, varies between 0.25 and 13.39. This proves that Tunisian banks are managed differently from each other. Some banks give considerable importance to non-traditional activities, while others specialize more in traditional activities such as deposit collection and lending.

Table 3. Descriptive statistics

Variable	Obs	Mean	Std.Dev.	Min	Max
Zscore	190	4.501	4.061	-3.71	13.493
DIV	190	0.744	1.456	0.251	13.393
TAILBQ	190	15.278	0.667	13.814	17.405
CAR	190	0.12	0.09	-0.062	0.956
LIQ	190	1.707	6.433	0.098	89.5
CRD	190	0.017	0.014	0.001	0.121
INF	190	4.449	1.362	2.037	7.455
PIB	190	0.023	0.034	-0.092	0.067
CONC	190	53.82	20.737	5.61	86.42
ROA	190	0.009	0.012	-0.104	0.029
PETR	190	25.162	25.891	0	64.24
PINS	190	32.348	25.119	0	88.54
PPUB	190	9.28	16.123	0	71.54

This observation supports the interest of testing the impact of diversification on the level of risk within banks.

Concerning the variables of the ownership structure, the average value of the ownership concentration is 53.82% with a minimum value of 5% and a maximum value of 86%. There is a great disparity within Tunisian banks. This disparity cannot be without effects on the management strategies and the way managers control, and consequently on the performance and level of risk of these banks. Similarly, the nature of ownership differs considerably from one bank to another. The average bank is held in the order of 9.28% by the state, 32.34% by domestic private investors and 25.16% by foreign investors. This may indicate that institutional and foreign investors may be responsible for better monitoring, as the literature indicates. For the control variables used, the average size of the banks is 15.27. The capital is an average of 12% we note that the Tunisian banks respect the conditions of regulatory capital. The average of the variable apprehending liquidity is 17.07% which varies between 0.098 and 89.5, This indicates that some Tunisian banks are in a more comfortable liquidity situation than others. The average credit rating is 1.7% with a minimum value of 1% and a maximum value of 12.1%, so we note that some banks focus more on traditional activities than others. Finally, we note that one bank has an economic return of 2.9%, while another has a negative economic return of 10.4%. This variable indicates that the performance of Tunisian banks varies greatly from one bank to another. Knowing that a bank's performance undoubtedly ensures its strength, we believed it is important to take this variable into account when explaining the level of risk.

4.2. Regression Analysis

Before proceeding with multiple regression, we checked the independence of the explanatory variables by establishing the correlation matrix. This showed that there is a strong correlation between the variables PPUB, PETR and PINST, representing respectively the percentage of public ownership, that of foreign ownership and finally that of institutional ownership. To overcome this problem and avoid biased results, we introduced these variables separately into the model. We also performed the VIF test to verify the absence of a multi-colinearity problem in the data structure of the selected sample. The result of this test shows that there is no multi-colinearity problem. The sample used in this research is made up of panel data. The choice of the appropriate estimator therefore requires the use of preliminary tests, namely the Fisher test (F-test) and the Breushe Pagan Lagrange Multiplier test (LM). The results of these tests reject the existence of a perfectly homogeneous panel structure. Therefore, the model could be either fixed individual effects or random individual effects. Therefore, we conducted the Hausman test. The result of this test shows that

Table 4. Correlation matrix

Variables	(1)	(2)	(3)	(4)	(5)	(6)	(7)	(8)	(9)	(10)	(11)	(12)	(13)
(1) zscore	1.000												
(2) DIV	-0.072	1.000											
(3) TAILBQ	-0.223	0.083	1.000										
(4) CAR	0.218	0.008	0.024	1.000									
(5) LIQ	-0.057	0.001	0.060	-0.020	1.000								
(6) CRD	-0.307	0.142	-0.064	-0.168	-0.051	1.000							
(7) INF	0.025	0.199	0.587	0.050	-0.019	-0.097	1.000						
(8) PIB	0.004	-0.164	-0.397	-0.102	0.003	0.150	-0.489	1.000					
(9) CONC	-0.001	0.148	0.317	-0.058	-0.017	-0.160	0.513	-0.400	1.000				
(10) ROA	0.400	0.093	0.129	0.268	-0.038	-0.457	0.139	-0.130	0.065	1.000			
(11) PETR	-0.026	0.143	-0.343	-0.051	-0.053	-0.112	0.002	-0.008	0.389	-0.051	1.000		
(12) PINST	0.207	0.103	-0.341	-0.063	-0.066	-0.116	-0.026	-0.007	0.351	-0.044	0.796	1.000	
(13) PETR	-0.439	-0.113	0.380	-0.110	0.059	0.184	0.083	-0.055	-0.069	-0.097	-0.551	-0.636	1.000

the model which adapts to the structure of the data of the selected sample is that with fixed random effects. Nevertheless, examination of the residues of the estimated regression functions shows that in the residues there is a contemporary correlation (cross-sectional correlation), a problem of heteroscedasticity between the panels, and also a problem of first-order autocorrelation. As a result, we used the FGLS method to estimate the specified model. The results of the resulting estimates are presented below in Table 4.

With ZSCORE level of banking risk; DIV is diversification of banking activity TAILBQ is the natural logarithm of total assets; and CAR is equal to the ratio of equity to the total assets of the bank. ; RLIQ = short-term assets divided by short-term liabilities; CRD is the ratio of loan provisions to all loans; inflation is measured by the consumer price index. ; GDP is economic growth measured by the Consumer Price Index; ROA = Net Income/Total Assets; PPUB is the total number of shares owned by the State; PINST is the total number of shares owned by institutional investors; PETR is the total number of shares owned by foreigners; CONC is the

Table 5. Results of the panel data estimation on the risk profile of Tunisian banks

	(1)	(2)	(3)
VARIABLES	zscore	zscore	zscore
DIV	0.049*	0.062**	0.071***
	(0.025)	(0.024)	(0.022)
TAILBQ	-0.857***	-1.057***	-0.975***
	(0.155)	(0.153)	(0.161)
CAR	1.388**	1.872***	1.836***
	(0.609)	(0.569)	(0.594)
LIQ	0.000	-0.003	-0.003
	(0.008)	(0.004)	(0.004)
CRD	-32.611***	-37.083***	-35.807***
	(3.929)	(3.548)	(3.351)
L.INF	0.100*	0.112**	0.089*
	(0.052)	(0.047)	(0.053)
PIB	4.319***	3.749***	2.805***
	(1.340)	(1.303)	(1.072)
CONC	0.006*	0.007**	0.009**
	(0.004)	(0.004)	(0.004)
ROA	12.764**	7.141	4.571
	(5.380)	(4.737)	(4.675)
PPUB	-0.061***		
	(0.008)		
PINST		0.010***	
		(0.004)	
PETR			-0.012***
			(0.004)
Constant	17.625***	19.718***	19.012***
	(2.245)	(2.261)	(2.394)
Observations	180	180	180
Number of panel	10	10	10

Standard errors in parentheses *** $p<0.01$, ** $p<0.05$, * $p<0.1$

proportion of the total number of shares owned by the main shareholders who hold more than 5% of the total capital.

With ZSCORE level of banking risk; DIV is diversification of banking activity TAILBQ is the natural logarithm of total assets; and CAR is equal to the ratio of equity to the total assets of the bank. ; RLIQ = short-term assets divided by short-term liabilities; CRD is the ratio of loan provisions to all loans; inflation is measured by the consumer price index. ; GDP is economic growth measured by the Consumer Price Index; ROA = Net Income/Total Assets; PPUB is the total number of shares owned by the State; PINST is the total number of shares owned by institutional investors; PETR is the total number of shares owned by foreigners; CONC is the proportion of the total number of shares owned by the main shareholders who hold more than 5% of the total capital.

Based on the results provided by the FGLS method, the first hypothesis is validated: diversification of banking activity has a positive impact on the strength of Tunisian banks at a significant threshold of 10%. This finding is consistent with (Diamond, 1984) which proposes that diversification helps to reduce risk in all types of enterprises, including financial intermediaries.

Similarly, Köhler (2015) highlighted the importance of noninterest income in total operating income which leads to significant stability of banks. According to the table, we noted that the relationship between ownership concentration and risk assessment of Tunisian banks presents a positive and significant sign, given that the dependent variable Z-score, which is considered an indicator of bank stability, we can therefore conclude that concentration of ownership is a factor that improves the strength of banks, we validated our second hypothesis. This result contradicts that of Haw, (2010) which demonstrated that bank concentration has a positive impact on the level of risk.

However, the result obtained corroborates that of García-Marco, (2008), which explains the negative link between ownership concentration and the level of risk within banks by the fact that management control by shareholders, may have two consequences for the banks' risk. If managers wish to safeguard their equity investment and therefore express risk-averse behaviour, then the agency problem will be reduced, and fewer risks will be taken.

Similarly, the results show that the third hypothesis (H3) is validated, we found that public ownership has an unfavourable effect on the ratio Z-score which measures stability and bank solidity and is statically significant at the threshold of 1%, The more public ownership increases the bank's financial strength decreases.

This result could be explained by the fact that the State finances projects that are not effective for political reasons (Vishny, 1994; Salman, 2013; La Porta, 2000). This conclusion is consistent with the results of previous studies (e.g., Berger, 2005;

Iannotta, 2007; Cornett, 2010; Angkinand, 2010 and Lassoued, 2016), which also find that public ownership encourages risk-taking by managers.

In addition, the fourth hypothesis (H4) is validated. Institutional ownership is positively and significantly associated with the financial strength of banks. This result is consistent with the assumptions of Jensen (1993) that institutional shareholders are considered experts and may impose more relevant control over managers when they hold large capital shares. On the other hand, institutional investors can have a negative impact on the level of banking risk when they are actively involved in the control process within banks (Levine, 2009).

Concerning the fifth hypothesis (H5), we also found that it is validated, There is a negative and statistically significant relationship between foreign ownership and the financial soundness of Tunisian banks. As a result, foreign ownership is associated with higher risk-taking within Tunisian banks. This result contradicts those of Gormley (2007); Berger (2005); and Megginson (2005), who find that foreign ownership reduces risk and explain this relationship as it reduces conflicts between board members and thus banking fragility. In addition, the results obtained corroborate those of (La Porta, 1999) and (Höglund, 2016) that foreign shareholdings allow problems of asymmetry of information and that these are mainly due to linguistic and cultural differences. The positive result linking foreign ownership with fragility can also be explained by the fact that foreign banks can also suffer from distance problems and that large banks are disadvantaged in the qualitative analysis of information (Stein, 2002). The research results show that the capital of banks has a positive impact on the solidity, so it has a negative impact on the level of risk of Tunisian banking firms and is statistically significant at 5%.

This conclusion is consistent with Akhtar (2011) and Iqbal (2012) and demonstrates that capital has a positive and significant impact on the strength of Islamic and traditional banks.

However, Calem (1999) concludes that the relationship between capital and bank risk-taking is in the form of a U, when capital is below the minimum required by regulation, banks select a portfolio of high-risk loans to improve the transfer benefits of deposit insurance risk. In addition, the size of the bank has a negative effect and significantly at a threshold of 1% on the level of solidity therefore a positive level on the risk. This means that large entities may be more attracted by excessive risk-taking, reduced market discipline and distortions of competition because they know they will be bailed out.

This research is compatible with De Jonghe (2010) and Uhde (2009) who found that large banking firms tend to be riskier because of a moral hazard problem. As far as the performance variable is concerned, the results indicate that there is a favourable influence on the financial strength, thus reducing the bank risk. This positive relationship indicates that the higher the performance, the more stable the bank becomes, which automatically reduces the level of risk. These results claim that the most profitable banking firms are generally still stable, a statement that is widely accepted in publications, such as, (Köhler, 2015). The results also show that the liquidity variable has no significant effect on the level of Tunisian banking stability. These results are not consistent with (Vazquez, 2015) which analyzes that banks with low liquidity structures and high levels of debt before the crisis were the most vulnerable to bankruptcy.

Similarly, the empirical results of the study prove that there is a negative link between the credit variable and the level of bank stability therefore has a positive effect on the bank's risk profile with a statistical significance of 1%, indicating that the bank that awards more credits, they are faced with a higher level of risk. This result confirms the first hypothesis that banks diversifying their activities are characterised by a lower level of risk.

This idea has been supported by the findings of NIKOMARAM (2013) that the increase in non-refundable debt reduced the level of solvency and financial soundness of banks in times of crisis. Research such as (Chen, 2017), (He, 2012) (Ericsson, 2006) (Chen, 2005), (Hund, 2008), (Acharya, 2011), (Acharya, 2015), (Ghosh, 2016) and (Ahçı, 2017) indicate that counterparty risk interacts and influences bank stability. The results indicate that macro-economic variables, such as the inflation rate variable have a positive and statistically significant coefficient on the level of financial stability of Tunisian banks automatically has a negative effect on the 1% threshold risk. This result is identical to previous research (Uhde, 2009) which states that the effect of changes in inflation rates depends on the fact that inflation is anticipated by banks and coincides with general economic fragility. Also, the results indicate that there is a positive and significant relationship at the 1% threshold between economic growth and the level of financial stability that necessarily has a negative impact on the risk of Tunisian banks, confirming the view that banks are clearly pro-cyclical. In times of economic recovery, banks are inclined to be overly optimistic, and few problematic loans are identified. Contrarywise, in times of slowdown, banking risk surges due to high defaults.

5. CONCLUSION

In recent years, a wave of changes has had an impact on the Tunisian financial context and also a significant change during the centralised planning phase and the decentralization phase. In view of the multitude of studies which have analysed the relationship between the diversification of trading activity on the level of strength and stability of banking firms in other countries, we have therefore sought to carry out work in accordance with the same research, by positioning ourselves on the context of Tunisian banks. The result of the FGLS regression showed that the separation between traditional and non-traditional activity has a beneficial effect on banking stability due to the fact that the diversification of activities allows banks to establish synergies between the different sectors, thus increasing the level of stability of banking firms by reducing the level of risk. One can thus confirm the hypothesis that the financial strength of Tunisian banks is positively influenced by the degree of diversification of banks' sources of income. We noted that on the one hand, the review of empirical research shows that a high concentration of ownership is positively linked to the stability and strength of Tunisian banks. On the other hand, the strong presence of public properties is high, the higher the level of risk of Tunisian banks, this indicates that these results correspond to the idea that governments generally use their holdings in the capital of banking firms to achieve objectives they consider strategic. Moreover, the presence of institutional investors in the composition of capital is positively associated with the solvency of banks. We concluded that the governance variable is considered very important since it has a positive impact on the strength of the Tunisian banking sector. While foreign participation has a positive impact on the risks of Tunisian banks. This result could indicate that the presence of foreign investors is perceived as an incentive to increase risk-taking by the leaders of Tunisian banking firms. Finally, the results of this research confirm the crucial role of the ownership structure in determining the level of risk of Tunisian banks, this allows us to conclude that the poor functioning of the banking governance system is likely to be responsible for the high level of risk of Tunisian banks.

REFERENCES

Acharya, V. V., Schaefer, S., & Zhang, Y. (2015). Liquidity risk and correlation risk: A clinical study of the General Motors and Ford Downgrade of May 2005. *The Quarterly Journal of Finance*, *5*(02), 1550006. doi:10.1142/S2010139215500068

Acharya, V. V., & Viswanathan, S. X. (2011). Leverage, moral hazard, and liquidity. *The Journal of Finance*, *66*(1), 99–138. doi:10.1111/j.1540-6261.2010.01627.x

Agrawal, A., & Mandelker, G. N. (1990). Large shareholders and the monitoring of managers: The case of antitakeover charter amendments. *Journal of Financial and Quantitative Analysis*, *25*(2), 143–161. doi:10.2307/2330821

Ahçi, M. (2017) *Dynamic interaction between liquidity and sovereign credit risk: Evidence from Turkey* [Master's thesis]. Ekonomi ve Sosyal Bilimler Enstitüsü. https://repository.bilkent.edu.tr/server/api/core/bitstreams/f008f56b-274d-4e5d-99f9-9a56e7fb215e/content

Ahmed, N., Akhtar, M. F., & Usman, M. (2011). Risk management practices and Islamic banks: An empirical investigation from Pakistan. *Interdisciplinary Journal of Research in Business*, *1*(6), 50–57.

Allen, J., & Cebula, J. (2008). *Risk and Resilience: Considerations for Information Security Risk Assessment and Management. J. Cebula*. CERT.

Angkinand, A., & Wihlborg, C. (2010). Deposit insurance coverage, ownership, and banks' risk-taking in emerging markets. *Journal of International Money and Finance*, *29*(2), 252–274. doi:10.1016/j.jimonfin.2009.08.001

Azofra, V., & Santamaría, M. (2011). Ownership, control, and pyramids in Spanish commercial banks. *Journal of Banking & Finance*, *35*(6), 1464–1476. doi:10.1016/j.jbankfin.2010.10.029

Barry, T. A. (2010). *Structure actionnariale des banques, risque et efficience* [Doctoral dissertation]. New York University.

Barth, J. R., Caprio, G., & Levine, R. (2008). *Rethinking bank regulation: Till angels govern*. Cambridge University Press.

Beck, T., De Jonghe, O., & Mulier, K. (2017). *Bank sectoral concentration and (systemic) risk: Evidence from a worldwide sample of banks*. Academic Press.

Ben-Hassoun, A., Aloui, C., & Ben-Nasr, H. (2018). Demand for audit quality in newly privatized firms in MENA region: Role of internal corporate governance mechanisms audit. *Research in International Business and Finance*, *45*, 334–348. doi:10.1016/j.ribaf.2017.07.167

Berger, A. N., Clarke, G. R., Cull, R., Klapper, L., & Udell, G. F. (2005). Corporate governance and bank performance: A joint analysis of the static, selection, and dynamic effects of domestic, foreign, and state ownership. *Journal of Banking & Finance*, *29*(8-9), 2179–2221. doi:10.1016/j.jbankfin.2005.03.013

Berger, A. N., & Di Patti, E. B. (2006). Capital structure and firm performance: A new approach to testing agency theory and an application to the banking industry. *Journal of Banking & Finance*, *30*(4), 1065–1102. doi:10.1016/j.jbankfin.2005.05.015

Bhagat, S., Bolton, B., & Lu, J. (2015). Size, leverage, and risk-taking of financial institutions. *Journal of Banking & Finance*, *59*, 520–537. doi:10.1016/j.jbankfin.2015.06.018

Bikker, J. A., & Metzemakers, P. A. (2005). Bank provisioning behaviour and procyclicality. *Journal of International Financial Markets, Institutions and Money*, *15*(2), 141–157. doi:10.1016/j.intfin.2004.03.004

Bonin, J. P., Hasan, I., & Wachtel, P. (2005). Bank performance, efficiency and ownership in transition countries. *Journal of Banking & Finance*, *29*(1), 31–53. doi:10.1016/j.jbankfin.2004.06.015

Borisova, G., Brockman, P., Salas, J. M., & Zagorchev, A. (2012). Government ownership and corporate governance: Evidence from the EU. *Journal of Banking & Finance*, *36*(11), 2917–2934. doi:10.1016/j.jbankfin.2012.01.008

Bouaziz, W., & Bouri, A. (2012). Ownership structure and financial institutes risk taking: evidence from Tunisian quoted bankOwnership structure and financial institutes risk taking: evidence from Tunisian quoted bank (financial institute). *International Journal of Managerial and Financial Accounting*, *4*(1), 47–60. doi:10.1504/IJMFA.2012.044836

Bourkhis, K., & Nabi, M. S. (2013). Islamic and conventional banks' soundness during the 2007–2008 financial crisis. *Review of Financial Economics*, *22*(2), 68–77. doi:10.1016/j.rfe.2013.01.001

Boussaada, R., & Karmani, M. (2015). Ownership concentration and bank performance: Evidence from MENA banks. *International Journal of Business and Management*, *10*(3), 189. doi:10.5539/ijbm.v10n3p189

Boyd, J. H., & Runkle, D. E. (1993). Size and performance of banking firms: Testing the predictions of theory. *Journal of Monetary Economics*, *31*(1), 47–67. doi:10.1016/0304-3932(93)90016-9

Burkart, M., Gromb, D., & Panunzi, F. (1997). Large shareholders, monitoring, and the value of the firm. *The Quarterly Journal of Economics*, *112*(3), 693–728. doi:10.1162/003355397555325

Calem, P., & Rob, R. (1999). The impact of capital-based regulation on bank risk-taking. *Journal of Financial Intermediation*, *8*(4), 317–352. doi:10.1006/jfin.1999.0276

Chaney, P. K., Faccio, M., & Parsley, D. (2011). The quality of accounting information in politically connected firms. *Journal of Accounting and Economics*, *51*(1-2), 58–76. doi:10.1016/j.jacceco.2010.07.003

Chau, G. K., & Gray, S. J. (2002). Ownership structure and corporate voluntary disclosure in Hong Kong and Singapore. *The International Journal of Accounting*, *37*(2), 247–265. doi:10.1016/S0020-7063(02)00153-X

Choi, J. J. (Ed.). (2001). *Asian Financial Crisis Financial, Structural and International Dimensions*. Emerald Group Publishing Limited. doi:10.1016/S1569-3767(2001)1

Claessens, S. (2006). Corporate governance and development. *The World Bank Research Observer*, *21*(1), 91–122. doi:10.1093/wbro/lkj004

Claessens, S., Demirgüç-Kunt, A., & Huizinga, H. (2001). How does foreign entry affect domestic banking markets? *Journal of Banking & Finance*, *25*(5), 891–911. doi:10.1016/S0378-4266(00)00102-3

Claessens, S., & Van Horen, N. (2014). Foreign banks: Trends and impact. *Journal of Money, Credit and Banking*, *46*(s1), 295–326. doi:10.1111/jmcb.12092

Cornett, M. M., Guo, L., Khaksari, S., & Tehranian, H. (2010). The impact of state ownership on performance differences in privately-owned versus state-owned banks: An international comparison. *Journal of Financial Intermediation*, *19*(1), 74–94. doi:10.1016/j.jfi.2008.09.005

Daniels, R. J., & Halpern, P. (1996). Too close for comfort: The role of the closely held public corporation in the Canadian economy and the implications for public policy. *Can. Bus. LJ*, *26*, 11.

De Jonghe, O. (2010). Back to the basics in banking? A micro-analysis of banking system stability. *Journal of Financial Intermediation*, *19*(3), 387–417. doi:10.1016/j.jfi.2009.04.001

Delis, M. D., & Staikouras, P. K. (2011). Supervisory effectiveness and bank risk. *Review of Finance*, *15*(3), 511–543. doi:10.1093/rof/rfq035

Demirgüç-Kunt, A., & Detragiache, E. (2002). Does deposit insurance increase banking system stability? An empirical investigation. *Journal of Monetary Economics*, *49*(7), 1373–1406. doi:10.1016/S0304-3932(02)00171-X

Demirgüç-Kunt, A., & Huizinga, H. (2010). Bank activity and funding strategies: The impact on risk and returns. *Journal of Financial Economics*, *98*(3), 626–650. doi:10.1016/j.jfineco.2010.06.004

Deng, S., & Jia, J. (2007). Institutional Ownership, Diversification, and Risk Taking in BHCs. Academic Press.

Deng, S. E., Elyasiani, E., & Mao, C. X. (2007). Diversification and the cost of debt of bank holding companies. *Journal of Banking & Finance, 31*(8), 2453–2473. doi:10.1016/j.jbankfin.2006.10.024

Diamond, D. W., & Rajan, R. G. (2001). Liquidity risk, liquidity creation, and financial fragility: A theory of banking. *Journal of Political Economy, 109*(2), 287–327. doi:10.1086/319552

Dicko, S. (2016). The impact of political connections on the quality of corporate governance. *International Journal of Corporate Governance, 7*(3), 247–273. doi:10.1504/IJCG.2016.080683

Dicko, S. (2017). Political connections, ownership structure and quality of governance. *International Journal of Managerial Finance, 13*(4), 358–377. doi:10.1108/IJMF-01-2017-0010

Dickstein, D. I., & Flast, R. H. (2008). *No excuses: a business process approach to managing operational risk*. John Wiley & Sons.

Doidge, C., Karolyi, G. A., Lins, K. V., Miller, D. P., & Stulz, R. M. (2009). Private benefits of control, ownership, and the cross-listing decision. *The Journal of Finance, 64*(1), 425–466. doi:10.1111/j.1540-6261.2008.01438.x

Dolde, W., & Knopf, J. (2006). *Impact of corporate ownership and governance on risk-taking and returns at thrift institutions*. University of Connecticut.

Ellul, A., & Yerramilli, V. (2013). Stronger risk controls, lower risk: Evidence from US bank holding companies. *The Journal of Finance, 68*(5), 1757–1803. doi:10.1111/jofi.12057

Elyasiani, E., & Jia, J. J. (2008). Institutional ownership stability and BHC performance. *Journal of Banking & Finance, 32*(9), 1767–1781. doi:10.1016/j.jbankfin.2007.12.010

Ericsson, J., & Renault, O. (2006). Liquidity and credit risk. *The Journal of Finance, 61*(5), 2219–2250. doi:10.1111/j.1540-6261.2006.01056.x

Faccio, M., Masulis, R. W., & McConnell, J. J. (2006). Political connections and corporate bailouts. *The Journal of Finance, 61*(6), 2597–2635. doi:10.1111/j.1540-6261.2006.01000.x

Fernández, C., & Arrondo, R. (2005). Alternative internal controls as substitutes of the board of directors. *Corporate Governance*, *13*(6), 856–866. doi:10.1111/j.1467-8683.2005.00476.x

García-Marco, T., & Robles-Fernandez, M. D. (2008). Risk-taking behaviour and ownership in the banking industry: The Spanish evidence. *Journal of Economics and Business*, *60*(4), 332–354. doi:10.1016/j.jeconbus.2007.04.008

Ghosh, S. (2016). Capital buffer, credit risk and liquidity behaviour: Evidence for GCC banks. *Comparative Economic Studies*, *58*(4), 539–569. doi:10.1057/s41294-016-0005-1

Goddard, J., Molyneux, P., & Wilson, J. O. (2004). The profitability of European banks: A cross-sectional and dynamic panel analysis. *Manchester School*, *72*(3), 363–381. doi:10.1111/j.1467-9957.2004.00397.x

Gormley, T. A. (2005). *Banking competition in developing countries: does foreign bank entry improve credit access?* Department of Economics, MIT.

Guedhami, O., Pittman, J. A., & Saffar, W. (2009). Auditor choice in privatized firms: Empirical evidence on the role of state and foreign owners. *Journal of Accounting and Economics*, *48*(2-3), 151–171. doi:10.1016/j.jacceco.2009.08.003

Gulamhussen, M. A., & Guerreiro, L. (2009). The influence of foreign equity and board membership on corporate strategy and internal cost management in Portuguese banks. *Management Accounting Research*, *20*(1), 6–17. doi:10.1016/j.mar.2008.10.006

Guo, R., Langston, V., & Hadley, L. (2012). Business cycle, corporate governance, and bank performance. *Research in Business and Economics Journal*, *5*(1), 1–11.

Gursoy, G., & Aydogan, K. (2002). Equity ownership structure, risk taking, and performance. *Russian & East European Finance & Trade*, *38*(6), 6–6.

Hasnan, S., Marzuki, H., & Shuhidan, S. M. (2017). Effects of board characteristics on financial restatement in Malaysia. *Pertanika Journal of Social Science & Humanities*, 255–263.

Haw, I. M., Ho, S. S., Hu, B., & Wu, D. (2010). Concentrated control, institutions, and banking sector: An international study. *Journal of Banking & Finance*, *34*(3), 485–497. doi:10.1016/j.jbankfin.2009.08.013

He, Z., & Xiong, W. (2012). Rollover risk and credit risk. *The Journal of Finance*, *67*(2), 391–430. doi:10.1111/j.1540-6261.2012.01721.x

Höglund, H., & Sundvik, D. (2016). Financial reporting quality and outsourcing of accounting tasks: Evidence from small private firms. *Advances in Accounting*, *35*, 125–134. doi:10.1016/j.adiac.2016.03.001

Houcine, A. (2017). The effect of financial reporting quality on corporate investment efficiency: Evidence from the Tunisian stock market. *Research in International Business and Finance*, *42*, 321–337. doi:10.1016/j.ribaf.2017.07.066

Htay, S. N. N., Rashid, H. M., Adnan, M. A., & Meera, A. K. M. (2011). Corporate governance and risk management information disclosure in Malaysian listed banks: Panel data analysis. *International Review of Business Research Papers*, *7*(4), 159–176.

Iannotta, G., Nocera, G., & Sironi, A. (2007). Ownership structure, risk and performance in the European banking industry. *Journal of Banking & Finance*, *31*(7), 2127–2149. doi:10.1016/j.jbankfin.2006.07.013

Iannotta, G., Nocera, G., & Sironi, A. (2013). The impact of government ownership on bank risk. *Journal of Financial Intermediation*, *22*(2), 152–176. doi:10.1016/j.jfi.2012.11.002

Iqbal, A. (2012). Liquidity risk management: A comparative study between conventional and Islamic banks of Pakistan. *Global Journal of Management and Business Research*, *12*(5), 54–64.

Jensen, M. C. (1993). The modern industrial revolution, exit, and the failure of internal control systems. *The Journal of Finance, 48*(3), 831-880.

Jensen, M. C., & Meckling, W. H. (2019). Theory of the firm: Managerial behavior, agency costs and ownership structure. In *Corporate governance* (pp. 77–132). Gower.

Kamani, E. F. (2019). The effect of non-traditional banking activities on systemic risk: Does bank size matter? *Finance Research Letters*, *30*, 297–305. doi:10.1016/j.frl.2018.10.013

Klai, N., & Omri, A. (2011). Corporate governance and financial reporting quality: The case of Tunisian firms. *International Business Research*, *4*(1), 158–166.

Köhler, M. (2015). Which banks are more risky? The impact of business models on bank stability. *Journal of Financial Stability*, *16*, 195–212. doi:10.1016/j.jfs.2014.02.005

Konishi, M., & Yasuda, Y. (2004). Factors affecting bank risk taking: Evidence from Japan. *Journal of Banking & Finance*, *28*(1), 215–232. doi:10.1016/S0378-4266(02)00405-3

La Porta, R., Lopez-de-Silanes, F., & Shleifer, A. (1999). Corporate ownership around the world. *The Journal of Finance*, *54*(2), 471–517. doi:10.1111/0022-1082.00115

La Porta, R., Lopez-de-Silanes, F., & Shleifer, A. (2002). Government ownership of banks. *The Journal of Finance*, *57*(1), 265–301. doi:10.1111/1540-6261.00422

La Porta, R., Lopez-de-Silanes, F., Shleifer, A., & Vishny, R. (2000). Investor protection and corporate governance. *Journal of Financial Economics*, *58*(1-2), 3–27. doi:10.1016/S0304-405X(00)00065-9

Laeven, L., & Levine, R. (2009). Bank governance, regulation and risk taking. *Journal of Financial Economics*, *93*(2), 259–275. doi:10.1016/j.jfineco.2008.09.003

Laeven, L., & Majnoni, G. (2003). Loan loss provisioning and economic slowdowns: Too much, too late? *Journal of Financial Intermediation*, *12*(2), 178–197. doi:10.1016/S1042-9573(03)00016-0

Laidroo, L. (2009). Association between ownership structure and public announcements' disclosures. *Corporate Governance*, *17*(1), 13–34. doi:10.1111/j.1467-8683.2008.00717.x

Lassoued, N., Sassi, H., & Attia, M. B. R. (2016). The impact of state and foreign ownership on banking risk: Evidence from the MENA countries. *Research in International Business and Finance*, *36*, 167–178. doi:10.1016/j.ribaf.2015.09.014

Levine, R. (1996). Foreign banks, financial development, and economic. *International financial markets: Harmonization versus competition, 224.*

Lobez, F. (2010). Too big to fail: Gouvernance et régulation des banques. *Revue d'Economie Financiere*, *100*(4), 187–199. doi:10.3406/ecofi.2010.5830

Maechler, A., Mitra, S., & Worrell, D. (2005, October). Exploring financial risks and vulnerabilities in new and potential EU member states. In *Second Annual DG ECFIN Research Conference: "Financial Stability and the Convergence Process in Europe," October* (pp. 6-7). Academic Press.

Männasoo, K., & Mayes, D. G. (2009). Explaining bank distress in Eastern European transition economies. *Journal of Banking & Finance*, *33*(2), 244–253. doi:10.1016/j.jbankfin.2008.07.016

Means, G. (2017). *The modern corporation and private property*. Routledge. doi:10.4324/9781315133188

Megginson, W. L. (2005). The economics of bank privatization. *Journal of Banking & Finance*, *29*(8-9), 1931–1980. doi:10.1016/j.jbankfin.2005.03.005

Micco, A., Panizza, U., & Yanez, M. (2007). Bank ownership and performance. Does politics matter? *Journal of Banking & Finance*, *31*(1), 219–241. doi:10.1016/j.jbankfin.2006.02.007

Mohamad, A. A. S., Mohamad, M. T., & Samsudin, M. L. (2013). How Islamic banks of Malaysia managing liquidity? An emphasis on confronting economic cycles. *International Journal of Business and Social Science*, *4*(7), 253–263.

Moshirian, F., Sahgal, S., & Zhang, B. (2011, November). *Non-interest income and systemic risk: The role of concentration*. In Global Systemic Risk Conference. working paper.

Munteanu, I. (2012). Bank liquidity and its determinants in Romania. *Procedia Economics and Finance*, *3*, 993–998. doi:10.1016/S2212-5671(12)00263-8

Nikomaram, H., Taghavi, M., & Diman, S. (2013). The relationship between liquidity risk and credit risk in Islamic banking industry of Iran. *Management Science Letters*, *3*(4), 1223–1232. doi:10.5267/j.msl.2013.02.025

Nouha, K., & Walid, K. (2016). Le rôle des mécanismes de gouvernance dans la prévention de la fraude managériale. *Management Accounting Research*.

Pathan, S. (2009). Strong boards, CEO power and bank risk-taking. *Journal of Banking & Finance*, *33*(7), 1340–1350. doi:10.1016/j.jbankfin.2009.02.001

Pathan, S., Skully, M., & Wickramanayake, J. (2007). Board size, independence and performance: An analysis of Thai banks. *Asia-Pacific Financial Markets*, *14*(3), 211–227. doi:10.1007/s10690-007-9060-y

Pearce, J. A. II, & Zahra, S. A. (1992). Board composition from a strategic contingency perspective. *Journal of Management Studies*, *29*(4), 411–438. doi:10.1111/j.1467-6486.1992.tb00672.x

Pichard-Stamford, J. P. (2000). Légitimité et enracinement du dirigeant par le réseau des administrateurs. *Revue Finance Contrãle Stratãgie, 3*(4), 143-178.

Salas, V., & Saurina, J. (2002). Credit risk in two institutional regimes: Spanish commercial and savings banks. *Journal of Financial Services Research*, *22*(3), 203–224. doi:10.1023/A:1019781109676

Salhi, B., & Boujelbene, Y. (2012). Effect of internal banking mechanisms of governance on the risk taking by the Tunisian banks. *International Journal of Economics, Finance and Management*, *1*(1).

Salman, F., & Siddiqui, K. (2013). Mehrangate Scandal: Corporate Governance Failure. *The IUP Journal of Corporate Governance*, *12*(4), 41–46.

Saunders, A., Strock, E., & Travlos, N. G. (1990). Ownership structure, deregulation, and bank risk taking. *The Journal of Finance, 45*(2), 643-654.

Schaede, U. (1994). The" Old Boy" network and government-business relationships in Japan (Vol. 94, No. 12). Graduate School of International Relations and Pacific Studies, University of California, San Diego.

Scialom, L. (2011). Stratégies et instruments d'une régulation macroprudentielle. *Revue d'Economie Financiere*, (3), 171–186.

Shehzad, C. T., De Haan, J., & Scholtens, B. (2010). The impact of bank ownership concentration on impaired loans and capital adequacy. *Journal of Banking & Finance*, *34*(2), 399–408. doi:10.1016/j.jbankfin.2009.08.007

Shen, C. H., Lin, C. Y., & Wang, Y. C. (2015). Do strong corporate governance firms still require political connection, and vice versa? *International Review of Economics & Finance*, *39*, 107–120. doi:10.1016/j.iref.2015.06.006

Shleifer, A., & Vishny, R. W. (1994). Politicians and firms. *The Quarterly Journal of Economics*, *109*(4), 995–1025. doi:10.2307/2118354

Stein, J. C. (2002). Information production and capital allocation: Decentralized versus hierarchical firms. *The Journal of Finance*, *57*(5), 1891–1921. doi:10.1111/0022-1082.00483

Stiroh, K. J. (2004). Diversification in banking: Is noninterest income the answer? *Journal of Money, Credit and Banking*, *36*(5), 853–882. doi:10.1353/mcb.2004.0076

Talwar, S. P. (2001). Competition, consolidation and systemic stability in the Indian banking industry. *BIS Papers*, (4).

Uhde, A., & Heimeshoff, U. (2009). Consolidation in banking and financial stability in Europe: Empirical evidence. *Journal of Banking & Finance*, *33*(7), 1299–1311. doi:10.1016/j.jbankfin.2009.01.006

Vazquez, F., & Federico, P. (2015). Bank funding structures and risk: Evidence from the global financial crisis. *Journal of Banking & Finance*, *61*, 1–14. doi:10.1016/j.jbankfin.2015.08.023

Whidbee, D. A. (1997). Board composition and control of shareholder voting rights in the banking industry. *Financial Management*, *26*(4), 27–41. doi:10.2307/3666125

Zhang, G. (2012). Determinants of Financial Restatements in the Listed Companies in China. *Data Mining and Knowledge Discovery*, 725–730.

Zheng, C., Moudud-Ul-Huq, S., Rahman, M. M., & Ashraf, B. N. (2017). Does the ownership structure matter for banks' capital regulation and risk-taking behavior? Empirical evidence from a developing country. *Research in International Business and Finance*, *42*, 404–421. doi:10.1016/j.ribaf.2017.07.035

ENDNOTE

1 www.bvmt.com.tn

Chapter 8
Digitalization and the Rise of Green Finance:
Opportunities, Challenges, and the Path Forward

Kaushikkumar Patel
https://orcid.org/0009-0005-9197-2765
TransUnion LLC, USA

ABSTRACT

This chapter provides a comprehensive exploration of the intersection between digitalization and green finance, emphasizing its pivotal role in advancing environmental sustainability. Through a meticulous literature review, the authors identify the current state of digital green finance, highlighting both its transformative potential and the challenges it presents. The chapter offers a deeper understanding of the existing issues, controversies, and problems faced by practitioners and stakeholders in this domain. In response, the authors present well-reasoned solutions and recommendations, drawing from empirical evidence and innovative thinking. The chapter also ventures into future research directions, discussing emerging technologies and methodologies that promise to redefine the landscape of digital green finance. In conclusion, the authors reflect on the broader socio-economic and environmental implications of integrating digital tools in green finance, emphasizing the critical role they play in shaping a sustainable and resilient future.

DOI: 10.4018/979-8-3693-1678-8.ch008

1. INTRODUCTION

In today's rapidly evolving world, the fusion of technology and finance is revolutionizing our approach to environmental sustainability. This era is marked by an urgent need for innovative financial strategies to support projects aimed at combating climate change, mitigating resource depletion, and addressing environmental degradation. At the heart of this movement is green finance, an emerging field dedicated to funneling financial investments into projects with significant positive environmental impacts. The real game-changer, however, has been the advent of digitalization, which has significantly expanded the scope, efficiency, and influence of green finance initiatives.

The digital revolution, with its vast data networks, sophisticated analytics, and interconnected technologies, is transforming not only our daily lives and work environments but also our perspectives on finance, investment, and environmental stewardship. Digital platforms are making green finance more accessible than ever, breaking down barriers to entry and allowing a diverse range of stakeholders to contribute to and benefit from sustainable projects. These digital tools are enhancing the transparency and accountability of green finance, making it an increasingly attractive option for investors and stakeholders alike.

However, this transformative journey is not without its hurdles. The integration of digitalization into green finance introduces complex challenges, including data security risks, regulatory hurdles, and ethical considerations. These issues must be carefully navigated to ensure that the digital-green finance nexus can effectively contribute to our collective goal of a sustainable future.

This chapter seeks to provide an in-depth analysis of the digital aspects of green finance, examining both the vast opportunities and the significant challenges that arise from the integration of digital tools into this field. By drawing on empirical research, case studies, and a comprehensive review of existing literature, this chapter aims to shed light on the practical implications of digitalization in green finance. Furthermore, it will explore the future landscape of this integration, considering the impact of emerging technologies and the changing socio-economic environment.

The objectives of this chapter are multifaceted: to elucidate the transformative impact of digitalization on green finance, to investigate the opportunities and challenges at this intersection, to showcase practical examples and case studies that highlight the application of digital tools in green finance, to anticipate the future direction of digital green finance in light of emerging technological advancements, and to provide valuable insights and recommendations for stakeholders within the green finance ecosystem, steering them towards a path of sustainability and resilience.

2. LITERATURE REVIEW

Integrating digital technologies into green finance is revolutionizing how we approach sustainable investment, drawing significant attention from scholars, policymakers, and industry practitioners. This literature review explores the intricate relationship between digitalization and green finance, utilizing a broad spectrum of research, including seminal works and empirical studies, to provide a comprehensive overview of this evolving field.

Puschmann and Leifer (2020) delve into the transformative potential of FinTech, InsurTech, and blockchain technologies, positing them as pivotal forces in sculpting a better world through sustainable digital finance. Their insights lay the groundwork for understanding the instrumental role these technologies play in enhancing the efficacy and reach of green finance initiatives. Otto and Thornton (2023) further expand on this narrative by examining the symbiotic relationship between digital finance and technological innovation in propelling the green economy forward, thereby underscoring the critical role digital advancements play in fostering environmental sustainability.

Macchiavello and Siri (2022) navigate the confluence of sustainable finance and fintech, probing the capacity of technological innovations to contribute to environmental objectives. Their exploration into the realms of 'green fintech' and 'sustainable digital finance' unveils the burgeoning intersection of financial technology with environmental stewardship. Yan et al. (2023) provide a detailed analysis of eco-digitalization and green finance policies, particularly focusing on the engagements of multinational corporations within selected MENA countries and their impact on sustainable environmental practices.

Zhou, Zhu, and Luo (2022) investigate the ramifications of fintech innovation on green growth in China, with a special emphasis on the mediating role played by green finance. Their research highlights the indispensable role of financial technology in catalyzing environmentally sustainable economic growth. Taghizadeh-Hesary and Hyun (2022) compile a comprehensive overview of green digital finance in alignment with Sustainable Development Goals, offering a panoramic view of how digital solutions are being integrated into green finance initiatives to achieve broader sustainability objectives.

Ryszawska (2018) articulates a paradigm shift in sustainable finance, reflecting on the transformative trends that are reshaping financial practices to support sustainability. This shift underscores the evolving landscape of finance in response to the pressing need for environmental sustainability. Moşteanu, Faccia, and Cavaliere (2020) discuss the significant changes digitalization brings to the green economy, emphasizing the profound impact of digital advancements on business perspectives and practices that foster sustainability.

Yang and Masron (2022) explore the influence of digital finance on enhancing energy efficiency within the framework of sustainable development, shedding light on the potential of digital tools to bolster environmental sustainability efforts. Zhou (2022) investigates the application trends of digital finance and technological innovation in nurturing the green economy, providing valuable insights into how digital solutions are being employed to advance environmental initiatives.

Lei et al. (2024) present an empirical analysis of the relationship between digitalization and sustainable development across OECD countries, offering evidence of digital advancements' positive impact on sustainability efforts. Han, Li, and Wang (2023) delve into the intricate dynamics between digital finance, environmental regulation, and the efficiency of green development in China, presenting a nuanced examination of how digital finance can be leveraged to support and enhance environmental policies and practices.

This expanded literature review, enriched by diverse authoritative sources, offers a comprehensive exploration of the dynamic relationship between digitalization and green finance. It highlights the myriad opportunities presented by this convergence and addresses the multifaceted challenges that accompany it. The review underscores the imperative for ongoing research, multidisciplinary collaboration, and innovative thinking to fully exploit the potential of digital technologies in advancing the cause of sustainable finance, thereby paving the way for a future that is not only environmentally sustainable but also inclusive and equitable.

3. ISSUES, CONTROVERSIES, PROBLEMS

The digitalization of green finance marks a significant turning point in the financing and oversight of environmental initiatives. While the advantages of integrating digital tools into green finance are vast, offering unprecedented opportunities for scalability, efficiency, and global participation, this transformation is not without its complexities and challenges.

Deepening Cybersecurity Concerns: As the adoption of digital green finance platforms expands, so does their allure as targets for cyber threats. The integration of digital technologies, essential for broadening the scope of green finance, brings with it various vulnerabilities that could potentially be exploited by cybercriminals. As highlighted by Yannakogeorgos (2021), this digital expansion introduces a range of security challenges that must be addressed to safeguard the integrity of green finance initiatives. These threats are not limited to mere data breaches, which in themselves pose significant risks by exposing sensitive investor information, but extend to more sophisticated attacks that could undermine the very integrity of green investment platforms. The repercussions of such cybersecurity challenges are twofold: they jeopardize the financial assets at stake and, perhaps more critically, they can significantly erode trust in the digital green finance ecosystem. To counteract these risks, the implementation of stringent cybersecurity measures is imperative. This includes the adoption of encryption protocols, the enforcement of multi-factor authentication, and the conduct of regular security audits. Moreover, cultivating a culture of cybersecurity awareness among all stakeholders is essential for the proactive defense of digital green finance platforms against potential cyber threats.

Bridging the Digital Divide: The digitization of green finance also brings to light the issue of the digital divide, a significant barrier that could prevent wide sections of the population from accessing and participating in green finance initiatives due to limited access to digital tools and technologies. This divide not only restricts the inclusivity and reach of green finance programs but also raises concerns about equity and social justice in the transition to a sustainable financial ecosystem. To address this, there is a pressing need for digital green finance solutions that are universally accessible and user-friendly. Initiatives such as the development of mobile-based green finance applications and the implementation of community-driven digital literacy programs are vital steps towards bridging this divide. These efforts ensure that the advantages of digital green finance are shared more equitably, making the sustainable financial system inclusive and accessible to a broader demographic.

The Greenwashing Dilemma: A notable issue within digital green finance is the risk of greenwashing, where projects are inaccurately marketed as “green” or “sustainable” on digital platforms without substantial evidence or metrics to support such claims. This deceptive practice can mislead investors and the public, potentially discrediting the integrity of genuinely sustainable projects. Combatting greenwashing requires a multifaceted approach, including the establishment of stringent verification processes, the development of standardized sustainability metrics, and the promotion of transparency in the reporting and auditing of green projects.

Ensuring Data Integrity and Reliability: The reliance on digital tools for the monitoring and reporting of the environmental impact of funded projects introduces concerns regarding data integrity and reliability. Investors face the challenge of verifying the accuracy of data, which is crucial for maintaining trust in digital green finance platforms. Addressing this issue necessitates the implementation of robust data management practices, the adoption of transparent reporting standards, and the integration of third-party verification processes to ensure the authenticity and accuracy of environmental impact data.

Navigating the complexities of regulation presents a significant challenge in the rapidly evolving domain of digital green finance. As Pashang and Weber (2023) articulate, the swift advancement of digital tools in the sector often surpasses the development rate of corresponding regulatory frameworks, creating a notable regulatory void. This gap is problematic, as numerous digital green finance platforms find themselves operating within ambiguous regulatory boundaries, heightening the potential for misuse and fraudulent activities. To address these concerns, there's a pressing necessity to establish adaptive regulatory frameworks capable of keeping pace with the rapid technological progress in digital finance. Such frameworks should aim to delineate clear operational guidelines, ensure the accountability of platforms, safeguard investor interests, and simultaneously encourage the innovation and expansion of the green finance sector.

The deployment of AI and machine learning technologies in the assessment and oversight of green finance projects brings to the fore intricate ethical considerations. Vikas, Venegas, and Aiyer (2022) discuss how the application of AI algorithms in determining the sustainability of projects necessitates a nuanced approach to ensure evaluations are transparent and equitable. The potential for AI to inadvertently overlook valuable projects due to inflexible or erroneous criteria underscores the need for a thorough review of these algorithms. It is imperative to develop ethical guidelines tailored to the use of AI within the realm of green finance and to advocate for human involvement in the decision-making processes guided by AI, ensuring a balanced and fair assessment of all projects.

In conclusion, while the digital transformation of green finance presents a promising avenue for advancing environmental sustainability, it is accompanied by a series of issues, controversies, and challenges that necessitate careful consideration and strategic action. Addressing these challenges head-on is essential for ensuring that the digitalization of green finance achieves its full potential in contributing to a sustainable and equitable future.

Table 1. Issues, challenges, and problems in digital green finance

Issue/Challenge	Description
Digitalization and Greenwashing	Risk of projects being portrayed as "green" without substantial evidence, leading to misleading investors.
Data Integrity and Reliability	Concerns about the accuracy and authenticity of data reported by digital green finance platforms.
Regulatory Challenges	The rapid evolution of digital tools has outpaced the development of regulatory frameworks, leading to potential misuse.
Ethical Dilemmas in Digital Green Finance	Ethical concerns arise with the integration of AI in assessing and monitoring green projects.

4. CASE STUDIES OF DIGITAL GREEN FINANCE IN ACTION

Introduction to Real-World Applications: The integration of digital technologies into green finance has opened new avenues for funding environmentally sustainable projects, showcasing the tangible benefits and challenges of such endeavors. This expanded section delves deeper into diverse case studies, illustrating the innovative use of digital tools in green finance across various sectors and geographies. These examples highlight the practical applications of digital green finance and offer insights into overcoming obstacles and maximizing impact.

The proliferation of green crowdfunding platforms exemplifies the innovative use of digital technologies to foster sustainable investment. Dabbous, Barakat, and Tarhini (2024) highlight how one such platform has effectively harnessed digital marketing and social networking to bridge the gap between potential investors and a diverse array of sustainable projects, ranging from solar energy initiatives to local recycling programs. The platform's success is attributed to its engaging use of interactive tools and the incorporation of social proof elements like regular project updates and compelling success narratives. These features cultivate trust and stimulate community involvement, making sustainable investment more accessible to the broader public. By streamlining the investment process and offering transparent, quantifiable impact assessments, the platform has played a pivotal role in expanding the reach and appeal of green finance among the general populace.

Blockchain for Supply Chain Transparency: In the fashion industry, a groundbreaking project leveraged blockchain technology to enhance supply chain transparency by tracking the lifecycle of products from their origin to the retail shelf. Dorfleitner and Braun (2019) discuss how this initiative utilized blockchain to create a reliable and unalterable record of each product's environmental impact, ensuring adherence to sustainability standards. This approach effectively met the increasing consumer demand for sustainable products by providing clear visibility into the supply chain, thereby setting a model for transparency that other industries could emulate. This case study underscores the potential of blockchain technology as a tool for achieving greater transparency and sustainability in various sectors.

AI-Driven Environmental Impact Assessments: In the realm of infrastructure development, an AI-powered platform was developed to conduct comprehensive environmental impact assessments. This platform uses machine learning algorithms to analyze satellite imagery and environmental data, predicting the potential impacts of large-scale construction projects on local ecosystems. By providing developers and financiers with detailed risk assessments, the platform facilitates more informed decision-making, ensuring that only projects with minimal environmental disruption receive funding.

Big Data Analytics for Sustainable Investment Insights: The utilization of big data analytics by an investment firm specializing in sustainable investments represents a significant advancement in the field. Mondejar et al. (2021) describe how the firm developed a dynamic Environmental, Social, and Governance (ESG) scoring system that leverages real-time data to assess the sustainability performance of companies. This innovative approach, which incorporates data visualization and predictive analytics, simplifies the complexity of ESG data, empowering investors with the insights needed to make more informed and strategic decisions regarding sustainable investments. This advancement in data analytics has facilitated a deeper understanding and increased strategic investment in businesses that prioritize sustainability, marking a pivotal step towards achieving sustainable development goals.

Overcoming Challenges through Innovation: Each case study presented unique challenges, from ensuring data accuracy and privacy to managing stakeholder expectations and adapting to regulatory changes. Innovative solutions, such as employing advanced encryption for data security, developing user-friendly interfaces for diverse audiences, and engaging in policy advocacy for supportive regulatory environments, were key to overcoming these obstacles.

Learning from Diverse Implementations: These case studies reveal the importance of tailoring digital green finance solutions to specific contexts and needs. For instance, the success of the green crowdfunding platform was largely due to its community-centric approach, while the blockchain initiative in the fashion industry succeeded because of its focus on consumer transparency. These examples underscore the need for flexibility and customization in the application of digital tools in green finance.

Synthesizing Key Insights for Future Endeavors: The collective insights from these case studies emphasize the transformative potential of digitalization in green finance when coupled with strategic planning, stakeholder engagement, and continuous innovation. They highlight the critical role of transparency, user engagement, and data integrity in building trust and scaling up sustainable investments.

In wrapping up, the detailed exploration of these case studies serves as a rich source of inspiration and guidance for future digital green finance initiatives. They illustrate not only the power of digital technologies to facilitate sustainable development but also the importance of a holistic approach that considers technological, social, and environmental factors. As the field of digital green finance continues to evolve, these real-world examples provide valuable lessons on leveraging technology to achieve greater environmental sustainability and social impact.

Table 2. Impactful implementations of digital green finance: A global perspective

Case Study	Sector	Digital Tool Used	Key Achievements	Challenges Overcome	Insights Gained
Green Crowdfunding Platform	Renewable Energy & Sustainability	Crowdfunding Platform	Democratized investment in green projects, broadened public participation	Data privacy, user engagement	Importance of community-centric approaches, interactive tools for trust-building
Blockchain in Fashion Industry	Fashion & Retail	Blockchain Technology	Enhanced supply chain transparency, ensured sustainability compliance	Supply chain complexity, stakeholder skepticism	Need for verifiable sustainability standards, consumer demand for transparency
AI in Environmental Impact Assessments	Infrastructure & Development	Artificial Intelligence	Detailed risk assessments for projects, minimized environmental disruption	Data accuracy, regulatory adaptation	Value of predictive analytics in environmental conservation, strategic decision-making
Big Data in Sustainable Investments	Finance & Investment	Big Data Analytics	Developed dynamic ESG scoring system, facilitated strategic sustainable investments	Managing complex ESG data, real-time data analysis	Role of data visualization and predictive analytics in simplifying ESG investment decisions

5. INNOVATIVE TECHNOLOGIES SHAPING THE FUTURE OF GREEN FINANCE

Introduction to Technological Frontiers in Green Finance: The realm of green finance is undergoing a profound transformation, propelled by the advent of groundbreaking technologies. This expanded section delves into the myriad of innovative technologies that are set to redefine green finance, enhancing its effectiveness in promoting environmental sustainability. From the nuanced applications of the Internet of Things (IoT) to the vast potential of quantum computing, these technologies herald a new era for green finance, offering novel approaches to funding, monitoring, and evaluating sustainable projects.

The Internet of Things (IoT) for Comprehensive Environmental Monitoring: The IoT's expansive network of sensors and devices offers unparalleled opportunities for real-time monitoring of environmental parameters, providing a granular view of the impact of green finance projects. Deployed across diverse ecosystems, IoT devices can track a wide array of environmental indicators, from forest regeneration rates to the carbon sequestration capabilities of new green projects. This level of detailed monitoring not only ensures the accountability of investments but also allows for adaptive management of projects based on real-time data, significantly enhancing the precision and impact of green finance initiatives.

Advancements in Distributed Ledger Technologies: The exploration of DLTs extends beyond the conventional realm of blockchain, venturing into innovative alternatives like Directed Acyclic Graphs (DAGs) and Holochain, which hold the potential to revolutionize transactional mechanisms within green finance. Schulz, Gstrein, and Zwitter (2020) delve into how these advanced DLTs offer scalable and energy-efficient solutions for transaction recording, addressing some of the scalability and environmental challenges inherent in traditional blockchain systems. The adoption of these novel DLTs could pave the way for more sustainable and effective infrastructures for green finance transactions, enhancing both trust and adoption rates in these emerging systems.

Machine Learning and Predictive Analytics in Green Finance: The utilization of machine learning in green finance transcends traditional risk assessment, heralding a new era of possibilities in detecting environmental trends, refining green investment strategies, and forecasting the sustainability of initiatives. Yigitcanlar, Mehmood, and Corchado (2021) emphasize how machine learning, through the analysis of extensive datasets, can reveal underlying patterns and provide valuable insights. This empowers more informed and strategic decision-making within the realm of green finance, potentially fostering the creation of investment strategies that encompass a wider array of environmental and social considerations. Such advancements in predictive analytics are steering green finance towards outcomes that are not only more impactful but also inherently sustainable.

Immersive Technologies for Stakeholder Engagement: VR and AR technologies are poised to revolutionize stakeholder engagement in green finance by providing immersive and interactive experiences. These technologies can bring distant environmental projects to life for investors and the public, fostering a deeper emotional connection and understanding of the importance of sustainable investments. By visualizing the direct impact of their investments in virtual environments, stakeholders can gain a more profound appreciation for the value of green finance, potentially driving increased interest and investment in sustainable projects.

Harnessing Quantum Computing for Complex Environmental Simulations: The extraordinary computational power of quantum computing could enable the simulation of complex environmental systems and financial models with unprecedented accuracy and speed. This capability could be instrumental in assessing the viability and environmental impact of large-scale green finance projects, offering insights that could reshape investment strategies and policy decisions. The exploration of quantum computing in green finance could unlock new dimensions of understanding and managing the intricate interplay between financial investments and environmental sustainability.

Addressing Ethical and Social Considerations: The incorporation of cutting-edge technologies into the sphere of green finance brings to light significant ethical and social issues that necessitate careful consideration. Tuyon, Onyia, Ahmi, and Huang (2023) highlight the critical need to ensure that these technologies are accessible to all segments of society, to mitigate biases in AI algorithms, and to uphold stringent standards of privacy and data protection. The development of future research and policy should be directed towards establishing comprehensive ethical guidelines and frameworks that oversee the application of these technologies within green finance. Such measures are essential to ensure that these innovations not only align with but actively promote societal well-being and the broader objectives of environmental sustainability.

Fostering Interdisciplinary Innovation for Sustainable Solutions: The convergence of insights from various disciplines can catalyze the development of comprehensive and innovative solutions in green finance. By fostering collaboration between environmental scientists, technologists, economists, and social scientists, the green finance sector can develop holistic approaches that not only meet environmental targets but also resonate with diverse stakeholders. This interdisciplinary synergy is crucial for designing financial products and services that are not only environmentally sustainable but also socially inclusive and economically viable.

Regulatory Adaptation to Technological Innovation: As green finance continues to evolve with technological advancements, the regulatory landscape must also adapt to ensure these technologies are used responsibly and effectively. Future research should explore the development of adaptive regulatory frameworks that can keep pace with technological innovation, ensuring that green finance remains a safe, transparent, and effective tool for promoting environmental sustainability.

Envisioning the Future with Technology-Driven Green Finance: The integration of innovative technologies into green finance presents a promising horizon filled with opportunities to enhance the sector's impact on global sustainability efforts. By embracing these technologies and addressing the associated challenges, the green finance sector can pave the way for a future where financial investments are seamlessly aligned with environmental conservation and sustainability goals. This future vision of green finance, powered by technological innovation, holds the potential to drive significant positive change, but it requires careful stewardship, ethical considerations, and collaborative efforts across sectors to fully realize its transformative impact.

Table 3. Emerging technologies revolutionizing green finance

Technology	Application in Green Finance	Potential Benefits	Key Challenges	Future Research Directions
Internet of Things (IoT)	Real-time environmental monitoring and project impact assessment	Enhanced transparency and accountability, adaptive project management	Data privacy, integration with existing systems	Developing secure IoT frameworks for scalable environmental monitoring
Distributed Ledger Technologies (DLTs)	Transactional transparency and efficiency in green finance operations	Scalable and energy-efficient transaction management, enhanced trust	Technological complexity, regulatory acceptance	Exploring DLT alternatives to blockchain for green finance
Machine Learning	Predictive analytics for environmental trends and green investment optimization	Informed decision-making, strategic investment planning	Bias in algorithms, interpretability of models	Enhancing predictive models for environmental and financial data analysis
Virtual and Augmented Reality (VR/AR)	Stakeholder engagement through immersive experiences	Increased investor engagement, improved understanding of project impacts	High development costs, technological accessibility	Creating accessible VR/AR platforms for diverse stakeholder education
Quantum Computing	Complex environmental simulations and financial modeling	Unprecedented computational power, enhanced risk assessment	Technological maturity, ethical considerations	Investigating quantum algorithms for environmental risk modeling
Ethical and Social Considerations	Framework development for responsible technology use	Ensuring equitable access, preventing bias, maintaining data security	Ethical governance, social equity	Developing guidelines for ethical AI use in green finance
Interdisciplinary Innovation	Integration of environmental science, economics, and digital technology insights	Holistic and innovative green finance solutions, broader impact	Cross-disciplinary collaboration, knowledge sharing	Fostering interdisciplinary research initiatives in green finance
Regulatory Adaptation	Adaptive frameworks for emerging technology governance	Safe and effective use of technologies, investor protection	Keeping pace with rapid technological advancements	Crafting dynamic regulatory standards for technology-driven green finance

6. SOLUTIONS AND RECOMMENDATIONS

The integration of digital technologies into the realm of green finance heralds a promising avenue for addressing environmental challenges more effectively. However, this fusion also introduces a spectrum of challenges that necessitate thoughtful solutions and strategic approaches. Drawing from a blend of personal insights and industry best practices, I propose comprehensive solutions to overcome these hurdles and maximize the potential of green finance in the digital era.

Developing Dynamic Regulatory Frameworks: The inherently fluid nature of digital green finance calls for regulatory frameworks that are both nimble and forward-thinking. Traditional regulatory models often fall short in accommodating the novel challenges and opportunities that digital technologies bring to green finance. For example, the decentralized characteristic of blockchain technology, which is crucial for enhancing transparency in green finance transactions, presents unique regulatory challenges in terms of jurisdiction and compliance. To navigate these complexities, it is essential for policymakers and regulatory bodies to engage in ongoing dialogues with technology experts and financial institutions. Such collaborative efforts can pave the way for the creation of regulatory frameworks that protect investor interests and uphold market integrity and encourage innovation and growth within the green finance sector.

Fostering Synergy Between Technology and Regulation: The swift pace of advancements in technologies such as AI, blockchain, and big data analytics often outpaces the regulatory framework's ability to adapt. This discrepancy can lead to a regulatory void that may impede the progress and efficacy of digital green finance initiatives. Bridging this gap is crucial, and one effective approach is the establishment of regulatory sandboxes. These sandboxes provide a controlled environment where emerging technologies can be tested and evaluated under regulatory oversight. This setup allows for the real-time assessment of the impact of digital technologies on green finance, enabling regulators to devise regulations that are both informed and adaptable. Such a proactive approach ensures that regulatory frameworks evolve in tandem with technological advancements, fostering a conducive environment for innovation and the development of new financial products and services that bolster environmental sustainability.

Enhancing Digital Literacy Among Stakeholders: The disparity in digital literacy levels among stakeholders presents a notable challenge to the full integration of digital tools within green finance. Mondejar et al. (2021) stress the importance of bridging this gap through the establishment of extensive training programs and interactive workshops aimed at clarifying the functionalities of digital technologies and improving user skills. By enhancing the accessibility and ease of use of digital tools, stakeholders are empowered to more actively participate in green finance initiatives, thus expanding the scope of investment in projects that contribute to sustainability.

Strengthening Data Security Measures: In today's digital landscape, ensuring the security of sensitive information is crucial, particularly within the realm of green finance, where the details of investors and the specifics of financial transactions are at stake. Devidze (2022) underscores the necessity of prioritizing cybersecurity initiatives, including conducting regular system audits, implementing robust encryption protocols, and adopting multi-factor authentication techniques, to protect digital green finance platforms from potential cyber threats. Additionally, fostering a cybersecurity-aware culture among all stakeholders can significantly strengthen the security framework of digital green finance systems, safeguarding them against potential vulnerabilities.

Promoting Transparency and Accountability: Trust is the cornerstone of any financial system, and in the realm of digital green finance, this trust is predicated on transparency and accountability. Utilizing digital platforms to provide real-time updates on project progress and financial transactions can significantly enhance stakeholder confidence. Additionally, the adoption of smart contracts, which automatically execute transactions based on predefined criteria, can ensure that financial commitments are fulfilled transparently and efficiently.

Encouraging Collaborative Innovation: The challenges inherent in green finance are multifaceted and require collaborative solutions. Establishing platforms for dialogue and innovation among technology developers, financial experts, and environmental scientists can lead to the development of bespoke solutions tailored to the unique needs of green finance. This collaborative approach can spur the creation of innovative financial products and services that not only meet environmental objectives but also offer viable investment opportunities.

Diversifying the Portfolio of Green Projects: Broadening the range of projects eligible for green finance is essential to captivate a more diverse group of investors. Altunina and Alieva (2021) emphasize the importance of extending green finance initiatives beyond the conventional focus on renewable energy to include ventures in sustainable agriculture, eco-friendly transportation, and effective waste management. This expansion not only caters to a wider array of investor preferences but also fosters a more holistic approach to environmental sustainability, encompassing various sectors and disciplines.

Simplifying the Investment Process: The complexity of investment processes can often deter potential investors. Streamlining these processes through user-friendly digital platforms, clear investment guidelines, and readily available support can enhance the investor experience, making it easier for individuals and institutions to participate in green finance.

Raising Awareness About Green Finance: Despite its growing importance, green finance is still a relatively new concept to many potential investors. Launching educational campaigns that highlight the environmental and financial benefits of green investments can increase awareness and participation. Sharing success stories and case studies can also illustrate the tangible impacts of green finance, further encouraging investment in sustainable projects.

Offering Incentives for Green Investments: Incentives can play a pivotal role in motivating investors to engage with green finance. Fiscal incentives such as tax breaks or grants for investors in green projects, along with competitive interest rates for green investments, can make sustainable investing more attractive.

Prioritizing Continuous Innovation: In the ever-evolving landscape of green finance, staying at the forefront of technological and financial innovations is key. Allocating resources for research and development, exploring emerging technologies, and fostering partnerships for innovation can ensure that green finance continues to adapt and thrive in the digital age.

In conclusion, while integrating digital tools into green finance presents certain challenges, these obstacles are surmountable with strategic planning, collaboration, and innovation. The recommendations provided here aim to serve as a practical guide for stakeholders in navigating the complexities of digital green finance, ultimately unlocking its full potential to contribute to a sustainable and prosperous future.

Table 4. Potential solutions and recommendations for digital green finance

Challenges	My Suggestions
Boosting Digital Proficiency	Organize hands-on training and interactive sessions. Demystify digital tools to make them more approachable.
Fortifying Data Protection	Prioritize cybersecurity. Adopt technologies like blockchain and ensure regular system checks and timely updates.
Refining Regulatory Approaches	Foster open dialogues between tech experts, financial leaders, and policymakers for informed and flexible regulations.
Championing Openness and Responsibility	Use digital platforms for real-time project updates. Implement smart contracts to ensure commitments are met.
Cultivating Team Efforts	Create brainstorming platforms for tailored solutions for tech innovators, financial experts, and environmentalists.
Broadening Green Initiatives	Diversify the green project portfolio. Explore ventures in sustainable farming, eco-transport, and waste reduction.
Demystifying Investment Steps	Streamline processes using intuitive digital platforms. Offer clear guidelines and 24/7 online assistance.
Spreading the Word	Launch campaigns spotlighting the dual benefits of green investments. Share real-world success stories.
Rolling Out Attractive Offers	Introduce fiscal incentives like tax reductions or grants. Offer competitive interest rates for green investments.
Prioritizing Innovation	Allocate resources for innovation. Explore emerging tech and its potential synergies with green finance.

7. FUTURE RESEARCH DIRECTIONS

The fusion of digital technologies with green finance is carving out an exciting frontier in the quest for sustainable financial solutions. As environmental concerns become increasingly urgent, the role of digital tools in enhancing the efficacy and reach of green finance becomes ever more critical. This section aims to unfold the emerging trends within this domain, shedding light on the promising future directions that digital green finance might take.

Expanding the Role of AI in Green Finance: The integration of Artificial Intelligence (AI), alongside blockchain and big data analytics, stands at the forefront of innovation within green finance, holding the promise to drastically elevate the impact and efficiency of sustainable investments. AI's sophisticated predictive capabilities are set to transform the evaluation and monitoring processes of green projects, providing deeper insights into their environmental contributions and long-term sustainability. AI algorithms, with their ability to sift through and analyze extensive datasets, could predict project outcomes, evaluate risks, and tailor investment portfolios to favor more eco-friendly options. This advancement is expected to not only refine decision-making processes but also ensure that financial investments are more closely aligned with overarching sustainability goals.

Blockchain and Big Data as Catalysts for Transparency: Blockchain technology offers an unparalleled level of transparency and security in the transactions within green finance. By documenting these transactions on a decentralized ledger, blockchain technology guarantees the traceability and verifiability of financial flows directed towards green projects, making it an essential tool in combating greenwashing. This is achieved by maintaining a transparent record of fund allocation and utilization within projects claiming sustainability. In parallel, big data analytics stands to harness the extensive environmental and financial data generated, providing critical insights into market trends, investor behaviors, and the tangible environmental impacts of financial activities. The synergy of these technologies promises to foster a more robust, transparent, and efficient green finance ecosystem, propelling the sector towards achieving more significant and accountable sustainable investments.

Decentralized Finance (DeFi) and Its Potential in Green Finance: The advent of blockchain technology has catalyzed the growth of decentralized finance (DeFi) platforms, which are beginning to play a pivotal role in green finance. Future research should delve into how DeFi can be leveraged to democratize access to green finance, enabling a wider array of investors to engage in and support sustainable projects. This exploration could reveal how DeFi platforms can lower entry barriers to investment in green projects, potentially democratizing the financial landscape of environmental sustainability.

Quantum Computing's Emerging Role in Green Finance: With its extraordinary computational power, quantum computing has the potential to revolutionize aspects of green finance such as risk assessment, data analysis, and predictive modeling. Future investigations into quantum computing's applications within green finance could uncover new methodologies for evaluating and managing the complexities of sustainable investments, offering a leap in accuracy and efficiency in decision-making processes within the sector.

Navigating the Ethical Terrain of AI in Decision-Making: As AI becomes increasingly integrated into the decision-making frameworks of green finance, the ethical dimensions of its application come to the fore. There is a pressing need for research into the development of ethical frameworks that ensure decisions driven by AI in green finance are transparent, fair, and aligned with sustainability objectives. Such research could provide guidelines for the responsible use of AI, ensuring that it contributes positively to the goals of green finance without compromising ethical standards.

Interdisciplinary Research in Green Finance: The intersection of environmental science, finance, and digital technology presents a fertile ground for interdisciplinary research. Future studies could explore how insights from diverse fields such as ecology, behavioral economics, and data science can be amalgamated into green finance, potentially unveiling novel approaches and solutions to the financing of environmental sustainability.

Towards Global Regulatory Alignment: As digital green finance platforms increasingly operate on a global scale, the need for cohesive regulatory frameworks becomes evident. Future research should aim at establishing international standards and best practices that guide the ethical and responsible use of digital tools in green finance, ensuring a harmonized approach to regulation that supports the global nature of environmental challenges and solutions.

The Influence of Digital Narratives on Green Investments: In an era dominated by social media and digital storytelling, the impact of digital narratives on green investment decisions warrants thorough exploration. Understanding how influencers, digital campaigns, and online communities shape investor perceptions and behaviors could offer valuable insights into the mechanisms driving investment in green projects, highlighting the power of narrative in shaping the future of green finance.

Addressing Scalability Challenges in Digital Green Finance Platforms: As digital green finance platforms continue to grow, they face scalability challenges that encompass data management, cybersecurity, and user experience. Future research should focus on developing scalable, secure, and user-friendly solutions that can accommodate the expanding scope of digital green finance, ensuring that these platforms can sustain their growth without compromising security or efficiency.

Table 5. Future research directions

Research Area	Description	Potential Impact
Decentralized Finance (DeFi)	Exploring the role of blockchain in democratizing access to green finance.	Broadening the investor base for green projects.
Integration of Quantum Computing	Harnessing quantum computational capabilities for risk assessment and predictive modeling.	Enhanced accuracy and efficiency in decision-making.
Ethical Implications of AI	Creating frameworks for transparent and unbiased AI-driven decisions in green finance.	Ensuring ethical and responsible AI applications in finance.

In summary, the trajectory of digital green finance is laden with opportunities that, if navigated wisely, could significantly reshape the financial landscape to support a more sustainable and equitable future. The path forward will require ongoing research, innovation, and cross-sector collaboration to harness the full potential of digital technologies in advancing the goals of green finance.

8. CONCLUSION

The convergence of digitalization with green finance marks a pivotal shift towards achieving global environmental sustainability goals. This chapter has delved into how the advent of digital technologies has revolutionized the green finance sector, significantly broadening its scope, enhancing its operational efficiency, and magnifying its impact on sustainable projects. Digitalization has democratized the accessibility of green finance, enabling diverse stakeholders to engage in sustainable projects through platforms like crowdfunding, and has brought about a new level of transparency and accountability through the adoption of advanced data analytics and blockchain technologies.

Yet, this transformative journey is accompanied by a spectrum of challenges that necessitate careful navigation. Issues such as data security breaches, the complexities of establishing comprehensive regulatory frameworks, and the ethical considerations surrounding the deployment of technologies like AI in financial decision-making processes highlight the intricate balance required in leveraging digitalization for green finance. The literature explored throughout this chapter, encompassing a wide array of authoritative sources, offers a holistic view of the digital green finance landscape, shedding light on both the promising opportunities it presents and the hurdles that lie in its path.

The solutions and strategic recommendations put forth in this chapter underscore the critical need for ongoing innovation, fostering collaborative ecosystems, and developing flexible regulatory frameworks that can adapt to the rapid pace of technological advancements. The future research directions proposed herein, ranging from the exploration of decentralized finance (DeFi) platforms to the in-depth analysis of AI's ethical implications in financial contexts, set forth a comprehensive agenda for advancing the field of digital green finance.

As this chapter navigates the intricate interplay between finance and technology, it becomes increasingly important to remain agile, foresee emerging challenges, and craft proactive strategies to address them. The roadmap for future research provided in this chapter aims to guide academics, industry practitioners, and policymakers through the evolving terrain of digital green finance, encouraging a concerted effort to push the boundaries of what is possible in this domain.

In sum, the synergy between digitalization and green finance offers a beacon of hope for a more sustainable and equitable future. Despite the obstacles that may arise, the collective commitment to informed decision-making, collaborative innovation, and the pursuit of adaptable regulatory measures can unlock the full potential of this powerful convergence. This chapter not only celebrates the transformative impact of digital tools on green finance but also calls upon all stakeholders to embrace their shared responsibility in harnessing these advancements for the betterment of our planet and future generations.

REFERENCES

Altunina, V. V., & Alieva, I. A. (2021). Current trends in the development of a green finance system: Methodology and practice. *Baltic Region, 13*(2), 64-89.

Dabbous, A., Barakat, K. A., & Tarhini, A. (2024). Digitalization, crowdfunding, eco-innovation and financial development for sustainability transitions and sustainable competitiveness: Insights from complexity theory. *Journal of Innovation & Knowledge*, *9*(1), 100460. doi:10.1016/j.jik.2023.100460

Devidze, N. (2022). Current State of Green Digital Financing and the Associated Challenges. In Green Digital Finance and Sustainable Development Goals (pp. 29-50). Singapore: Springer Nature Singapore. doi:10.1007/978-981-19-2662-4_2

Dorfleitner, G., & Braun, D. (2019). Fintech, digitalization and blockchain: possible applications for green finance. *The rise of green finance in Europe: opportunities and challenges for issuers, investors and marketplaces*, 207-237.

Han, Y., Li, Y., & Wang, Q. (2023). Digital finance, environmental regulation, and green development efficiency of China. *Frontiers in Environmental Science*, *11*, 1131058. doi:10.3389/fenvs.2023.1131058

Lei, X., Shen, Z. Y., Štreimikienė, D., Baležentis, T., Wang, G., & Mu, Y. (2024). Digitalization and sustainable development: Evidence from OECD countries. *Applied Energy, 357*, 122480. doi:10.1016/j.apenergy.2023.122480

Macchiavello, E., & Siri, M. (2022). Sustainable finance and fintech: Can technology contribute to achieving environmental goals? A preliminary assessment of 'green fintech'and 'sustainable digital finance'. *European Company and Financial Law Review, 19*(1), 128–174. doi:10.1515/ecfr-2022-0005

Mondejar, M. E., Avtar, R., Diaz, H. L. B., Dubey, R. K., Esteban, J., Gómez-Morales, A., Hallam, B., Mbungu, N. T., Okolo, C. C., Prasad, K. A., She, Q., & Garcia-Segura, S. (2021). Digitalization to achieve sustainable development goals: Steps towards a Smart Green Planet. [Reference Link]. *The Science of the Total Environment, 794*, 148539. doi:10.1016/j.scitotenv.2021.148539 PMID:34323742

Moşteanu, N. R., Faccia, A., & Cavaliere, L. P. L. (2020, August). Digitalization and green economy-changes of business perspectives. In *Proceedings of the 2020 4th International Conference on Cloud and Big Data Computing* (pp. 108-112). 10.1145/3416921.3416929

Otto, M., & Thornton, J. (2023). The Role Of Digital Finance And Technological Innovation In The Growth Of The Green Economy. *Qo 'qon universiteti xabarnomasi, 7*, 19-22.

Pashang, S., & Weber, O. (2023). AI for Sustainable Finance: Governance Mechanisms for Institutional and Societal Approaches. In *The Ethics of Artificial Intelligence for the Sustainable Development Goals* (pp. 203–229). Springer International Publishing. doi:10.1007/978-3-031-21147-8_12

Puschmann, T., & Leifer, L. (2020). *Sustainable Digital Finance: The Role of FinTech*. InsurTech & Blockchain for Shaping the World for the Better.

Ryszawska, B. (2018). Sustainable finance: Paradigm shift. In *Finance and Sustainability: Proceedings from the Finance and Sustainability Conference, Wroclaw 2017* (pp. 219-231). Springer International Publishing.

Schulz, K. A., Gstrein, O. J., & Zwitter, A. J. (2020). Exploring the governance and implementation of sustainable development initiatives through blockchain technology. *Futures, 122*, 102611. doi:10.1016/j.futures.2020.102611

Taghizadeh-Hesary, F., & Hyun, S. (Eds.). (2022). *Green Digital Finance and Sustainable Development Goals*. Springer Nature. doi:10.1007/978-981-19-2662-4

Tuyon, J., Onyia, O. P., Ahmi, A., & Huang, C. H. (2023). Sustainable financial services: Reflection and future perspectives. *Journal of Financial Services Marketing*, *28*(4), 664–690. doi:10.1057/s41264-022-00187-4

Vikas, N., Venegas, P., & Aiyer, S. (2022). Role of Banks and Other Financial Institutions in Enhancing Green Digital Finance. In *Green Digital Finance and Sustainable Development Goals* (pp. 329–352). Springer Nature Singapore. doi:10.1007/978-981-19-2662-4_16

Yan, Y., Ibrahim, R. L., Al-Faryan, M. A. S., & Oke, D. M. (2023). Embracing Eco-Digitalization and Green Finance Policies for Sustainable Environment: Do the Engagements of Multinational Corporations Make or Mar the Target for Selected MENA Countries? *Sustainability (Basel)*, *15*(15), 12046. doi:10.3390/su151512046

Yang, C., & Masron, T. A. (2022). Impact of digital finance on energy efficiency in the context of green sustainable development. *Sustainability (Basel)*, *14*(18), 11250. doi:10.3390/su141811250

Yannakogeorgos, P. (2021). Cyber Competition and Global Stability. In C. Ankersen & W. P. S. Sidhu (Eds.), *The Future of Global Affairs*. Palgrave Macmillan. doi:10.1007/978-3-030-56470-4_10

Yigitcanlar, T., Mehmood, R., & Corchado, J. M. (2021). Green artificial intelligence: Towards an efficient, sustainable and equitable technology for smart cities and futures. *Sustainability (Basel)*, *13*(16), 8952. doi:10.3390/su13168952

Zhou, G., Zhu, J., & Luo, S. (2022). The impact of fintech innovation on green growth in China: Mediating effect of green finance. *Ecological Economics*, *193*, 107308. doi:10.1016/j.ecolecon.2021.107308

Zhou, Y. (2022). The application trend of digital finance and technological innovation in the development of green economy. *Journal of Environmental and Public Health*, *2022*, 2022. doi:10.1155/2022/1064558 PMID:35865872

Chapter 9
Digitalization of Tax Administration and Tax Avoidance:
Evidence on Tax Reform Dynamics in Morocco

Rida Belahouaoui
https://orcid.org/0000-0003-1625-6732
Cadi Ayyad University, Morocco

El Houssain Attak
Cadi Ayyad University, Morocco

ABSTRACT

This chapter delves into the Moroccan tax system's challenges, underscored by a significant tax shortfall as reported by the IMF. At its core, the study explores the nexus between digitalization in tax administration and taxpayer behavior, particularly focusing on tax avoidance. Conducted within the Moroccan reform context, the research utilizes qualitative insights from interviews with 30 tax administrators. The findings highlight that while digitalization and service facilitation promote tax compliance, a lack of trust and transparency can exacerbate tax avoidance. The study emphasizes the critical need for comprehensive tax reform in Morocco, targeting fairness and a robust relationship between tax authorities and taxpayers. Such reforms are essential to foster a business-friendly environment conducive to investment. This research contributes to the understanding of digital governance's role in tax administration and its potential to influence taxpayer behavior.

DOI: 10.4018/979-8-3693-1678-8.ch009

INTRODUCTION

Morocco has embarked on a transformative journey since the 1980s, with a concerted effort to modernize its tax administration. This initiative is not only a response to the urgent need for revenue enhancement but also aligns with global best practices in governance. At the forefront of this endeavor is the enactment of framework law 69-19 on tax reform (Kingdom of Morocco, 2021), a comprehensive legislation set to unfold progressively until 2026. Rooted in the objectives of modernization, digitalization, and measures against tax avoidance, this legislation stands as a testament to Morocco's commitment to merging digital progress with robust fiscal discipline.

However, despite these proactive measures, Morocco faces a significant tax gap, estimated at approximately 12% of the GDP by the IMF in 2023 (IMF, 2023). The crux of this challenge lies in the prevalence of tax avoidance, a legal practice that minimizes tax liability and can critically impact a nation's fiscal system. Even with Morocco's strides in digitizing tax administration to address this gap, the intricate relationship between digitization and tax avoidance persists. While digitization promises enhanced efficiency, transparency, and reduced errors in tax collection, it may also unveil pre-existing avoidance schemes that were previously concealed in manual systems.

Recent scholarly contributions by Bassey et al. (2022) and Canares (2016) have underscored the global trend of digitization in tax administrations. While Canares (2016) highlights the positive impact of information and communication technologies (ICT) on local governance and revenue generation in the Philippines, Bassey et al. (2022) present a conceptual framework emphasizing efficiency gains and increased job motivation reported by tax authorities. Nevertheless, a nuanced perspective, as advocated by Bellon et al. (2022), is essential, particularly when assessing the costs and benefits of digital tax services.

Despite the wealth of literature on global digitization trends, a noticeable gap exists in studies directly addressing the impact of tax administration digitalization on tax avoidance within the unique socio-economic and administrative dynamics of Morocco. This research lacuna is particularly significant, offering an opportunity for distinct insights into the interplay between digital reforms and tax behaviors in the Moroccan context. Furthermore, a dearth of qualitative research methodologies prevails in the existing literature, with a predominant reliance on quantitative analyses.

The absence of qualitative research not only signifies untapped experiential data from stakeholders but also highlights the opportunity for a comprehensive understanding of the human and organizational aspects influencing the success or limitations of digital transformations. Consequently, the objective of this study is twofold: firstly, to provide a granular analysis of the degree to which the Moroccan tax administration has been digitized, encompassing technological tools, processes, and digital penetration in both urban and rural tax collection centers. Secondly, the study aims to correlate this level of digitization with patterns of tax avoidance in Morocco, discerning whether digital reforms have had a deterring impact on aggressive tax avoidance behaviors or whether other factors mask the potential benefits of digitization.

The central research question is formulated as follows: How does the digitalization of tax administration impact tax avoidance in Morocco, considering the tax reform dynamics?

This research aims to contribute valuable insights not only to the Moroccan context but also to the broader scholarly discourse on the intricate dynamics between digital governance and tax behaviors. The chapter structure follows a standard academic format, commencing with a literature review that addresses tax avoidance, trust in tax authorities, and the impact of digitalization on tax administration. Subsequently, the methodological approach, encompassing data collection and analysis, is outlined, leading to a conclusion that discusses the results and their implications for ongoing tax reform efforts in Morocco.

LITERATURE REVIEW

This section systematically delves into Tax Avoidance, Trust in tax authorities, Digitalization of tax administration, and the intricate Interplay of tax administration digitalization, trust, and tax avoidance. Through this review, it synthesizes insights from current research, identifies gaps in the literature, and strategically shapes the research questions to discuss Morocco's ongoing digital transformation in tax administration.

Tax Avoidance

In the literature, definitions and determinants of tax avoidance have primarily been based on an economic perspective of taxpayer behavior. This follows the standard model of tax compliance by Allingham & Sandmo (1972), In terms of tax avoidance, this model assumes that tax payments are made solely because of economic deterrence. Milliron (1985) define tax avoidance behavior as the evasion of income reporting and tax liabilities, and the avoidance of tax payments to authorities, contrary to relevant tax laws, regulations, and ordinances. Roth (1989) emphasize that avoidance means evading tax obligations inaccurately and in contravention of the legal framework. Slemrod & Yitzhaki (2002) delve into the integration of tax avoidance and evasion in taxation models, examining their impact on equity, efficiency, and tax policy. They analyze both empirical data and theoretical models, suggesting optimal tax systems that account for administrative costs and behavioral responses. Their work expands the marginal efficiency cost concept to encompass avoidance and evasion strategies. The study of tax avoidance has thus evolved over the past fifty years, and contributions from diverse scientific disciplines such as psychology, sociology, and economics have led to significant advancements in this field (Kirchler, 2007). Recent theoretical developments in the field of tax avoidance consider social variables to be just as important to study as deterrence variables, focusing on the broader influences on tax avoidance behavior (Kirchler et al., 2008).

Recent studies in tax avoidance offer diverse insights into this complex area. Agusti & Rahman (2023) highlight the importance of tax literacy, trust, and power in shaping tax attitudes among Indonesian SMEs, revealing that trust and authority mediate the relationship between tax literacy and voluntary compliance. Dyreng et al. (2022) explore corporate tax avoidance, finding that firms with shareholders bearing less of the corporate tax burden engage in less avoidance, influenced by factors like labor supply elasticity and the productivity of capital. McClure (2023) develops a structural model to quantify the costs of tax avoidance, revealing significant nontax costs and explaining why firms might underutilize tax avoidance strategies. Hutchens et al. (2023) use latent class mixture models to examine the relationship between tax avoidance and firm risk, finding varied associations across different firm characteristics. Lastly, Mashuri (2023) investigates the impact of institutional ownership and corporate social responsibility on tax avoidance in Indonesian mining companies, with audit quality as a moderating factor, revealing complex relationships between these variables and tax avoidance behavior.

Trust in Tax Authorities

The works of Allingham & Sandmo (1972) and Feld & Frey (2007) have shown that trust in tax authorities encompasses a range of measures related to fair procedures among different taxpayer categories. This is based on the perception of fiscal equity, particularly procedural fairness, which leads to taxpayers' trust in the tax administration. Kirchler et al. (2008) propose a framework for tax compliance in which the power of tax authorities and trust in tax authorities are relevant dimensions for understanding both voluntary and enforced compliance of taxpayers. Kogler et al. (2023) examined the slippery slope framework, finding that trust in and power of tax authorities significantly reduce the informal economy and corruption, underscoring their role in promoting tax compliance. Cahyonowati et al. (2023) also tackled tax compliance, emphasizing the importance of trust and social norms, but noted that economic factors did not significantly influence tax compliance, suggesting that psychological factors might play a more substantial role than previously considered. On a related note, Ayoola et al. (2023) studied the Nigerian tax system and discovered that both the tax administration and the taxpayers' trust in it notably enhance compliance, with trust serving as a positive moderator. Similarly, Prinz (2023) investigated cultural factors, revealing that in "tight" societies, trust is paramount for tax compliance, while in "loose" societies, authority is more influential. This body of research collectively illustrates the complex interplay of trust, power, and cultural contexts in shaping tax compliance behavior.

Digitalization of Tax Administration

Tax administrations are the driving force of any economy and are essential to the success of the government's digital program. In the context of the broader digital transformation of government, the main mission of tax administration has also evolved. As noted by Vasconcellos & Rua (2005), tax authorities no longer see themselves merely as tax collectors, but as providers of a range of tax services, from providing information to assisting taxpayers and offering tax education. Digital taxation is thus a system that fits an ecosystem approach, as it arguably relies heavily on the engagement of actors external to the tax authorities for success. This is due to the wide impact that taxation can have on the economy, ranging from changing taxpayer behavior to facilitating business, and affecting inequalities, poverty, and fiscal policy (Okafor, 2022; Petutschnig, 2017). Therefore, aligned with Canares (2016), the argument posits that the ecosystem of digital taxation should recognize specific elements. These encompass the role of stakeholders, their motivations, and behaviors in relations with the tax administration and interactions among themselves. Additionally, it underscores the significance of context, particularly in the facilitation and encouragement of digital taxation within a local environment. The availability and accessibility of e-taxation services, covering both software and hardware aspects, are crucial considerations. Finally, an exploration of the outcomes of applying e-taxation evaluates its expected costs and benefits.

Katua (2019) found that digitizing tax administration positively impacts SME tax avoidance behaviors in Nairobi by streamlining processes and improving data reliability, which eases their tax obligations and reduces non-compliance risks. Wahab & Bakar (2021) address the challenges of taxing the digital economy in Malaysia, emphasizing the need for better tax avoidance mitigation and suggesting analytic models to improve the detection of taxpayers' compliance levels. Other researchers, such as Gangodawilage et al. (2021), investigate the influence of technology on tax avoidance decisions within the digital economy, highlighting the critical role of trust in technology and the power of the tax authority. Etim et al. (2020) observed a negative influence of digitalization on tax avoidance in Nigeria, suggesting the need for tax policies tailored to electronic transactions. Fanea-Ivanovici et al. (2019) connect the fight against corruption and enhancement of tax compliance to the use of digital public services, underscoring the importance of trust and transparency. This body of work collectively indicates that while digitalization offers tools to combat tax avoidance, its effectiveness is contingent on the trust in and the capability of the technology employed by tax authorities.

Interplay of Tax Administration Digitalization, Trust, and Tax Avoidance

Research on developing governmental policies to improve compliance suggests three "paradigms" for tax administration (Alm, 2019). These begin with a government compliance strategy focused on detection and punishment but also extend beyond this, encompassing a range of additional policies with significant theoretical and empirical support.

In the first "traditional paradigm," the focus is exclusively on detecting illegal behaviors through frequent audits and severe sanctions. This is the classic paradigm of tax administrations throughout history, aligning well with the standard portfolio model of tax evasion based on the economics of crime theory. However, more recent literature on tax administration reform emphasizes a new paradigm, the "service paradigm," recognizing the role of tax administration as a facilitator and service provider to taxpayer-citizens, assisting taxpayers at every step of their income reporting and tax payments. A third paradigm is also suggested by recent work, especially emerging studies that view the taxpayer as a member of a broader group, as a social creature whose behavior depends on their own moral values (and those of others), as well as their perception of the quality, credibility, and reliability of the tax administration. The "trust paradigm" aligns with the role of various behavioral economic factors such as broadly defined social norms in the compliance decision (Alm, 2019).

Given this discussion, designing strategies to combat tax evasion/fraud falls into three main categories, each corresponding to one of the three paradigms: increasing the probability and threat of sanctions, improving the delivery of tax services, and changing the tax culture. Specifically:

- Firstly, it's possible to enhance policies aimed at increasing detection and sanctions;
- Secondly, the services of the tax administration can be improved to be more accessible and easier for taxpayers, in line with the service paradigm;
- Thirdly, it might be possible to induce a change in the culture of tax payment, in line with the trust paradigm.

Drawing on prior research on the determinants of tax compliance, a framework for tax compliance is suggested by Kirchler et al. (2008). This framework posits that the power of tax authorities and trust in tax authorities are relevant dimensions for understanding both enforced and voluntary compliance. The dynamic interactions between power and trust are considered. Using the framework as a conceptual tool, factors studied in previous research, such as fines, audit probabilities, tax rates, knowledge, attitudes, norms, and equity, are examined and discussed in reference to the dimensions of power and trust. Utilizing the framework as an operational tool, reactive regulatory approaches to increase tax compliance are discussed.

Kirchler et al. (2007, 2008) have endeavored to integrate economic and psychological factors into a comprehensive two-dimensional framework, the Slippery Slope Model. The power dimension of authorities aggregates economic determinants and is defined by taxpayers' perception of the authorities' ability to detect and punish tax fraudsters. The trust dimension in authorities covers the psychological bases of tax compliance, resulting from the general opinion of taxpayers that tax legislation and regulation are clear and easy to follow, and that tax authorities act fairly and benevolently in the interest of the community. The Slippery Slope Model (Figure 1) asserts that the power of authorities and trust in authorities can resolve the social dilemma of tax compliance.

Figure 1. The slippery slope framework
Source: Gangl et al. (2015)
Note. This figure illustrates the essential components of the Slippery Slope Model, emphasizing the influential factors of authority power and trust in resolving the social dilemma of tax compliance.

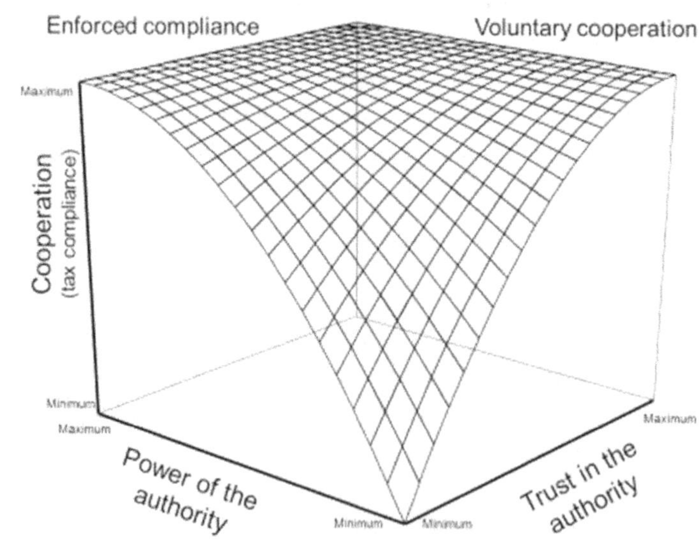

At the individual taxpayer level, the framework differentiates between two motivations for complying with tax legislation: enforced compliance and voluntary cooperation. Enforced compliance results from the power of tax authorities, while voluntary cooperation is motivated by taxpayers' trust in these authorities. On a broader level, the Slippery Slope Framework (SSF) posits that power and trust define different interaction climates between tax authorities and taxpayers: while the exercise of strong power by authorities fosters an antagonistic climate, high trust is a prerequisite for a synergistic climate (Kirchler et al., 2008). Figure 1 depicts power and trust as independent dimensions, positively linked to enforced compliance and voluntary cooperation, respectively, and to an antagonistic and synergistic climate, respectively.

The work of Hofmann et al. (2014) on improving tax compliance through the coercive and legitimate power of tax authorities, while simultaneously diminishing or facilitating trust in these authorities, has shown that coercion, such as strict audits and fines, and legitimate procedures, like assistance from tax authorities, are often cited as means to enhance tax compliance. However, the psychological mechanisms determining the effectiveness of each strategy are not clear. While highly relevant, there is limited empirical literature examining the effects of both strategies applied in combination. It's assumed that coercion decreases implicit trust in tax authorities, leading to the perception of a hostile and antagonistic tax climate and enforced compliance. Conversely, it's suggested that legitimate power increases reason-based trust in tax authorities, leading to the perception of a service climate and possibly voluntary cooperation. Combining both strategies is presumed to result in higher expected levels of compliance than each strategy alone. This analysis can also be extended to understanding tax avoidance behaviors, where the balance between coercion and trust could play a pivotal role in influencing taxpayers' decisions to either comply or avoid taxes.

Tax compliance represents a social dilemma where the short-term personal interest of minimizing tax payments conflicts with the long-term collective interest of providing sufficient fiscal funds for public goods. The Slippery Slope Framework (Figure 1) suggests that this social dilemma can be resolved and tax compliance ensured through the power of tax authorities and trust in them. However, the framework doesn't fully address the dynamics between power and trust. This theoretical paper aims to conceptualize the dynamics between power and trust by differentiating between coercive and legitimate power, and between reason-based and implicit trust. Insights into this dynamic are drawn from integrating a wide range of literature, including on organizational behavior and social influence. Conclusions are drawn about the effect of the dynamics between power and trust on the interaction climate between authorities and individuals and the subsequent individual motivation for cooperation in social dilemmas such as tax contributions. Practically, assumptions about the

Figure 2. Power, trust, and cooperative compliance
Source: Gangl et al. (2015)
Note. This figure showcases dynamics between power and trust affecting climates of cooperation and motivations to comply.

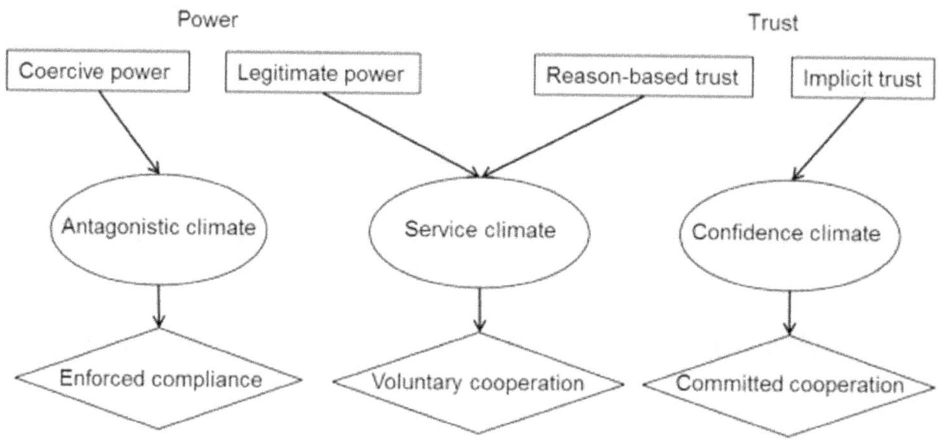

dynamics can be used by authorities to increase cooperation and shift the interaction climate from antagonistic to service-oriented and trusting. With rapid technical and technological progress, and according to recent studies on the digitalization of tax administration (Bassey et al., 2022; Canares, 2016), tax administrations worldwide have significantly digitized, offering a diverse and sophisticated array of electronic services to improve taxpayer compliance. The conceptual framework identifies fifteen themes for policymakers to consider when designing digital services in tax administrations, grouped around four categories (Figure 2): Context, Stakeholders, Technology, and Demonstrated Outcomes.

The contributions from Canares (2016) on the digitalization of tax administration and taxpayer compliance join the growing body of literature advocating for the use of Information and Communication Technologies (ICT) in local governance, particularly in public finance management. Using a case study in the Philippines, this study examined the impact of ICT on tax revenue generation by analyzing quantitative and qualitative data from 15 municipalities that used e-taxation. This study argues that ICT can enable more transparent and accountable tax revenue generation systems, benefiting both the government and taxpayers. As with any new public sector reform, it's crucial to evaluate the success of digital tax services by assessing associated costs and benefits, as explored in a study by Bassey et al. (2022). Digital taxation has achieved notable gains for taxpayers and tax officials. There are efficiency gains such as error elimination and fewer administrative checks, and effectiveness gains like the availability of e-tax services anytime and anywhere, automated confirmation of declarations and payments, the potential to deploy more people on the front line, personal portals for taxpayers, and easier and faster tax form filling (Beynon-Davies, 2005). Tax authorities also report increased work motivation due to the system's speed (Dečman & Klun, 2015). Bassey et al. (2022) presented (Figure 3) a conceptual framework of the digitalization of tax administration.

In the context of tax avoidance, these developments suggest a nuanced view where the digitization of tax administration could potentially alter the dynamics of taxpayer behavior, influencing decisions between compliance and avoidance. While digitalization offers efficiencies and transparency that might encourage compliance, it also changes the landscape of how and where avoidance can occur, requiring a deeper understanding of these evolving dynamics.

Figure 3. Digital tax administration conceptual framework
Source: Bassey et al. (2022)
Note. This figure illustrates the key elements guiding the digitalization of tax administration, offering a concise conceptual overview.

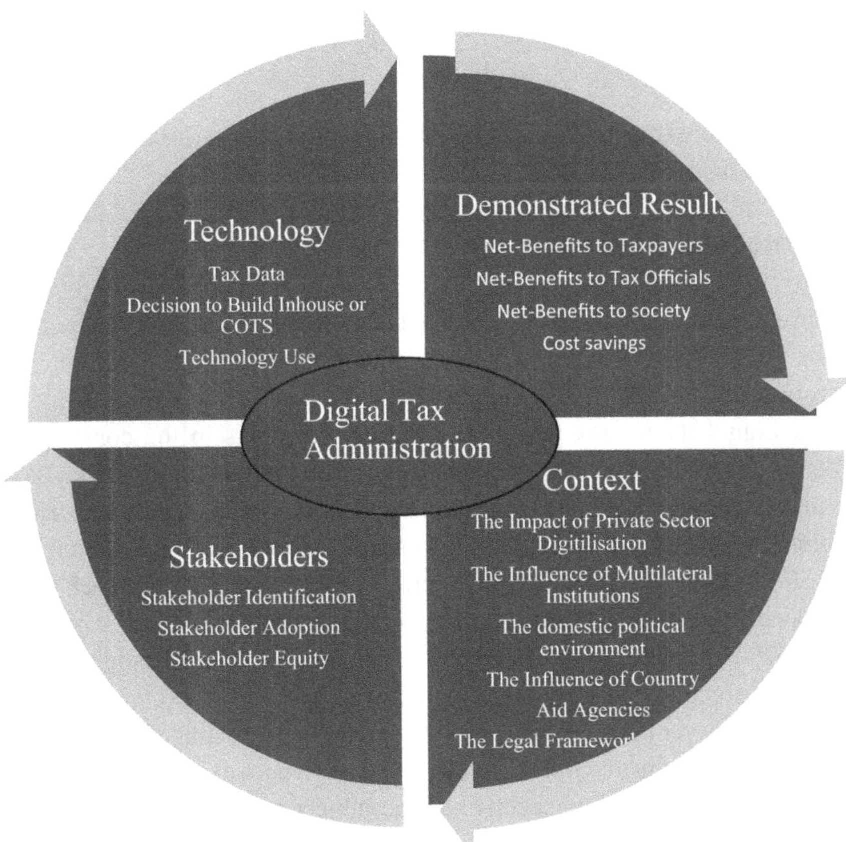

Bellon et al. (2022) found that digital transformation increases VAT declaration obligations by more than 5% annually in Peru, suggesting that digitization enhances compliance by reducing compliance costs and strengthening deterrence. This indicates that digitization should be complemented by other reforms to improve tax revenue mobilization. Digital transformation emerges as a key lever in reshaping tax management practices, with studies indicating it plays a critical role in mitigating tax stickiness and promoting compliance. These investigations collectively suggest that the integration of digital technologies within tax systems not only aids in strategic tax avoidance to navigate economic adversities but also bolsters internal controls, leading to a more equitable and controlled business environment. Moreover, in sectors like tourism, the move towards digitalization has been shown to deter aggressive tax avoidance by enhancing corporate governance mechanisms, suggesting a broader influence on managerial decision-making regarding tax strategies. These findings have significant implications for both business managers and policymakers in understanding the evolving landscape of tax administration in the digital age (Su, 2023; Tiantian et al., 2023; Zhou et al., 2022).

METHOD

This section outlines the methodological approach and details the processes of data collection and analysis.

Methodological Approach

In this investigation, a qualitative research design was employed, with a particular emphasis on conducting structured focus groups. The selection of a qualitative framework was informed by the study's goal to explore the dynamics influencing the interactions between tax administration and taxpayers in the context of tax compliance. Qualitative methods are adept at probing into complex issues as they unfold in real-life situations, unearthing nuanced understandings of the experiences, perceptions, and actions of individuals (Korstjens & Moser, 2018; L. Haven & Van Grootel, 2019; Tenny et al., 2017). As Dworkin (2012) notes, this approach seeks to uncover deep insights into phenomena, concentrating on the "how" and "why" behind specific issues or circumstances. This method favors an inductive reasoning process, prioritizing the generation of data-derived categories and the exploration of their interconnections over broad generalizations or hypothesis testing. The overarching objective is to document and interpret the lived experiences of the participants, thus offering a rich and detailed perspective on the subject matter under examination.

Data Collection and Analysis

For the investigation, data collection utilized in-person interviews guided by a semi-structured interview protocol (Appendix). This protocol, derived from an extensive literature review, consisted of various sections. The initial segment focused on gathering personal data from respondents while prioritizing anonymity. Divergent scholarly views exist on optimal sample sizes. Baker & Edwards (2012) propose around 12 participants, generally not exceeding 20, whereas Saunders et al. (2018) suggest a range of 5 to 25 for semi-structured interviews. Commonly endorsed by qualitative research literature, including Boddy (2016), Creswell & Poth (2016), and Marshall et al. (2013), is a participant ceiling of 30. To align with these scholarly perspectives, engagement occurred with 30 Moroccan tax officials, as detailed in Table 1.

All interviews were meticulously transcribed, resulting in an extensive textual database. The initial analysis phase utilized the IRAMUTEQ software, following Ratinaud's (2009) methodology. This software proves particularly effective for sorting and analyzing data from semi-structured interview dialogues (Chaves et al., 2017). Employing Discursive Textual Analysis, IRAMUTEQ enhances the process by providing efficiency, novel insights, and accuracy in qualitative data analysis, in line with Ramos et al.'s (2018) findings. The adopted tripartite analysis strategy, influenced by Bueno et al. (2021), began with a lexicographic assessment, followed by a cluster analysis using the top-down hierarchical classification (Reinert method). The analysis also included factorial correspondence analysis, concluding with a similarity analysis, ensuring a comprehensive evaluation of the textual data.

FINDING

This section synthesizes the collected data and resulting insights, providing a critical examination of the relationship between the qualifications and experiences of tax administration officials in the context of tax compliance. The assessment of respondents' characteristics, detailed in Table 2, considers the diverse educational backgrounds and professional experiences of 30 tax administrators, encompassing roles such as tax inspectors, auditors, and finance officers. This diversity is crucial for comprehending the intricacies and depth of knowledge that impact tax avoidance behaviors and strategies within the administrative framework.

Analyzing data from the interviews, Table 2 showcases the 30 most frequently used active words, highlighting key themes, particularly the digitalization of tax administration and tax avoidance. This lexicometric analysis, generated through

Table 1. Characteristics of respondents

Tax inspectors	Masters in Finance, Accounting & Tax	10	5-10 years	12
	PhD	5	11-15 years	3
Tax auditors	Masters in Finance, Accounting & Tax	8	5-10 years	6
	PhD	2	16-20 years	4
Tax finance officers	Masters in Finance, Accounting & Tax	3	10-15 years	4
	PhD	2	Over 20 years	1
Total		30		30

Source: The authors

Note. This table outlines respondent characteristics specific to their positions within tax administration, encompassing qualifications and experience.

Table 2. The 30 most frequently used active words from IRaMuTeQ

Order	Active Forms	Freq.	Order	Active Forms	Freq.
01	Taxpayers	136	16	Simplification	13
02	Tax authorities	92	17	Mistrust	12
03	Relationship	87	18	Transparency	12
04	Tax administration	51	19	Confidence	11
05	Tax avoidance	39	20	Tax citizenship	10
06	Trust	39	21	Tax evasion	10
07	Digitalization	39	22	Technology	10
08	Tax compliance	39	23	Access	9
09	Tax	34	24	Businesses	9
10	Impact	28	25	Comply	9
11	Services	20	26	Digital	9
12	Lack	19	27	Tax collection	9
13	Moroccan Taxpayers	15	28	Tax procedures	9
14	Tax System	15	29	Challenge	8
15	Quality	14	30	Complex	8

Source: The authors

Note. This table highlights the 30 most frequently employed active words, providing insight into recurring language patterns or key terms within the context of the study.

IRaMuTeQ software, sheds light on the primary concerns and focal areas within the domain of tax administration as perceived by the participants.

The frequent mention of terms like "digitalization," "tax avoidance," and "technology" indicates a significant focus on how the digital transformation of tax administration is perceived as impacting tax avoidance behaviors. The juxtaposition of "trust" and "tax compliance" with "tax avoidance" reflects a nuanced understanding of the challenges and opportunities presented by digitalization in the realm of tax administration. The occurrence of words like "complex" alongside "digitalization"

Figure 4. Descending hierarchical classification from IRaMuTeQ
Source: The authors
Note. This figure categorizes terms into clusters based on similarities and differences, offering a structured view of groupings and subgroups within the analyzed dataset.

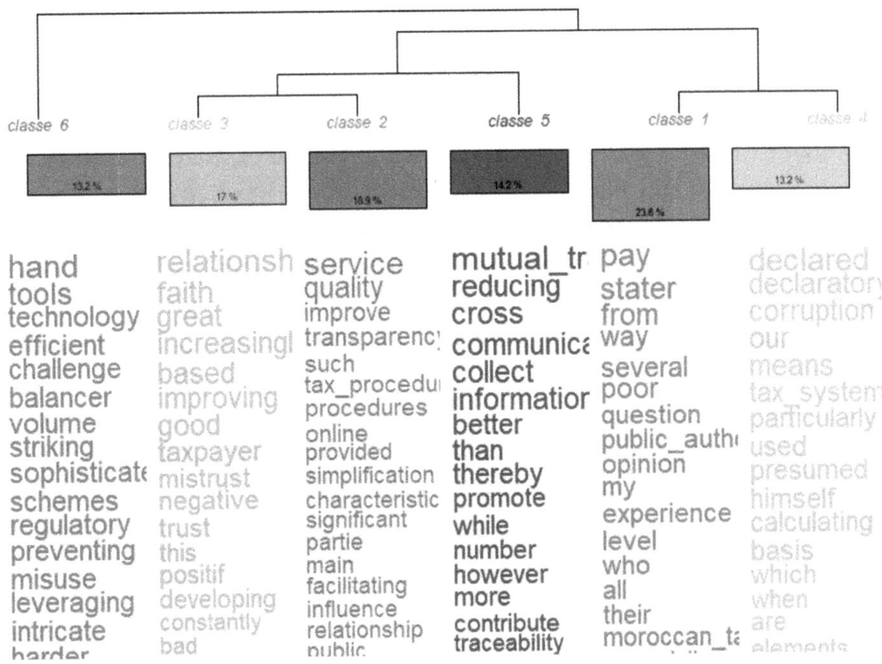

and "technology" suggests an awareness of the complexities inherent in integrating new technologies into existing systems. These insights reveal the importance of managing the balance between the adoption of digital technologies and addressing tax avoidance. The data suggests a need for strategies that not only embrace technological advancements but also foster trust and understanding among taxpayers to enhance compliance and effectively tackle tax avoidance. This analysis provides a foundation for discussing how digitalization can be leveraged to simplify the tax system, improve transparency, and ultimately contribute to a more efficient and fair tax administration.

Continuing the analysis, a hierarchical descending classification of the active words was performed using the Reinert method. This process revealed four primary lexical clusters, illustrated in Figure 4. To delve into the specific lexical content of each cluster, Table 3 provides a detailed overview, listing the 15 most significant words from each group. These selections are based on a high level of statistical relevance (p<0.001) and exclude verbs and base word forms.

Examining Figure 4 reveals a dendrogram visually organizing the identified clusters, encapsulating key themes derived from the lexical analysis. Each cluster, distinguished by a specific color, encapsulates a thematic concentration of words that are statistically significant and contextually related. For example, Cluster 1 (red) might represent themes around direct tax-related terms, while Cluster 2 (green) seems to emphasize interpersonal aspects such as trust and relationships. Clusters 3 (blue) and 4 (purple) also showcase their respective thematic focuses which may relate to the operational and technological aspects of tax administration. This dendrogram provides a structured overview, revealing patterns in the data that point to overarching themes such as the importance of technology in tax administration (Cluster 6, purple) and the interplay between service quality and transparency (Cluster 3, blue). The branches connecting the clusters suggest interrelated themes that reflect the complex nature of tax administration discourse, particularly around digitalization and tax avoidance.

To summarize the predominant themes from the lexical analysis, the results have been organized into a table titled "Thematic classifications of lexical clusters". Table 3 delineates the thematic essence and corresponding descriptions for each class identified through the hierarchical descending classification process. It serves as a comprehensive guide to the thematic undercurrents that permeate the discourse among tax administration officials, particularly highlighting their perspectives

Table 3. Thematic classifications of lexical clusters

Class	Thematic	Description
Class 1	Tax Compliance and Tax Authorities	This class appears to concentrate on the direct interaction between taxpayers and tax authorities, emphasizing the role of tax compliance and the authority's influence in the tax system.
Class 2	Trust and Relationship Dynamics between taxpayers & tax authorities	Focused on the interpersonal dynamics between the tax administration and taxpayers, highlighting the importance of trust and the quality of relationships.
Class 3	Service Quality and Transparency	Encompasses themes related to the quality of service provided by tax authorities and the transparency of tax processes.
Class 4	Tax Avoidance and System Complexity	Likely represents discussions around the complexities of the tax system that may contribute to tax avoidance behaviors.
Class 5	Impact of Technology & Digitalization on Tax Avoidance	Technology & Digitalization in Tax Avoidance Examines the influence of technological advancements and digitalization on the strategies and prevalence of tax avoidance within the administration process.
Class 6	Operational Efficiency and Challenges	Centers on the operational aspects of tax administration, including the challenges and efficiency of the system, possibly indicating the influence of sophisticated tools and technology.

Source: The authors

Note. This table delineates thematic classifications within lexical clusters, providing a comprehensive overview of the identified themes and their respective groupings.

on compliance, relationships, service quality, and the impact of technology and digitalization on tax administration.

This synthesis incorporates lexical clusters into distinct themes, establishing a framework to discuss the contributions of each cluster to the understanding of the tax administration landscape. It highlights the multifaceted nature of the discourse, revealing nuanced perspectives on how tax officials interpret and respond to the evolving challenges and innovations in their field.

Figure 5 presents a Factorial Correspondence Analysis (FCA), a statistical method used to graphically illustrate the relationships between the lexical clusters obtained from the interview transcripts. This visualization is instrumental in understanding how various themes interconnect and potentially influence each other.

In the FCA, the proximity between words indicates a stronger association in the dataset, meaning they often appear in similar contexts or are frequently mentioned together by participants. Conversely, words positioned further apart are less likely to be associated or are mentioned in different contexts. Observing the figure reveals discernible groupings of words that may correspond to specific clusters. Notably, words such as "technology," "hand," "tools," "leveraging," and "schemes" are closely linked, indicating discussions related to the practical aspects of tax avoidance, potentially involving the use of technology to either facilitate or counter such practices.

Another noticeable grouping involves terms like "tax avoidance," "tax evasion," and "complex," which are somewhat distanced from positive terms like "service," "quality," "trust," and "transparency." This separation may indicate a dichotomy in the discourse, where discussions about tax avoidance and evasion are conceptually separated from those centered around improving service quality and transparency. The positioning of "tax collection," "volume," "businesses," and "digital" in relation to "tax avoidance" and "tax evasion" might reflect a discourse on how digitalization affects the volume of tax collection and its potential to both expose and prevent tax avoidance and evasion in businesses.

Overall, this FCA suggests that while there is a conversation about leveraging technology for better tax administration, there's also an awareness of its role in tax avoidance strategies. The analysis underscores the need for a balanced approach in digital tax administration, one that harnesses technology for efficiency and transparency, while also mitigating the risk of its misuse in tax avoidance schemes.

Figure 6 illustrates a similarity analysis, which is a visual representation of the connections between different terms based on how frequently they are mentioned together in the dataset. The analysis forms clusters that are graphically separated, with each cluster representing a different thematic area based on the similarity of the terms within.

The figure displays three distinct clusters, each represented by a different color, implying thematic cohesion within each group. The red cluster, labeled "taxpayers,"

Figure 5. Correspondence factor analysis generated by IRAMUTEQ
Source: The authors
Note. The diagram illustrates the arrangement of terms within a multidimensional space, emphasizing their relative proximity or separation from one another.

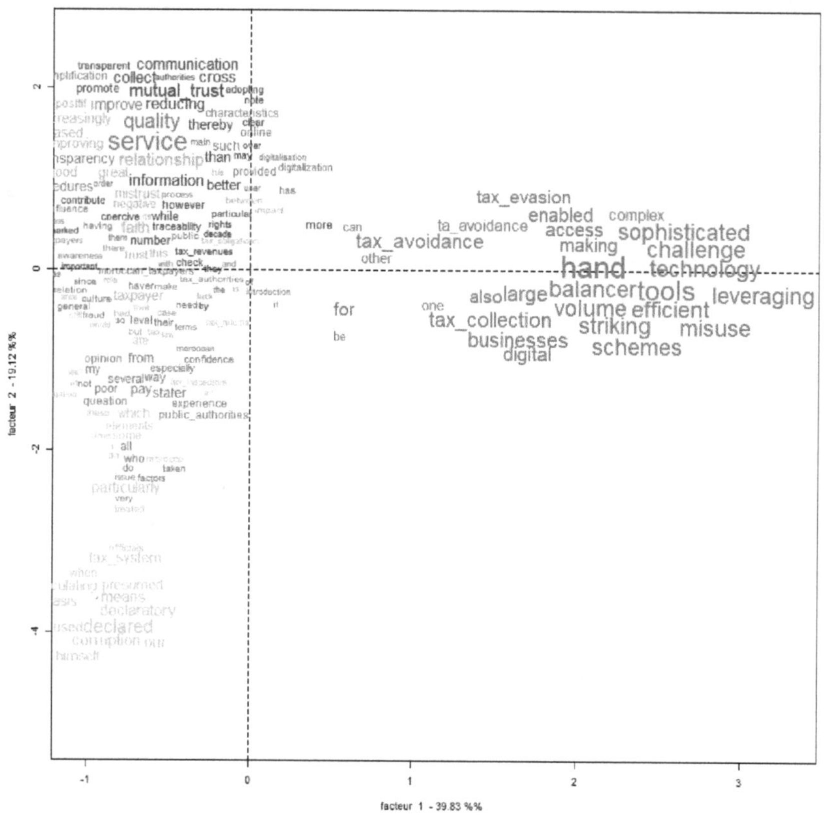

is closely associated with terms such as "tax administration," "digitalization," and "tax system," suggesting a focus on the relationship between taxpayers and the mechanisms of tax administration, including the impact of digital technologies. The green cluster, titled "tax compliance," includes "quality," "transparency," and "tax procedures," indicating discussions centered on the quality of tax compliance procedures and the transparency of the tax system, which are crucial for ensuring compliance. The blue cluster is labeled with terms like "tax avoidance," "tax evasion," "technology," and "digital," pointing to discussions about the challenges and risks associated with tax avoidance and evasion, especially in the context of new technologies and digital platforms. These clusters show the nuanced discourse within the tax administration field. The close proximity between "digital" and "tax avoidance" in the blue cluster, for example, might imply concerns about how digital

Figure 6. Similarity analysis results from IRaMuTeQ
Source: The authors
Note. This figure depicts the co-occurrence and connections between words derived from the Similarity Analysis method.

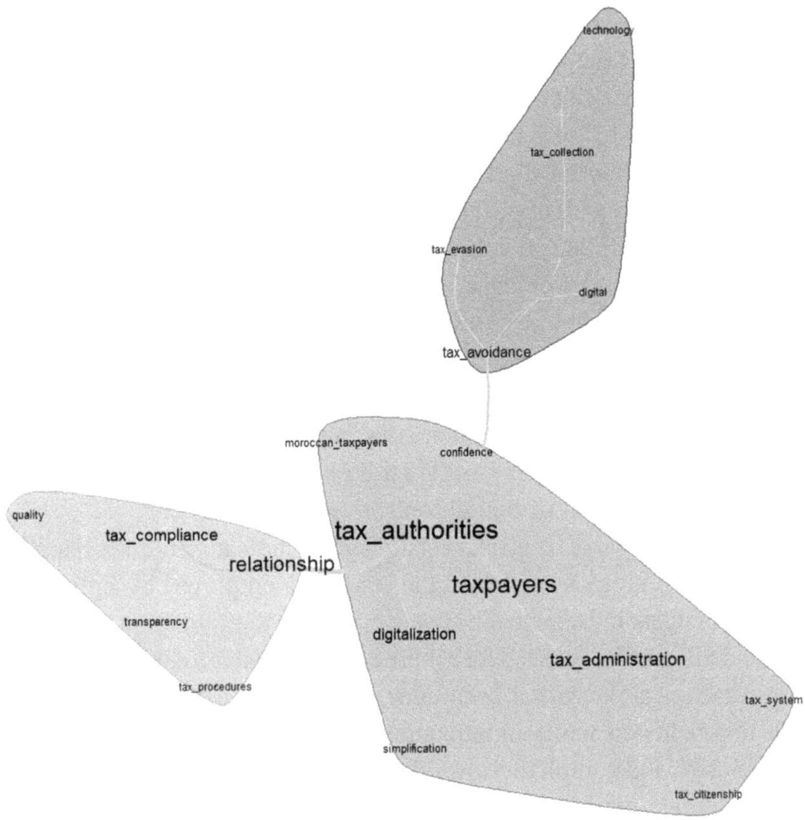

advancements could be facilitating avoidance behaviors. Meanwhile, the green cluster's focus on "tax compliance" suggests a dialogue on improving compliance through better service quality and transparent procedures. The proximity of "tax authorities" to both "taxpayers" and "tax compliance" indicates a perceived interdependence between the authorities' role and the achievement of effective tax compliance, as well as the management of tax avoidance. This similarity analysis thus provides a visual summary of the study's findings, offering insights into the interconnected themes that emerged from the participants' discourse.

CONCLUSION

In the conclusion section of the chapter, the understanding of how digitalization affects tax administration is synthesized, the significance of trust is examined, and tax avoidance patterns are explored against the backdrop of Morocco's tax reform initiatives. The findings suggest that digitalization is a double-edged sword. It holds the potential to enhance tax collection and administration efficiency, as indicated by frequent references to "technology," "digital," and "tax collection" in the lexical analysis. The deployment of digital tools is perceived as a catalyst for improving procedural transparency and simplifying tax-related processes, which can lead to better taxpayer compliance. On the other hand, there are concerns that such advancements could also facilitate tax avoidance, with sophisticated schemes emerging as a byproduct of the same technology designed to curb them. Trust emerged as a pivotal theme, closely linked with tax compliance and the perception of tax authorities. The data suggest that fostering trust between taxpayers and tax authorities can lead to a more cooperative relationship, which is essential for voluntary compliance and minimizing tax avoidance behaviors. Trust is seen as a foundational element that influences the effectiveness of digital tools in tax administration.

Tax avoidance remains a significant challenge, as indicated by discussions around the complexity of the tax system and the strategies employed by individuals and businesses to navigate it. Despite the advancements in digitalization, the persistence of tax avoidance signifies the need for a more comprehensive approach that combines technological innovation with a keen understanding of human behavior and trust dynamics. In conclusion, while digitalization offers promising avenues for enhancing tax administration and compliance, its efficacy is contingent upon the development of a trustworthy relationship between tax authorities and taxpayers. The Moroccan context, mirroring global trends, suggests that successful tax reform dynamics must address both the technological and the human facets of tax administration.

Theoretical and Managerial Implications

From a theoretical perspective, this study enhances the understanding of how digitalization influences tax systems, especially within the context of Morocco. It demonstrates the dual role of digital tools, simplifying tax administration while inadvertently creating new avenues for tax avoidance. On a practical managerial level, especially for small and medium-sized enterprises (SEMs) which are vital to Morocco's economy, the study offers significant implications. For SEMs managers, the findings highlight the need to stay abreast of evolving digital tax systems and leverage these advancements for efficient tax management. This involves understanding and adapting to digital tax platforms, ensuring compliance, and using digital tools to gain insights for better fiscal planning and decision-making.

For tax authorities and policymakers, the study underscores the necessity of implementing balanced digital strategies. Such strategies should not only focus on optimizing tax collection but also on designing systems that minimize opportunities for avoidance. Moreover, fostering trust between SEMs and tax authorities is paramount. Trust-building initiatives could include transparent communication, consistent and fair tax practices, and providing support and education to SEMs on navigating the digital tax system. These measures can encourage voluntary compliance and strengthen the overall tax ecosystem, ultimately contributing to a more robust and resilient economic environment in Morocco.

Limitations and Perspectives

While this study offers valuable insights, it is not without limitations. The focus on Moroccan tax administrators provides a context-specific perspective that may not be generalizable to other settings. Additionally, the reliance on qualitative data may introduce subjective biases. Future research could delve into the sustained impact of digitalization on tax systems, scrutinizing the quality and efficacy of digital and e-tax systems in relation to tax avoidance and evasion. Such studies would be crucial in understanding how digitalization influences taxpayer behavior over time, particularly in terms of enhancing fiscal compliance and reducing avoidance and evasion tactics. Moreover, investigating the maturation of taxpayer trust in the context of increasingly digital tax environments would offer deeper insights into the interplay between technological adoption and taxpayer engagement.

REFERENCES

Agusti, R. R., & Rahman, A. F. (2023). Determinants of tax attitude in small and medium enterprises: Evidence from Indonesia. *Cogent Business & Management*, *10*(1), 2160585. doi:10.1080/23311975.2022.2160585

Allingham, M. G., & Sandmo, A. (1972). Income tax evasion: A theoretical analysis. *Taxation: Critical Perspectives on the World Economy*, *3*(1), 323–338.

Alm, J. (2019). What motivates tax compliance? *Journal of Economic Surveys*, *33*(2), 353–388. doi:10.1111/joes.12272

Ayoola, T. J., Olaniyi, O. O., Kolawole, P. E., Aregbesola, O. D., & Wright, O. (2023). *Tax administration, trust in tax authorities, and personal income tax compliance: Evidence from Nigeria*. Academic Press.

Baker, S. E., & Edwards, R. (2012). *How many qualitative interviews is enough*. Academic Press.

Bassey, E., Mulligan, E., & Ojo, A. (2022). A conceptual framework for digital tax administration-A systematic review. *Government Information Quarterly, 39*(4), 101754. doi:10.1016/j.giq.2022.101754

Bellon, M., Dabla-Norris, E., Khalid, S., & Lima, F. (2022). Digitalization to improve tax compliance: Evidence from VAT e-Invoicing in Peru. *Journal of Public Economics, 210*, 104661. doi:10.1016/j.jpubeco.2022.104661 PMID:35711616

Beynon-Davies, P. (2005). Constructing electronic government: The case of the UK inland revenue. *International Journal of Information Management, 25*(1), 3–20. doi:10.1016/j.ijinfomgt.2004.08.002

Boddy, C. R. (2016). Sample size for qualitative research. *Qualitative Market Research, 19*(4), 426–432. doi:10.1108/QMR-06-2016-0053

Bueno, S., Banuls, V. A., & Gallego, M. D. (2021). Is urban resilience a phenomenon on the rise? A systematic literature review for the years 2019 and 2020 using textometry. *International Journal of Disaster Risk Reduction, 66*, 102588. doi:10.1016/j.ijdrr.2021.102588

Cahyonowati, N., Ratmono, D., & Juliarto, A. (2023). The role of social norms and trust in authority in tax compliance dilemmas. *Cogent Business & Management, 10*(1), 2174084. doi:10.1080/23311975.2023.2174084

Canares, M. P. (2016). Creating the Enabling Environment for More Transparent and Better-resourced Local Governments: A Case of E-taxation in the Philippines. *Information Technology for Development, 22*(sup1), 121–138. doi:10.1080/02681102.2015.1121857

Chaves, M. M. N., dos Santos, A. P. R., dos Santosa, N. P., & Larocca, L. M. (2017). Use of the software IRaMuTeQ in qualitative research: An experience report. *Computer Supported Qualitative Research*, 39–48.

Creswell, J. W., & Poth, C. N. (2016). *Qualitative inquiry and research design: Choosing among five approaches*. Sage publications.

de Vasconcellos, M. V., & das Graças Rua, M. (2005). Impacts of internet use on public administration: A case study of the Brazilian tax administration. *Electronic Journal of E-Government, 3*(1), 49–58.

Dečman, M., & Klun, M. (2015). The Impact of Information Systems on Taxation: A Case of Users Experience With an e-Recovery Information System. *Electronic Journal of E-Government, 13*(2), 110–121.

Dworkin, S. L. (2012). Sample size policy for qualitative studies using in-depth interviews. [). Springer.]. *Archives of Sexual Behavior, 41*(6), 1319–1320. doi:10.1007/s10508-012-0016-6 PMID:22968493

Dyreng, S. D., Jacob, M., Jiang, X., & Müller, M. A. (2022). Tax incidence and tax avoidance. *Contemporary Accounting Research, 39*(4), 2622–2656. doi:10.1111/1911-3846.12797

Etim, R. S., Jeremiah, M. S., & Dan, P. B. (2020). Tax Compliance and Digitalization of Nigerian Economy: The Empirical Review. *American International Journal of Social Science, 9*(2), 42–50. doi:10.30845/aijss.v9n2p5

Fanea-Ivanovici, M., Muşetescu, R.-C., Pană, M.-C., & Voicu, C. (2019). Fighting corruption and enhancing tax compliance through digitization: Achieving sustainable development in Romania. *Sustainability (Basel), 11*(5), 1480. doi:10.3390/su11051480

Feld, L. P., & Frey, B. S. (2007). Tax compliance as the result of a psychological tax contract: The role of incentives and responsive regulation. *Law & Policy, 29*(1), 102–120. doi:10.1111/j.1467-9930.2007.00248.x

Gangl, K., Hofmann, E., & Kirchler, E. (2015). Tax authorities' interaction with taxpayers: A conception of compliance in social dilemmas by power and trust. *New Ideas in Psychology, 37*, 13–23. doi:10.1016/j.newideapsych.2014.12.001 PMID:25859096

Gangodawilage, D., Madurapperuma, W., & Aluthge, C. (2021). Use of technology to manage tax compliance behavior of entrepreneurs in the digital economy. *International Journal of Scientific and Research Publications, 11*(3), 366–370. doi:10.29322/IJSRP.11.03.2021.p11150

Haven, T., & Van Grootel, D. L. (2019). Preregistering qualitative research. *Accountability in Research, 26*(3), 229–244. doi:10.1080/08989621.2019.1580147 PMID:30741570

Hofmann, E., Gangl, K., Kirchler, E., & Stark, J. (2014). Enhancing T ax Compliance through Coercive and Legitimate Power of T ax Authorities by Concurrently Diminishing or Facilitating Trust in T ax Authorities. *Law & Policy*, *36*(3), 290–313. doi:10.1111/lapo.12021 PMID:26074656

Hutchens, M., Rego, S. O., & Williams, B. (2023). Tax avoidance, uncertainty, and firm risk. *Uncertainty, and Firm Risk.*

IMF. (2023). *Morocco: 2022 Article IV Consultation-Press Release and Staff Report.* IMF Country Report No. 23/42; December 16, 2022. http://www.imf.org

Katua, C. M. (2019). *Digitization Of Tax Administration, Technology And Tax Compliance By Small And Medium Sized Enterprises In Nairobi Central Business District* [Doctoral Dissertation]. University of Nairobi.

Kingdom of Morocco. (2021). *Framework Law 69-19 on Tax Reform.* Author.

Kirchler, E. (2007). *The economic psychology of tax behaviour.* Cambridge University Press. doi:10.1017/CBO9780511628238

Kirchler, E., Hoelzl, E., & Wahl, I. (2008). Enforced versus voluntary tax compliance: The "slippery slope" framework. *Journal of Economic Psychology*, *29*(2), 210–225. doi:10.1016/j.joep.2007.05.004

Kogler, C., Olsen, J., Kirchler, E., Batrancea, L. M., & Nichita, A. (2023). Perceptions of trust and power are associated with tax compliance: A cross-cultural study. *Economic and Political Studies*, *11*(3), 365–381. doi:10.1080/20954816.2022.2130501

Korstjens, I., & Moser, A. (2018). Series: Practical guidance to qualitative research. Part 4: Trustworthiness and publishing. *The European Journal of General Practice*, *24*(1), 120–124. doi:10.1080/13814788.2017.1375092 PMID:29202616

Marshall, B., Cardon, P., Poddar, A., & Fontenot, R. (2013). Does sample size matter in qualitative research?: A review of qualitative interviews in IS research. *Journal of Computer Information Systems*, *54*(1), 11–22. doi:10.1080/08874417.2013.11645667

Mashuri, A. A. S. (2023). Determinants of Tax Avoidance and Audit Quality as a Moderating Variable. *Ilomata International Journal of Tax and Accounting*, *4*(1), 117–127. doi:10.52728/ijtc.v4i1.661

McClure, C. G. (2023). How costly is tax avoidance? evidence from structural estimation. *The Accounting Review*, *98*(6), 1–28. doi:10.2308/TAR-2020-0465

Milliron, V. C. (1985). A behavioral study of the meaning and influence of tax complexity. *Journal of Accounting Research*, *23*(2), 794–816. doi:10.2307/2490838

Okafor, O. N. (2022). Shaming of tax evaders: Empirical evidence on perceptions of retributive justice and tax Compliance intentions. *Journal of Business Ethics*, 1–19.

Petutschnig, M. (2017). Future orientation and taxes: Evidence from big data. *Journal of International Accounting, Auditing & Taxation*, *29*, 14–31. doi:10.1016/j.intaccaudtax.2017.03.003

Prinz, A. (2023). Cultural tightness, trust, and power in enforcing tax compliance. *Economic and Political Studies*, 1–28. doi:10.1080/20954816.2023.2203306

Ramos, M. G., do Rosário Lima, V. M., & Amaral-Rosa, M. P. (2018). IRaMuTeQ Software and discursive textual analysis: interpretive possibilities. *World Conference on Qualitative Research*, 58–72.

Ratinaud, P. (2009). *IRaMuTeQ: Interface de R pour les analyses multidimensionnelles de textes et de questionnaires* [IRaMuTeQ: R interface for multidimensional analysis of texts and questionnaires]. Academic Press.

Roth, J. A. (1989). Taxpayer compliance: Vol. 1. *An agenda for research.* University of Pennsylvania Press.

Saunders, B., Sim, J., Kingstone, T., Baker, S., Waterfield, J., Bartlam, B., Burroughs, H., & Jinks, C. (2018). Saturation in qualitative research: Exploring its conceptualization and operationalization. *Quality & Quantity*, *52*(4), 1893–1907. doi:10.1007/s11135-017-0574-8 PMID:29937585

Slemrod, J., & Yitzhaki, S. (2002). Tax avoidance, evasion, and administration. In *Handbook of public economics* (Vol. 3, pp. 1423–1470). Elsevier.

Su, L. (2023). *Tax Administration Digitization and Corporate Tax Avoidance: A Quasi-Natural Experiment Based on the Golden Tax III Project in China*. Academic Press.

Tenny, S., Brannan, J. M., & Brannan, G. D. (2017). *Qualitative study*. Academic Press.

Tiantian, G., Hailin, C., Zhou, X., Ai, S., & Siyao, W. (2023). Does corporate digital transformation affect the level of corporate tax avoidance? Empirical evidence from Chinese listed tourism companies. *Finance Research Letters*, *57*, 104271. doi:10.1016/j.frl.2023.104271

Wahab, R., & Bakar, A. (2021). Digital economy tax compliance model in malaysia using machine learning approach. *Sains Malaysiana*, *50*(7), 2059–2077. doi:10.17576/jsm-2021-5007-20

Zhou, S., Zhou, P., & Ji, H. (2022). Can digital transformation alleviate corporate tax stickiness: The mediation effect of tax avoidance. *Technological Forecasting and Social Change*, *184*, 122028. doi:10.1016/j.techfore.2022.122028

KEY TERMS AND DEFINITIONS

Digitalization of Tax Administration: The ongoing transformation of tax administration processes through electronic technologies including digital platforms, data analytics, and automation.

Tax Avoidance: The intentional arrangement of financial activities to minimize tax liability within legal boundaries involving strategic decision-making to optimize the use of legal provisions and incentives.

Tax Compliance: The adherence and conformity of individuals businesses, or entities to the tax laws and regulations set forth by the government. It involves accurately reporting income, fulfilling tax obligations, and meeting deadlines to ensure legal compliance.

Trust in Tax Authorities: The reliance and belief individuals and businesses place in tax authorities indicating perceptions of fairness, transparency, and ethical conduct in taxation matters.

APPENDIX

Interview questions:

1. What specific digital tools have been most impactful in altering tax avoidance strategies?
2. In what ways have taxpayers adapted their practices in response to the digitalization of tax administration?
3. How do taxpayers perceive the objectives and outcomes of recent tax reforms in the context of digitalization?
4. What behavioral shifts are observed among taxpayers in response to the specific digital aspects of recent tax reforms?
5. How is trust in tax authorities influenced by the implementation of digital systems in tax administration?
6. In what ways does trust impact taxpayer cooperation and compliance with digitalized tax reforms aimed at reducing avoidance?

Chapter 10
Exploring the Risks, Challenges, and Opportunities of Using Digital Financial Technologies for Green Finance

Muhammad Arslan
https://orcid.org/0000-0001-5046-7627
Open Polytechnic, New Zealand

Alimshan Faizulayev
https://orcid.org/0000-0002-0212-0538
KIMEP University, Kazakhstan

Dana Abeuova
KIMEP University, Kazakhstan

Umar Nawaz Kayani
https://orcid.org/0000-0003-1404-5288
Al Ain University, UAE

ABSTRACT

The use of digital financial technologies (DFTs) for green finance has been evolving and has created new risks and challenges for the environment and users. This chapter aims to explore the risks, challenges, and opportunities that are associated with the use of DFTs for green finance. In this chapter, authors used Google Scholar, Scopus, and Web of Science databases as sources for article collection. They initially collected over 245 articles for the period 2000 to 2023 through keyword searches, and their final sample consisted of 183 articles. They applied a thematic analysis and explored four themes (i.e., green innovation; green investment and sustainability; a data-driven approach; and the risks and challenges of using DFTs for green finance). In this chapter, the authors found that the DFTs offer several opportunities

DOI: 10.4018/979-8-3693-1678-8.ch010

for green finance. However, the DFTs also pose several risks and challenges (such as cybercrime, fraud, scams, tax evasion, capital-intensive technologies, a lack of awareness, uncertain policies, and an absence of protection mechanisms) that need to be addressed.

1. INTRODUCTION AND BACKGROUND

In the presence of global sustainability and environmental challenges, the relationship of digital financial technologies (DFTs) with green finance has emerged (Arnone & Crovella, 2023). Digital financial technologies encompass a wide range of innovations, including artificial intelligence, blockchain, cloud computing, big data, crypto assets, etc., which are increasingly being leveraged to reshape the landscape of green finance. There is a dire need for a transition towards a low-carbon and environmentally responsible future. Consequently, DFTs, encompassing technologies like blockchain, artificial intelligence, and big data, play a pivotal role in reshaping the landscape of financial systems dedicated to fostering sustainable development (Maheswar & Kanagachidambaresan, 2020). Institutional theory has been widely used in exploring environmental management (Hoffman, 1999), corporate social responsibility (Wong, Lai, Shang, Lu, & Leung, 2012), and the green supply chain (DiMaggio & Powell, 1983; Sarkis, Zhu, & Lai, 2011). DFTs have profoundly changed industries, firms, and even society, and institutional theory offers a rich array of perspectives on both the content and dynamics of such changes (Schildt, 2022).

Xiao and Peng (2023) argued that curbing rising global temperatures and reducing greenhouse gases have received increased attention in the wake of global climate crises. The use of digital technologies may help in decision-making by providing real-time data collection and monitoring; however, such digital technologies may also have environmental costs. Consequently, the incorporation of DFTs for green finance signifies a vigorous merging of environmental stewardship and financial innovation. This synergy not only enhances the efficiency and accessibility of financial services but also introduces novel approaches to address the complex and interconnected challenges posed by climate change, biodiversity loss, and resource depletion. The use of DFTs for green finance signifies a paradigm shift, bringing about unprecedented opportunities, mitigating risks, and fostering inclusivity in the pursuit of a more sustainable global economy. The majority of the countries around the globe are committed to the Paris Agreement and aim to achieve "*the increase in the global average temperature to well below 2 °C above pre-industrial levels and pursue efforts to limit the temperature increase to 1.5 °C above pre-industrial levels*" (UNFCCC, 2015, p. 3). Loiseau et al. (2016) argued that emerging countries have different definitions of green economy compared to their developed counterparts, and its link with sustainability is not clear. Digital finance is pivotal for the transition to a green economy, and digital technology can play an important role in the development of a green economy. Digital green financial products may attract corporate social responsibility investors if the link between green financial products and a carbon-neutral economy is certified and transparent. However, Campiglio (2016) argued that the transition to a climate-resilient and low-carbon economy needs significant investment in green sectors. It is estimated that approximately 2% of the global GDP is required for the delivery of a green economy over 2010–2050 (UNEP, 2011).

Scholars argued that technological advancement and innovation can help in overcoming the operational barriers and bottlenecks that might prevent green finance from scaling up, such as the limited access to reliable data and the statistical complexity of the climate change model (Savignac, 2008; Yang, Wang, Deng, & Xiang, 2023). Yang and Masron (2022) highlighted the need for green finance to promote environmental governance and protection with innovative digital technologies. They further argued for the need for integration between financial development and digital technology for long-term ecological benefits. Green finance, along with digital finance, can serve as a bridge to balance industrial development and reach the vision of carbon neutrality. Digital finance can improve energy utilisation and reduce environmental pollution without compromising the ecology (Yang & Masron, 2022). Scholars have argued that digital financial technologies can promote green technology innovation, reduce costs, and increase efficient services. (Kaur, 2023). DFTs such as blockchain, with their decentralised and transparent nature, have the potential to revolutionise green finance by ensuring efficiency, traceability, and accountability in green finance. In addition, digital finance has more potential in developing countries, which have weak regulations and financial development. Digital financial technologies have significantly improved accessibility to financial services and enabled the development of innovative financing models, particularly in regions with limited infrastructure (Pazarbasioglu et al., 2020). This increased accessibility is crucial for promoting green finance, as it allows a broader range of stakeholders, including small and medium-sized enterprises (SMEs) and individuals, to participate in environmentally friendly initiatives. For example, crowdfunding platforms, peer-to-peer lending, and digital marketplaces connect investors directly with green projects, bypassing traditional financial intermediaries. This disintermediation not only reduces transaction costs but also fosters a more direct and transparent connection between investors and sustainable initiatives. Similarly, mobile banking and fintech solutions enable users to make investments in green projects, fostering a more inclusive and sustainable financial ecosystem. The Global Findex Database showed that more and more adults have a formal financial account in developing countries (Demirgüç-Kunt, Klapper, Singer, & Ansar, 2022) in the wake of COVID-19. The Global Findex showed that the number rose to 71% in

2021, which was only 42% a decade ago (Demirgüç-Kunt et al., 2022). In addition, two-thirds of adults use digital payments globally (Demirgüç-Kunt et al., 2022).

Smart contracts that are run on blockchain platforms can automate and verify the fulfilment of environmental commitments, such as carbon offset projects or sustainable supply chain practices (Secinaro, Calandra, & Biancone, 2021; Vigna & Casey, 2019). This enhances the credibility of green finance projects, ensures compliance with regulations, enhances transaction security, and attracts more investors who seek transparency and accountability in their sustainable investments. Similarly, advanced data analytics, such as big data, play a fundamental role in evaluating the risks associated with green finance projects (Payne, 2014). By analysing vast amounts of environmental and financial data, machine learning algorithms can identify potential risks and predict the success of green investments (Richins, Stapleton, Stratopoulos, & Wong, 2017). Scholars (e.g., Andrianaivo and Kpodar (2011); Ozili, Ademiju, and Rachid (2023)) argued that digital financial services can provide easier access to banking services to consumers at the time of financial crises and help in expanding the client base and reducing costs. It also has the potential to improve financial security by enhancing transaction security, compliance with regulations, and access to financial services. However, digital financial services are not available to all users, and there is a need to boost efforts to ensure digital financial services are inclusive and sustainable and that their benefits are accessible to all, including vulnerable consumers.

DFTs and green finance present numerous opportunities; however, these also come with challenges that must be addressed. In today's digital age, the use of DFTs has become more prevalent, and consequently, it has increased the risks of cyber threats such as cybercrime, fraud, opaque pricing, etc. (Tolzmann, 2022) and financial exploitation and data privacy concerns, mostly among vulnerable populations (Zhang, Morris, McNiel, & Binder, 2023). Therefore, it is paramount to protect green finance initiatives from cyberattacks to maintain the integrity and security of sustainable investments. There is also a need for a consumer-centric approach where consumers need to be protected and their private information should be secured sustainably. In addition, customers may not be able to complete transactions during downtime or service interruptions of digital financial services, and they can become frustrated. Therefore, it is essential to protect customers against poor outages, and their feedback should be incorporated. It may not be the case in developing countries due to a lack of regulations and/or resources (Xun, Guanghua, Jiajia, & Zongyue, 2020). On the other side, the risks of scams and frauds are growing considerably with the evolving use of electronic funds transfers, social media, and payment apps (Zhang et al., 2023). Several countries are facing this challenge, and people have lost billions of dollars in such scams. According to an MBIE survey, Kiwis lost $220 million to scams in 2022 (RNZ, 2023). Similarly, it is reported that Australians lost $3.1 billion in

2022 (Kelly, 2023). This number is even bigger in the USA, where scams cost $8.8 billion in 2022, up 30% from 2021 (Walrack, 2023). This highlights the need for a regulatory framework by governments. However, the regulatory landscape for DFTs for green finance is still evolving. Clear and standardised regulatory frameworks are essential to ensure that these innovations adhere to ethical and sustainable practices, protecting both investors and the environment. It is also pivotal to provide proper education and awareness to consumers to exert responsible financial behaviour in the era of digitalisation (Bulyga, Vasyukova, Grigoryeva, & Dimov, 2022). This chapter explores the interdependent association between digital financial technologies and green finance, emphasising risks, challenges, and opportunities to accelerate the transition towards a more sustainable and environmentally friendly global economy. In particular, the chapter aims to explore the risks, challenges, and opportunities that are associated with the use of DFTs for green finance.

2. METHODOLOGY

This chapter aims to explore the risks, challenges, and opportunities that are associated with the use of DFTs for green finance. In line with scholars (e.g., Arslan (2020a); Arslan and Alqatan (2020); Moher, Liberati, Tetzlaff, Altman, and Group* (2009)), the authors of this chapter employed a two-stage process. In the first stage, the authors of this chapter searched the relevant journal articles from Google Scholar, Web of Science, and Scopus databases with keyword searches. They only considered those relevant journal articles that were published in English from 2000 to 2023. A total of 245 papers were identified in the initial search process. The duplicate and some other irrelevant articles were removed, and the final sample was 183 articles. In the second stage, the chapter authors applied a thematic approach because this chapter aims to explore the risks, challenges, and opportunities that are associated with the use of DFTs for green finance. The thematic approach was the right choice for analysing and understanding published papers. In this approach, the text is analysed and coded into different categories and concepts. These categories are well-established elements of grounded theory (Corbin & Strauss, 1990). Several researchers (e.g., Arslan (2020a, 2020b, 2022)) have already used a similar approach.

In this chapter, the authors applied three coding methods (i.e., open coding, axial coding, and selective coding) for extracting the themes. In the first coding method (open coding), the authors of this chapter went through the articles to abridge the raw data into discrete parts and create open codes for labelling. This stage resulted in 50 open codes. In the next stage (axial coding), they started drawing connections among the open codes and organising them to create categories. This stage resulted in 15 categories. These categories were fundamental to their next stage of coding.

In the end, the authors of this chapter applied selective coding to the data, where they discovered the aggregate themes (core categories) by connecting the existing categories. The following four aggregate themes were extracted:

I. Green Innovation
II. Green Investment and Sustainability
III. Data-Driven Approach
IV. Risks and Challenges of DFTs for Green Finance

3. RESULTS AND DISCUSSION

This section presents the findings of the thematic analysis. This section also discusses the themes and supports existing studies.

3.1 Green Innovation

Technology, particularly digital financial technologies, emerges as a catalyst for innovation in green finance. Blockchain, artificial intelligence, and data analytics are leveraged to enhance transparency, efficiency, and accountability in sustainable finance projects. These technologies facilitate the development of new models for financing, monitoring, and reporting on green initiatives. Wang, Song, and Qi (2023) conducted a study in China and found that digital inclusive finance helped innovative SMEs access credit and stimulated consumption, which led to urban green innovation. They further argued that digitally inclusive finance is more effective for green innovation in eastern and high-environmental-regulation cities. In a similar vein, scholars argued that innovation is significantly affected by characteristics of the external environment, including financial constraints and supervision (Xu, Yao, & Zhou, 2023) and green finance (Liu, Zhao, Dong, Wang, & Sun, 2023). In addition, the government's financial intervention can play a pivotal role in promoting innovation. Shen, Fu, and Song (2023) conducted a study and found that digital finance enhances the scope of green credit, enhances green innovation, and has a heterogeneous effect on sustainable total factor eco-efficiency. Scholars also found a positive link between coordinated digital financial development and green innovation (Yu & Peng, 2023). Xue and Zhang (2022) found that digital financial inclusion alleviates financial mismatches and corporate financing constraints, which enhances the green innovation of enterprises. Scholars also argued that digital finance stimulates technological innovation through research and development and dynamic consumer demand (Li, Ye, & Zhang, 2023). In addition, digital finance supports technological innovation by fostering the supply of non-financial funds (Li et al.,

2023). Jin and Wang (2024) found that two-way FDI can promote green technology innovation while digital finance plays a moderating role.

The existing studies reveal that digital finance promotes innovation in several ways, removes financial constraints, and offers investment opportunities to investors and financial institutions.

3.2 Green Investment and Sustainability

Research indicates a growing trend in the development of innovative financial instruments to support green projects. These instruments include green bonds, sustainability-linked loans, and green investment funds (Coulthard, 2020). These financial mechanisms aim to attract capital for eco-friendly initiatives by aligning financial returns with positive environmental outcomes. Research highlights the pivotal role of the private sector in driving innovation in green finance. Environmental, social, and governance (ESG) considerations and sustainability initiatives contribute to the emergence of innovative financial solutions. Scholars argued that digital finance predominantly facilitates corporate ESG development (Mo, Che, & Ning, 2023) and improves internal control efficiency and pollution control capabilities (Kong & Liu, 2023). Zhang (2023a) argued that digital finance empowerment alleviates financial constraints, hence reducing financial costs, which leads to a reduction in extreme ESG hypocrisy resistance. Scholars argued that DFTs reduce corporate financial volatility (Tang, Chen, Zhang, & Zhang, 2023), minimise the risk of greenwashing, and allocate credit resources efficiently, which promotes green investment and sustainability (Kaur, 2023). The EU has shown a positive attitude towards green finance and provided several incentives for institutional and private investors (Afzal, Rasoulinezhad, & Malik, 2022; Migliorelli & Dessertine, 2019). Mavlutova et al. (2023) conducted a study in EU and OECD countries to identify the benefits and challenges and investigate the trends in green finance. They found a positive impact of green bonds on renewable energy supply and carbon reduction. Ma (2023) argued that several SMEs were able to secure funding for green projects through digital financial platforms, such as peer-to-peer lending, crowdfunding, and other alternative financing models. However, the private sector must play its role in scaling up green finance innovation. Zhang (2023b) conducted a study and found that digital finance empowerment plays a positive role in increasing green innovation performance. Similarly, Migliorelli and Dessertine (2019) also found a negative relationship between financial development and four measures of environmental degradation. Yuan, Cen, and Du (2023) argued that digital finance enhances governance and protects the ecological environment. However, Qiu, Li, and Wu (2023) conducted a study to examine the effect of direct financing on regional green development and found mixed results. They documented a positive relationship in the western and central regions and a negative effect in the eastern regions. The existing studies reveal that DFTs promote green investment and sustainability. It also helps reduce ESG hypocrisy and protects the ecological environment.

3.3 Data-Driven Approach

Digital financial technologies promote a data-driven decision approach for green finance by leveraging digital transformation and innovation. Successful green finance innovation often involves active engagement with local communities and various stakeholders. The existing studies highlight the importance of understanding the needs and concerns of local communities in the design and implementation of green finance initiatives (Wang et al., 2023). The inclusive approaches that involve diverse stakeholders contribute to the success and sustainability of green finance projects. In addition, the integration of digital financial technologies enables risk management and reforms in green finance (Boskov & Drakulevski, 2017). Li (2003) argued that technology will keep affecting the future development of financial risk management. In addition, Kong, Sun, Sun, and Song (2022) argued that big data helps digital financial institutions alleviate information asymmetry and foster green innovation. Similarly, Ai, Sun, and Kong (2023) found that digital finance reduces agency costs, increases information transparency, and reduces the risk of stock price collapse. Scholars also studied the nexus between artificial intelligence and green innovation and found a positive correlation (Wang, Sun, & Li, 2024). Hasan, Popp, and Oláh (2020) found a significant positive effect of big data on risk analysis, financial institutions, financial markets, and fraud detection. However, it is paramount to mention that digital financial technologies also introduce new risks and unintended consequences for the environment and users, such as negative environmental effects, cybercrime, and disposal of software and hardware.

3.4 Risks and Challenges of DFTs for Green Finance

Digital financial technologies provide several opportunities. However, these also raise risks and challenges. Rapid technological advancement has raised challenges in the disposal of older technology, such as hardware and software (Morgan, 2022). Similarly, the risks of cybercrimes, fraud, possible tax evasion, and illicit financial flows have multiplied (Morgan, 2022). The rapid growth in online users in the wake of COVID-19 has raised several ethical challenges. Globally, there is a surge in cybercrimes such as stealing sensitive corporate and consumer financial data through different fraudulent means and theft of online financial assets. Scholars argue that consumers understand the environmental benefits of using digital financial technologies; however, they are concerned about fraud and scams (Shankaranarayana,

Ramaswamy, Bagrecha, Hiremath, & Madhavi, 2023) and lack awareness and relevant education. On the other side, several scholars have criticised the use of digital finance for increasing carbon emissions (Xuan, Ge, Yang, & Zhang, 2024). Several scholars have argued that it is a challenge to protect consumers from cybercrimes due to a lack of policies and regulations (Boskov & Drakulevski, 2017; Delina, 2023; Morgan, 2022). Those countries that have clear and robust regulations related to environmental standards and sustainable finance tend to see more innovation in financial products and services that align with green objectives (Shao & Chen, 2023). Otto and Thornton (2023) also argued for the need for regulatory frameworks and the potential risk of technology being misused. Scholars highlighted the need for green credit incentives to promote digital financial technologies for green finance in regions with a lower level of green development (Du et al., 2022). It is evident that digital financial technologies pose several risks and challenges; however, there is a need to address the policy gaps without compromising innovation (Pavlidis, 2021).

4. CONCLUSION, RECOMMENDATIONS, SIGNIFICANCE, AND FUTURE RESEARCH DIRECTIONS

This chapter explores the interdependent association between digital financial technologies and green finance, emphasising risks, challenges, and opportunities to accelerate the transition towards a more sustainable and environmentally friendly global economy. The thematic analysis explored four themes, i.e., green innovation, green investment and sustainability, data-driven approaches, and the risks and challenges of DFTs for green finance. The findings reveal that DFTs can play a critical role in green innovation, creating opportunities, and combating environmental crises without posing additional risks. For example, there are fintech services for green finance, blockchain for transparency and trust, and AI for data analysis and interpretation. DFTs reshape the financial systems, thus increasing the resilience of financial institutions, which is paramount for supporting activities that contribute to reducing carbon emissions and fighting against climate change. The findings also reveal that the DFTs offer several opportunities for green finance, provide long-term value, provide environmental protection, and create sustainable investment portfolios.

Green finance projects need substantive investment, and they bring opportunities for investors, asset managers, or lending institutions. These findings are consistent with Falcone and Sica (2019), who also argued that green finance is a win-win solution. In addition, the findings reveal that DFTs gather a lot of data and help in making informed decisions for green finance. It also helps in tracking the progress of green finance projects and provides opportunities for SMEs to access funding for green innovation. However, the DFTs also pose several risks and challenges (such as cybercrime, fraud, scams, tax evasion, capital-intensive technologies, a lack of awareness, uncertain policies, and an absence of protection mechanisms) that need to be addressed. The findings reveal that many consumers are victims of financial scams and frauds, are exposed to cyber threats, and thus have lost billions of dollars. This is due to a lack of awareness, uncertain policies, and the absence of protection mechanisms. On the other side, people can use DFTs for tax evasion. Drawing on the notion of institutional theory, the authors of this chapter argued that institutional and social pressure may force governments and regulatory bodies to take swift action to address these risks and challenges. They also recommended that the regulatory framework should prioritise risk assessment, provide incentives, expand international cooperation, and contribute to cyber security and consumer protection. In addition, the government and regulators should run awareness campaigns and provide relevant education. Hence, educational institutes can also play an imperative role in addressing these challenges to fully utilise the benefits of DFTs for green finance. This chapter contributes to the existing literature on DFTs for green finance and has several practical implications for scholars and policymakers. The findings can be used by policymakers and regulators to identify the true benefits of DFTs for green finance and will help in developing relevant policies and regulations. The educational institutes can use the findings as a foundation and make relevant changes to the curriculum to equip the learners for the future. This chapter also has some limitations. In this chapter, the authors only used secondary data for thematic analysis; future researchers may also use a combination of primary and secondary data. Due to limited time and cost, the authors of this chapter only collected articles from 2000 to 2023 and ignored the dot-com bubble. Future research can be conducted by including the dot-com bubble and linking it with disruptive technologies such as artificial intelligence and blockchain.

REFERENCES

Afzal, A., Rasoulinezhad, E., & Malik, Z. (2022). Green finance and sustainable development in Europe. *Economic research-. Ekonomska Istrazivanja*, *35*(1), 5150–5163. doi:10.1080/1331677X.2021.2024081

Ai, Y., Sun, G., & Kong, T. (2023). Digital finance and stock price crash risk. *International Review of Economics & Finance*, *88*(November), 607–619. doi:10.1016/j.iref.2023.07.003

Andrianaivo, M., & Kpodar, K. (2011). *ICT, financial inclusion, and growth: Evidence from African countries.* IMF Working Paper. International Monetary Fund. Retrieved from https://www.imf.org/external/pubs/ft/wp/2011/wp1173.pdf

Arnone, M., & Crovella, T. (2023). The Role of Green Finance in Supporting Maritime Sustainable Development. In Fintech and Sustainability: How Financial Technologies Can Help Address Today's Environmental and Societal Challenges (pp. 53-87). Springer. doi:10.1007/978-3-031-40647-8_4

Arslan, M. (2020a). Corporate social sustainability in supply chain management: A literature review. *Journal of Global Responsibility*, *11*(3), 233–255. doi:10.1108/JGR-11-2019-0108

Arslan, M. (2020b). Mechanisms of labour exploitation: The case of Pakistan. *International Journal of Law and Management*, *62*(1), 1–21. doi:10.1108/IJLMA-07-2018-0145

Arslan, M. (2022). Succession Planning in Family-Owned Business Evidence From an Emerging Economy. In *Research Anthology on Strategies for Maintaining Successful Family Firms* (pp. 504–528). IGI Global. doi:10.4018/978-1-6684-3550-2.ch022

Arslan, M., & Alqatan, A. (2020). Role of institutions in shaping corporate governance system: Evidence from emerging economy. *Heliyon*, *6*(3), 1–17. doi:10.1016/j.heliyon.2020.e03520 PMID:32181393

Boskov, T., & Drakulevski, L. (2017). Addressing the role of risk management and digital finance technology on financial inclusion. *Quality - Access to Success*, *18*(161), 113–115.

Bulyga, E. S., Vasyukova, L. K., Grigoryeva, V. I., & Dimov, R. P. (2022). Digital transformation of the financial market: Risks and opportunities. *Наука Красноярья*, *11*(2), 49–67. doi:10.12731/2070-7568-2022-11-2-49-67

Campiglio, E. (2016). Beyond carbon pricing: The role of banking and monetary policy in financing the transition to a low-carbon economy. *Ecological Economics*, *121*, 220–230. doi:10.1016/j.ecolecon.2015.03.020

Corbin, J. M., & Strauss, A. (1990). Grounded theory research: Procedures, canons, and evaluative criteria. *Qualitative Sociology*, *13*(1), 3–21. doi:10.1007/BF00988593

Coulthard, E. B. (2020). *Green bonds and blockchain: How technology may help navigate the increasingly complex world of sustainability regulation* [Master Thesis]. University of Oslo, Norway. Retrieved from https://www.duo.uio.no/bitstream/handle/10852/84662/1/Master-thesis-final.pdf

Delina, L. L. (2023). Fintech RE in a global finance centre: Expert perceptions of the benefits of and challenges to digital financing of distributed and decentralised renewables in Hong Kong. *Energy Research & Social Science*, *97*(March), 102997. doi:10.1016/j.erss.2023.102997

Demirgüç-Kunt, A., Klapper, L., Singer, D., & Ansar, S. (2022). *The Global Findex Database 2021: Financial inclusion, digital payments, and resilience in the age of COVID-19*. World Bank Publications. doi:10.1596/978-1-4648-1897-4

DiMaggio, P. J., & Powell, W. W. (1983). The iron cage revisited: Institutional isomorphism and collective rationality in organizational fields. *American Sociological Review*, *48*(2), 147–160. doi:10.2307/2095101

Du, M., Zhang, R., Chai, S., Li, Q., Sun, R., & Chu, W. (2022). Can green finance policies stimulate technological innovation and financial performance? Evidence from Chinese listed green enterprises. *Sustainability (Basel)*, *14*(15), 9287. doi:10.3390/su14159287

Falcone, P. M., & Sica, E. (2019). Assessing the opportunities and challenges of green finance in Italy: An analysis of the biomass production sector. *Sustainability (Basel)*, *11*(2), 517. doi:10.3390/su11020517

Hasan, M. M., Popp, J., & Oláh, J. (2020). Current landscape and influence of big data on finance. *Journal of Big Data*, *7*(1), 1–17. doi:10.1186/s40537-020-00291-z

Hoffman, S. D. (1999). School texts, the written word, and political indoctrination: A review of moral education curricula in modern Japan (1886–1997). *History of Education*, *28*(1), 87–96. doi:10.1080/004676099284816

Jin, Q., & Wang, K. (2024). Exploring the moderating role of digital finance in the two-way foreign direct investment and green technology innovation nexus: an empirical evidence from China. *Environmental Science and Pollution Research*, 1-10. doi:10.1007/s11356-024-31896-z

Kaur, G. (2023). Application of Blockchain for Sustaining Green Finance. In *Perspectives on Blockchain Technology and Responsible Investing* (pp. 226–235). IGI Global. doi:10.4018/978-1-6684-8361-9.ch011

Kelly, C. (2023). Australians report record $3.1bn losses to scams, with real amount even higher. *The Guardian*. Retrieved from https://www.theguardian.com/australia-news/2023/apr/17/australians-report-record-31bn-losses-to-scams-with-real-amount-even-higher-accc-says

Kong, D., & Liu, B. (2023). Digital technology and corporate social responsibility: Evidence from China. *Emerging Markets Finance & Trade*, *59*(9), 1–27. doi:10.1080/1540496X.2023.2199122

Kong, T., Sun, R., Sun, G., & Song, Y. (2022). Effects of digital finance on green innovation considering information asymmetry: An empirical study based on Chinese listed firms. *Emerging Markets Finance & Trade*, *58*(15), 4399–4411. doi:10.1080/1540496X.2022.2083953

Li, J., Ye, S., & Zhang, Y. (2023). How digital finance promotes technological innovation: Evidence from China. *Finance Research Letters*, *58*(December), 104298. doi:10.1016/j.frl.2023.104298

Li, S. (2003). Future trends and challenges of financial risk management in the digital economy. *Managerial Finance*, *29*(5/6), 111–125. doi:10.1108/03074350310768797

Liu, Y., Zhao, C., Dong, K., Wang, K., & Sun, L. (2023). How does green finance achieve urban carbon unlocking? Evidence from China. *Urban Climate*, *52*, 101742. doi:10.1016/j.uclim.2023.101742

Loiseau, E., Saikku, L., Antikainen, R., Droste, N., Hansjürgens, B., Pitkänen, K., Leskinen, P., Kuikman, P., & Thomsen, M. (2016). Green economy and related concepts: An overview. *Journal of Cleaner Production*, *139*, 361–371. doi:10.1016/j.jclepro.2016.08.024

Ma, J. (2023). How digital finance promotes renewable energy consumption in China? *Environmental Science and Pollution Research International*, *30*(46), 102490–102503. doi:10.1007/s11356-023-29504-7 PMID:37667128

Maheswar, R., & Kanagachidambaresan, G. (2020). Sustainable development through Internet of Things. *Wireless Networks*, *26*(May), 2305–2306. doi:10.1007/s11276-020-02269-4

Mavlutova, I., Spilbergs, A., Verdenhofs, A., Kuzmina, J., Arefjevs, I., & Natrins, A. (2023). The Role of Green Finance in Fostering the Sustainability of the Economy and Renewable Energy Supply: Recent Issues and Challenges. *Energies*, *16*(23), 7712. doi:10.3390/en16237712

Migliorelli, M., & Dessertine, P. (2019). *The rise of green finance in Europe* (Vol. 2). Palgrave Macmillan Cham. doi:10.1007/978-3-030-22510-0

Mo, Y., Che, Y., & Ning, W. (2023). Digital Finance Promotes Corporate ESG Performance: Evidence from China. *Sustainability (Basel)*, *15*(14), 11323. doi:10.3390/su151411323

Moher, D., Liberati, A., Tetzlaff, J., & Altman, D. G. (2009). Preferred reporting items for systematic reviews and meta-analyses: The PRISMA statement. *Annals of Internal Medicine*, *151*(4), 264–269. doi:10.7326/0003-4819-151-4-200908180-00135 PMID:19622511

Morgan, P. J. (2022). Assessing the risks associated with green digital finance and policies for coping with them. In *Green Digital Finance and Sustainable Development Goals* (pp. 51–68). Springer. doi:10.1007/978-981-19-2662-4_3

Otto, M., & Thornton, J. (2023). The Role Of Digital Finance And Technological Innovation In The Growth Of The Green Economy. *Qo 'qon universiteti xabarnomasi, 7*(7), 19-22. doi:10.54613/ku.v7i7.771

Ozili, P. K., Ademiju, A., & Rachid, S. (2023). Impact of financial inclusion on economic growth: Review of existing literature and directions for future research. *International Journal of Social Economics*, *50*(8), 1105–1122. doi:10.1108/IJSE-05-2022-0339

Pavlidis, G. (2021). Europe in the digital age: Regulating digital finance without suffocating innovation. *Law, Innovation and Technology*, *13*(2), 464–477. doi:10.1080/17579961.2021.1977222

Payne, R. (2014). Discussion of 'Digitisation,' Big Data' and the transformation of accounting information' by Alnoor Bhimani and Leslie Willcocks (2014). *Accounting and Business Research*, *44*(4), 491–495. doi:10.1080/00014788.2014.910053

Pazarbasioglu, C., Mora, A. G., Uttamchandani, M., Natarajan, H., Feyen, E., & Saal, M. (2020). *Digital financial services*. World Bank. Retrieved from https://pubdocs.worldbank.org/en/230281588169110691/Digital-Financial-Services.pdf

Qiu, W., Li, Y., & Wu, H. (2023). The role of direct financing on regional green development: Inhibition or promotion? *Economic Change and Restructuring*, *56*(5), 3665–3699. doi:10.1007/s10644-023-09546-0

Richins, G., Stapleton, A., Stratopoulos, T. C., & Wong, C. (2017). Big data analytics: Opportunity or threat for the accounting profession? *Journal of Information Systems*, *31*(3), 63–79. doi:10.2308/isys-51805

RNZ. (2023). *Scams cost Kiwis almost $200m - Ministry of Business, Innovation and Employment (MBIE)*. Retrieved from https://www.nzherald.co.nz/nz/scams-cost-kiwis-almost-200m-ministry-of-business-innovation-and-employment-report/7BA6OADPBBGNLDXU765DEXUFQM/

Sarkis, J., Zhu, Q., & Lai, K. (2011). An organizational theoretic review of green supply chain management literature. *International Journal of Production Economics*, *130*(1), 1–15. doi:10.1016/j.ijpe.2010.11.010

Savignac, F. (2008). Impact of financial constraints on innovation: What can be learned from a direct measure? *Economics of Innovation and New Technology*, *17*(6), 553–569. doi:10.1080/10438590701538432

Schildt, H. (2022). The Institutional Logic of Digitalization. In T. Gegenhuber, D. Logue, C. R. Hinings, & M. Barrett (Eds.), *Digital Transformation and Institutional Theory* (Vol. 83, pp. 235–251). Emerald Publishing Limited. doi:10.1108/S0733-558X20220000083010

Secinaro, S., Calandra, D., & Biancone, P. (2021). *Blockchain, trust, and trust accounting: Can blockchain technology substitute trust created by intermediaries in trust accounting?* Retrieved from https://money.usnews.com/money/personal-finance/family-finance/articles/what-fraud-costs-consumers#:~:text=American%20consumers%20lost%20%248.8%20billion,report%20median%20of%20about%20%24650

Shankaranarayana, R., Ramaswamy, S., Bagrecha, C., Hiremath, K., & Madhavi, A. (2023). Promoting Economic Sustainability Through the Adoption of Digital Payment Systems. In *The Sustainable Fintech Revolution: Building a Greener Future for Finance* (pp. 145–161). IGI Global. doi:10.4018/979-8-3693-0008-4.ch008

Shao, L., & Chen, J. (2023). Digital finance and regional green innovation: The perspective of environmental regulation. *Environmental Science and Pollution Research International*, *30*(36), 85592–85610. doi:10.1007/s11356-023-28356-5 PMID:37391561

Shen, Y., Fu, Y., & Song, M. (2023). Digital finance promotes sustainable total factor eco-efficiency: Evidence from China. *Applied Economics*, 1–15. doi:10.1080/00036846.2023.2211337

Tang, D., Chen, W., Zhang, Q., & Zhang, J. (2023). Impact of Digital Finance on Green Technology Innovation: The Mediating Effect of Financial Constraints. *Sustainability (Basel)*, *15*(4), 3393. doi:10.3390/su15043393

Tolzmann, M. (2022). *CGAP Funder Survey 2020*. World Bank. Retrieved from https://www.cgap.org/sites/default/files/publications/2022_01_Focus_Note_2020_Funder_Survey.pdf

UNEP. (2011). *Towards a Green Economy: Pathways to Sustainable Development and Poverty Eradication*. United Nations Environment Programme.

UNFCCC. (2015). *United Nations framework convention on climate change: The Paris Agreement.* Retrieved from https://unfccc.int/process-and-meetings/the-paris-agreement/the-paris-agreement

Vigna, P., & Casey, M. J. (2019). *The truth machine: the blockchain and the future of everything*. St. Martin's Press.

Wang, M., Song, W., & Qi, X. (2023). Digital inclusive finance, government intervention, and urban green technology innovation. *Environmental Science and Pollution Research International*, (October), 1–14. doi:10.1007/s11356-023-29395-8 PMID:37848800

Wang, Q., Sun, T., & Li, R. (2024). Does artificial intelligence promote green innovation? An assessment based on direct, indirect, spillover, and heterogeneity effects. *Energy & Environment.*

Wong, C. W., Lai, K., Shang, K.-C., Lu, C.-S., & Leung, T. (2012). Green operations and the moderating role of environmental management capability of suppliers on manufacturing firm performance. *International Journal of Production Economics*, *140*(1), 283–294. doi:10.1016/j.ijpe.2011.08.031

Xiao, M., & Peng, X. (2023). Decomposition of carbon emission influencing factors and research on emission reduction performance of energy consumption in China. *Frontiers in Environmental Science*, *10*, 1096650. doi:10.3389/fenvs.2022.1096650

Xu, R., Yao, D., & Zhou, M. (2023). Does the development of digital inclusive finance improve the enthusiasm and quality of corporate green technology innovation? *Journal of Innovation & Knowledge*, *8*(3), 100382. doi:10.1016/j.jik.2023.100382

Xuan, S., Ge, W., Yang, P., & Zhang, Y. (2024). Exploring digital finance, financial regulations and carbon emission nexus: New insight from resources efficiency, industrial structure and green innovation in China. *Resources Policy*, *88*, 104452. doi:10.1016/j.resourpol.2023.104452

Xue, L., & Zhang, X. (2022). Can digital financial inclusion promote green innovation in heavily polluting companies? *International Journal of Environmental Research and Public Health*, *19*(12), 7323. doi:10.3390/ijerph19127323 PMID:35742571

Xun, Z., Guanghua, W., Jiajia, Z., & Zongyue, H. (2020). Digital economy, financial inclusion and inclusive growth. *Chinese Economy*, *15*(3), 92–105.

Yang, C., & Masron, T. A. (2022). Impact of digital finance on energy efficiency in the context of green sustainable development. *Sustainability (Basel)*, *14*(18), 11250. doi:10.3390/su141811250

Yang, G., Wang, F., Deng, F., & Xiang, X. (2023). Impact of digital transformation on enterprise carbon intensity: The Moderating Role of Digital Information Resources. *International Journal of Environmental Research and Public Health*, *20*(3), 2178. doi:10.3390/ijerph20032178 PMID:36767545

Yuan, H., Cen, W., & Du, T. (2023). Digital Finance and County Ecological Performance—New Evidence from China Counties. *Sustainability (Basel)*, *15*(24), 16691. doi:10.3390/su152416691

Zhang, D. (2023a). Can digital finance empowerment reduce extreme ESG hypocrisy resistance to improve green innovation? *Energy Economics*, *125*(September), 106756. doi:10.1016/j.eneco.2023.106756

Zhang, D. (2023b). Can digital finance empowerment reduce extreme ESG hypocrisy resistance to improve green innovation? *Energy Economics*, *125*, 106756. doi:10.1016/j.eneco.2023.106756

Zhang, T., Morris, N. P., McNiel, D. E., & Binder, R. (2023). Elder Financial Exploitation in the Digital Age. *The Journal of the American Academy of Psychiatry and the Law*, *51*(2), 173–180. doi:10.29158/jaapl.220047-21 PMID:36928135

KEY TERMS AND DEFINITIONS

Artificial Intelligence: Is the process of simulating human intelligence through machines and computer systems.

Blockchain: Refers to an advanced database mechanism that allows secure and transparent information sharing within a network.

Digital Finance: Is a term that refers to expounding on the impact of new technologies on the financial services industry.

Financial Technology: Refers to the use of new technologies such as artificial intelligence, blockchain, cloud computing, and big data (referred to as ABCD) to provide financial services along with traditional financial methods.

Green Finance: Refers to financial products and services that promote and adopt sustainable practices.

Green Innovation: Is a combination of technological innovation and environmental protection.

Green Investment: Means allocating financial resources to sustainable projects and/or practices.

Chapter 11
Navigating the Digital Transformation Landscape:
Implications for Accounting

Shuchita Pal
Christ University, India

Meesha Singh
Christ University, India

Manjari Sharma
Christ University, India

ABSTRACT

Digitalization brings significant changes to the world, particularly in industries where information technology is essential. Accounting is one profession that has benefited from digital developments. The goal of this chapter is to synthesize recent academic studies on accounting digitalization and provide some suggestions for future research. Because of the short- and long-term effects of environmental factors on both the corporate and financial sectors, it is clear that business leaders and investors must measure and manage environmental risks to address the impact on business and society. This chapter aims to contribute to these critical discussions by providing new insights of digitalization, tax avoidance, reporting, accounting, and green finance.

DOI: 10.4018/979-8-3693-1678-8.ch011

INTRODUCTION

The digital transformation can spur innovation and productivity growth across many activities, transform public services, and improve wellbeing as information, knowledge and data become more widely available (Brynjolfsson & McAfee, 2014; Arntz et al., 2016; Mokyr, 2014). This transformation has impacted virtually every sector, and one field that has experienced substantial disruption is accounting (Brynjolfsson & McAfee, 2014; Arntz et al., 2016). This chapter embarks on a comprehensive exploration of the far-reaching consequences of technological innovation and the pervasive use of digital tools, with a particular emphasis on their influence on digitalization within four critical domains: reporting practices, tax avoidance strategies, accounting procedures, and the burgeoning field of green finance.

The primary objective of this chapter is to provide readers with a thorough understanding of how digitalization has revolutionized these vital areas of financial practice (Brynjolfsson & McAfee, 2014; Arntz et al., 2016). Through rigorous analysis and empirical evidence, we illuminate the profound shifts in reporting practices, the transformation of traditional tax avoidance methods, the evolution of accounting protocols, and the ascent of green finance as a prominent player in the modern financial landscape.

In essence, this research endeavors to offer a cross-national perspective on the economic consequences of technological innovation, particularly within the realm of financial market development. The central question guiding our exploration revolves around the causal relationship between financial market development and technological innovation (Schumpeter, 1934; Levine, 1982; Bresnahan & Trajtenberg, 1995). To tackle this question effectively, we grapple with the challenges inherent in addressing reverse causality and the omission of pertinent variables (Levine, 1982; Bresnahan & Trajtenberg, 1995).

To contextualize this discussion, it is imperative to draw insights from the established body of research that examines the intricate interplay between financial markets and technological innovation. A key finding from this extensive literature is the understanding that financial markets often emerge in economies with substantial growth potential (Bresnahan & Trajtenberg, 1995; Goldin, C., & Katz, L., 1998). These markets serve as crucial sources of capital, facilitating the pursuit of ambitious growth opportunities that, in turn, fuel technological innovation (Bresnahan & Trajtenberg, 1995; Goldin, C., & Katz, L., 1998). In such contexts, it is the dynamism of the economy that takes the lead, with finance playing a pivotal role in propelling growth and innovation.

In this introductory section, we delineate the key areas of focus for this chapter: reporting practices, tax avoidance, accounting procedures, and green finance. Additionally, we provide an overview of the research methodology employed in our study, including the measures taken to address potential challenges associated with causality and omitted variables.

Digitalization of Reporting Practices

In the context of tax reporting, "digitalization" refers to the full integration and application of cutting-edge digital technology for the purpose of streamlining, automating, and optimizing a variety of processes associated with tax-related operations. It entails switching from manual, conventional processes to digital platforms and tools that make use of blockchain, data analytics, and artificial intelligence (AI). The goal of this change is to make tax reporting processes more accurate, transparent, and efficient.

The initial area of exploration within this chapter centers on the digitalization of reporting practices (Brynjolfsson & McAfee, 2014; Corlin Christensen, R., & Lips, W.,2021). Conventional financial reporting has been profoundly impacted by the digital age, marked by a transition from manual data entry to automated systems capable of generating real-time financial. As businesses adapt to this evolving landscape, the transparency, accuracy, and timeliness of financial reporting have witnessed substantial enhancements (Liu, Y., & Chen, L., 2022). This transformation has not only bolstered the decision-making process for stakeholders but has also engendered discussions surrounding data security and the imperative need for updated regulatory frameworks.

Evolving Tax Avoidance Strategies in the Digital Era

The second critical domain of investigation delves into the evolving strategies employed in tax avoidance. The advent of digitalization has created opportunities for multinational corporations to optimize their tax liabilities through intricate financial structures, transfer pricing mechanisms, and the utilization of tax. In contrast, tax authorities worldwide are harnessing digital tools to combat tax evasion and enforce compliance. This dynamic landscape has engendered a continuous battle between corporations seeking to minimize tax burdens and governments striving to safeguard their revenue streams.

Digital Transformation of Reporting Practices

The adoption of digital solutions has catalyzed a significant shift in reporting practices across industries (Fosso Wamba,2019). Companies are increasingly leveraging digital tools and technologies to enhance the accuracy, timeliness, and transparency of their financial reporting (Fosso Wamba,2019). This transformation has been particularly instrumental in improving the efficiency of data collection, analysis, and dissemination, empowering stakeholders with real-time insights into financial performance. For instance, cloud-based financial reporting systems have become commonplace, enabling businesses to streamline their reporting processes and provide stakeholders with instant access to critical financial information.

Understanding how digitization affects formal and informal standards in financial and environmental reporting frameworks is made easier with the help of institutional theory. In this sense, "institutions" refers to the established practices, conventions, and structures that guide the conduct of organizations. Digitalization has a significant impact on these institutional environments as it continues to change the corporate landscape.

Formal Regulations in Accounting: The Impact of Digitalization

Financial reporting has been transformed by digitalization, which has made it possible to analyze data in real-time, automate tasks, and employ sophisticated analytical tools. Formal regulations controlling reporting standards and procedures are directly impacted by this. For example, the use of extensible Business Reporting Language (XBRL) makes financial data more uniform and machine-readable, improving report comparability and transparency. Furthermore, the possibility of using blockchain technology to create transparent, safe, and unchangeable financial records is being investigated.

Changing Institutional Environments

As a result of these technical developments, governments, standard-setting bodies, and regulatory agencies are compelled to adjust to the ever-changing environment. As these organizations adapt to the opportunities and difficulties posed by digitization, the institutional environment is shaped. Regulatory agencies might, for instance, modify reporting requirements to take new technologies into account and make sure that the formal regulations match the functionalities of digital tools.

Informal Guidelines for Environmental Reporting: The Impact of Digitization

When it comes to environmental reporting, where businesses are being forced to reveal their sustainability initiatives, digitalization is essential. The gathering, processing, and reporting of environmental data are made easier by the use of digital tools. An organization's eco-friendly actions can be more accurately and comprehensively portrayed thanks to the real-time monitoring and reporting of environmental data using machine learning algorithms and Internet of Things (IoT) devices.

Changing Institutional Environments

Digitalization has an impact on the informal norms that exist inside the environmental reporting system in addition to the statutory regulations. Consumers and investors alike are become more environmentally sensitive as stakeholders. Organizations are therefore encouraged to implement sustainable practices and openly share their progress. Organizations now have to abide by a new set of unwritten norms in order to remain legitimate and acceptable in society as a result of the stakeholders' changing values.

Transformation of Accounting Procedures

Our analysis extends further to the transformation of accounting procedures in the digital age. With the automation of routine tasks, accountants now find themselves with more time to engage in strategic analysis and decision support. The integration of artificial intelligence and machine learning into accounting software has unlocked new horizons for predictive analytics and risk assessment. Nevertheless, this transformation has also engendered discussions about the future role of accountants and the requisite upskilling needed to remain relevant in this evolving landscape.

Challenges to Traditional Accounting Procedures

The advent of digitalization has posed both challenges and opportunities to traditional accounting procedures. Automation and the integration of artificial intelligence have led to the automation of routine accounting tasks, freeing up accountants to engage in higher-value strategic. However, this transformation has also raised questions about the evolving role of accountants and the need for continuous upskilling to navigate the changing landscape effectively.

Addressing Tax Avoidance in the Digital Era

Digitalization has presented both challenges and opportunities in the realm of tax avoidance (Niels Johannesen and Gabriel Zucman., 2014). On one hand, multinational corporations have employed digital tools to optimize their tax strategies through complex financial structures and cross-border transactions (Johannesen and Gabriel Zucman., 2014). On the other hand, tax authorities worldwide have harnessed technology to combat tax evasion and enhance transparency (Johannesen and

Gabriel Zucman., 2014). Initiatives such as the Common Reporting Standard (CRS) and the digitalization of tax administration have played pivotal roles in addressing tax avoidance in the digital era (OECD 2019). Effect on Strategies for Avoiding Taxation are Advanced Data Analysis and Blockchain Technology for Transparency. Tax experts may perform comprehensive studies using data analytics, which makes it more difficult for organizations to falsify or conceal financial information. This has the potential to discourage tax avoidance and evasion. Businesses may find it increasingly difficult to participate in aggressive tax evasion tactics due to the transparency this technology offers. Transactions on the blockchain can be tracked down and verified because of its immutability.

The Emergence of Green Finance

Financial goods, services, and investments with an eye toward supporting ecologically friendly initiatives are referred to as "green finance." It includes a variety of financial instruments that are aimed at undertakings and projects that have a good influence on the environment, such as bonds, investment funds, and loans. By allocating funds to environmentally and socially conscious enterprises, green finance seeks to alleviate environmental issues, mitigate climate change, and advance sustainable development. Sustainability reporting, which includes disclosing an organization's environmental, social, and governance (ESG) performance, is strongly related to green financing. Sustainability reports are a common tool used by green financing companies to demonstrate their dedication to eco-friendly operations. An organization's environmental actions, resource usage, and overall influence on the earth are transparently disclosed to stakeholders through sustainability reporting, which also includes investors and the general public. It is an accountability instrument that lets stakeholders evaluate the environmental performance of a business.

Lastly, we delve into the emergence of green finance as a pivotal force in the contemporary financial sector. Digitalization has facilitated the development of innovative financial instruments aimed at supporting environmentally sustainable projects. Examples include green bonds, financing for renewable energy initiatives, and the burgeoning field of ESG (Environmental, Social, and Governance). As the global community increasingly acknowledges the urgency of mitigating climate change, green finance has ascended as a potent means to mobilize capital for a sustainable future.

Digitalization for Environmental Sustainability in Finance

Digitalization has emerged as a powerful enabler of environmental sustainability in finance (Christ, K. L., & Burritt, R. L., 2019). The rise of green finance, encompassing green bonds, sustainable investments, and environmentally responsible lending, has been facilitated by digital platforms and tools. These innovations have enabled the mobilization of capital toward eco-friendly projects, offering investors opportunities to align their financial portfolios with sustainability goals.

Tools for Evaluating Environmental Impacts

Life Cycle Assessment (LCA): Using digital tools such as LCA software, organizations may evaluate how items or processes will affect the environment over the course of their whole existence. This covers the extraction, production, distribution, use, and disposal of raw materials.

Systems for Environmental Management

Digital Systems for Collection of Data: To gather, examine, and handle environmental data, organizations employ digital environmental management systems. The process of obtaining data on energy use, emissions, and trash production is streamlined by these technologies.

Digitalization to Tackle Tax Evasion

The utilization of digitalization to combat tax evasion is a pressing concern in the modern financial landscape (Slemrod, J., & Velayudhan, T., 2022; OECD, 2021). Digital tools and data analytics are increasingly employed by tax authorities to detect irregularities and ensure tax compliance (Slemrod, J., & Velayudhan, T., 2022; OECD, 2021). The automation of tax reporting, real-time data sharing, and international cooperation through digital platforms have significantly bolstered efforts to curtail tax evasion and promote equitable tax collection (OECD, 2021; Slemrod, J., & Velayudhan, T., 2022).

In conclusion, the infusion of digitalization into finance has ushered in a paradigm shift across reporting practices, accounting procedures, tax avoidance, and sustainability endeavors. This chapter will delve deeper into these transformative dynamics, exploring the multifaceted impact of digitalization on these vital aspects of the financial landscape. Real-world examples and empirical evidence will be presented to underscore the practical implications and significance of these digitalization-driven changes.

OBJECTIVES

The primary objective of green financing lies in its pursuit of stimulating corporate innovation in green technology as a strategic means to foster sustainable development. By facilitating corporations' access to financial resources, establishing streamlined procedures, and offering incentivizing mechanisms, green finance endeavors to empower companies to invest in and nurture environmentally sustainable technologies and practices. This overarching aim is aligned with broader sustainability goals, including the reduction of carbon emissions, the preservation of natural resources, and the collective endeavor to combat climate change.

Furthermore, green finance seeks to alleviate financial constraints while nurturing a culture of innovation within the realm of green technology. Its core mission is to channel capital and funding towards projects and initiatives that bear a positive ecological footprint, ensuring adaptability and responsiveness to the evolving industrial landscape brought about by digitalization.

Within the domain of accounting, the objectives are two-fold. Firstly, accounting endeavors to equip accounting professionals, encompassing both seasoned accountants and accounting apprentices, with the knowledge and competencies essential for thriving in a dynamically evolving workplace. This entails not only the cultivation of skills for prudent decision-making but also the cultivation of awareness regarding the potential opportunities and challenges engendered by digitalization.

Secondly, accounting transcends its traditional role of maintaining financial records, encompassing a broader purview in the context of the digital era. It necessitates a profound comprehension of and adept navigation through the digital revolution. The transformation is such that accounting professionals must become adept at leveraging digital tools and technologies to harness the full spectrum of their capabilities, transcending mere record-keeping to assume an instrumental role in strategic financial management.

Lastly, a pivotal facet of these objectives pertains to the recognition of gender-neutral perspectives in elucidating how digital transformation has impacted the accounting profession. Emphasizing inclusivity and equal opportunity, this dimension of the objectives seeks to comprehensively understand and address the nuanced ways in which digitalization has shaped the accounting landscape, ensuring that the profession remains accessible and equitable for all.

METHODOLOGY AND CHALLENGES

To fulfill our research objectives, we have conducted an exhaustive analysis of existing literature and amassed cross-national data to scrutinize the economic ramifications of financial market development from the vantage point of technological innovation (Bresnahan & Trajtenberg, 1995; Goldin, C., & Katz, L., 1998). Our research methodology entails the employment of a rigorous statistical approach designed to disentangle the intricate relationship between financial market development and technological innovation (Bresnahan & Trajtenberg, 1995; Goldin, C., & Katz, L., 1998). Nevertheless, we remain cognizant of the challenges posed by potential reverse causality and omitted variables, which are inherent in such analyses (Bresnahan & Trajtenberg, 1995; Goldin, C., & Katz, L., 1998). To address these challenges robustly, we have implemented specific measures, including the utilization of instrumental variables and sensitivity analyses (Bresnahan & Trajtenberg, 1995; Goldin, C., & Katz, L., 1998).

Challenges and Ethical Dilemmas Posed by Digital Transformation

1. Privacy Issues:
    a) **Challenge**: Concerns regarding privacy infringement are raised by the gathering and analysis of enormous volumes of personal data. Data breaches and unauthorized usage are becoming more likely as organizations collect more data for insights and customized offerings.
    b) **Ethical Dilemma**: An ongoing ethical dilemma is how to strike a balance between the advantages of data-driven innovation and the requirement to preserve people's privacy. Effective security measures and transparent data regulations are necessary to strike the correct balance.
2. Digital Disparities:
    a) **Challenge:** There is still a digital divide, with certain people and groups not having access to the tools and knowledge required to fully engage in the digital economy.
    b) **Ethical Dilemma:** To address digital inequality, proactive measures must be taken to guarantee that everyone may profit from the digital transition. Promoting inclusion and preventing the escalation of current social and economic inequalities are two examples of ethical considerations.
3. Job Displacement:
    a) **Challenge:** In some industries, automation and artificial intelligence may result in job displacement, affecting workers' livelihoods and necessitating reskilling.
    b) **Ethical Dilemma:** The loss of jobs presents ethical challenges for businesses and society as a whole. These challenges include helping impacted employees, developing new skills, and guaranteeing a fair shift to a digital workforce.

4. Algorithmic Bias:
   a) **Challenge:** Machine learning algorithms may carry over biases from training data, which could result in unfair outcomes, particularly in the employment, lending, and law enforcement sectors.
   b) **Ethical Dilemma:** Issues of justice, accountability, and openness are ethically relevant when addressing algorithmic prejudice. It is a difficult ethical task to strike a balance between algorithmic efficiency and preventing unfair consequences.
5. Disinformation and Misinformation:
   a) **Challenge:** The ease with which information may now be shared online has resulted in the spread of misinformation and disinformation, which has an effect on public opinion and decision-making.
   b) **Ethical Dilemma:** Users and platforms are faced with moral conundrums about the dissemination of incorrect information, the duty to ensure content accuracy, and the possible effects on people and society.

RESEARCH MOTIVATION: MANAGERIAL CONTRIBUTIONS

1. Making Strategic Decisions in the Digital Age:

This study offers managers crucial information to help them navigate the challenges of digital transformation. Managers may implement pertinent technologies, streamline procedures, and match financial practices with sustainability goals by having a thorough understanding of how digitalization affects tax reporting, accounting, and green finance.

2. Tax Reporting & Risk Mitigation:

The study looks at how digital tools might reduce risks in tax reporting, which directly addresses the concerns of financial managers and tax professionals. In order to support more reliable and compliant financial operations, the research investigates the possibilities for decreased errors, increased transparency, and the use of sophisticated analytics to identify and manage tax-related issues.

3. Financial Reporting's Efficiency and Accuracy:

The work provides executives and finance managers with an understanding of how digital accounting practices are changing. Financial reporting procedures are made more accurate and efficient by integrating automation, real-time reporting, and cloud-based solutions. Managerial choices about the adoption of technology, the distribution of resources, and process improvement depend heavily on this understanding.

4. Eco-Friendly Banking Methods:

By examining the relationship between sustainability reporting and green finance concepts, the study offers managers practical advice. Financial managers may satisfy the growing need for environmentally responsible business operations by incorporating sustainable practices into their financial strategy and understanding how digital tools simplify the monitoring and reporting of environmental consequences.

5. Handling Regulatory Shifts:

In an ever-evolving regulatory landscape, managers must remain ahead of compliance demands. Examining how digitalization affects official and informal regulations in financial and environmental reporting frameworks, this work aids managers. This knowledge is necessary to ensure compliance, adjust to changes in regulations, and stay out of trouble with the law.

6. Improving Relations with Stakeholders:

The study offers insights into sustainable financial practices for businesses that are dedicated to stakeholder engagement and transparency. Managers may strengthen their relationships with investors, customers, and other stakeholders who value environmentally responsible business operations by integrating digital tools for accurate reporting and making financial decisions that are in line with green finance principles.

LITERATURE REVIEW

The literature surrounding the concept of tax evasion is often juxtaposed with tax avoidance, emphasizing the fundamental distinction between the two. Tax evasion entails the deliberate use of deceptive tactics by taxpayers to evade tax payments, creating a false representation of financial reality (Alm, 2011). Recent research on the determinants of tax evasion has revealed a multifaceted interplay of economic and non-economic factors (Gabor, D., & Brooks, S, 2017; Riahi-Belkaoui, 2004; Tsakumis et al., 2007). Drawing from these studies, Khlif, (2023) categorize these determinants into four distinct factor categories: demographic factors (including age, gender, education, urbanization, religion, and unemployment), cultural and behavioral factors (encompassing tax morale, culture, masculinity, individualism, and risk-aversion), legal and institutional factors (comprising corruption, the legal system, and bureaucracy), and economic factors (encompassing economic development, economic freedom, and government policies).

Additionally, contemporary research on corporate tax avoidance predominantly approaches the subject from two perspectives: external influencing factors and internal influencing factors. Regarding external influencers, international scholars have posited that the effectiveness of tax administration significantly impacts corporate tax evasion, with more effective tax administrations correlating with lower corporate tax avoidance (Deng et al.,2019). Government subsidies, as suggested by (Deng et al.,2019) can serve as a deterrent against corporate tax evasion. Institutional cross-shareholding, as demonstrated by Xing et al., can reduce incentives for company tax avoidance by enhancing corporate governance and alleviating financing constraints.

Green technology innovation, as conceptualized by Brawn and Wield, pertains to production and manufacturing techniques aimed at reducing resource consumption, such as energy and raw materials, while mitigating environmental degradation. The application of innovative green technology has a transformative effect, converting corporate environmental knowledge into tangible environmental performance by bolstering production efficiency and minimizing environmental harm. Literature often discusses the intersection of green technology innovation and environmental legislation. Porter contends that effective environmental regulations facilitate the development of green technologies, a claim corroborated by several scholars. However, Lin et al. present an opposing view, asserting that environmental regulations can stifle green technology development by increasing compliance costs for heavily polluting companies. Behera et al. introduce the concept of a U-shaped shifting pattern between the development of green technology and environmental legislation, adding complexity to this relationship.

In the realm of digital finance, the convergence of information technology and finance has become increasingly indispensable. Extensive research highlights the macroeconomic benefits of digital finance, including its capacity to enhance and diversify the industrial structure, positively moderating the impact of environmental legislation on robust economic growth. Digital finance also has the potential to stimulate consumer spending and reduce income inequality by promoting online transactions and equalizing consumption disparities among farmers. Moreover, the growth of inclusive finance can be facilitated through digital finance.

This publication advances research in several ways. While prior studies have explored the economic and environmental effects of digital transformation (Li, 2022; Wang et al., 2022), limited attention has been given to internal factors influencing digital transformation in businesses (Feliciano-Cestero et al., 2023). This report contributes by focusing on external policy considerations, investigating how green finance policies impact businesses' digital transformation. It provides empirical evidence that environmental and financial policies collaborate to compel heavily polluting businesses to adapt and evolve.

Hypothesis 1: Digital Finance Can Advance Green Technology Innovation

An important possibility for encouraging the development of green technology innovation is the incorporation of digital finance into the field of green finance. This idea emphasizes how adopting digital financial tools, platforms, and technologies can have a tremendous impact on how innovations that are environmentally sustainable develop. Digitalization possesses the transformative capacity required to hasten the development and adoption of green technologies by enabling better access to capital, fostering enhanced transparency, introducing novel financing structures, and improving data-driven decision-making processes. The intersection of digital finance and green finance offers an appropriate avenue towards addressing urgent environmental concerns and guiding a more sustainable future, it becomes clear as we examine this idea in greater detail. The area of capital access is one important factor. Funding for green technology efforts has historically been difficult to obtain due to factors including high transaction costs and a small audience. But digital finance provides creative answers to these difficulties. Digitalization has made it possible for crowdfunding platforms to provide equal investment options for initiatives that value the environment and draw supporters from around the world. By putting borrowers and lenders in direct contact, peer-to-peer lending—another breakthrough in digital finance—simplifies the process of raising money for entrepreneurs in the green technology sector. Additionally, by leveraging blockchain technology to tokenize assets, new fundraising opportunities are opened up, improving the liquidity and transparency of the green finance industry. Digital finance-supported innovative funding methods offer additional support for the theory. Environmental project financing is done with the help of green bonds. Their creation and trading could be revolutionized by digital platforms. Due to these platforms' effective capacity to issue and trade green bonds, investors can support environmental projects while also gaining from secondary market liquidity. Digital marketplaces can safely track and trade carbon credit markets thanks to blockchain technology. As a result, the funding process for green initiatives that reduce carbon footprints is enhanced, demonstrating the innovative potential of digital finance to promote sustainability.

Hypothesis 2: Business Organizations Are Constantly Working to Develop Their Accounting Information Systems in Line With the Requirements of Digital Transformation

A turning point has been reached in the field of accounting with the incorporation of digitalization, which has the potential to profoundly alter how financial information is managed, reported, and used. According to this theory, the adoption of digital technologies such as blockchain, artificial intelligence (AI), and cloud computing may result in a new era of accounting practices that are distinguished by increased efficiency, unmatched accuracy, and improved decision-making skills. A new era of more effective financial management, compliance, and strategic decision-making is about to emerge largely to the transformative power of digitalization, which has been demonstrated across a wide range of industries. Business organizations are actively developing their accounting information systems in reaction to digital transformation, in addition to embracing it. This continual work ensures that these systems stay in line with the organization's strategic imperatives, regulatory needs, and the ever-changing technological world. The continual process of improving commercial organization's accounting information systems is actively ongoing. This suggests that they are committed to a continual and adaptive strategy rather than just adopting digital technologies once. These organizations understand that embracing digital transformation requires them to adapt their accounting systems in step with technological developments rather than viewing it as a final destination that never changes. As a result, companies are spending money on cloud-based accounting software to make sure their systems are flexible and scalable enough to meet changing customer demands.

Hypothesis 3: There Is a High Degree of Challenges Related to Digital Transformation Within the Accounting Information Systems

While the digital transformation of accounting holds a lot of potential advantages, it also poses a number of major challenges that businesses must overcome in order to properly convert their accounting information systems.

The requirement for significant financial investments is one of the main challenges in this situation. Modern accounting information system implementation that supports digital transformation frequently necessitates a sizable financial commitment. Resources must be set aside by organizations for the purchase of software, hardware upgrades, employee training, and continuous maintenance. For smaller firms and organizations with tighter budgets, this financial load can be particularly difficult. Another significant issue is privacy and data security worries. Organizations must be careful in protecting sensitive financial data as accounting information is increasingly housed digitally and accessed remotely. Another difficult issue is integration with outdated systems. Many businesses still use accounting systems that date back many years and weren't created with the digital transformation in mind. It can be a challenging and resource-intensive procedure to upgrade to new, digitalized systems while assuring compatibility and data migration. Problems with compatibility between new and existing technologies could prevent smooth financial operations. Accounting professionals face a difficulty in terms of human resources because of skills and training gaps. Although essential, the skills required to use new software, analyze data analytics, and utilize artificial intelligence may present organizations with a significant learning curve. A successful digital transformation requires addressing this skills gap through extensive training programs. Employees must receive training to develop digital skills if they want to properly utilize the capabilities of digitalized accounting systems. organizations may face major challenges due to the knowledge and skills needed to use new software, understand data analytics, and utilize artificial intelligence. For the digital transition to be effective, this skills gap must be closed. Challenges with compliance and regulation are also common. On this digital journey, compliance and regulatory concerns are very common. Regulatory organizations are evolving to address new concerns about data security, financial reporting, and taxation as the digital landscape changes. It takes constant awareness and adaptability to be in compliance with these constantly changing rules and reporting requirements. Compliance is a constant challenge for businesses since they must constantly modify their accounting information systems to satisfy changing regulations. Digital transformation attempts can be severely hampered by organizational culture issues and reluctance to change. Employees could be wary of switching from established procedures and tools to digital alternatives. Adoption of transformed accounting practices may be hampered by an organizational culture that isn't fundamentally receptive of innovation and change. To overcome these cultural obstacles, it is essential to manage change effectively, promote an innovative culture, and address employee concerns.

MAIN FOCUS OF THE CHAPTER

Issues, Controversies, and Problems

This chapter delves into the profound implications of digitization on tax avoidance, shedding light on the evolving landscape of tax strategies in the digital era. It further explores the moderating role of corruption in shaping the intricate relationship between digitization and tax evasion. In a comprehensive analysis spanning both high- and low-corruption contexts, this chapter investigates how corruption influences the nexus between tax evasion and digitization. This research holds significant policy implications, particularly in elucidating the pivotal role of digitization in mitigating tax evasion behaviors.

The contemporary business environment has undergone a rapid and transformative evolution characterized by heightened complexity, market globalization, and intensified competition. Consequently, modern enterprises must keenly harness the vast array of data emerging from both their internal operations and the external environment. Leveraging modern technologies for data collection empowers these firms to identify and capitalize on their strengths, seize opportunities, address weaknesses, and proactively mitigate threats. The effective utilization of data in decision-making has become paramount in navigating this dynamic business landscape (Davenport & Harris, 2007).

To ensure that sustainability initiatives wield a substantial impact, the domain of green finance confronts multifaceted challenges. One such challenge pertains to the effective mobilization and allocation of funds for sustainability projects. Equally daunting is the labyrinth of regulatory and policy frameworks governing green finance. In the absence of standardized and consistent regulations, both investors and organizations may grapple with uncertainty, potentially hindering the flow of capital into green technology ventures. Overcoming this challenge necessitates the establishment of robust regulatory frameworks that offer transparency and clarity, fostering confidence among stakeholders (Zhang, 2023).

Mitigating financial constraints and market barriers emerges as another imperative. Certain green technology initiatives may demand substantial upfront investments, rendering them financially daunting, especially for smaller enterprises. To ensure inclusivity and broad accessibility, it becomes paramount to dismantle these obstacles and facilitate equitable access to green financing options. This endeavor underscores the importance of addressing both market and budgetary limitations to propel sustainable technological innovations across diverse organizational scales (Flammer & Bansal, 2017).

A significant challenge on the horizon pertains to the adaptation of accounting professionals to the demands of the digital age. The rapid pace of technological change necessitates continuous learning and upskilling, enabling professionals to harness digital tools, data analytics, and artificial intelligence to their fullest potential. The imperative to bridge this skills gap underscores the transformative nature of digital technology and the essential role of education and training in ensuring professionals remain proficient in an ever-evolving landscape.

Additionally, the burgeoning reliance on digital technologies has raised concerns regarding data security and privacy. Accountants grapple with cybersecurity risks, data breaches, and the inherent need to safeguard the confidentiality and accuracy of financial information in an increasingly interconnected digital world. These issues highlight the critical importance of data protection measures, robust cybersecurity protocols, and ethical considerations in the practice of accounting (Liu, Y., & Chen, L.2022).

In essence, this chapter delves into these multifaceted issues, controversies, and challenges, offering a comprehensive exploration of the intricacies surrounding tax strategies, green finance, digital transformation, and data security in the contemporary financial landscape.

DISCUSSION

The advent of digitalization and technological advancements has ushered in transformative changes in how taxes are reported, monitored, and audited on a global scale. This digital metamorphosis has not only revolutionized the speed, quality, and accuracy of data used in tax-related processes but has also garnered recognition and adoption across various stakeholders, including tax authorities, policymakers, regulators, accountants, and taxpayers. These stakeholders have embraced a myriad of digital tools and platforms, such as e-services, applications, websites, and specialized software, to streamline tax-related activities.

One of the central implications of digitalization in taxation is its potential to strengthen data collection mechanisms, enhance control frameworks, and augment overall operational efficiency. By leveraging digital technologies, tax authorities can access real-time data, conduct more sophisticated data analysis, and implement robust control mechanisms, thereby bolstering their ability to detect and prevent tax evasion. However, this digital transformation also introduces new opportunities for tax evasion, necessitating vigilant oversight and adaptation of tax enforcement strategies.

Taxation stands as a cornerstone of government revenue generation, making tax avoidance a significant concern. Tax avoidance strategies, when left unchecked, have the potential to undermine a fair distribution of economic outcomes. When instances of tax evasion come to light, businesses are not only liable to repay back taxes but may also face substantial penalties, magnifying the stakes of this complex game involving businesses and tax authorities.

The impact of technology advancements extends beyond tax evasion concerns, profoundly altering traditional tax concepts and mechanisms. The globalization of the world economy, coupled with businesses' ability to exploit gaps and variations in domestic tax rules, challenges established tax paradigms. In response to these shifts, the emergence of digital service taxes (DSTs), applied to digital rather than physical presence, has become a notable phenomenon in recent years. DSTs serve as a means for numerous nations to boost their revenue streams, reflecting the evolving digital economy.

However, it's worth noting that unilateral DSTs and similar measures are subject to ongoing international negotiations and agreements. Under the OECD's two-pillar strategy, such measures are slated for elimination, with participating nations committing to refraining from enacting comparable measures in the future. Multilateral agreements have been forged to address transitional steps regarding DSTs and to navigate potential double taxation issues under Pillar One and existing DSTs. This progression builds upon the foundational work initiated by the Base Erosion and Profit Shifting (BEPS) initiative launched in 2013, which has evolved into a comprehensive reshaping of the international tax landscape.

Pillar One of the two-pillar structure, commonly referred to as BEPS 2.0, aims to reallocate a portion of taxable revenue to market countries, thereby affecting effective tax rates, cash tax obligations, and existing transfer pricing agreements. This realignment has implications for businesses, particularly major multinationals, as it introduces a fundamental change in the distribution of tax liabilities and profits.

The adoption of Pillar One hinges on the acceptance of a sufficient number of jurisdictions, with the exact timeline remaining uncertain. While these changes represent simplifications compared to earlier proposals, they still encompass a global scope and present technical intricacies. In conjunction with Pillar Two, focused on global minimum taxes, the international tax landscape is poised for a significant transformation.

Pillar Two, known as the Global Anti-Base Erosion (GloBE) Rules, is designed to ensure the equitable imposition and collection of income taxes. These rules are underpinned by a common approach, targeting a 15% global minimum tax rate for multinational corporations with annual revenues exceeding EUR750 million. The implementation timeline varies across jurisdictions, with some planning to enact Pillar Two in 2025 and others, including the European Union (EU), aiming for implementation in 2024.

The Undertaxed Payments Rule (UTPR), part of Pillar Two, is scheduled to take effect in 2024, with the Pillar Two regulations anticipated to be enacted into law in 2023. Notably, the scope of these rules extends to include wholly domestic groups with EU presence, signaling a broader impact.

The COVID-19 pandemic has underscored the critical importance of technology and digital infrastructure in business operations, emphasizing the need for effective communication, collaboration, and addressing contemporary environmental challenges. Alongside the broader digitalization of businesses, a significant enhancement in information quality has been observed, particularly within financial accounting reporting systems (Xu, 2022). In response to the pandemic, businesses have been compelled to swiftly reorganize and digitize their management and decision-making processes, with financial accounting reporting assuming a pivotal role in this digital transformation (Zhang, 2023). The COVID-19 epidemic caused a sharp increase in the use of telemedicine. Remote patient consultations with medical experts lower the possibility of virus transmission. With the use of remote monitoring tools, medical professionals could remotely monitor patients' vital signs and take care of their chronic illnesses.

While tax avoidance strategies may offer short-term tax savings, the evolving landscape of regulations, improved tax authority enforcement methods, and enhanced tax collection and management efficiency have elevated the risk of detection by tax regulators (De Simone, 2018). Consequently, businesses face the prospect of harsh penalties and reputational damage in addition to financial losses when caught evading taxes. As regulatory and tax law systems gradually improve, companies are increasingly inclined to adopt a "compliance" orientation. This approach enables them to carefully evaluate the benefits of tax avoidance, manage associated risks, and minimize the costs of non-compliance by reducing the extent of tax avoidance.

Finance also plays a crucial role in addressing environmental concerns. Environmental finance theory emphasizes the importance of financial technology innovation, the enhancement of financial products, and the rationalization of financial structures to provide effective support for environmental protection (Li, T., & Yang, L.2021). In alignment with sustainable development principles, digital finance has undergone a green transformation through the integration of information technology, resulting in reduced resource consumption within the financial industry and improved operational efficiency. Compared to traditional finance, digital finance assumes a more prominent role in supporting and promoting green industries and technologies, contributing significantly to economic and societal sustainability (Cai, C., 2023). Digital finance's ability to reduce resource consumption and enhance resource allocation efficiency within the financial sector underscores its notable "green effect".

Furthermore, digital finance extends the coverage and depth of financial services, directing more financial resources towards low-carbon, environmentally friendly, and high-tech industries (Li, 2021). It acts as a catalyst, accelerating the transition towards green technologies, pollution reduction, and energy conservation. Additionally, digital finance facilitates the free flow and effective allocation of capital, information, digital assets, and technology, serving as a lubricant in the financial ecosystem (Liu, Y., & Chen, L, 2022). Global education was transformed by the widespread adoption of online learning platforms like Zoom, Google Classroom, and Moodle. Teachers and students adjusted to online learning environments, making education accessible from any location. But new issues also arose, such as the digital divide and the requirement for innovative teaching strategies. Also, the retail sector has changed significantly with the emergence of e-commerce giants like Amazon and

Alibaba. Before making a purchase, customers can shop online, compare costs, and read reviews. With the simplicity and effectiveness of digital payment options such as PayPal and mobile wallets, traditional cash transactions have been supplanted. Similarly, Traditional banking has been impacted by the emergence of financial technology, or FinTech. With the help of mobile banking apps like Revolut or Square Cash, consumers can easily manage their finances, transfer money, and make payments. People's interactions with their money have evolved and financial inclusion has expanded as a result.

In response to the rapidly evolving business environment characterized by increasing complexity, market openness, and heightened competition, modern enterprises must closely monitor data emerging from both internal and external sources. They must harness modern technologies to collect, analyze, and interpret this data, enabling them to identify strengths, seize opportunities, address weaknesses, and mitigate threats effectively. The digital revolution, marked by the proliferation of the Internet and communication networks, necessitates organizations to transition their accounting and management information systems from traditional approaches to modern digital methods. This transition encompasses technologies such as artificial intelligence, the Internet of Things, Blockchain, Big Data, Cloud Computing, and others. These technologies enhance transparency, reduce costs, save time and effort, improve data access, ensure data security, and enhance the efficiency of accounting information systems.

The integration of digital tools and sustainability reporting has become a significant trend in recent years, transforming the way companies convey their social and environmental obligations. This integration is a calculated step in the direction of accountability, transparency, and matching financial procedures to more general objectives of social and environmental sustainability.

Global Reporting Initiative-developed GRI Standards are now considered industry standard practice for sustainability reporting. These guidelines, which were first released in 2000, offer businesses a thorough framework for disclosing their environmental, social, and governance (ESG) performance. Due to their organized approach to measuring and reporting on many areas of sustainability, the GRI Standards have had a significant impact on the standardization of sustainability reporting standards. Consistency is ensured and data-driven insights are facilitated through the integration of digital tools with these standards.

The Financial Stability Board created the TCFD, which is centered on financial disclosures pertaining to climate change. The TCFD recommendations were introduced in 2017 and offer a structured approach for firms to openly reveal their climate-related risks and opportunities in financial reports. This had an effect on the TCFD recommendations, which highlighted the financial costs of climate change and provided guidance to organizations on how to disclose climate-related data.

Companies can improve the accuracy of climate-related financial information and expedite the disclosure process by integrating TCFD recommendations with digital tools.

The GRI Standards and TCFD Recommendations, for example, show how sustainability reporting may be integrated with digital tools to create a more open, effective, and internationally accessible way to report on social and environmental consequences. In the modern company environment, this integration not only improves accountability but also synchronizes financial processes with the necessity of sustainable and ethical business operations.

Blockchain operates as a distributed network consisting of multiple nodes, with each node functioning as both a database and a ledger. Transactions within the network undergo verification and validation by other participating nodes to ensure their authenticity. This technology plays a pivotal role in shaping accounting information systems by enhancing transparency and transitioning from traditional double-entry bookkeeping to a more automated triple-entry system. By enabling transactions to be directly recorded in a shared ledger accessible to all network participants, accounting systems become more streamlined, reducing the potential for errors and simplifying the tasks of accountants. The integrity of transactions pertaining to taxes is guaranteed by the decentralized, tamper-resistant ledger that blockchain technology offers. By establishing a single source of truth that all parties involved may access, it improves transparency and lowers the possibility of fraud or manipulation in tax reporting.

Traditional accounting methods have been completely transformed by blockchain technology, which introduces transparent and decentralized ledger systems. This invention, which is frequently linked to cryptocurrencies like Bitcoin, has broad ramifications, especially for auditing practices and transaction verification in the accounting industry.

Blockchain technology was first introduced with the release of the Bitcoin whitepaper in 2008 by the enigmatic person known only as Satoshi Nakamoto. It unveiled a peer-to-peer, decentralized electronic cash system built on the groundbreaking blockchain ledger. This had an impact on Nakamoto's work and signaled the beginning of blockchain as a system that guarantees safe, open, and unchangeable record-keeping. The initial use case for a decentralized money was the blockchain of Bitcoin, which opened the door for more widespread accounting applications.

Accounting practices are changing as a result of the introduction of blockchain technology, as demonstrated by Nakamoto's groundbreaking work on Bitcoin. This technology ushers in a new era of financial record-keeping that is transparent, trustworthy, and efficient. It has an impact on conventional accounting procedures and creates opportunities for cutting-edge applications like decentralized finance (DeFi) and smart contracts. Blockchain technology is expected to revolutionize the accounting profession by providing never-before-seen levels of security and transparency in financial transactions.

Cloud Computing represents a digital transformation in the field of accounting that goes beyond mere technical solutions or server-based storage. The emergence of cloud-based accounting platforms in the 21st century brought about a revolutionary change in the accounting landscape. These platforms, which provide unmatched flexibility, accessibility, and real-time capability, turned heads and changed the game. The use of cloud-based financial management resulted in a fundamental transformation in the way firms handled accounting procedures. The types of cloud computing system are:

1. **Centralized Data Storage:** Financial data can be centrally stored thanks to cloud-based accounting solutions. This encourages cooperation amongst stakeholders by making accessibility possible from any location with an internet connection.
2. **Flexibility and Scalability:** Cloud systems offer firms the flexibility to modify their accounting infrastructure in response to changing circumstances. This flexibility is especially helpful for expanding companies whose accounting needs change over time.

It offers numerous advantages, including cost reduction through labor and time savings, enhanced processing speed, efficient data storage, scalability, robust data security measures, seamless data connectivity, uninterrupted service availability, and the utilization of extensive cloud infrastructure resources.

When Intuit released QuickBooks Online in 2000, it was a major turning point for cloud-based accounting. It promoted cooperation amongst various stakeholders by enabling users to access financial data at any time and from any location. Accounting procedures were made more accessible with the launch of QuickBooks Online, enabling companies of all sizes to effectively manage their money without being limited by physical location.

Also, Xero, which debuted in 2006, pioneered cloud-based accounting solutions. For accountants and businesses, it provided a real-time collaboration platform, strong capabilities, and an easy-to-use design. This affected Xero's focus on accessibility and simplicity, which helped cloud-based accounting become widely used. It made financial duties more efficient and improved teamwork when handling financial data.

A change in perspective was brought about by the advent of cloud-based accounting systems. Collaboration and accessibility were restricted by the need for local server installs for traditional accounting applications. Cloud-based programs like Xero and QuickBooks Online allowed businesses to easily accept remote work. Collaboration and real-time data processing have evolved from benefits to requirements in a fast-paced business environment.

The revolutionary incorporation of automation and artificial intelligence (AI) into the accounting field characterizes the modern era. This integration represents a paradigm change that will improve decision support systems while also reinventing ordinary accounting procedures. AI's efficiency improvements and insights have thrust accounting operations into a new, highly sophisticated technological era.

Big Data refers to vast volumes of intricate data that exceed the capabilities of conventional computer programs and conventional data processing methods. In the realm of accounting, Big Data holds significant potential. It enables businesses to identify their target markets and predict the outcomes of their marketing and sales efforts by analyzing data from sources such as social media and financial markets. This data-driven approach enhances decision-making and allows for more informed strategies in various accounting functions.

One of the first investigations on the use of AI in auditing was concentrated on the influence of expert systems on audit judgment. The research explores how expert systems can improve auditors' ability to make decisions. This had an influence on Alles' study and established the groundwork for comprehending how AI technologies—specifically, expert systems—could improve the auditing process. It emphasized how automation may improve the efficiency and judgment of audits.

The use of artificial intelligence (AI) and automation into accounting procedures, as demonstrated by influential studies like Michael Alles', signifies a revolutionary development for the field. This advancement in technology not only simplifies repetitive work but also gives accountants access to sophisticated analytical tools, which improves accuracy, productivity, and strategic decision-making in the industry. The future of AI in accounting is expected to completely change the function of accountants and how they contribute to the success of their organizations.

SOLUTIONS

In this study, the authors will delve into the impact of technological advancements on various aspects of accounting procedures, reporting practices, and tax avoidance, highlighting both the benefits and challenges they pose for accounting professionals. To the best of our knowledge, this research represents the first comprehensive investigation into how tax evasion may be influenced by multiple dimensions of digitalization adoption, encompassing individuals, businesses, and governmental entities.

Examining the interplay between a corrupt environment and the relationship between digital transformation and tax evasion constitutes a pivotal contribution to this research. As organizations undergo significant transformations fueled by the digital revolution, accounting information systems have experienced substantial enhancements, adaptations, and modernizations. These systems now function as output providers rather than merely handling tasks such as data storage, categorization, and summarization. With the seamless integration of data from smart devices into the information flow of the system, it is widely anticipated that the role of traditional accounting personnel will undergo substantial changes during the process of digital transformation.

Our study revealed several key insights. Firstly, scholars have dedicated considerable attention to reevaluating accounting standards, particularly in light of how they can be effectively applied to the digital era's evolving reporting needs. Secondly, a significant body of research has focused on the impact of professional regulatory bodies on the digitization of accounting, addressing new regulations and guidelines and their implications for reporting practices. Lastly, a substantial portion of the research has centered on the realm of green financing, exploring areas that stand to benefit from the integration of digital process automation.

One of the key findings of this research is the substantial reduction in corporate tax evasion facilitated by digital transformation. This reduction is attributed to the elevation of internal corporate controls, and its magnitude varies significantly when firms are subject to different levels of tax enforcement activities and government subsidies. Furthermore, this decrease in corporate tax evasion is accompanied by an enhancement in the efficiency of corporate investments.

In broader terms, our findings hold substantial real-world implications. They serve to underscore the potency of digital transformation as a formidable tool in the fight against tax evasion. However, it is worth noting that our research reveals that a high-corruption environment can diminish the effectiveness of digital transformation in deterring tax fraud, thereby warranting increased vigilance from regulatory bodies and stakeholders alike.

Mitigation Strategies

Openness in the application of AI algorithms is required by ethical accounting standards. It is imperative to conduct routine audits of automated processes, disclose algorithms, and make attempts to reduce biases. Furthermore, it is imperative that professionals receive continual ethical training in order to comprehend and handle the consequences of AI in accounting.

And to stop data breaches, strong cybersecurity measures are essential. These include encryption, access controls, and frequent security audits. Proactive risk assessments, implementing industry best practices, and having quick response plans in place in case of a breach are all components of ethical practices. Strict access controls, secure data transmission, and secure storage procedures need to be put in place by ethical accountants. Client informed permission and well-defined policies around data sharing are essential. Accounting practitioners are guaranteed to be up to date on the latest rules by receiving regular training on data privacy legislation and compliance.

Also, performing data validation tests, keeping audit trails, and routinely balancing digital records are all part of ethical accounting procedures. In order to guarantee data integrity and accuracy, professionals should embrace a culture of accountability and ongoing oversight.

RECOMMENDATIONS

1. Privacy and Data Security

Ethical Consideration: Data security and privacy are issues that are brought up by the processing and storing of financial data in digital systems. Building confidence and adhering to ethical norms require the protection of sensitive financial data.

Social Impact: To promote trust in digital accounting systems, people and organizations need to feel confident that their financial information is secure. Financial loss, identity theft, and reputational harm are all possible outcomes of breaches.

2. Accuracy and Reliability

Ethical Consideration: In accounting, ensuring the dependability and correctness of financial data is a basic ethical duty. Digital technologies and automation need to be utilized carefully to avoid mistakes and misrepresentations.

Social Impact: Investors, regulators, and the general public are among the stakeholders for whom accurate financial reporting is crucial. Errors may result in legal problems, financial mismanagement, and a decline in the credibility of companies and accounting experts.

3. Digital Gap in Technology Access

Ethical Consideration: Ethical questions of inclusion and fair access to accounting tools are brought up by the digital gap, which occurs when certain people or companies do not have access to the required technologies.

Social Impact: Inequalities in financial reporting capacities could be sustained by unequal access, which would impede the expansion and prosperity of companies unable to afford digital accounting procedures.

4. Professional Competence and Training

Ethical Consideration: In order to respect ethical standards, accountants and other financial professionals need to stay proficient with digital tools and technologies. To guarantee competence and moral decision-making in a digitalized setting, ongoing training is crucial.

Social Impact: Errors, fraud, and unethical behavior can result from a lack of professional expertise in digital accounting. Sufficient training guarantees that accountants are capable of handling digital technologies sensibly.

FUTURE RESEARCH DIRECTIONS

This chapter has served the purpose of elucidating the transformative impact of digitalization on accounting practices, tax avoidance strategies, reporting methodologies, and the broader landscape of accounting. It has also shed light on how digitalization has contributed to the growth of green finance. However, in this evolving landscape, policymakers face numerous challenges. The dynamic nature of these changes necessitates that tax policy formulation and implementation be designed to accommodate the ever-shifting environment while providing the requisite stability and clarity to foster long-term and sustainable economic growth. In such scenarios, the economy assumes the lead role, with finance following suit.

CONCLUSION

The research chapter concludes by exploring the complex effects of digitalization on tax reporting, accounting procedures, and the incorporation of sustainability principles. The institutional theory-based theoretical framework offers a prism through which to view the changing dynamics influenced by technological breakthroughs. Fundamental ideas clarify the nature of digitization and highlight its significance for tax reporting, the development of accounting, and the incorporation of green finance.

Corporate tax avoidance is a pivotal factor influencing corporate financial decision-making, as it represents a substantial burden for businesses, adding to their financial pressures. On one hand, tax avoidance strategies can reduce the tax burden, resulting in increased operating profits that align with or surpass analysts' forecasts, generating a "cash flow effect" and elevating profitability levels. Our findings underscore the multifaceted examination of accounting digitalization in the scholarly discourse. Within the publications analyzed, three factors emerged as potentially significant in this context. Our research confirms that digitalization serves as an effective means of curbing tax evasion. The results illuminate the inherent conflict between tax avoidance strategies and the adoption of digitalization by businesses and individuals. Furthermore, the findings substantiate that digitalization, whether in environments characterized by high or low corruption, leads to a decrease in tax evasion.

To the best of our knowledge, this study represents the inaugural exploration into the potential impact of various dimensions of digitalization adoption—spanning individuals, businesses, and governments—on tax evasion. In broad terms, our discoveries bear substantial real-world implications. They underscore the potency of digital transformation as a formidable tool for combating tax evasion. However, it is noteworthy that our research reveals a diminishing effectiveness of digital transformation in deterring tax fraud in environments characterized by high corruption, raising potential concerns for regulatory authorities.

In a broader context, tax authorities should emphasize the significance of robust tax administration, embark on the digital transformation of tax collection and administration processes, and employ indirect means to elevate the cost of tax evasion for managers. These efforts will contribute to heightened tax collection rates and improved compliance levels. Additionally, businesses should proactively support tax administration and collection endeavors by providing timely information and cooperating during audits. Corporate tax evasion practices should be integrated into businesses' internal control frameworks, overseen by shareholders, to effectively curb management's self-serving behavior and enhance oversight roles.

REFERENCES

Alm, J. (2011). Measuring, explaining, and controlling tax evasion: Lessons from theory, experiments, and field studies. *International Tax and Public Finance*, *19*(1), 54–77. doi:10.1007/s10797-011-9171-2

Arbolino, R., Boffardi, R., & De Simone, L. (2018). Which are the factors influencing innovation performances? Evidence from Italian cohesion policy. *Social Indicators Research*, *146*(1-2), 221–247. doi:10.1007/s11205-018-1904-5

Arntz, M., Gregory, T., & Zierahn, U. (2016). *The Risk of Automation for Jobs in OECD Countries: a comparative analysis.* OECD Social, Employment and Migration Working Papers, No. 189. OECD Publishing. https://www.oecd-ilibrary.org/social-issues-migration-health/the-risk-ofautomation-for-jobs-in-oecd-countries_5jlz9h56dvq7-en

Bresnahan, T., & Trajtenberg, M. (1995). General purpose technologies: 'engines of growth'? *Journal of Econometrics*, *65*(1), 83–108. doi:10.1016/0304-4076(94)01598-T

Brynjolfsson, E., & McAfee, A. (2014). *The Second Machine Age: Work, Progress, and Prosperity in a Time of Brilliant Technologies*. W. W. Norton & Company.

Cai, C. (2023). *Customer–supplier digital transformation and corporate tax avoidance*. doi:10.2139/ssrn.4578455

Christ, K. L., & Burritt, R. L. (2019). Implementation of sustainable development goals: The role for business academics. *Australian Journal of Management*, *44*(4), 571–593. doi:10.1177/0312896219870575

Corlin Christensen, R., & Lips, W. (2021). *The politics of taxing the digital economy*. Handbook on the Politics of Taxation. doi:10.4337/9781788979429.00034

Davenport, T. H., & Harris, J. G. (2007). *Competing on analytics: The new science of winning*. Harvard Business Press.

Deng, J. L., & Li, J. (2019). Will government subsidies affect corporate tax avoidance? *Journal of Financial Economics*, *45*(1), 109–121.

Development Co-operation Report 2019. (2019). OECD. doi:10.1787/9a58c83f-en

Feliciano-Cestero, M. M., Ameen, N., Kotabe, M., Paul, J., & Signoret, M. (2023). Is digital transformation threatened? A systematic literature review of the factors influencing firms' digital transformation and internationalization. *Journal of Business Research*, *157*, 113546. doi:10.1016/j.jbusres.2022.113546

Flammer, C., & Bansal, P. (2017). Does long-term orientation create value? Evidence from a regression discontinuity. *Strategic Management Journal*, *38*(9), 1827–1847. doi:10.1002/smj.2629

Fosso Wamba, S., Kala Kamdjoug, J. R., Epie Bawack, R., & Keogh, J. G. (2019). Bitcoin, blockchain and Fintech: A systematic review and case studies in the supply chain. *Production Planning and Control*, *31*(2-3), 115–142. doi:10.1080/09537287.2019.1631460

Gabor, D., & Brooks, S. (2017). The digital revolution in financial inclusion: International development in the fintech era. *New Political Economy*, *22*(4), 423–436. doi:10.1080/13563467.2017.1259298

Goldin, C., & Katz, L. (1998). *The origins of technology-skill complementarity*. doi:10.3386/w5657

Johannesen, N., & Zucman, G. (2014). The End of Bank Secrecy? An Evaluation of the G20 Tax Haven Crackdown. *American Economic Journal. Economic Policy*, *6*(1), 66. doi:10.1257/pol.6.1.65

Khelil, I., Khlif, H., & Achek, I. (2023). The economic consequences of money laundering: A review of empirical literature. *Journal of Money Laundering Control*. doi:10.1108/JMLC-09-2023-0143

Levin, R. C. (1982). The semiconductor industry. In R. R. Nelson (Ed.), *Government and Technical Progress: A Cross-Industry Analysis* (pp. 9–100). Pergamon Press.

Li, T., & Yang, L. (2021). The effects of tax reduction and fee reduction policies on the digital economy. *Sustainability (Basel)*, *13*(14), 7611. doi:10.3390/su13147611

Liu, Y., & Chen, L. (2022). The impact of digital finance on green innovation: Resource effect and information effect. *Environmental Science and Pollution Research International*, *29*(57), 86771–86795. doi:10.1007/s11356-022-21802-w PMID:35794335

Mokyr, J. (2014). *Secular Stagnation? Not in Your Life. In Secular Stagnation: Facts, Causes, and Cures*. CEPR Press.

OECD Competition Trends 2021. (2021). doi:10.1787/308565fd-en

Riahi-Belkaoui, A. (2004). Relationship between tax compliance internationally and selected determinants of tax morale. *Journal of International Accounting, Auditing & Taxation*, *13*(2), 135–143. doi:10.1016/j.intaccaudtax.2004.09.001

Schumpeter, J. A. (1934). *The Theory of Economic Development*. Harvard University Press.

Slemrod, J., & Velayudhan, T. (2022). The VAT at 100: A retrospective survey and agenda for future research. *Public Finance Review*, *50*(1), 4–32. doi:10.1177/10911421221094595

Tsakumis, G. T., Curatola, A. P., & Porcano, T. M. (2007). The relation between national cultural dimensions and tax evasion. *Journal of International Accounting, Auditing & Taxation*, *16*(2), 131–147. doi:10.1016/j.intaccaudtax.2007.06.004

Xu, Y., Li, S., Zhou, X., Shahzad, U., & Zhao, X. (2022). How environmental regulations affect the development of green finance: Recent evidence from polluting firms in China. *Renewable Energy*, *189*, 917–926. doi:10.1016/j.renene.2022.03.020

Zhang, X., Li, J., Xiang, D., & Worthington, A. C. (2023). Digitalization, financial inclusion, and small and medium-sized enterprise financing: Evidence from China. *Economic Modelling*, *126*, 106410. doi:10.1016/j.econmod.2023.106410

Chapter 12
The Impact of Blockchain Technology on the Financial Audit

Mohamed Ali Bejjar
https://orcid.org/0009-0004-8051-7559
Higher Business School of Sfax, Tunisia

Yosr Siala
https://orcid.org/0009-0007-4593-4586
Higher Business School of Sfax, Tunisia

ABSTRACT

This chapter focuses on exploring the implications of blockchain technology on the practice of financial auditing. It begins by explaining the fundamentals of financial auditing, and then provides a historical context for digitization within auditing. This is followed by a thorough examination of blockchain technology, including its architecture, characteristics, and categorizations. The chapter then highlights the integration of blockchain into financial auditing, highlighting benefits such as improved risk management, automated audit processes, fraud reduction, cost savings, and the emergence of a continuous audit model. The changing role of auditors in this technologically evolving landscape is also discussed. This synthesis provides an in-depth perspective on the transformative potential of blockchain to improve the efficiency and transparency of financial audit.

DOI: 10.4018/979-8-3693-1678-8.ch012

INTRODUCTION

In recent decades, the advent of digitalization has brought about significant changes in the financial audit landscape. Information and communication technologies (ICT) have orchestrated a fundamental change in the mechanisms for collecting, processing, and analyzing accounting and financial information. Since the 1980s, the widespread computerization of business has driven the development of computer-aided audit techniques (CAATs), which allow the direct extraction of digitized data from the information systems of audited entities, thereby facilitating their aggregation and examination (Debreceny et al., 2005).

More recently, financial auditing has embraced the paradigms of artificial intelligence and machine learning, facilitating the automation of repetitive tasks and the ability to analyze large volumes of data to extract relevant information (Zhang et al., 20-22). The adaptation of financial auditing practices to technological advances is driven by the inherent need to ensure the robustness and relevance of audit procedures in an environment characterized by constant innovation. Technological advances bring new and complex challenges, such as data security and fraud detection.

As a result, the need to integrate technological skills into the audit process is critical, not only to maintain public confidence and ensure regulatory compliance, but also to meet the demands of an increasingly digital business environment. However, in a dynamic economic context characterized by the continuous progress of digitalization, the intersection between blockchain technology and the discipline of financial auditing raises issues of eminent complexity.

Fundamentally, this convergence raises the following issue:

How does the incorporation of blockchain technology into the financial audit process lead to a substantial redefinition of traditional audit parameters?

The fundamental objective of this study is to explore in depth the impact of blockchain technology on financial auditing. It aims to meticulously analyze how blockchain has changed the nature of auditing by automating traditionally manual procedures, enhancing data security, and creating unprecedented transparency in financial transactions. This comprehensive analysis is intended to provide informed perspectives for audit practitioners, contribute to the profession's proactive adaptation to the changes brought about by blockchain, and enrich the body of knowledge in this ever-evolving field.

This research also consists of four distinct sections. The first section sets the stage by introducing the field of financial auditing. The second section explores digitalization and financial audit. The third section focuses on the blockchain technology. Finally, the fourth section highlights the impact of blockchain technology on the financial auditing.

THE FINANCIAL AUDIT

Financial auditing is a crucial discipline that plays a leading role in the verification, authentication and validation of organizations' financial and accounting data. In this section, we will focus on an in-depth exploration of three essential facets of this profession: the definition of financial audit, the structuring and hierarchization within the field, and the constituent stages of the audit process.

Definition of a Financial Audit

Financial audit is defined as "the critical examination carried out by an independent professional external to the company in order to express a reasoned opinion on the fairness of the image given by the company's financial documents" (translated from Obert, 1994).

This definition can be supplemented as follows: "Financial auditing is the examination by a competent, independent professional of a company's financial statements with a view to expressing an opinion on their fairness and accuracy" (translated from Raffegeau et al., 1994).

According to ISA 200 of the International Auditing and Assurance Standards Board (IAASB) of the International Federation of Automatic Control (IFAC): "The objective of an audit of financial statements is to enable the auditor to express an opinion that the financial statements have been prepared, in all material respects, in accordance with an applicable financial reporting framework".

In conclusion, a financial audit is a methodical and documented examination of a company's financial statements performed by an independent external auditor. The objective is to determine the accuracy, compliance with accounting principles and laws, and reliability of financial information to provide a sound basis for financial decisions.

Financial Audit Structure and Hierarchy

The audit profession is regulated by professional organizations such as accounting bodies and financial market regulators. These organizations set standards of quality and professional practice to which auditors must adhere. For example, IFAC publishes international auditing standards, while the Securities and Exchange Commission (SEC) in the United States regulates auditors of publicly traded companies.

Audit firms are characterized by a hierarchical structure in which each level has not only specific and defined responsibilities in the technical performance of audit engagements, but also behaviors and mentalities that reflect progressive socialization (Fogarty, 1992). The structure of the accounting profession includes the following levels: partners/Directors, managers and senior executives, senior/experienced auditors and junior auditors or internal auditors.

Partners or directors are the most senior people in an accounting firm. They handle the overall management of the firm, setting strategic goals, supervising audit engagements, and making major decisions regarding audit engagements.

Managers and senior executives are responsible for managing audit teams. They supervise audit work, coordinate engagements, communicate with clients, and ensure the quality of audit work.

Senior or experienced auditors are responsible for performing audit work in the field. They supervise junior team members, perform audit tests, assess risks and internal controls, and assist in the preparation of audit reports.

Junior auditors or internal auditors are the least experienced members of the audit team. They perform specific audit tasks, such as gathering data, performing tests, and preparing working papers, under the supervision of managers and supervisors.

Financial Audit Process

Within the discipline of financial auditing, the audit process represents the cardinal element, methodical and systematic in nature, designed to assess the veracity and relevance of the accounting data presented by a company. At the heart of this phase lies the overarching mission to attest to the accuracy of financial information, ensure compliance with accounting standards, and bring to light any significant irregularities that could affect the financial health of an organization.

Customer Acceptance and Planning (ISA 210 and ISA 300)

According to ISA 210, client acceptance is the first step in any audit. The auditor must carefully evaluate the potential client before accepting the engagement. This includes understanding the nature of the client's business, its reputation, its financial history, and the potential risks associated with the relationship. The objective of this step is to ensure that the auditor can objectively and independently perform an audit engagement in accordance with applicable auditing standards and regulations. This may include ethical and deontological considerations, such as respect for confidentiality and the absence of conflicts of interest. Once the auditor has accepted the engagement, he or she needs to plan the audit rigorously.

According to ISA 300, audit planning includes defining the scope of the audit, establishing an overall audit strategy, identifying key audit areas, and determining the timing and resources required to complete the engagement. This planning phase is essential to ensure audit effectiveness, compliance with auditing standards, and risk management. The auditor must consider the risks inherent in the client's business, control risks, and other factors that may affect the nature and extent of audit procedures.

Understanding the Entity, Its Environment, and Assessing the Risk of Material Misstatement (ISA 315)

The auditor must first obtain a thorough understanding of the entity being audited. This includes understanding the nature of the entity's business, its principal objectives and strategies, its organizational structure, its governance, and its business model. The auditor also needs to consider the factors that affect the entity, such as economic, political, regulatory, and competitive factors. The objective of this step is to immerse oneself in the entity's universe to better assess potential risks.

In addition to the entity itself, the auditor must carefully consider the environment in which the entity operates. This may include elements such as the industry, market, economic conditions, regulatory and legal constraints, and stakeholders. This understanding of the environment enables the auditor to identify external factors that may influence the entity's risks.

Once the auditor has a thorough understanding of the entity and its environment, he or she can move on to assessing the risks of material misstatement in the financial statements. This involves identifying financial areas where there is a significant risk of material misstatement, meaning, material inaccuracies in the financial statements that could affect users' decisions. The auditor must also assess the likelihood of such misstatements and their potential impact. This risk assessment guides the design of audit procedures, focusing on the areas of greatest risk.

Risk Assessment and Response (ISA 330)

The auditor begins by assessing the risks associated with the audit engagement. These risks may be of several types, such as risks related to material errors in the financial statements, potential fraud, deficiencies in internal control, or other factors that could affect the reliability of the financial information. Risk assessment involves determining the likelihood and impact of these risks. It is based on an understanding of the entity and its environment, as discussed in ISA 315.

Once risks have been identified and assessed, the auditor must design and perform audit procedures to address those risks. These procedures are tailored to the nature and extent of the risks identified. They fall into two main categories:

Tests of controls: The auditor may decide to test the internal controls implemented by the entity to ensure their effectiveness in mitigating risks. The purpose of these tests is to assess whether the controls are operating as intended and whether they can prevent or detect errors or fraud. The results of these tests influence the scope of substantive audit procedures.

Substantive Audit Procedures: The auditor performs substantive audit procedures to obtain direct, independent evidence about the amounts and transactions included in the financial statements. These procedures are designed to minimize the risk of material misstatement. They may include analyses, confirmations, physical inspections, calculations, and other procedures to test the accuracy and completeness of the financial information.

Gathering Evidence (ISA 500, 501, 505, 510, 520, 530)

Audit evidence is the information and documentation that the auditor uses to assess the reliability of the entity's financial information. Audit evidence must be both sufficient (in quantity) and appropriate (in quality) to enable the auditor to form an informed opinion. In other words, it must be sufficient in number and relevant to support the auditor's conclusions. The auditor may use various methods to obtain audit evidence. These include inspection, observation, confirmation, replication, analytical procedures, and inquiry.

Obtaining audit evidence is fundamental to the audit because it reduces the risk of material misstatement and fraud in the financial statements. Audit evidence forms the basis for the auditor's opinion on the fairness and compliance of the financial statements. Obtaining appropriate audit evidence enhances the credibility of the entity's financial reports, which is important to investors, creditors, and other stakeholders who rely on this information to make important financial decisions.

Forming an Opinion and Preparing the Audit Report (ISA 700, 705, 706)

After performing all the audit steps, including understanding the entity, assessing the risks, and obtaining audit evidence, the auditor has gathered sufficient information to assess the fairness and compliance of the audited entity's financial statements. At this stage, the auditor uses the audit evidence to form an opinion on the financial statements. This opinion may be one of several types, including an unqualified (favorable) opinion, a qualified opinion (when certain matters remain unresolved or qualifications have been imposed by the entity), or an adverse opinion (when the financial statements are considered inadequate or unreliable).

Once an opinion has been expressed, the auditor prepares an auditor's report that clearly expresses the auditor's opinion on the entity's financial statements. The auditor's report is intended for users of the financial statements, such as shareholders, investors, creditors, and other stakeholders. This report is addressed to the entity's management (board of directors or senior management) and must comply with auditing standards to ensure clear and transparent communication of the auditor's opinion.

DIGITALIZATION AND FINANCIAL AUDIT

Within the evolving continuum of financial auditing practices, the unprecedented influence of digital technology is of undeniable importance. The purpose of this section is to methodically explore and deepen our understanding of the implications of the technological revolution on the financial audit landscape, highlighting its impact on the efficiency, accuracy, and relevance of the audit process.

History of Digitalization on Financial Auditing

Before the computer age, auditing was based on manual processes and physical practices. Auditors had to handle physical documents such as ledgers, invoices, and bank statements. They used mechanical tools such as calculators and adding machines to perform calculations and verifications (Ajao et al., 2016).

The computer age, which spanned from the 1950s to the 1970s, marked a period of notable change for auditing. Indeed, the introduction of the first computers brought benefits to auditors by automating certain calculation and data processing tasks. Accounting software made it possible to simplify bookkeeping and financial reporting. In addition, computer systems began to be used to store financial data, making it easier to access and manage this information. This development contributed to the transformation of auditing processes by enabling auditors to use IT (Information Technology) tools to analyze and verify financial data more efficiently (Shaikh et al., 2018).

The microcomputer era, from the 1970s to the 1990s, was a pivotal time for auditing, marked by the widespread adoption of personal computers. As personal computers became more accessible, auditors were able to automate accounting tasks and analyze data more efficiently. Accounting management software also evolved, offering advanced features such as payroll, inventory, and cost accounting, allowing companies to manage their financial operations more efficiently. In addition, auditors now use specific audit software to organize and document their procedures, facilitating planning, follow-up, and structured documentation of audit findings (Shaikh et al., 2018).

The computer-Assisted Auditing (CAATs) era, which spanned from the 1990s to the 2000s, saw significant technological advances that had a profound impact on the way auditors conduct their engagements. Indeed, CAATs tools have been developed to help auditors automate data collection, compliance testing, and financial data

Figure 1. Audit evolution continuum

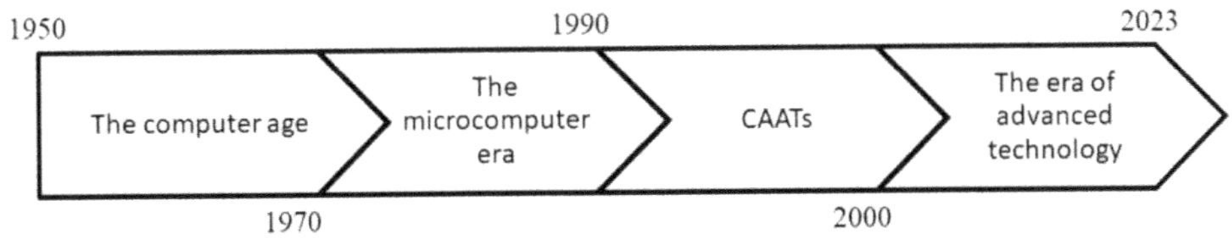

analysis. In addition, relational databases have enabled auditors to store and retrieve information efficiently (Marei et al., 2019).

The era of advanced technology, which began in the 2000s and continues today, has brought significant changes to the field of auditing. In fact, digital technology, particularly artificial intelligence and big data analytics, can improve audit quality. Indeed, recent advances in machine learning and artificial intelligence (AI), particularly in the areas of deep learning, natural language processing (NLP), and computer vision, have enabled the development of algorithms capable of analyzing large volumes of structured and unstructured data for fraud and anomaly detection. Their integration is transforming audit processes by enabling continuous, real-time risk assessment (Issa et al., 2016). Technology has also enabled remote auditing, which was particularly relevant during the COVID-19 pandemic (Ramdi, 2021).

Indeed, the future of auditing is being shaped by several important technological trends. Han et al. (2023) focuses primarily on the increasing integration of blockchain technology into auditing to improve the traceability of transactions. Blockchain offers features such as immutability, sequential data addition, and multi-party auditing, which enhance transparency and trust in accounting practices. In addition, the use of AI in auditing can improve assurance and efficiency by providing real-time data from verified blockchain protocols. This can enable auditors to use AI to analyze risks in a more predictive manner. In conclusion, Figure 1 represents a summary continuum.

Technology and Financial Audit

The evolution of technology has significantly reshaped the financial audit landscape over the last few decades, ushering in a significant transition towards more advanced methodologies and tools. This transformation, which is linked to the rise of digitalization, revolves around a redefinition of audit practices, characterized by increased agility and optimization of procedures. In this context of constant innovation, several emerging technologies have taken a prominent place, each contributing in a unique way to the reconfiguration of the financial audit landscape.

Computer-Assisted Audit Techniques (CAATs)

Computer-Assisted Audit Techniques (CAATs) are computer-assisted audit processes that rely on software and computer tools to streamline and enhance the financial audit process. These computer techniques are integrated by auditors with the aim of automating certain phases of the audit, analyzing substantial volumes of data, detecting irregularities, and increasing the efficiency of audit procedures (Marei et al., 2019). CAATs encompass various applications, such as data audit software, computer queries, computer-assisted sampling methods, and other specialized tools. These instruments allow auditors to perform a quick analysis of large data sets, identify patterns, and isolate anomalies that require further inspection.

Expert Systems

Expert systems are computer systems that use artificial intelligence to simulate the reasoning of a human audit expert. These systems are designed to help auditors make decisions and solve complex problems based on pre-defined rules and knowledge (Chukwuani & Egiyi, 2020; Hasan, 2021). These systems combine a knowledge base that contains audit rules and information about audit procedures with an inference engine that applies these rules to solve specific problems. They can ask questions, analyze financial data, and make recommendations based on the available information (Yang & Vasarhelyi, 1995). They are used in various areas of financial auditing, including risk assessment, fraud detection, compliance, and audit planning (Yang & Vasarhelyi, 1995; Hasan, 2021).

Cloud Computing

The widespread adoption of cloud computing has had a significant impact on the conduct of financial audits. The increased convenience of accessing financial data hosted in the cloud has undoubtedly made it easier for auditors to obtain critical information. However, this increased accessibility has raised significant concerns about the security and confidentiality of data, requiring a thorough evaluation of the security policies implemented by cloud service providers. Ensuring data integrity remains a paramount concern, as auditors must be able to certify that stored financial data has not been altered. In addition, data traceability requires rigorous audit mechanisms to ensure accurate verification. The economic benefits and inherent scalability of cloud computing are undeniable, but its use requires careful monitoring of costs and strict adherence to regulatory standards (Chou, 2015; Moghadasi et al., 2018). Financial auditors play an essential role in the meticulous evaluation of these issues, working to ensure the compliance, security, and reliability of cloud operations to maintain the integrity of the financial audit process.

Artificial Intelligence (AI)

AI is an academic field of study that deals with the creation of computers and software capable of intelligent behavior. AI aims to build machines that can react in an equivalent way to humans (Chukwuani & Egiyi, 2020). It encompasses various technologies such as robotic process automation (RPA), machine learning, neural networks, and fuzzy systems (Stancheva-Todorova, 2018; Chukwuani & Egiyi, 2020; Zheng et al., 2020).

According to Kokina and Davenport (2017) and Zemankova (2019), AI enables the automation of repetitive and labor-intensive auditing tasks. Structured tasks such as verification, recalculation, and reconciliation can be performed more efficiently and accurately thanks to AI. This frees up time for human auditors to focus on more complex tasks that require in-depth expertise and analysis.

Blockchain

Recognized as a decentralized and immutable technology, blockchain has had a profound impact on the discipline of financial auditing, fundamentally reshaping the methodologies for recording, verifying, and auditing financial transactions. The symbiosis between blockchain and financial auditing is underscored by an intrinsic alignment of their respective characteristics, resulting in mutual benefits. The prospect of integrating blockchain into financial auditing anticipates a significant improvement in critical parameters, particularly transparency, security, and efficiency in the field of financial auditing. This convergence represents a promising path towards a more robust and technologically sophisticated framework for auditing financial transactions, confirming the transformative potential inherent in the assimilation of blockchain technology into the financial audit.

BLOCKCHAIN TECHNOLOGY

Blockchain technology has emerged as a major disruptive force in the financial audit landscape and far beyond. This section undertakes to break down the complexities inherent in blockchain, starting with an exploration of its architecture, fundamental

Figure 2. Example of blockchain
Source: Zheng et al., 2017

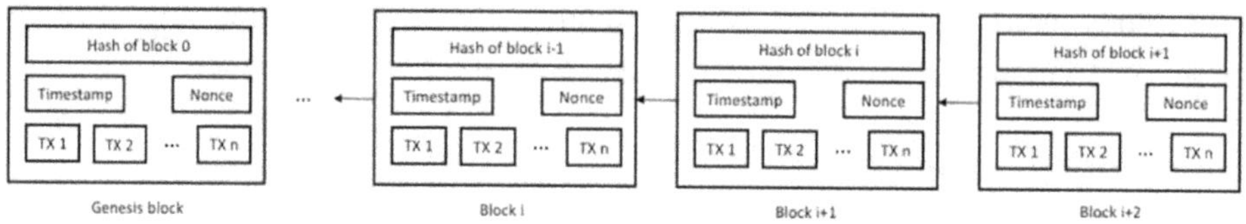

characteristics, various categories of blockchain, and widespread applications that have redefined the paradigms of trust, security, and traceability in various sectors.

Blockchain Technology Architecture

Blockchain is a disruptive technology based on distributed registers (Nofer et al., 2017; Schmitz & Leoni, 2019; Zemankova, 2019; Demirkan et al., 2020). In fact, blockchain is described as a peer-to-peer network. In this type of network, tasks and decisions are distributed among the participating peers. Each participant in the network maintains an identical copy of the register in which information is recorded. These registries contain all transactions that have occurred since the register was created (Schmitz & Leoni, 2019).

A blockchain is a chain of blocks of data. Each block contains a set of transactions (Nofer et al., 2017). The blocks of the blockchain are validated by the network using cryptographic means (Nofer et al., 2017). Figure 2 illustrates how blockchain works.

Each block references the immediately preceding block via a hash value that is the hash value of the preceding block, called the parent block. It is important to note that the hashes associated with the uncles (children of the block's ancestors) are also stored on the Ethereum blockchain. The first component of a blockchain is called the genesis block this block has no direct parent (Zheng at al., 2017).

Transactions are organized into blocks, and validation of the block must take place before it is added to the blockchain (Nofer at al., 2017). The validation process is performed by network participants, also known as miners. Miners assess the legitimacy of transactions and ensure that they comply with the rules of the protocol (Nofer et al., 2017).

The blockchain uses a consensus mechanism that is responsible for reaching agreement on the state of the blockchain and the transactions that are added to it (Nofer et al., 2017). The most common consensus mechanism is proof-of-work. In this mechanism, miners must solve complex mathematical problems to verify a block of transactions. Once a miner has solved the problem, he or she posts the verified

Figure 3. Block structure
Source: Zheng et al., 2017

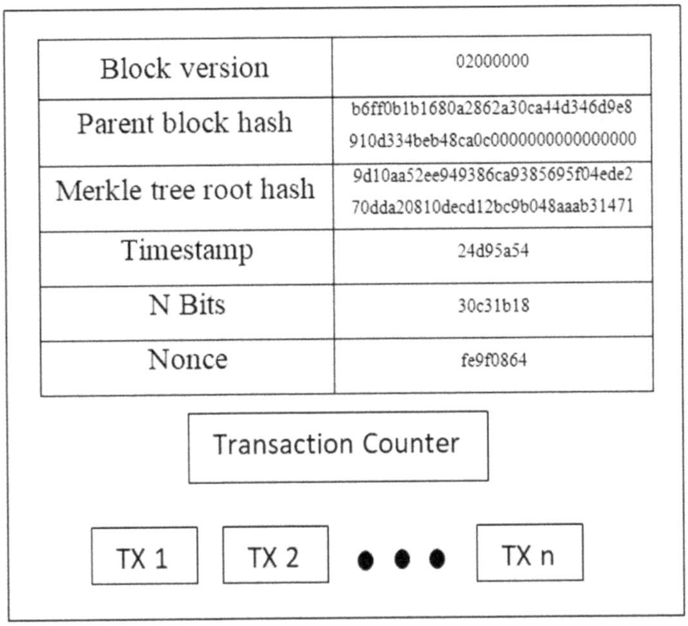

block to the network, and other miners evaluate the legitimacy of the block before adding it to their blockchain (Nofer et al., 2017).

A block consists of a block header and a block body (Zheng al., 2017). Figure 3 shows the block structure.

More specifically, according to Zheng et al. (2017) and Dai et al. (2019), the block header contains: block version: indicates the following validation blocks, parent block hash: a 256-bit hash value referring to the previous block, merkle tree root hash: the hash value of each transaction in the block, timestamp: The current time in seconds since January 1, 1970, at 0:00 UTC, N bits: the current hash value in compact format and nonce: a 4-byte field that typically starts at 0 and increments by hash values.

Characteristics of Blockchain

Blockchain, as an innovative technological paradigm, manifests several distinctive characteristics that delineate its importance in the field of financial auditing and extend its ramifications beyond. These characteristics, as illustrated in Figure 4, collectively form the basic framework that underpins the capabilities inherent in blockchain technology.

Figure 4. Blockchain's key features

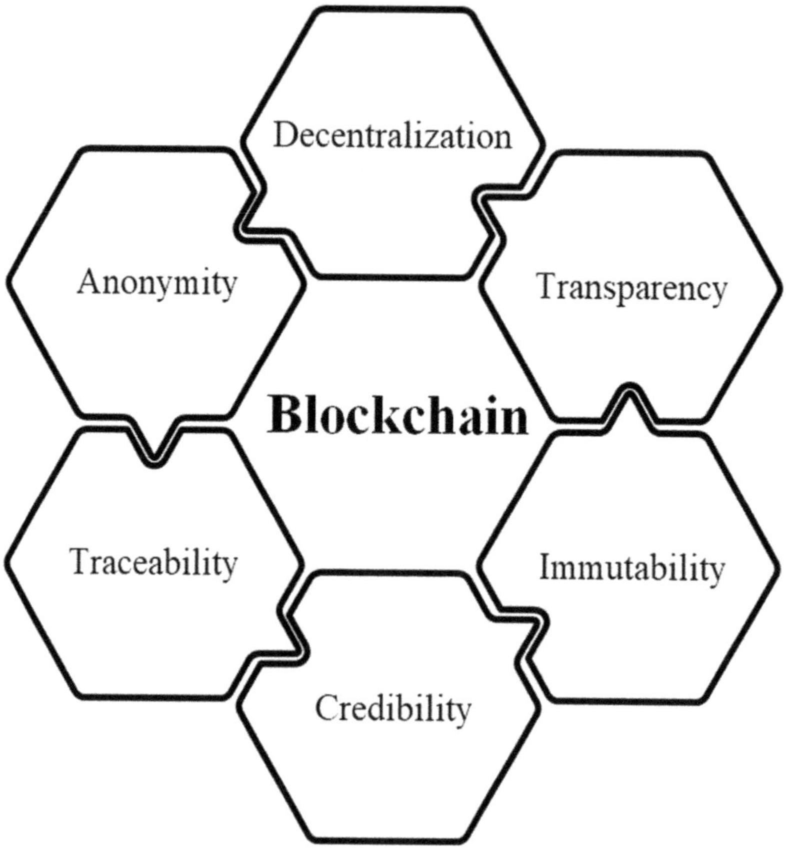

Decentralization which means that blockchain is a distributed technology that operates on a network of interconnected nodes, meaning that there is no single central authority that controls the system, allowing for decentralized management of transactions (Zheng et al., 2017; Dai et al., 2019; Lu, 2019).

Anonymity which means that blockchain provides a degree of anonymity, as users can conduct transactions without revealing their identity. Transactions are associated with cryptographic keys rather than names or personal identifiers (Zheng et al., 2017; Lu, 2019).

Transparency which means that the blockchain ledger is transparent, meaning that all network participants can view and verify transactions and data stored on the blockchain. This transparency strengthens trust among participants and promotes accountability (Dai et al.,2019; Lu, 2019).

Immutability which means that once a transaction is recorded on the blockchain, it becomes immutable. Data recorded in blocks cannot be altered or deleted later, ensuring the integrity and traceability of information (Dai et al., 2019).

Traceability which means that each transaction recorded in the blockchain is associated with a timestamp and can be traced back to its origin. This makes it possible to track the history of transactions and gain full visibility of the exchanges made (Dai et al., 2019; Lu, 2019).

Credibility which means that blockchain operates without human intervention through the self-monitoring of each node, which performs powerful computations to protect itself from external attacks (Lu, 2019).

These characteristics make blockchain a promising technology with a wide range of potential applications in various fields, especially in auditing.

Blockchain Categories

There are three categories of blockchain, including public blockchain, private blockchain, and consortium blockchain (Dai et al., 2019; Lu, 2019).

Public blockchain is accessible to everyone and anyone can participate. It is a decentralized network in which everyone can see and verify transactions, making it transparent and secure.

Private blockchain is more exclusive and controlled by a specific group or organization. It offers stricter security measures and limits access to selected participants.

Blockchain consortium is a hybrid of public and private blockchains. In this case, several organizations come together to form a network where they collaborate and share data securely.

These various categories give us an overview of the vast possibilities of blockchain technology in different sectors, such as auditing.

Common Blockchain Technology Applications

Beyond its reputation as a medium for cryptocurrencies, blockchain technology offers a range of innovative solutions that transcend the boundaries of traditional business sectors. This section focuses on two key applications of blockchain, namely smart contracts and triple-entry accounting, which have revolutionized the way transactions are executed and recorded.

Smart Contract Application

The concept of smart contracts was proposed by Nick Szabo. Smart contracts are self-executing computer programs that automatically facilitate, verify, and execute the terms of a contract between the parties involved without the need for an intermediary (Dai &Vasarhelyi, 2017). These contracts are based on blockchain 2.0 technology. In fact, smart contracts are used to facilitate and secure the exchange of value. They guarantee the transparent execution of agreements between stakeholders and ensure that all predefined conditions are met before a transaction is approved (Lu, 2019).

Smart contracts can be used in a variety of fields, such as financial services, auditing, and so on. According to Taherdoost (2023), the Ethereum platform enables the creation and execution of smart contracts using the Solidity programming language. In fact, Ethereum is a popular blockchain platform that is specifically designed to support smart contracts. Ethereum has been widely adopted for the development of Decentralized Applications (DApps) based on smart contracts. Smart contracts offer many advantages, including cost reduction, process acceleration, elimination of human error, and the elimination of intermediaries (Lu, 2019). However, their implementation requires careful attention to correct programming and risk management, as errors in a smart contract can have financial and legal consequences. In conclusion, smart contract applications are one of the key areas of research and practice related to blockchain technology in accounting and auditing.

Triple-Entry-Accounting

Triple-entry accounting is an innovative approach that combines the principles of double-entry accounting with advances in financial cryptography (Grigg, 2005). In traditional double-entry accounting, each transaction is recorded with a debit and a credit entry to ensure that the accounting ledgers balance. Triple-entry accounting goes beyond this model by introducing a third entry that is verified by a public ledger (Grigg, 2005; Dai &Vasarhelyi, 2019), which is the blockchain. According to Dai &Vasarhelyi (2019), the triple-entry system requires an independent intermediary to verify each transaction, which has limitations.

However, blockchain technology can solve these problems by automating and securing the process of recording and verifying transactions. Blockchain provides a transparent, secure and self-verifying system where confirmed transactions are impossible to alter or delete. The use of blockchain technology in triple-entry accounting increases trust and transparency by providing a decentralized and immutable source of truth (Cai, 2021). Accounting information stored on the blockchain can be accessed by all authorized stakeholders (Dai &Vasarhelyi, 2019;

Cai, 2021). This reduces the risk of fraud and facilitates independent verification of transactions.

BLOCKCHAIN TECHNOLOGY AND FINANCIAL AUDITING

The integration of blockchain technology into the financial audit ecosystem has ushered in an era of profound and substantial change. In this section, we aim to provide a detailed analysis of the remarkable consequences of the adoption of blockchain in the financial audit. We carefully analyze six key dimensions of this transformation, namely improved risk management, automation of audit processes, reduction of anomalies and fraud, potential cost savings, emergence of a new continuous audit model, enhancement of audit quality and the changing role of the auditor.

Improved Risk Management

The adoption of blockchain technology by companies significantly improves their risk management, thanks to a better assessment of these risks by auditors. According to Elommal and Manita (2022), blockchain technology would enable auditors to quickly and remotely extract data and verify many transactions already validated by blockchain actors, significantly reducing the number of accounting entries to be verified. This would allow auditors to focus on the risks associated with unvalidated transactions and areas of risk, rather than spending time verifying transactions that have already been validated.

In fact, blockchain guarantees the traceability of every transaction in a secure and immutable manner. This gives auditors real-time access to all financial data in a reliable, tamper-proof form. This total transparency allows auditors to analyze all operations in detail, to trace flows precisely, and to verify compliance at every stage. They can pinpoint any risk points within the audited financial processes. Thanks to this refined understanding of inherent risks made possible by blockchain traceability, auditors can make more targeted and effective risk management recommendations. These recommendations help the company to concretely strengthen its processes to better respond to identified risks and secure its long-term financial performance.

Audit Process Automation

Automating audit processes with blockchain means that certain manual and repetitive tasks can be automated, saving auditors time and allowing them to focus on more value-added activities. Traditionally, auditors have had to collect and validate a large amount of data from multiple sources when conducting an audit. This can be a tedious and time-consuming process that requires significant resources.

With blockchain, financial and operational data can be recorded transparently and immutably. Transactions are recorded in blocks of data, making it easier to collect and verify audit-relevant information. Auditors can access the blockchain ledger directly to obtain the data they need, eliminating the need to gather information from disparate sources. In addition, blockchain uses smart contracts, which are self-executing contracts based on predefined rules. These contracts can automate processes such as invoice payment, expense reporting, audit sampling, and compliance processes. This makes it easier to control and monitor accounting information and harder to hide financial fraud (Han et al., 2023).

By automating data collection and validation, auditors can spend more time on higher value-added activities, such as in-depth analysis of financial information, detecting potential fraud, and providing strategic advice to clients. This improves overall audit efficiency and enables auditors to provide better service to their clients (Garanina et al., 2022).

However, the automation of audit processes through blockchain does not completely replace the role of auditors. Auditors still play a critical role in interpreting data, assessing risk, and exercising professional judgment. Blockchain simply facilitates their work by automating administrative tasks and providing easier access to relevant data.

Reducing Anomalies and Fraud

Due to its immutable and transparent nature, blockchain offers opportunities to more easily detect anomalies, errors or potential fraud in transactions. The blockchain records all transactions transparently and chronologically. Each transaction is recorded in a block of data that is cryptographically linked to the previous blocks, forming a blockchain. This transparency allows auditors to access detailed information about each transaction, including origin, destination, amount, and time. This makes it easier to track and verify transaction flows, reducing the risk of fraud or hidden errors.

Once a transaction is registered on the blockchain, it becomes immutable, meaning it cannot be altered or deleted without the consensus of the network. This guarantees data integrity and prevents fraudulent retroactive manipulation. For example, Sarker et al. (2021) points out that auditors can rely on the accuracy and authenticity of information recorded on the blockchain, reducing the risk of error or falsification.

Transactions recorded on the blockchain are verifiable by all network participants. Auditors can examine transactions in real time and verify their validity (Gad et al., 2022). This makes it easier to detect anomalies or suspicious behavior, such as unusual transactions or unusually substantial amounts. Auditors can also use algorithms and analytical tools to monitor transaction patterns and identify potentially fraudulent behavior.

Although blockchain is transparent, it also provides privacy and security mechanisms. Sensitive data can be encrypted, and only authorized parties can access it. This reduces the risk of disclosure of sensitive information and protects the confidentiality of the data of parties involved in transactions.

Cost Reduction

By using blockchain, auditors can effectively benefit from a reduction in the cost and time associated with traditional auditing. Blockchain allows transactions to be stored transparently and securely. Auditors can access data in real time, without having to wait until the end of the audit period to collect the necessary information. This eliminates the need for manual data collection processes, which can be time consuming and costly. As a result, auditors have instant access to relevant information, speeding up the audit process.

Automating audit processes with blockchain technology has a direct impact on costs (Ramdi, 2021). For example, transactions recorded on the blockchain can automatically trigger pre-defined checks and controls. This reduces the need for manual intervention and multiple reviews, saving time and resources. Audit firms can optimize their internal processes, reducing the overhead associated with conducting audits. Fewer staff may be required to perform administrative tasks, as automation simplifies many aspects of the audit process.

New Financial Audit Model: Continuous Auditing

Blockchain-based continuous auditing can be defined as an auditing approach that leverages the intrinsic characteristics of blockchain technology to perform real-time monitoring of an organization's financial and operational transactions. This auditing methodology relies on the use of smart contracts and decentralized applications to continuously collect, validate, record, and analyze transaction data within a blockchain.

A key aspect of continuous auditing is near real-time reporting. This means that audit results are available almost immediately after the audit procedures are performed. Audit procedures are automated and run regularly, allowing data to be collected and analyzed in real time (Schmitz & Leoni, 2019; Barandi et al., 2019). This allows auditors and stakeholders to have a constant view of the company's financial and operational performance.

Another important feature of continuous auditing is continuous monitoring through tests embedded in smart contracts. Smart contracts are autonomous computer programs that run on a blockchain. For example, compliance rules can be programmed into a smart contract to automatically verify that transactions comply with established policies and regulations. If a violation is detected, alerts can be generated for immediate action.

However, Barandi et al. (2020) point out that despite the implementation of blockchain-based continuous auditing, auditors will still need to exercise professional judgment and gather evidence to assess assertions that are not covered by blockchain technology. While blockchain technology will not completely replace the role of auditors, it provides a powerful tool to enhance and improve audit processes. As a result, this approach delivers faster results, identifies issues earlier, and improves transparency and data security.

Improving Audit Quality

The use of blockchain technology can certainly help to improve audit quality in several ways, including increasing transparency for stakeholders, facilitating comprehensive verification of all data, and ensuring the permanent preservation of audit evidence.

Blockchain provides a decentralized, immutable ledger system that is accessible to all relevant stakeholders. This means that information stored on the blockchain is transparent, verifiable, and cannot be changed without network consensus. Stakeholders, such as shareholders, regulators or investors, can therefore have greater transparency and confidence in the company's financial and operational data.

In a traditional audit, verification may be limited to a sample of data due to time and resource constraints. With blockchain technology, however, it becomes possible to perform comprehensive audits of all data stored on the blockchain.

Audit evidence, such as accounting records, audit reports, or certifications, can be stored permanently on the blockchain (Elommal&Manita, 2021). The immutable nature of the blockchain ensures that such evidence cannot be altered or deleted. This facilitates the long-term preservation and accessibility of audit evidence, which is essential for compliance, regulatory, or potential litigation purposes.

It should be noted, however, that the widespread adoption of blockchain technology in auditing will require close collaboration between auditors, companies and regulators to establish appropriate standards, protocols and regulations. In addition, technical expertise in blockchain will be necessary for auditors to effectively use this technology in their audit processes.

The Changing Role of Auditor

By automating audit tasks with blockchain, auditors can spend more time on risk analysis and strategic consulting. Instead of focusing on data collection and verification, they can focus on identifying potential risks to the business and making

Figure 5. Impact of blockchain technology on the financial auditing
Source: Bejjar and Siala, 2023

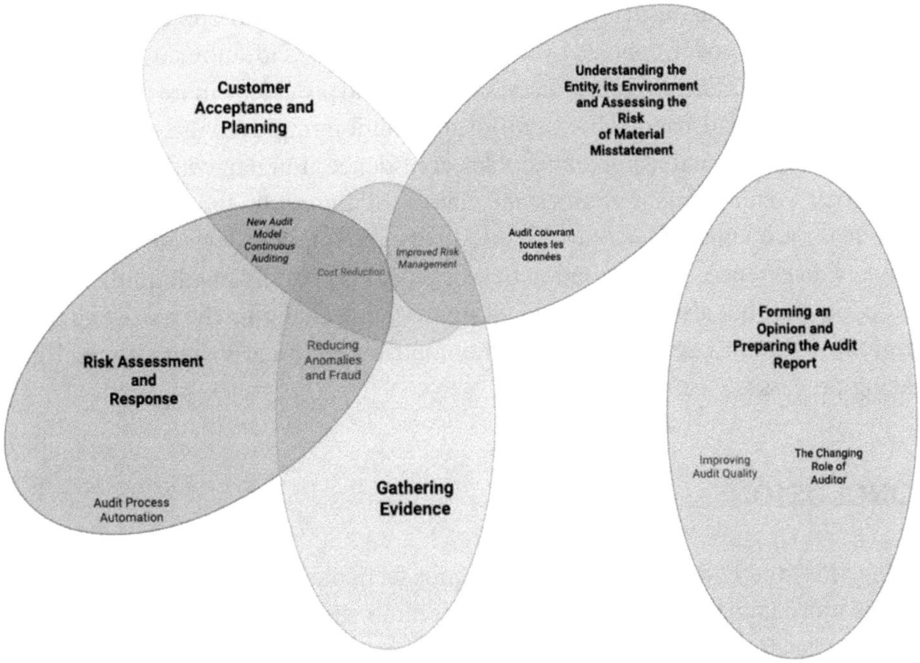

recommendations to mitigate them. According to Elommal & Manita (2021), this adds value to the audit by providing strategic information for decision-making.

With the advent of blockchain and other technologies, it is becoming increasingly important for auditors to understand the technical and IT aspects of information systems. Therefore, audit teams are increasingly composed of multidisciplinary profiles, including information technology (IT) experts (Secinaro et al., 2021). These IT experts contribute their expertise in assessing system security, verifying technical data, and understanding computerized processes. This allows for a more comprehensive approach to the audit, considering both financial and technological aspects.

This evolution enables auditors to add significant value by providing strategic recommendations based on a deep understanding of the risks and opportunities associated with technology and data.

To sum up, the integration of blockchain technology in the context of financial audit is creating a transformative landscape. The decentralized and transparent nature of blockchain significantly improves risk management, while reducing operational costs through streamlined and automated processes. Blockchain's inherent ability to encompass all data provides comprehensiveness to the audit, limiting the risk of omission or error. In addition, blockchain acts as an effective deterrent against anomalies and fraud, ensuring the integrity of financial data. The emergence of a continuous audit model, enabled by real-time monitoring and automation, represents a departure from traditional periodic assessments and provides a more dynamic view of the financial landscape. This significant evolution improves the overall quality of audits, thereby increasing stakeholder confidence. Fundamentally, blockchain technology significantly redefines the nature of the audit function as auditors move from a manual role to a strategic oversight function leveraging advanced analytics. In essence, the integration of blockchain is not only revolutionizing audit methodologies, but also profoundly and significantly changing the role of auditors, positioning them as strategic actors who contribute critical insights to decision-making processes (see Figure 5).

CONCLUSION

During this study, we found that blockchain technology has intrinsic properties such as transparency, immutability and decentralization that have the potential to radically transform the audit industry. These characteristics allow for a significant improvement in risk management, increased automation of audit processes, and a significant reduction in anomalies and fraud. The use of blockchain can also lead to significant cost savings for audit firms and create a new financial audit model - continuous auditing.

What is more, the application of blockchain technology in auditing expands the traditional role of the auditor. Auditors should become blockchain experts, capable of understanding blockchain systems, auditing them effectively, and advising clients on their use. This paves the way for the auditor's role to evolve into a more strategic advisory function.

The study also highlighted several promising areas for future research. First, there is a need to further explore how blockchain technology can be more thoroughly integrated into audit processes, including the use of smart contracts and asset traceability. Further research is needed to understand how auditors can adapt their skills and methodologies to take full advantage of this technology. In addition, it is imperative to monitor the evolution of regulations and standards in the audit sector in response to the growing adoption of blockchain. This regulatory evolution will have a significant impact on the way audit firms operate and provide services to their clients. Finally, it is critical to keep a close eye on technological developments and innovations in the blockchain space, as new advances may have a significant impact on auditing. Auditors need to stay at the forefront of technology to remain relevant in an ever-changing environment.

In conclusion, blockchain technology represents a notable change for financial auditing. It offers significant benefits in terms of efficiency, security and quality of audit work. However, its adoption requires an adaptation of methodologies, skills and regulations. Auditors who embrace this technology will have the opportunity to play a key role in transforming the audit industry and provide more valuable services to their clients.

REFERENCES

Ajao, O. S., Olamide, J. O., &Temitope, A. A. (2016). Evolution and development of auditing. *Unique Journal of Business Management Research, 3*(1), 32-40.

Akbar, H., Zubair, M., & Malik, M. S. (2023). Security Issues and challenges in Cloud Computing. *International Journal for Electronic Crime Investigation*, *7*(1), 13–32. doi:10.54692/ijeci.2023.0701125

Arpaci, I., Yardimci, Y. C., Ozkan, S., & Turetken, O. (2012). Organizational adoption of information technologies: A literature review. *International Journal of ebusiness and egovernment. Studies*, *4*(2), 37–50.

Barandi, Z., Lawson-Body, A., Lawson-Body, L., & Willoughby, L. (2020). Impact of blockchain technology on the continuous auditing: mediating role of transaction cost theory. *Issues in Information Systems*, *21*(2).

Brody, P., & Giuseppe, P. (n.d.-a). *EY OpsChain Traceability.* EY. https://www.ey.com/en_us/blockchain-platforms/opschain-traceability

Brody, P., & Giuseppe, P. (n.d.-b). *EY Blockchain Analyzer: Explorer & Visualizer.* EY. https://www.ey.com/en_us/blockchain-platforms/explorer-visualizer

Cai, C. W. (2021). Triple-entry accounting with blockchain: How far have we come? *Accounting and Finance*, *61*(1), 71–93. doi:10.1111/acfi.12556

Chan, D. Y., Chiu, V., & Vasarhelyi, M. A. (2018). New Perspective: Data analytics as a precursor to audit automation. In Continuous Auditing (pp. 315-322). Emerald Publishing Limited.

Chou, D. C. (2015). Cloud computing risk and audit issues. *Computer Standards & Interfaces*, *42*, 137–142. doi:10.1016/j.csi.2015.06.005

Chukwuani, V. N., & Egiyi, M. A. (2020). Automation of accounting processes: Impact of artificial intelligence. *International Journal of Research and Innovation in Social Science*, *4*(8), 444–449.

Cunningham, L. A. (2004). A new product for the state corporation law market: Audit committee certifications. *Berkeley Bus. LJ*, *1*, 327.

Dai, H. N., Zheng, Z., & Zhang, Y. (2019). Blockchain for Internet of Things: A survey. *IEEE Internet of Things Journal*, *6*(5), 8076–8094. doi:10.1109/JIOT.2019.2920987

Dai, J., & Vasarhelyi, M. A. (2017). Toward blockchain-based accounting and assurance. *Journal of Information Systems*, *31*(3), 5–21. doi:10.2308/isys-51804

Davies, M. (2019). PwC *launches solution supporting audit of cryptocurrency*. PWC. https://www.pwc.com/gx/en/archive/news-room/press-releases/cryptocurrenc-audit.html

De Andrés, J., & Lorca, P. (2021). On the impact of smart contracts on auditing. *The International Journal of Digital Accounting Research*, 21. doi:10.4192/1577-8517-v21_6

Debreceny, R., Lee, S. L., Neo, W., & Shuling Toh, J. (2005). Employing generalized audit software in the financial services sector: Challenges and opportunities. *Managerial Auditing Journal*, *20*(6), 605–618. doi:10.1108/02686900510606092

Demirkan, S., Demirkan, I., & McKee, A. (2020). Blockchain technology in the future of business cyber security and accounting. *Journal of Management Analytics*, *7*(2), 189–208. doi:10.1080/23270012.2020.1731721

DiMaggio, P. J., & Powell, W. W. (1983). The iron cage revisited: Institutional isomorphism and collective rationality in organizational fields. *American Sociological Review*, *48*(2), 147–160. doi:10.2307/2095101

Du, H., & Cong, Y. (2010). Cloud computing, accounting, auditing, and beyond. *The CPA Journal*, *80*(10), 66.

Elommal, N., &Manita, R. (2021). How blockchain innovation could affect the audit profession: a qualitative study. *Journal of Innovation Economics & Management*, I103-27.

Fogarty, T. J. (1992). Financial accounting standard setting as an institutionalized action field: Constraints, opportunities and dilemmas. *Journal of Accounting and Public Policy*, *11*(4), 331–355. doi:10.1016/0278-4254(92)90003-G

Gad, A. G., Mosa, D. T., Abualigah, L., & Abohany, A. A. (2022). Emerging trends in blockchain technology and applications: A review and outlook. *Journal of King Saud University. Computer and Information Sciences*, *34*(9), 6719–6742. doi:10.1016/j.jksuci.2022.03.007

Garanina, T., Ranta, M., & Dumay, J. (2022). Blockchain in accounting research: Current trends and emerging topics. *Accounting, Auditing & Accountability Journal*, *35*(7), 1507–1533. doi:10.1108/AAAJ-10-2020-4991

Gepp, A., Linnenluecke, M. K., O'Neill, T. J., & Smith, T. (2018). Big data techniques in auditing research and practice: Current trends and future opportunities. *Journal of Accounting Literature*, *40*(1), 102–115. doi:10.1016/j.acclit.2017.05.003

Grigg, I. (2005). Triple entry accounting. *SystemicsInc*, 1-10.

Han, H., Shiwakoti, R. K., Jarvis, R., Mordi, C., & Botchie, D. (2023). Accounting and auditing with blockchain technology and artificial Intelligence: A literature review. *International Journal of Accounting Information Systems*, *48*, 100598. doi:10.1016/j.accinf.2022.100598

Hasan, A. R. (2021). Artificial Intelligence (AI) in accounting & auditing: A Literature review. *Open Journal of Business and Management*, *10*(1), 440–465. doi:10.4236/ojbm.2022.101026

Hezam, Y. A., Anthonysamy, L., & Suppiah, S. D. K. (2023). Big Data Analytics and Auditing: A Review and Synthesis of Literature. *Emerging Science Journal*, *7*(2), 629–642. doi:10.28991/ESJ-2023-07-02-023

International Auditing and Assurance Standards Board (IAASB). (2008a). *ISA 200: Overall objectives of the independent auditor and the conduct of an audit in accordance with international standards on auditing*. Retrieved October 7, 2023, from https://eis.international-standards.org/standards/iaasb/2020?section=MASTER_7#MASTER_7

International Auditing and Assurance Standards Board (IAASB). (2008b). *ISA 210: Agreeing the terms of audit engagements*. Retrieved October 7, 2023, from https://eis.international-standards.org/standards/iaasb/2020?section=MASTER_8#MASTER_8

International Auditing and Assurance Standards Board (IAASB). (2008c). *ISA 330: The auditor's responses to assessed risks*. Retrieved October 7, 2023, from https://eis.international-standards.org/standards/iaasb/2020?section=MASTER_18#MASTER_18

International Auditing and Assurance Standards Board (IAASB). (2008d). *ISA 500: Audit evidence*. Retrieved October 7, 2023, from https://eis.international-standards.org/standards/iaasb/2020?section=MASTER_21#MASTER_21

International Auditing and Assurance Standards Board (IAASB). (2008e). *ISA 501: Audit evidence—Specific considerations for selected items*. Retrieved October 7, 2023, from https://eis.international-standards.org/standards/iaasb/2020?section=MASTER_22#MASTER_22

International Auditing and Assurance Standards Board (IAASB). (2008f). *ISA 505: External confirmations*. Retrieved October 7, 2023, from https://eis.international-standards.org/standards/iaasb/2020?section=MASTER_23#MASTER_23

International Auditing and Assurance Standards Board (IAASB). (2008g). *ISA 510: Initial audit engagements—Opening balances*. Retrieved October 7, 2023, from https://eis.international-standards.org/standards/iaasb/2020?section=MASTER_24#MASTER_24

International Auditing and Assurance Standards Board (IAASB). (2008h). *ISA 520: Analytical procedures*. Retrieved October 7, 2023, from https://eis.international-standards.org/standards/iaasb/2020?section=MASTER_25#MASTER_25

International Auditing and Assurance Standards Board (IAASB). (2008i). *ISA 530: Audit sampling*. Retrieved October 7, 2023, from https://eis.international-standards.org/standards/iaasb/2020?section=MASTER_26#MASTER_26

International Auditing and Assurance Standards Board (IAASB). (2012). *ISA 315: Identifying and assessing the risks of material misstatement through understanding the entity and its environment*. Retrieved October 7, 2023, from https://eis.international standards.org/standards/iaasb/2020?section=MASTER_16#MASTER_16

International Auditing and Assurance Standards Board (IAASB). (2015a). *ISA 700 (Revised): Forming an Opinion and Reporting on Financial Statements*. Retrieved October 7, 2023, from https://eis.international-standards.org/standards/iaasb/2020?section=MASTER_35#MASTER_35

International Auditing and Assurance Standards Board (IAASB). (2015b). *ISA 705 (Revised): Modifications to the opinion in the independent auditor's report*. Retrieved October 7, 2023, from https://eis.international-standards.org/standards/iaasb/2020?section=MASTER_37#MASTER_37

International Auditing and Assurance Standards Board (IAASB). (2015c). *ISA 706: Emphasis of matter paragraphs and other matter paragraphs in the independent auditor's report*. Retrieved October 7, 2023, from https://eis.international-standards.org/standards/iaasb/2020?section=MASTER_38#MASTER_38

Issa, H., Sun, T., & Vasarhelyi, M. A. (2016). Research ideas for artificial intelligence in auditing: The formalization of audit and workforce supplementation. *Journal of Emerging Technologies in Accounting*, *13*(2), 1–20. doi:10.2308/jeta-10511

Karmańska, A. (2021). Internet of Things in the accounting field–benefits and challenges. *Operations Research and Decisions*, *31*(3), 23–39. doi:10.37190/ord210302

Kokina, J., & Davenport, T. H. (2017). The emergence of artificial intelligence: How automation is changing auditing. *Journal of Emerging Technologies in Accounting*, *14*(1), 115–122. doi:10.2308/jeta-51730

Laszlo, P. (n.d.). *KPMG Origins Bringing better transparency to global supply chain*. KPMG. https://kpmg.com/xx/en/home/insights/2021/04/kpmg-origins-transparency-global-supply-chains.html

Lu, Y. (2019). The blockchain: State-of-the-art and research challenges. *Journal of Industrial Information Integration*, *15*, 80–90. doi:10.1016/j.jii.2019.04.002

Luan, H., Geczy, P., Lai, H., Gobert, J., Yang, S. J., Ogata, H., Baltes, J., Guerra, R., Li, P., & Tsai, C. C. (2020). Challenges and future directions of big data and artificial intelligence in education. *Frontiers in Psychology*, *11*, 580820. doi:10.3389/fpsyg.2020.580820 PMID:33192896

Malik, S., Chadhar, M., Vatanasakdakul, S., & Chetty, M. (2021). Factors affecting the organizational adoption of blockchain technology: Extending the technology–organization–environment (TOE) framework in the Australian context. *Sustainability (Basel)*, *13*(16), 9404. doi:10.3390/su13169404

Marei, A., & Iskandar, E. D. T. B. M. (2019). The impact of Computer Assisted Auditing Techniques (CAATs) on development of audit process: An assessment of Performance Expectancy of by the auditors. *International Journal of Management and Commerce Innovations*, *7*(2), 1199–1205.

Matthews, D. (2006). *A history of auditing: the changing audit process in Britain from the nineteenth century to the present day* (Vol. 5). Routledge. doi:10.4324/9780203965634

Mearian, L. (2019). *Deloitte launches 'Blockchain in a Box' hands-on demonstrator.* Computerworld. https://www.computerworld.com/article/3433856/deloitte-launches-blockchain-in-a-box-hands-on-demonstrator.html

Moghadasi, M., Mousavi, S. M., & Fazekas, G. (2018). Cloud computing auditing. *International Journal of Advanced Computer Science and Applications*, *9*(12). Advance online publication. doi:10.14569/IJACSA.2018.091265

Montes, G. A., & Goertzel, B. (2019). Distributed, decentralized, and democratized artificial intelligence. *Technological Forecasting and Social Change*, *141*, 354–358. doi:10.1016/j.techfore.2018.11.010

Nofer, M., Gomber, P., Hinz, O., & Schiereck, D. (2017). Blockchain. *Business & Information Systems Engineering*, *59*(3), 183–187. doi:10.1007/s12599-017-0467-3

O'Leary, D. E. (2003). Auditor environmental assessments. *International Journal of Accounting Information Systems*, *4*(4), 275–294. doi:10.1016/j.accinf.2003.09.001

Obert, R. (1994). *Pratique internationale de la comptabilité et de l'audit.* No Title.

Raffegeau, J., Dufils, P., & De Ménonville, D. (1994). *L'audit financier.* Presses Universitaires De France.

Ramdi, I. (2021). La technologie digitale et la profession d'audit: Quel impact? *International Journal of Accounting, Finance, Auditing, Management and Economics*, *2*(6-1), 126-144.

Rogers, E. M. (1995). Diffusion of Innovations: modifications of a model for telecommunications. *Die diffusion von innovationen in der telekommunikation*, 25-38.

Sarker, S., Henningsson, S., Jensen, T., & Hedman, J. (2021). The use of blockchain as a resource for combating corruption in global shipping: An interpretive case study. *Journal of Management Information Systems*, *38*(2), 338–373. doi:10.1080/07421222.2021.1912919

Schmitz, J., & Leoni, G. (2019). Accounting and auditing at the time of blockchain technology: A research agenda. *Australian Accounting Review*, *29*(2), 331–342. doi:10.1111/auar.12286

Secinaro, S., Dal Mas, F., Brescia, V., & Calandra, D. (2021). Blockchain in the accounting, auditing and accountability fields: A bibliometric and coding analysis. *Accounting, Auditing & Accountability Journal*, *35*(9), 168–203. doi:10.1108/AAAJ-10-2020-4987

Shaikh, H., Jokhio, M. U., Maher, Z. A., Chandio, S., Manirajah, M., Abdullah, B., ... Shah, A. (2018). Beyond traditional audits: The implications of information technology on auditing. *International Journal of Engineering & Technology, 7*(2.34), 5-11.

Su, X., Xiao, Y., & Liu, S. (2022, March). Analysis on the Impact of Blockchain Technology on the Accounting Profession. In *7th International Conference on Economy, Management, Law and Education (EMLE 2021)* (pp. 10-14). Atlantis Press. 10.2991/aebmr.k.220306.002

Tabrizchi, H., & Kuchaki Rafsanjani, M. (2020). A survey on security challenges in cloud computing: Issues, threats, and solutions. *The Journal of Supercomputing, 76*(12), 9493–9532. doi:10.1007/s11227-020-03213-1

Taherdoost, H. (2023). Smart Contracts in Blockchain Technology: A Critical Review. *Information (Basel), 14*(2), 117. doi:10.3390/info14020117

Tapscott, D., & Tapscott, A. (2016). *Blockchain revolution: how the technology behind bitcoin is changing money, business, and the world.* Penguin.

Yang, D. C., & Vasarhelyi, M. A. (1995). The Application of Expert Systems in Accounting. *Unpublished Working Paper.*

Yilmaz, N. K., & Hazar, H. B. (2019). The rise of internet of things (IoT) and its applications in finance and accounting. *Press Academia Procedia, 10*(1), 32–35. doi:10.17261/Pressacademia.2019.1139

Zemankova, A. (2019). Artificial intelligence and blockchain in audit and accounting: Literature review. *WSEAS Transactions on Business and Economics, 16*(1), 568-581.

Zhang, C. A., Cho, S., & Vasarhelyi, M. (2022). Explainable artificial intelligence (xai) in auditing. *International Journal of Accounting Information Systems, 46*, 100572. doi:10.1016/j.accinf.2022.100572

Zheng, W., Lai, C. F., He, D., Kumar, N., & Chen, B. (2020). Secure storage auditing with efficient key updates for cognitive industrial IoT environment. *IEEE Transactions on Industrial Informatics, 17*(6), 4238–4247. doi:10.1109/TII.2020.2991204

Zheng, Z., Xie, S., Dai, H., Chen, X., & Wang, H. (2017, June). *An overview of blockchain technology: Architecture, consensus, and future trends. In 2017 IEEE international congress on big data (BigData congress).* IEEE.

KEY TERMS AND DEFINITIONS

Artificial Intelligence (AI): Artificial intelligence (AI) is the field of computer science that aims to reproduce human cognitive abilities in machines, such as learning, problem solving, language comprehension, image recognition, etc.

Blockchain: Blockchain is a decentralized technology for storing and transmitting information. Technically, it consists of a distributed database in which the information sent by users and the links within the database are verified and grouped into blocks at regular intervals, all secured by cryptography.

Continuous Auditing: Continuous auditing is an audit methodology that involves the ongoing examination and evaluation of an organization's operations and internal controls. Unlike the traditional periodic audit, continuous auditing is performed on an ongoing basis throughout the year.

Digitalization: Digitalization is the process of converting information from analog to digital format. This typically involves converting information in physical form (paper documents, photographs, films, etc.) into digital files that can be stored and processed by computers.

Financial Audit: A financial audit is an in-depth examination of a company's or organization's financial statements by an independent auditor. The objective is to ensure that the financial statements give a true and fair view of the financial position and results of operations of the audited entity.

Smart Contract: A smart contract is an automated computer program that executes the terms of a contract. It is an agreement whose terms are written directly in lines of code. The smart contract enables the exchange of value (money, property, shares, or other assets) by automatically verifying compliance with rules and obligations.

Compilation of References

AACSB. (2018). *Eligibility Procedures and Accreditation Standards for Accounting Accreditation*. The Association to Advance Collegiate Schools of Business.

Abbott, A. (2014). *The system of professions: An essay on the division of expert labor*. University of Chicago Press.

Abernethy, M. A., Bouwens, J., & Van Lent, L. (2013). The role of performance measures in the intertemporal decisions of business unit managers. *Contemporary Accounting Research*, *30*(3), 925–961. doi:10.1111/j.1911-3846.2012.01178.x

Acharya, V. V., Schaefer, S., & Zhang, Y. (2015). Liquidity risk and correlation risk: A clinical study of the General Motors and Ford Downgrade of May 2005. *The Quarterly Journal of Finance*, *5*(02), 1550006. doi:10.1142/S2010139215500068

Acharya, V. V., & Viswanathan, S. X. (2011). Leverage, moral hazard, and liquidity. *The Journal of Finance*, *66*(1), 99–138. doi:10.1111/j.1540-6261.2010.01627.x

Afzal, A., Rasoulinezhad, E., & Malik, Z. (2022). Green finance and sustainable development in Europe. *Economic research-. Ekonomska Istrazivanja*, *35*(1), 5150–5163. doi:10.1080/1331677X.2021.2024081

Agarwal, R. (2020). *Digital Transformation: A Path to Economic and Societal Value*. Retrieved from https://www.redalyc.org/journal/6381/638167728001/

Agrawal, A., & Mandelker, G. N. (1990). Large shareholders and the monitoring of managers: The case of antitakeover charter amendments. *Journal of Financial and Quantitative Analysis*, *25*(2), 143–161. doi:10.2307/2330821

Agusti, R. R., & Rahman, A. F. (2023). Determinants of tax attitude in small and medium enterprises: Evidence from Indonesia. *Cogent Business & Management*, *10*(1), 2160585. doi:10.1080/23311975.2022.2160585

Ahçi, M. (2017) *Dynamic interaction between liquidity and sovereign credit risk: Evidence from Turkey* [Master's thesis]. Ekonomi ve Sosyal Bilimler Enstitüsü. https://repository.bilkent.edu.tr/server/api/core/bitstreams/f008f56b-274d-4e5d-99f9-9a56e7fb215e/content

Ahmed, N., Akhtar, M. F., & Usman, M. (2011). Risk management practices and Islamic banks: An empirical investigation from Pakistan. *Interdisciplinary Journal of Research in Business, 1*(6), 50–57.

AICPA. (2020). *The Data-Driven Audit: How Automation and AI are Changing the Audit and the Role of the Auditor*. Retrieved from https://us.aicpa.org/content/dam/aicpa/interestareas/frc/assuranceadvisoryservices/downloadabledocuments/the-data-driven-audit.pdf

Ai, Y., Sun, G., & Kong, T. (2023). Digital finance and stock price crash risk. *International Review of Economics & Finance, 88*(November), 607–619. doi:10.1016/j.iref.2023.07.003

Ajao, O. S., Olamide, J. O., &Temitope, A. A. (2016). Evolution and development of auditing. *Unique Journal of Business Management Research, 3*(1), 32-40.

Akbar, H., Zubair, M., & Malik, M. S. (2023). Security Issues and challenges in Cloud Computing. *International Journal for Electronic Crime Investigation, 7*(1), 13–32. doi:10.54692/ijeci.2023.0701125

Alam, M. S., & Hossain, D. M. (2021). Management Accounting in the Era of Digitalization. *The Journal of Industrial Distribution & Business, 12*(11), 1–8.

Al-dmour, A., Al-Fawaz, K. M., Al-dmour, R., & Allozi, N. M. (2017). Accounting Information System and Its Role on Business Performance: A Theoretical Study. *Journal of Management and Strategy, 8*(4), 79. doi:10.5430/jms.v8n4p79

Al-Htaybat, K., & von Alberti-Alhtaybat, L. (2017). Big Data and corporate reporting: Impacts and paradoxes. *Accounting, Auditing & Accountability Journal, 30*(4), 850–873. doi:10.1108/AAAJ-07-2015-2139

Alkafaji, B. K. A., Dashtbayaz, M. L., & Salehi, M. (2023). The Impact of Blockchain on the Quality of Accounting Information: An Iraqi Case Study. *Risks, 11*(3), 58. doi:10.3390/risks11030058

Alkayed, H., Zighan, S., Qabajeh, M., & Almaharmeh, M. I. (2023). The role of XBRL adoption on enhancing transparency of information disclosure: A case study of Jordanian financial companies. *Cogent Business and Management, 10*(3), 2265082. Advance online publication. doi:10.1080/23311975.2023.2265082

Allen, J., & Cebula, J. (2008). *Risk and Resilience: Considerations for Information Security Risk Assessment and Management. J. Cebula*. CERT.

Allingham, M. G., & Sandmo, A. (1972). Income tax evasion: A theoretical analysis. *Journal of Public Economics, 1*(3-4), 323–338. doi:10.1016/0047-2727(72)90010-2

Allingham, M. G., & Sandmo, A. (1972). Income tax evasion: A theoretical analysis. *Taxation: Critical Perspectives on the World Economy, 3*(1), 323–338.

Al-Masharfi, M. H. R., & Matriano, M. T. (2022). The Role of Electronic Accounting Information System in Measuring Credit Risk in National Bank of Oman. *GSJ, 10*(1), 1789–1800. https://www.researchgate.net/profile/Maria-Teresa-Matriano/publication/358273351_The_Role_of_Electronic_Accounting_Information_System_in_Measuring_Credit_Risk_in_National_Bank_of_Oman/links/61f9dc3111a1090a79c9216e/The-Role-of-Electronic-Accounting-Inform

Alm, J. (2011). Measuring, explaining, and controlling tax evasion: Lessons from theory, experiments, and field studies. *International Tax and Public Finance, 19*(1), 54–77. doi:10.1007/s10797-011-9171-2

Alm, J. (2019). What motivates tax compliance? *Journal of Economic Surveys, 33*(2), 353–388. doi:10.1111/joes.12272

Al-Sabti, A. A. W. H. (2023). Implications for Enhancing the Financial Reporting Quality Brought on by the Digital Revolution of Internal Control. *International Journal of Professional Business Review, 8*(4), e01381. doi:10.26668/businessreview/2023.v8i4.1381

Alsulmani, A. H., Alkindi, S. S., & Ahmed, E. R. (2021). Customer Accounting Information and Omani Service Companies' Performance. *International Journal of Finance & Banking Studies, 10*(2), 79–88. doi:10.20525/ijfbs.v10i2.1245

Altunina, V. V., & Alieva, I. A. (2021). Current trends in the development of a green finance system: Methodology and practice. *Baltic Region, 13*(2), 64-89.

Andrianaivo, M., & Kpodar, K. (2011). *ICT, financial inclusion, and growth: Evidence from African countries*. IMF Working Paper. International Monetary Fund. Retrieved from https://www.imf.org/external/pubs/ft/wp/2011/wp1173.pdf

Angkinand, A., & Wihlborg, C. (2010). Deposit insurance coverage, ownership, and banks' risk-taking in emerging markets. *Journal of International Money and Finance, 29*(2), 252–274. doi:10.1016/j.jimonfin.2009.08.001

Anis, A. (2023). Blockchain in accounting and auditing: Unveiling challenges and unleashing opportunities for digital transformation in Egypt. *Journal of Humanties and Applied Sciences, 5*(4), 359–380. doi:10.1108/JHASS-06-2023-0072

Apochi, J. G., & Mustapha, L. O. I. (2022). FRS Adoption Financial Reporting Quality in Nigeria: A Conceptual Approach. European Journal of Accounting. *Audit and Finance Research, 10*, 9–18.

Appelbaum, M., Cooper, H., Kline, R. B., Mayo-Wilson, E., Nezu, A. M., & Rao, S. M. (2018). Journal article reporting standards for quantitative research in psychology: The APA Publications and Communications Board task force report. *The American Psychologist, 73*(1), 3–25. doi:10.1037/amp0000191 PMID:29345484

Arbolino, R., Boffardi, R., & De Simone, L. (2018). Which are the factors influencing innovation performances? Evidence from Italian cohesion policy. *Social Indicators Research, 146*(1-2), 221–247. doi:10.1007/s11205-018-1904-5

Arnaboldi, M., Busco, C., & Cuganesan, S. (2017). Accounting, accountability, social media and big data: Revolution or hype? *Accounting, Auditing & Accountability Journal, 30*(4), 762–776. doi:10.1108/AAAJ-03-2017-2880

Arnold, V. (2018). The changing technological environment and the future of behavioural research in accounting. *Accounting and Finance, 58*(2), 315–339. doi:10.1111/acfi.12218

Arnone, M., & Crovella, T. (2023). The Role of Green Finance in Supporting Maritime Sustainable Development. In Fintech and Sustainability: How Financial Technologies Can Help Address Today's Environmental and Societal Challenges (pp. 53-87). Springer. doi:10.1007/978-3-031-40647-8_4

Arntz, M., Gregory, T., & Zierahn, U. (2016). *The Risk of Automation for Jobs in OECD Countries: a comparative analysis.* OECD Social, Employment and Migration Working Papers, No. 189. OECD Publishing. https://www.oecd-ilibrary.org/social-issues-migration-health/the-risk-ofautomation-for-jobs-in-oecd-countries_5jlz9h56dvq7-en

Arpaci, I., Yardimci, Y. C., Ozkan, S., & Turetken, O. (2012). Organizational adoption of information technologies: A literature review. *International Journal of ebusiness and egovernment. Studies, 4*(2), 37–50.

Arslan, M. (2020). Corporate social sustainability in supply chain management: A literature review. *Journal of Global Responsibility, 11*(3), 233–255. doi:10.1108/JGR-11-2019-0108

Arslan, M. (2020b). Mechanisms of labour exploitation: The case of Pakistan. *International Journal of Law and Management, 62*(1), 1–21. doi:10.1108/IJLMA-07-2018-0145

Arslan, M. (2022). Succession Planning in Family-Owned Business Evidence From an Emerging Economy. In *Research Anthology on Strategies for Maintaining Successful Family Firms* (pp. 504–528). IGI Global. doi:10.4018/978-1-6684-3550-2.ch022

Arslan, M. (2023). CEO Compensation and Say on Pay: Does CEO-to-Employee Pay Ratio Matters? *Proceedings - Academy of Management, 2023*(1), 11035. doi:10.5465/AMPROC.2023.11035abstract

Arslan, M., & Alqatan, A. (2020). Role of institutions in shaping corporate governance system: Evidence from emerging economy. *Heliyon, 6*(3), e03520. doi:10.1016/j.heliyon.2020.e03520 PMID:32181393

Asian Development Bank. (2022). *Launching A Digital Tax Administration Transformation : What You Need to Know.* Asian Development Bank. doi:10.22617/TCS210343

Attias Assouline, A.-V., & Glon, G. (2018). Fiscalité du digital, digitalisation de la fiscalité. *Revue d'Economie Financiere, 131*(3), 217–232. doi:10.3917/ecofi.131.0217

AtzoriM. (2015). Blockchain technology and decentralized governance: Is the state still necessary? *Available at* SSRN 2709713. doi:10.2139/ssrn.2709713

Ayoola, T. J., Olaniyi, O. O., Kolawole, P. E., Aregbesola, O. D., & Wright, O. (2023). *Tax administration, trust in tax authorities, and personal income tax compliance: Evidence from Nigeria*. Academic Press.

Azofra, V., & Santamaría, M. (2011). Ownership, control, and pyramids in Spanish commercial banks. *Journal of Banking & Finance*, *35*(6), 1464–1476. doi:10.1016/j.jbankfin.2010.10.029

Bai, L., Koveos, P., & Liu, M. (2018). Applying an ontology-augmenting XBRL model to accounting information system for business integration. *Asia-Pacific Journal of Accounting & Economics*, *25*(1–2), 75–97. Advance online publication. doi:10.1080/16081625.2016.1170616

Baisalbayeva, K., Enden, E., Ion, V., & Tsavdaris, H. (2017). *Digital Transformation of Tax Administrators*. Microsoft and PwC.

Bajaher, M. S. (2023). Exploring user perception of XBRL adoption and its impact on accounting data in the Saudi context. *Electronic Journal of University of Aden for Humanity and Social Sciences*, *4*(1), 184–192. Advance online publication. doi:10.47372/ejua-hs.2023.1.242

Baker El-Ebiary, Y. A., & Alawi, N. A. M. (2020). The risks of accounting information systems. *International Journal of Engineering Trends and Technology*, *1*, 120–127. Advance online publication. doi:10.14445/22315381/CATI3P220

Baker, S. E., & Edwards, R. (2012). *How many qualitative interviews is enough*. Academic Press.

Barandi, Z., Lawson-Body, A., Lawson-Body, L., & Willoughby, L. (2020). Impact of blockchain technology on the continuous auditing: mediating role of transaction cost theory. *Issues in Information Systems*, *21*(2).

Barry, T. A. (2010). *Structure actionnariale des banques, risque et efficience* [Doctoral dissertation]. New York University.

Barth, J. R., Caprio, G., & Levine, R. (2008). *Rethinking bank regulation: Till angels govern*. Cambridge University Press.

Bassey, E., Mulligan, E., & Ojo, A. (2022). A conceptual framework for digital tax administration-A systematic review. *Government Information Quarterly*, *39*(4), 101754. doi:10.1016/j.giq.2022.101754

Bayrak, T. (2021). *Digital Future*. Peter Lang Verlag. doi:10.3726/b18869

Beck, T., De Jonghe, O., & Mulier, K. (2017). *Bank sectoral concentration and (systemic) risk: Evidence from a worldwide sample of banks*. Academic Press.

Belfo, F., & Trigo, A. (2013). Accounting information systems: Tradition and future directions. *Procedia Technology*, *9*, 536–546. doi:10.1016/j.protcy.2013.12.060

Bellon, M., Dabla-Norris, E., Khalid, S., & Lima, F. (2022). Digitalization to improve tax compliance : Evidence from VAT e-Invoicing in Peru. *Journal of Public Economics*, *210*, 104661. doi:10.1016/j.jpubeco.2022.104661 PMID:35711616

Bellucci, M., Cesa Bianchi, D., & Manetti, G. (2022). Blockchain in accounting practice and research: Systematic literature review. *Meditari Accountancy Research, 30*(7), 121–146. doi:10.1108/MEDAR-10-2021-1477

Ben-Hassoun, A., Aloui, C., & Ben-Nasr, H. (2018). Demand for audit quality in newly privatized firms in MENA region: Role of internal corporate governance mechanisms audit. *Research in International Business and Finance, 45*, 334–348. doi:10.1016/j.ribaf.2017.07.167

Berger, A. N., Clarke, G. R., Cull, R., Klapper, L., & Udell, G. F. (2005). Corporate governance and bank performance: A joint analysis of the static, selection, and dynamic effects of domestic, foreign, and state ownership. *Journal of Banking & Finance, 29*(8-9), 2179–2221. doi:10.1016/j.jbankfin.2005.03.013

Berger, A. N., & Di Patti, E. B. (2006). Capital structure and firm performance: A new approach to testing agency theory and an application to the banking industry. *Journal of Banking & Finance, 30*(4), 1065–1102. doi:10.1016/j.jbankfin.2005.05.015

Betti, N., & Sarens, G. (2021). Understanding the internal audit function in a digitalized business environment. *Journal of Accounting & Organizational Change, 17*(2), 197–216. doi:10.1108/JAOC-11-2019-0114

Beynon-Davies, P. (2005). Constructing electronic government: The case of the UK inland revenue. *International Journal of Information Management, 25*(1), 3–20. doi:10.1016/j.ijinfomgt.2004.08.002

Bhagat, S., Bolton, B., & Lu, J. (2015). Size, leverage, and risk-taking of financial institutions. *Journal of Banking & Finance, 59*, 520–537. doi:10.1016/j.jbankfin.2015.06.018

Bharadiya, J. P. (2023). A Comparative Study of Business Intelligence and Artificial Intelligence with Big Data Analytics. *American Journal of Artificial Intelligence, 7*(1), 24.

Bhaskar, R. (2020). Critical realism and the ontology of persons. *Journal of Critical Realism, 19*(2), 113–120. doi:10.1080/14767430.2020.1734736

Bikker, J. A., & Metzemakers, P. A. (2005). Bank provisioning behaviour and procyclicality. *Journal of International Financial Markets, Institutions and Money, 15*(2), 141–157. doi:10.1016/j.intfin.2004.03.004

Boddy, C. R. (2016). Sample size for qualitative research. *Qualitative Market Research, 19*(4), 426–432. doi:10.1108/QMR-06-2016-0053

Bonin, J. P., Hasan, I., & Wachtel, P. (2005). Bank performance, efficiency and ownership in transition countries. *Journal of Banking & Finance, 29*(1), 31–53. doi:10.1016/j.jbankfin.2004.06.015

Bonyuet, D. (2020). Overview and Impact of Blockchain on Auditing. *The International Journal of Digital Accounting Research, 20*, 31–43. doi:10.4192/1577-8517-v20_2

Borisova, G., Brockman, P., Salas, J. M., & Zagorchev, A. (2012). Government ownership and corporate governance: Evidence from the EU. *Journal of Banking & Finance*, *36*(11), 2917–2934. doi:10.1016/j.jbankfin.2012.01.008

Boskov, T., & Drakulevski, L. (2017). Addressing the role of risk management and digital finance technology on financial inclusion. *Quality - Access to Success*, *18*(161), 113–115.

Bouaziz, W., & Bouri, A. (2012). Ownership structure and financial institutes risk taking: evidence from Tunisian quoted bankOwnership structure and financial institutes risk taking: evidence from Tunisian quoted bank (financial institute). *International Journal of Managerial and Financial Accounting*, *4*(1), 47–60. doi:10.1504/IJMFA.2012.044836

Bourkhis, K., & Nabi, M. S. (2013). Islamic and conventional banks' soundness during the 2007–2008 financial crisis. *Review of Financial Economics*, *22*(2), 68–77. doi:10.1016/j.rfe.2013.01.001

Boussaada, R., & Karmani, M. (2015). Ownership concentration and bank performance: Evidence from MENA banks. *International Journal of Business and Management*, *10*(3), 189. doi:10.5539/ijbm.v10n3p189

Boyd, J. H., & Runkle, D. E. (1993). Size and performance of banking firms: Testing the predictions of theory. *Journal of Monetary Economics*, *31*(1), 47–67. doi:10.1016/0304-3932(93)90016-9

Boyle, T. (2000a). *CDEA General Ledger Schema*. Ledgerism. Available online: https://web.archive.org/web/20071001201740/http://www.ledgerism.net/GLSchema1.txt

Boyle, T. (2000b). *Draft Schema for General Ledger*. Ledgerism. Available online: http://web.archive.org/web/20051003224536 /http://ledgerism.net/GLSchemaDraft1.txt

Boyle, T. (2000c). *Re: Company Centric View Ends. Data Goes to the Net*. Available online: http://linas.org/mirrors/www.gldialtone.com/2001.07.14/ToddREAPost.htm

Boyle, T. (2000d). *The Public Transaction Repository (PTR) Project*. GL Dialtone. Available online: http://web.archive.org/web/20000622133330/http://www.gldialtone.com/PTR.htm

Boyle, T. (2001). *The Shared Transaction Repository (STR) ver. 0.60 spec*. Available at: http://linas.org/mirrors/www.gldialtone.com/2001.07.14/STR.htm

Boyle, T. (2003a). *The Argument to Abolish Double-Entry Accounting and Abolish the Assets=Liabilities + Owner's Equity Equation*. Available at http://web.archive.org/web/20031208235246/http://ledgerism.net/GLSchema2.txt

Boyle, T. (2003b). *Accounting Hypercubes on the Internet*. Available at http://web.archive.org/web/20060102014117/http://www.ledgerism.net/hypercub.htm

Boyle, T. (2003c). *File-Based Commerce (FBC) Architecture ver. 0.31 spec. Business Requirements Viewpoint*. Available at http://web.archive.org/web/20050211111755/http://ledgerism.net/fbc.htm

Boyle, T. (2003d). *General Ledgerism*. Available at http://web.archive.org/web/20060425114848/http://ledgerism.net/

Boyle, T. (2003e). *Shared Transaction Repository (STR) A High Level Software Specification.* Available at http://web.archive.org/web/20060102052824/http://www.ledgerism.net/STR.htm

Braun, V., & Clarke, V. (2006). Using thematic analysis in psychology. *Qualitative Research in Psychology, 3*(2), 77–101. doi:10.1191/1478088706qp063oa

Bresnahan, T., & Trajtenberg, M. (1995). General purpose technologies: 'engines of growth'? *Journal of Econometrics, 65*(1), 83–108. doi:10.1016/0304-4076(94)01598-T

Brody, P., & Giuseppe, P. (n.d.-a). *EY OpsChain Traceability.* EY. https://www.ey.com/en_us/blockchain-platforms/opschain-traceability

Brody, P., & Giuseppe, P. (n.d.-b). *EY Blockchain Analyzer: Explorer & Visualizer.* EY. https://www.ey.com/en_us/blockchain-platforms/explorer-visualizer

Brown-Liburd, H., Issa, H., & Lombardi, D. (2015). The behavioural implications of Big Data's impact on audit judgment, decision making, and future research directions. *Accounting Horizons, 29*(2), 451–468. doi:10.2308/acch-51023

Brown, P., Ly, T., Pham, H., & Sivabalan, P. (2020). Automation and management control in dynamic environments: Managing organisational flexibility and energy efficiency in service sectors. *The British Accounting Review, 52*(2), 100840. doi:10.1016/j.bar.2019.100840

Brynjolfsson, E., & McAfee, A. (2014). *The Second Machine Age: Work, Progress, and Prosperity in a Time of Brilliant Technologies.* W. W. Norton & Company.

Bueno, S., Banuls, V. A., & Gallego, M. D. (2021). Is urban resilience a phenomenon on the rise? A systematic literature review for the years 2019 and 2020 using textometry. *International Journal of Disaster Risk Reduction, 66*, 102588. doi:10.1016/j.ijdrr.2021.102588

Bulyga, E. S., Vasyukova, L. K., Grigoryeva, V. I., & Dimov, R. P. (2022). Digital transformation of the financial market: Risks and opportunities. *Наука Красноярья, 11*(2), 49–67. doi:10.12731/2070-7568-2022-11-2-49-67

Burkart, M., Gromb, D., & Panunzi, F. (1997). Large shareholders, monitoring, and the value of the firm. *The Quarterly Journal of Economics, 112*(3), 693–728. doi:10.1162/003355397555325

Caglio, A. (2003). Enterprise resource planning systems and accountants: Towards hybridization? *European Accounting Review, 12*(1), 123–153. doi:10.1080/0963818031000087853

Cahyonowati, N., Ratmono, D., & Juliarto, A. (2023). The role of social norms and trust in authority in tax compliance dilemmas. *Cogent Business & Management, 10*(1), 2174084. doi:10.1080/23311975.2023.2174084

Cai, C. (2023). *Customer–supplier digital transformation and corporate tax avoidance.* doi:10.2139/ssrn.4578455

Cai, C. W. (2019). Triple-entry Accounting with Blockchain: How far Have we Come? *Accounting and Finance, 61*(2), 71–93. doi:10.1111/acfi.12556

Calem, P., & Rob, R. (1999). The impact of capital-based regulation on bank risk-taking. *Journal of Financial Intermediation, 8*(4), 317–352. doi:10.1006/jfin.1999.0276

Campiglio, E. (2016). Beyond carbon pricing: The role of banking and monetary policy in financing the transition to a low-carbon economy. *Ecological Economics, 121*, 220–230. doi:10.1016/j.ecolecon.2015.03.020

Canares, M. P. (2016). Creating the Enabling Environment for More Transparent and Better-resourced Local Governments: A Case of E-taxation in the Philippines. *Information Technology for Development, 22*(sup1), 121–138. doi:10.1080/02681102.2015.1121857

Cao, X., Li, X., Zhu, Y., & Zhang, Z. (2015). A comparative study of environmental performance between prefabricated and traditional residential buildings in China. *Journal of Cleaner Production, 109*, 131–143. doi:10.1016/j.jclepro.2015.04.120

Casey, M. J., & Vigna, P. (2018). *The Truth Machine: The Blockchain and the Future of Everything*. St. Martin's Press.

Chan, D. Y., Chiu, V., & Vasarhelyi, M. A. (2018). New Perspective: Data analytics as a precursor to audit automation. In Continuous Auditing (pp. 315-322). Emerald Publishing Limited.

Chaney, P. K., Faccio, M., & Parsley, D. (2011). The quality of accounting information in politically connected firms. *Journal of Accounting and Economics, 51*(1-2), 58–76. doi:10.1016/j.jacceco.2010.07.003

Chan, K. S., & Zary, N. (2019). Applications and Challenges of Implementing Artificial Intelligence in Medical Education: Integrative Review. *JMIR Medical Education, 5*(1), e13930. Advance online publication. doi:10.2196/13930 PMID:31199295

Chapman, C. S., & Kihn, L.-A. (2009). Information system integration, enabling control and performance. *Accounting, Organizations and Society, 34*(2), 151–169. doi:10.1016/j.aos.2008.07.003

Chau, G. K., & Gray, S. J. (2002). Ownership structure and corporate voluntary disclosure in Hong Kong and Singapore. *The International Journal of Accounting, 37*(2), 247–265. doi:10.1016/S0020-7063(02)00153-X

Chaves, M. M. N., dos Santos, A. P. R., dos Santosa, N. P., & Larocca, L. M. (2017). Use of the software IRaMuTeQ in qualitative research: An experience report. *Computer Supported Qualitative Research*, 39–48.

Chen, H. (2019). *Success factors impacting artificial intelligence adoption: Perspective from the Telecom Industry in China*. Old Dominion University.

Chen, J. (2017). Testing and Implementing Digital Tax Administration. In *Digital Revolutions in Public Finance*. International Monetary Fund. doi:10.5089/9781484315224.071.ch005

Chen, Z., Xiao, Y., & Jiang, K. (2023). The impact of tax reform on firms' digitalization in China. *Technological Forecasting and Social Change, 187*, 122196. doi:10.1016/j.techfore.2022.122196

Chernousova, K. S. (2021). *Digital Transformation Of Tax Administration As A Function Of State Administration*. doi:10.15405/epsbs.2021.04.02.158

Chiu, V., Liu, Q., Muehlmann, B., & Baldwin, A. A. (2019). A bibliometric analysis of accounting information systems journals and their emerging technologies contributions. *International Journal of Accounting Information Systems*, *32*, 24–43. doi:10.1016/j.accinf.2018.11.003

Chiu, V., Liu, Q., & Vasarhelyi, M. A. (2014). The development and intellectual structure of continuous auditing research. *Journal of Accounting Literature*, *33*(1-2), 37–57. doi:10.1016/j.acclit.2014.08.001

Choi, J. J. (Ed.). (2001). *Asian Financial Crisis Financial, Structural and International Dimensions*. Emerald Group Publishing Limited. doi:10.1016/S1569-3767(2001)1

Chou, D. C. (2015). Cloud computing risk and audit issues. *Computer Standards & Interfaces*, *42*, 137–142. doi:10.1016/j.csi.2015.06.005

Christensen, C., Raynor, M. E., & McDonald, R. (2015). *Disruptive innovation*. Harvard Business Review. Retrieved from https://hbr.org/2015/12/what-is-disruptive-innovation

Christensen, C. M., Raynor, M. E., Dyer, J., & Gregersen, H. (2011). *Disruptive Innovation: The Christensen Collection (The Innovator's Dilemma, The Innovator's Solution, The Innovator's DNA, and Harvard Business Review article" How Will You Measure Your Life?")(4 Items)*. Harvard Business Press.

Christ, K. L., & Burritt, R. L. (2019). Implementation of sustainable development goals: The role for business academics. *Australian Journal of Management*, *44*(4), 571–593. doi:10.1177/0312896219870575

Chukwuani, V. N., & Egiyi, M. A. (2020). Automation of accounting processes: Impact of artificial intelligence. *International Journal of Research and Innovation in Social Science*, *4*(8), 444–449.

Chukwuani, V. N., & Egiyi, M. A. (2020). Automation of Accounting Processes: Impact of Artificial Intelligence. *International Journal of Research and Innovation in Social Science*, *4*, 444–449. https://www.rsisinternational.org/journals/ijriss/Digital-Library/volume-4-issue-8/444-449.pdf

Chu, M. K., & Yong, K. O. (2021). Big Data Analytics for Business Intelligence in Accounting and Audit. *Open Journal of Social Sciences*, *9*(9), 42–52. doi:10.4236/jss.2021.99004

Cipek, K. (2021). The Impact of Digitalisation on Tax Audit. *WCLF Tax und IP Gesprächsband 2019: Immaterielle Werte als zentrale Komponente internationaler Steuerstrategien*, 59-73.

Claessens, S. (2006). Corporate governance and development. *The World Bank Research Observer*, *21*(1), 91–122. doi:10.1093/wbro/lkj004

Claessens, S., Demirgüç-Kunt, A., & Huizinga, H. (2001). How does foreign entry affect domestic banking markets? *Journal of Banking & Finance*, *25*(5), 891–911. doi:10.1016/S0378-4266(00)00102-3

Claessens, S., & Van Horen, N. (2014). Foreign banks: Trends and impact. *Journal of Money, Credit and Banking*, *46*(s1), 295–326. doi:10.1111/jmcb.12092

CMA. (2020). *Capital Market Authority, Sultanate of Oman - XBRL*. https://cma.gov.om/Home/XBRL/aboutxbrl

Cooper, D. J., & Robson, K. (2006). Accounting, professions and regulation: Locating the sites of professionalization. *Accounting, Organizations and Society*, *31*(4-5), 415–444. doi:10.1016/j.aos.2006.03.003

Corbin, J. M., & Strauss, A. (1990). Grounded theory research: Procedures, canons, and evaluative criteria. *Qualitative Sociology*, *13*(1), 3–21. doi:10.1007/BF00988593

Corlin Christensen, R., & Lips, W. (2021). *The politics of taxing the digital economy*. Handbook on the Politics of Taxation. doi:10.4337/9781788979429.00034

Cormier, D., Dufour, D., Luu, P., Teller, P., & Teller, R. (2019). The Relevance of XBRL Voluntary Disclosure for Stock Market Valuation: The Role of Corporate Governance. *Canadian Journal of Administrative Sciences*, *36*(1), 113–127. Advance online publication. doi:10.1002/cjas.1483

Cornett, M. M., Guo, L., Khaksari, S., & Tehranian, H. (2010). The impact of state ownership on performance differences in privately-owned versus state-owned banks: An international comparison. *Journal of Financial Intermediation*, *19*(1), 74–94. doi:10.1016/j.jfi.2008.09.005

Coulthard, E. B. (2020). *Green bonds and blockchain: How technology may help navigate the increasingly complex world of sustainability regulation* [Master Thesis]. University of Oslo, Norway. Retrieved from https://www.duo.uio.no/bitstream/handle/10852/84662/1/Master-thesis-final.pdf

Coyne, J. G., & McMickle, P. L. (2017). Can blockchains serve an accounting purpose? *Journal of Emerging Technologies in Accounting*, *14*(2), 101–111. doi:10.2308/jeta-51910

Cremer, F., Sheehan, B., Fortmann, M., Kia, A. N., Mullins, M., Murphy, F., & Materne, S. (2022). Cyber risk and cybersecurity: A systematic review of data availability. *The Geneva Papers on Risk and Insurance. Issues and Practice*, *47*(4), 698–736. doi:10.1057/s41288-022-00266-6 PMID:35194352

Creswell, J. W., & Poth, C. N. (2016). *Qualitative inquiry and research design: Choosing among five approaches*. Sage publications.

Cross-Border Privacy Rules (CBPR) System. (n.d.). *CBPR System*. Retrieved February 12, 2024, from https://cbprs.org/

Cummings, M. (2021). Rethinking the maturity of artificial intelligence in safety-critical settings. *AI Magazine*, *42*(1), 6–15. doi:10.1002/j.2371-9621.2021.tb00005.x

Cunningham, L. A. (2004). A new product for the state corporation law market: Audit committee certifications. *Berkeley Bus. LJ*, *1*, 327.

D'Onza, G., & De Santis, F. (2020). Professional impact of digital audit-thinking beyond the realm of audit standards. *JOURNAL*, (1), 141–144.

Dabbous, A., Barakat, K. A., & Tarhini, A. (2024). Digitalization, crowdfunding, eco-innovation and financial development for sustainability transitions and sustainable competitiveness: Insights from complexity theory. *Journal of Innovation & Knowledge*, *9*(1), 100460. doi:10.1016/j.jik.2023.100460

Dagnino, G. B., & Quattrone, P. (2006). Comparing institutionalisms: Gino Zappa and John R. Commons' accounts of "institution" as a groundwork for a constructivist view. *Journal of Management History*, *12*(1), 36–52. doi:10.1108/13552520610638265

Dai, H. N., Zheng, Z., & Zhang, Y. (2019). Blockchain for Internet of Things: A survey. *IEEE Internet of Things Journal*, *6*(5), 8076–8094. doi:10.1109/JIOT.2019.2920987

Dai, J., & Vasarhelyi, M. A. (2017). Toward blockchain-based accounting and assurance. *Journal of Information Systems*, *31*(3), 5–21. Advance online publication. doi:10.2308/isys-51804

Dalal, R. S., Howard, D. J., Bennett, R. J., Posey, C., Zaccaro, S. J., & Brummel, B. J. (2022). Organizational science and cybersecurity: Abundant opportunities for research at the interface. *Journal of Business and Psychology*, *37*(1), 1–29. doi:10.1007/s10869-021-09732-9 PMID:33564206

Daniels, R. J., & Halpern, P. (1996). Too close for comfort: The role of the closely held public corporation in the Canadian economy and the implications for public policy. *Can. Bus. LJ*, *26*, 11.

Davenport, T. H., & Harris, J. G. (2007). *Competing on analytics: The new science of winning*. Harvard Business Press.

Davies, M. (2019). PwC *launches solution supporting audit of cryptocurrency.* PWC. https://www.pwc.com/gx/en/archive/news-room/press-releases/cryptocurrenc-audit.html

De Andrés, J., & Lorca, P. (2021). On the impact of smart contracts on auditing. *The International Journal of Digital Accounting Research*, 21. doi:10.4192/1577-8517-v21_6

De George, E. T., Ferguson, C. B., & Spear, N. A. (2013). How Much Does IFRS Cost? IFRS Adoption and Audit Fees. *The Accounting Review*, *88*(2), 429–462. doi:10.2308/accr-50317

De Jonghe, O. (2010). Back to the basics in banking? A micro-analysis of banking system stability. *Journal of Financial Intermediation*, *19*(3), 387–417. doi:10.1016/j.jfi.2009.04.001

de Vasconcellos, M. V., & das Graças Rua, M. (2005). Impacts of internet use on public administration: A case study of the Brazilian tax administration. *Electronic Journal of E-Government*, *3*(1), 49–58.

Debreceny, R., & Farewell, S. (2010). XBRL in the accounting curriculum. *Issues in Accounting Education*, *25*(3), 379–403. Advance online publication. doi:10.2308/iace.2010.25.3.379

Debreceny, R., Lee, S. L., Neo, W., & Shuling Toh, J. (2005). Employing generalized audit software in the financial services sector: Challenges and opportunities. *Managerial Auditing Journal, 20*(6), 605–618. doi:10.1108/02686900510606092

Dechow, N., & Mouritsen, J. (2005). Enterprise resource planning systems, management control and the quest for integration. *Accounting, Organizations and Society, 30*(7-8), 691–733. doi:10.1016/j.aos.2004.11.004

Dečman, M., & Klun, M. (2015). The Impact of Information Systems on Taxation: A Case of Users Experience With an e-Recovery Information System. *Electronic Journal of E-Government, 13*(2), 110–121.

Dečman, N., Sever Mališ, S., & Mamić Sačer, I. (2019). Digitalization of Accounting and Tax Processes-Challenges and Opportunities for Accountants and Tax Administrators. *Proceedings of FEB Zagreb International Odyssey Conference on Economics and Business, 1*(1), 30-40.

Delina, L. L. (2023). Fintech RE in a global finance centre: Expert perceptions of the benefits of and challenges to digital financing of distributed and decentralised renewables in Hong Kong. *Energy Research & Social Science, 97*(March), 102997. doi:10.1016/j.erss.2023.102997

Delis, M. D., & Staikouras, P. K. (2011). Supervisory effectiveness and bank risk. *Review of Finance, 15*(3), 511–543. doi:10.1093/rof/rfq035

Deloitte. (2016). *Blockchain Technology–A Game-Changer in Accounting*. White paper.

Deloitte. (2018). *Breaking blockchain open: Deloitte's 2018 global blockchain survey*. Available at: https://www2.deloitte.com/content/dam/Deloitte/cz/Documents/financial-services/cz-2018-deloitte-global-blockchain-survey.pdf

Demirgüç-Kunt, A., & Detragiache, E. (2002). Does deposit insurance increase banking system stability? An empirical investigation. *Journal of Monetary Economics, 49*(7), 1373–1406. doi:10.1016/S0304-3932(02)00171-X

Demirgüç-Kunt, A., & Huizinga, H. (2010). Bank activity and funding strategies: The impact on risk and returns. *Journal of Financial Economics, 98*(3), 626–650. doi:10.1016/j.jfineco.2010.06.004

Demirgüç-Kunt, A., Klapper, L., Singer, D., & Ansar, S. (2022). *The Global Findex Database 2021: Financial inclusion, digital payments, and resilience in the age of COVID-19*. World Bank Publications. doi:10.1596/978-1-4648-1897-4

Demirkan, S., Demirkan, I., & McKee, A. (2020). Blockchain technology in the future of business cyber security and accounting. *Journal of Management Analytics, 7*(2), 189–208. doi:10.1080/23270012.2020.1731721

Deng, S., & Jia, J. (2007). Institutional Ownership, Diversification, and Risk Taking in BHCs. Academic Press.

Deng, J. L., & Li, J. (2019). Will government subsidies affect corporate tax avoidance? *Journal of Financial Economics, 45*(1), 109–121.

Dengler, K., & Matthes, B. (2018). The impacts of digital transformation on the labour market: Substitution potentials of occupations in Germany. *Technological Forecasting and Social Change*, *137*, 304–316. doi:10.1016/j.techfore.2018.09.024

Deng, S. E., Elyasiani, E., & Mao, C. X. (2007). Diversification and the cost of debt of bank holding companies. *Journal of Banking & Finance*, *31*(8), 2453–2473. doi:10.1016/j.jbankfin.2006.10.024

Development Co-operation Report 2019. (2019). OECD. doi:10.1787/9a58c83f-en

Devidze, N. (2022). Current State of Green Digital Financing and the Associated Challenges. In Green Digital Finance and Sustainable Development Goals (pp. 29-50). Singapore: Springer Nature Singapore. doi:10.1007/978-981-19-2662-4_2

Diamond, D. W., & Rajan, R. G. (2001). Liquidity risk, liquidity creation, and financial fragility: A theory of banking. *Journal of Political Economy*, *109*(2), 287–327. doi:10.1086/319552

Dickey, G., Blanke, S., & Seaton, L. (2019). Machine Learning in Auditing: Current and Future Applications. *The CPA Journal*, *89*, 16–21.

Dicko, S. (2016). The impact of political connections on the quality of corporate governance. *International Journal of Corporate Governance*, *7*(3), 247–273. doi:10.1504/IJCG.2016.080683

Dicko, S. (2017). Political connections, ownership structure and quality of governance. *International Journal of Managerial Finance*, *13*(4), 358–377. doi:10.1108/IJMF-01-2017-0010

Dickstein, D. I., & Flast, R. H. (2008). *No excuses: a business process approach to managing operational risk*. John Wiley & Sons.

DiMaggio, P. J., & Powell, W. W. (1983). The iron cage revisited: Institutional isomorphism and collective rationality in organizational fields. *American Sociological Review*, *48*(2), 147–160. doi:10.2307/2095101

Dinesh, N., & Juvanna, I. (2017). Dynamic auditing and deduplication with secure data deletion in the Cloud. *Artificial Intelligence and Evolutionary Computations in Engineering Systems Proceedings of ICAIECES*, *2016*, 305–313.

Doidge, C., Karolyi, G. A., Lins, K. V., Miller, D. P., & Stulz, R. M. (2009). Private benefits of control, ownership, and the cross-listing decision. *The Journal of Finance*, *64*(1), 425–466. doi:10.1111/j.1540-6261.2008.01438.x

Dolde, W., & Knopf, J. (2006). *Impact of corporate ownership and governance on risk-taking and returns at thrift institutions*. University of Connecticut.

Dorfleitner, G., & Braun, D. (2019). Fintech, digitalization and blockchain: possible applications for green finance. *The rise of green finance in Europe: opportunities and challenges for issuers, investors and marketplaces*, 207-237.

dos Santos, B. L., Suave, R., Ferreira, M. M., & Altoé, S. M. L. (2020). Profissão contábil em tempos de mudança: Implicações do avanço tecnológico nas atividades em um escritório de contabilidade. *Revista de Contabilidade e Controladoria, 11*(3).

Du, H., & Cong, Y. (2010). Cloud computing, accounting, auditing, and beyond. *The CPA Journal, 80*(10), 66.

Du, M., Zhang, R., Chai, S., Li, Q., Sun, R., & Chu, W. (2022). Can green finance policies stimulate technological innovation and financial performance? Evidence from Chinese listed green enterprises. *Sustainability (Basel), 14*(15), 9287. doi:10.3390/su14159287

Durán Cabré, J. M., & Esteller Moré, A. (2020). Los retos de la Administración tributaria en la era de la digitalización. ICE. *Información Comercial Española, 917*(917). Advance online publication. doi:10.32796/ice.2020.917.7130

Dworkin, S. L. (2012). Sample size policy for qualitative studies using in-depth interviews. [). Springer.]. *Archives of Sexual Behavior, 41*(6), 1319–1320. doi:10.1007/s10508-012-0016-6 PMID:22968493

Dyreng, S. D., Jacob, M., Jiang, X., & Müller, M. A. (2022). Tax incidence and tax avoidance. *Contemporary Accounting Research, 39*(4), 2622–2656. doi:10.1111/1911-3846.12797

Ellul, A., & Yerramilli, V. (2013). Stronger risk controls, lower risk: Evidence from US bank holding companies. *The Journal of Finance, 68*(5), 1757–1803. doi:10.1111/jofi.12057

Elommal, N., &Manita, R. (2021). How blockchain innovation could affect the audit profession: a qualitative study. *Journal of Innovation Economics & Management*, I103-27.

Elyasiani, E., & Jia, J. J. (2008). Institutional ownership stability and BHC performance. *Journal of Banking & Finance, 32*(9), 1767–1781. doi:10.1016/j.jbankfin.2007.12.010

Enofe, A., Embele, K., & Obazee, E. P. (2019). Tax audit, investigation, and tax evasion. *Journal of Accounting and Financial Management, 5*(4), 47–66.

Ericsson, J., & Renault, O. (2006). Liquidity and credit risk. *The Journal of Finance, 61*(5), 2219–2250. doi:10.1111/j.1540-6261.2006.01056.x

Ernst & Young. (2017). *Tax technology and transformation.* https://assets.ey.com/content/dam/ey-sites/ey-com/en_gl/topics/digital/ey-tax-technology-transformation.pdf

Ernst and Young. (2017). *Tax Technology and Transformation: Tax Functions "Go Digital".* Ernst & Young LLP.

Etim, R. S., Jeremiah, M. S., & Dan, P. B. (2020). Tax Compliance and Digitalization of Nigerian Economy: The Empirical Review. *American International Journal of Social Science, 9*(2), 42–50. doi:10.30845/aijss.v9n2p5

European Commission, Directorate-General for Taxation and Customs Union. (2019). *TaxCompEU: EU tax competency framework: role descriptions – tax audit.* Publications Office. https://data.europa.eu/doi/10.2778/603542

European Commission. (2019). Commission delegated regulation 2018/815. *Official Journal of the European Union, 143*(2019), 1-792. https://eur-lex.europa.eu/legal-content/EN/TXT/PDF/?uri=CELEX:32019R0815&rid=1

EY. (2019). *EY Ops Chain industrializes the blockchain at scale for enterprises.* Available at: https://www.ey.com/en_gl/news/2019/04/ey-ops-chain-industrializes-the-blockchain-at-scale-for-enterprises

Faccio, M., Masulis, R. W., & McConnell, J. J. (2006). Political connections and corporate bailouts. *The Journal of Finance, 61*(6), 2597–2635. doi:10.1111/j.1540-6261.2006.01000.x

Fähndrich, J. (2023). A literature review on the impact of digitalisation on management control. *Journal of Management Control, 34*(1), 9–65. doi:10.1007/s00187-022-00349-4

Falcone, P. M., & Sica, E. (2019). Assessing the opportunities and challenges of green finance in Italy: An analysis of the biomass production sector. *Sustainability (Basel), 11*(2), 517. doi:10.3390/su11020517

Fan, H., Liu, Y., Qian, N., & Wen, J. (2018). *Computerizing VAT Invoices in China* (w24414). National Bureau of Economic Research. doi:10.3386/w24414

Fanea-Ivanovici, M., Muşetescu, R.-C., Pană, M.-C., & Voicu, C. (2019). Fighting corruption and enhancing tax compliance through digitization: Achieving sustainable development in Romania. *Sustainability (Basel), 11*(5), 1480. doi:10.3390/su11051480

Feld, L. P., & Frey, B. S. (2007). Tax compliance as the result of a psychological tax contract: The role of incentives and responsive regulation. *Law & Policy, 29*(1), 102–120. doi:10.1111/j.1467-9930.2007.00248.x

Feliciano-Cestero, M. M., Ameen, N., Kotabe, M., Paul, J., & Signoret, M. (2023). Is digital transformation threatened? A systematic literature review of the factors influencing firms' digital transformation and internationalization. *Journal of Business Research, 157*, 113546. doi:10.1016/j.jbusres.2022.113546

Fernández, C., & Arrondo, R. (2005). Alternative internal controls as substitutes of the board of directors. *Corporate Governance, 13*(6), 856–866. doi:10.1111/j.1467-8683.2005.00476.x

Flammer, C., & Bansal, P. (2017). Does long-term orientation create value? Evidence from a regression discontinuity. *Strategic Management Journal, 38*(9), 1827–1847. doi:10.1002/smj.2629

Fletcher, A. J. (2017). Applying critical realism in qualitative research: Methodology meets method. *International Journal of Social Research Methodology, 20*(2), 181–194. doi:10.1080/13645579.2016.1144401

Fogarty, T. J. (1992). Financial accounting standard setting as an institutionalized action field: Constraints, opportunities and dilemmas. *Journal of Accounting and Public Policy*, *11*(4), 331–355. doi:10.1016/0278-4254(92)90003-G

Fosso Wamba, S., Kala Kamdjoug, J. R., Epie Bawack, R., & Keogh, J. G. (2019). Bitcoin, blockchain and Fintech: A systematic review and case studies in the supply chain. *Production Planning and Control*, *31*(2-3), 115–142. doi:10.1080/09537287.2019.1631460

Fowler, M. (2005). *Event Sourcing*. Available at: https://martinfowler.com/eaaDev/EventSourcing.html

Fullana, O., & Ruiz, J. (2021). Accounting information systems in the blockchain era. *International Journal of Intellectual Property Management*, *11*(1), 63–80. doi:10.1504/IJIPM.2021.113357

Gabor, D., & Brooks, S. (2017). The digital revolution in financial inclusion: International development in the fintech era. *New Political Economy*, *22*(4), 423–436. doi:10.1080/13563467.2017.1259298

Gad, A. G., Mosa, D. T., Abualigah, L., & Abohany, A. A. (2022). Emerging trends in blockchain technology and applications: A review and outlook. *Journal of King Saud University. Computer and Information Sciences*, *34*(9), 6719–6742. doi:10.1016/j.jksuci.2022.03.007

Gal, G., & McCarthy, W. E. (1986). Operation of a Relational Accounting System. *Advances in Accounting*, *3*, 83–112.

Gangl, K., Hofmann, E., & Kirchler, E. (2015). Tax authorities' interaction with taxpayers: A conception of compliance in social dilemmas by power and trust. *New Ideas in Psychology*, *37*, 13–23. doi:10.1016/j.newideapsych.2014.12.001 PMID:25859096

Gangodawilage, D., Madurapperuma, W., & Aluthge, C. (2021). Use of technology to manage tax compliance behavior of entrepreneurs in the digital economy. *International Journal of Scientific and Research Publications*, *11*(3), 366–370. doi:10.29322/IJSRP.11.03.2021.p11150

Garanina, T., Ranta, M., & Dumay, J. (2022). Blockchain in accounting research: Current trends and emerging topics. *Accounting, Auditing & Accountability Journal*, *35*(7), 1507–1533. doi:10.1108/AAAJ-10-2020-4991

García-Marco, T., & Robles-Fernandez, M. D. (2008). Risk-taking behaviour and ownership in the banking industry: The Spanish evidence. *Journal of Economics and Business*, *60*(4), 332–354. doi:10.1016/j.jeconbus.2007.04.008

Gardi, B., Aga, M., & Abdullah, N. N. (2023). Corporate Governance and Financial Reporting Quality: The Mediation Role of IFRS. *Sustainability (Basel)*, *15*(13), 9869. doi:10.3390/su15139869

Gardner, E. C., & Bryson, J. R. (2022). The dark side of the industrialisation of accountancy: Innovation, commoditization, colonization and competitiveness. In *The Dark Side of Innovation* (pp. 56–71). Routledge.

Gartner. (2019). *Gartner AI Maturity Model.* Retrieved from https://www.gartner.com/smarterwithgartner/the-cios-guide-to-artificial-intelligence

Geerts, G. L., & McCarthy, W. E. (2006). Policy-Level Specifications in REA Enterprise Information Systems. *Journal of Information Systems, 20*(2), 37–63. doi:10.2308/jis.2006.20.2.37

George, K., & Patatoukas, P. N. (2021). The blockchain evolution and revolution of accounting. In Information for Efficient Decision Making: Big Data, Blockchain and Relevance (pp. 157-172). World Scientific.

George, D. S., & Diavastis, I. (2015). Tax audit effectiveness in Greek firms : Tax auditors perceptions. *Journal of Accounting and Taxation, 7*(7), 123–130. doi:10.5897/JAT2015.0186

Gepp, A., Linnenluecke, M. K., O'Neill, T. J., & Smith, T. (2018). Big data techniques in auditing research and practice: Current trends and future opportunities. *Journal of Accounting Literature, 40*(1), 102–115. doi:10.1016/j.acclit.2017.05.003

Ghosh, S. (2016). Capital buffer, credit risk and liquidity behaviour: Evidence for GCC banks. *Comparative Economic Studies, 58*(4), 539–569. doi:10.1057/s41294-016-0005-1

Goddard, J., Molyneux, P., & Wilson, J. O. (2004). The profitability of European banks: A cross-sectional and dynamic panel analysis. *Manchester School, 72*(3), 363–381. doi:10.1111/j.1467-9957.2004.00397.x

Goldin, C., & Katz, L. (1998). *The origins of technology-skill complementarity*. doi:10.3386/w5657

GomaaA.GomaaM.FaragM. (2019), The Creation of One Truth: Single-Ledger Entries for Multiple Stakeholders Using Blockchain Technology to Address the Reconciliation Problem. *Social Science Research Network* (SSRN*)*. Available at https://papers.ssrn.com/sol3/papers.cfm?abstract_id=3397684 doi:10.2139/ssrn.3397684

Goretzki, L., & Messner, M. (2019). Backstage and frontstage interactions in management accountants' identity work. *Accounting, Organizations and Society, 74*, 1–20. doi:10.1016/j.aos.2018.09.001

Gormley, T. A. (2005). *Banking competition in developing countries: does foreign bank entry improve credit access?* Department of Economics, MIT.

Grigg, I. (2005). *Triple Entry Accounting. Systemics.* Available at https://iang.org/papers/triple_entry.html

Grigg, I. (2005). Triple entry accounting. *SystemicsInc*, 1-10.

Grigg, I. (2016). *The Message is the Medium.* Available at https://steemit.com/eos/@iang/the-message-is-the-medium

Grigg, I. (2017a). *But it's not modelled there, it's only modelled up in the cloud. That's triple entry accounting at the triple A.* Twitter Post. Available at https://twitter.com/iang_fc/status/939243253060329475

Grigg, I. (2017b). *My thanks to Todd Boyle, originator of the concept of triple entry, for pointing out this video by Bill McCarthy* https://t.co/rwGAZZaHfo. Twitter Post. Available at https://twitter.com/iang_fc/status/939258799654924288

Grigg, I. (2017c). *Wildest dream: REA (triple entry accounting) is the Golden Spike that brings the conventional industry together with wild-eyed blockchain.* Twitter Post. Available at https://twitter.com/iang_fc/status/939256814314622976

Grigg, I. (2017d). *EOS – An Introduction.* EOS Whitepaper. Available at https://www.iang.org/papers/EOS_An_Introduction-BLACK-EDITION.pdf

Grigorieva, E. M., Chernyaev, M. V., & Kirichenko, O. S. (2020). Impact of Digitalisation on the Fiscal and Regulatory Functions of the Tax System. *Digital Finance 2020 (DF2020),* 93.

Gröblacher, M., & Mizdraković, V. (2019). *Triple-entry Bookkeeping: History and Benefits of the Concept.* Digitisation and Smart Financial Reporting.

Guedhami, O., Pittman, J. A., & Saffar, W. (2009). Auditor choice in privatized firms: Empirical evidence on the role of state and foreign owners. *Journal of Accounting and Economics, 48*(2-3), 151–171. doi:10.1016/j.jacceco.2009.08.003

Gulamhussen, M. A., & Guerreiro, L. (2009). The influence of foreign equity and board membership on corporate strategy and internal cost management in Portuguese banks. *Management Accounting Research, 20*(1), 6–17. doi:10.1016/j.mar.2008.10.006

Guo, R., Langston, V., & Hadley, L. (2012). Business cycle, corporate governance, and bank performance. *Research in Business and Economics Journal, 5*(1), 1–11.

Gursoy, G., & Aydogan, K. (2002). Equity ownership structure, risk taking, and performance. *Russian & East European Finance & Trade, 38*(6), 6–6.

Hamid, N., Saruji, S., Shamsuddin, R., & Othman, R. (2023). Determining the Factors of Tax Agents' Readiness Towards the Digitalisation of Tax Administration. *Revue d'Economie Financiere, 21,* 32–42. doi:10.55365/1923.x2023.21.4

Haner, J. K., & Knake, R. K. (2021). Breaking botnets: A quantitative analysis of individual, technical, isolationist, and multilateral approaches to cybersecurity. *Journal of Cybersecurity, 7*(1), tyab003. Advance online publication. doi:10.1093/cybsec/tyab003

Han, H., Shiwakoti, R. K., Jarvis, R., Mordi, C., & Botchie, D. (2023). Accounting and auditing with blockchain technology and artificial Intelligence: A literature review. *International Journal of Accounting Information Systems, 48,* 100598. doi:10.1016/j.accinf.2022.100598

Han, Y., Li, Y., & Wang, Q. (2023). Digital finance, environmental regulation, and green development efficiency of China. *Frontiers in Environmental Science, 11,* 1131058. doi:10.3389/fenvs.2023.1131058

Hasan, A. R. (2022). Artificial Intelligence (AI) in Accounting & Auditing: A Literature Review. *Open Journal of Business and Management, 10*(1), 440–465. doi:10.4236/ojbm.2022.101026

Hasan, M. M., Popp, J., & Oláh, J. (2020). Current landscape and influence of big data on finance. *Journal of Big Data*, *7*(1), 1–17. doi:10.1186/s40537-020-00291-z

Hashed, A., & Almaqtari, F. (2021). The Impact of Corporate Governance Mechanisms and IFRS on Earning Management in Saudi Arabia. *Accounting*, *7*, 207–224. doi:10.5267/j.ac.2020.9.015

Hasnan, S., Marzuki, H., & Shuhidan, S. M. (2017). Effects of board characteristics on financial restatement in Malaysia. *Pertanika Journal of Social Science & Humanities*, 255–263.

Haven, T., & Van Grootel, D. L. (2019). Preregistering qualitative research. *Accountability in Research*, *26*(3), 229–244. doi:10.1080/08989621.2019.1580147 PMID:30741570

Haw, I. M., Ho, S. S., Hu, B., & Wu, D. (2010). Concentrated control, institutions, and banking sector: An international study. *Journal of Banking & Finance*, *34*(3), 485–497. doi:10.1016/j.jbankfin.2009.08.013

Herath, S. K., & Joshi. (2023). Audit Data Analytics: A Game Changer for Audit Firms. *International Journal of Auditing and Accounting Studies*, *5*(1), 29–48. doi:10.47509/IJAAS.2023.v05i01.02

He, Y., & Yi, Y. (2023). Digitalization of tax administration and corporate performance : Evidence from China. *International Review of Financial Analysis*, *90*, 102859. doi:10.1016/j.irfa.2023.102859

He, Z., & Xiong, W. (2012). Rollover risk and credit risk. *The Journal of Finance*, *67*(2), 391–430. doi:10.1111/j.1540-6261.2012.01721.x

Hezam, Y. A., Anthonysamy, L., & Suppiah, S. D. K. (2023). Big Data Analytics and Auditing: A Review and Synthesis of Literature. *Emerging Science Journal*, *7*(2), 629–642. doi:10.28991/ESJ-2023-07-02-023

HilemanG.RauchsM. (2017). 2017 global blockchain benchmarking study. *Available at* SSRN 3040224.

Hoffman, S. D. (1999). School texts, the written word, and political indoctrination: A review of moral education curricula in modern Japan (1886–1997). *History of Education*, *28*(1), 87–96. doi:10.1080/004676099284816

Hofmann, P., Jöhnk, J., Protschky, D., & Urbach, N. (2020). *Developing Purposeful AI Use Cases-A Structured Method and Its Application in Project Management*. Symposium conducted at the meeting of the Wirtschaftsinformatik (Zentrale Tracks).

Hofmann, E., Gangl, K., Kirchler, E., & Stark, J. (2014). Enhancing T ax Compliance through Coercive and Legitimate Power of T ax Authorities by Concurrently Diminishing or Facilitating Trust in T ax Authorities. *Law & Policy*, *36*(3), 290–313. doi:10.1111/lapo.12021 PMID:26074656

Höglund, H., & Sundvik, D. (2016). Financial reporting quality and outsourcing of accounting tasks: Evidence from small private firms. *Advances in Accounting*, *35*, 125–134. doi:10.1016/j.adiac.2016.03.001

Hoitash, R., & Hoitash, U. (2018). Measuring accounting reporting complexity with XBRL. *The Accounting Review*, *93*(1), 259–287. Advance online publication. doi:10.2308/accr-51762

Holman, G. K. (2019). *Blockchain and eBusiness*. LinkedIn. Available at https://www.linkedin.com/pulse/blockchain-ebusiness-ken-holman/

Houcine, A. (2017). The effect of financial reporting quality on corporate investment efficiency: Evidence from the Tunisian stock market. *Research in International Business and Finance*, *42*, 321–337. doi:10.1016/j.ribaf.2017.07.066

Htay, S. N. N., Rashid, H. M., Adnan, M. A., & Meera, A. K. M. (2011). Corporate governance and risk management information disclosure in Malaysian listed banks: Panel data analysis. *International Review of Business Research Papers*, *7*(4), 159–176.

Hutchens, M., Rego, S. O., & Williams, B. (2023). Tax avoidance, uncertainty, and firm risk. *Uncertainty, and Firm Risk.*

IAASB (International Auditing and Assurance Standards Board). (2018). *Exploring the Growing Use of Technology in the Audit, with a Focus on Data Analytics*. International Auditing and Assurance Standards Board.

Iannotta, G., Nocera, G., & Sironi, A. (2007). Ownership structure, risk and performance in the European banking industry. *Journal of Banking & Finance*, *31*(7), 2127–2149. doi:10.1016/j.jbankfin.2006.07.013

Iannotta, G., Nocera, G., & Sironi, A. (2013). The impact of government ownership on bank risk. *Journal of Financial Intermediation*, *22*(2), 152–176. doi:10.1016/j.jfi.2012.11.002

ICAEW. (2019). *Digitalisation of tax : International perspectives*. https://www.icaew.com/-/media/corporate/files/technical/technology/thought-leadership/digital-tax.ashx

ICAEW. (2022). *Digitalisation of tax : International perspectives*. https://www.icaew.com/-/media/corporate/files/technical/technology/thought-leadership/digital-tax.ashx

IFRS. (2019). *IFRS Foundation publishes IFRS taxonomy 2019*. Available at: https://www.ifrs.org/news-and-events/2019/03/ifrs-foundation-publishes-ifrs-taxonomy-2019/

IFRS. (2020). *IFRS - IFRS Taxonomy 2020*. https://www.ifrs.org/issued-standards/ifrs-taxonomy/ifrs-taxonomy-2020/

Ijiri, Y. (1986). A framework for triple-entry bookkeeping. *The Accounting Review*, *61*(4), 745–759.

IMF. (2023). *Morocco: 2022 Article IV Consultation-Press Release and Staff Report.* IMF Country Report No. 23/42; December 16, 2022. http://www.imf.org

Inghirami, I. E. (2019). *Accounting Information Systems: the Scope of Blockchain Accounting*. Conference paper. ITAIS and MCIS 2019: 13th Mediterranean Conference on Information Systems and 16th Conference of the Italian Chapter of AIS (Pavia).

International Auditing and Assurance Standards Board (IAASB). (2008a). *ISA 200: Overall objectives of the independent auditor and the conduct of an audit in accordance with international standards on auditing*. Retrieved October 7, 2023, from https://eis.international-standards.org/standards/iaasb/2020?section=MASTER_7#MASTER_7

International Auditing and Assurance Standards Board (IAASB). (2008b). *ISA 210: Agreeing the terms of audit engagements*. Retrieved October 7, 2023, from https://eis.international-standards.org/standards/iaasb/2020?section=MASTER_8#MASTER_8

International Auditing and Assurance Standards Board (IAASB). (2008c). *ISA 330: The auditor's responses to assessed risks*. Retrieved October 7, 2023, from https://eis.international-standards.org/standards/iaasb/2020?section=MASTER_18#MASTER_18

International Auditing and Assurance Standards Board (IAASB). (2008d). *ISA 500: Audit evidence*. Retrieved October 7, 2023, from https://eis.international-standards.org/standards/iaasb/2020?section=MASTER_21#MASTER_21

International Auditing and Assurance Standards Board (IAASB). (2008e). *ISA 501: Audit evidence—Specific considerations for selected items*. Retrieved October 7, 2023, from https://eis.international-standards.org/standards/iaasb/2020?section=MASTER_22#MASTER_22

International Auditing and Assurance Standards Board (IAASB). (2008f). *ISA 505: External confirmations*. Retrieved October 7, 2023, from https://eis.international-standards.org/standards/iaasb/2020?section=MASTER_23#MASTER_23

International Auditing and Assurance Standards Board (IAASB). (2008g). *ISA 510: Initial audit engagements—Opening balances*. Retrieved October 7, 2023, from https://eis.international-standards.org/standards/iaasb/2020?section=MASTER_24#MASTER_24

International Auditing and Assurance Standards Board (IAASB). (2008h). *ISA 520: Analytical procedures*. Retrieved October 7, 2023, from https://eis.international-standards.org/standards/iaasb/2020?section=MASTER_25#MASTER_25

International Auditing and Assurance Standards Board (IAASB). (2008i). *ISA 530: Audit sampling*. Retrieved October 7, 2023, from https://eis.international-standards.org/standards/iaasb/2020?section=MASTER_26#MASTER_26

International Auditing and Assurance Standards Board (IAASB). (2012). *ISA 315: Identifying and assessing the risks of material misstatement through understanding the entity and its environment*. Retrieved October 7, 2023, from https://eis.international standards.org/standards/iaasb/2020?section=MASTER_16#MASTER_16

International Auditing and Assurance Standards Board (IAASB). (2015a). *ISA 700 (Revised): Forming an Opinion and Reporting on Financial Statements*. Retrieved October 7, 2023, from https://eis.international-standards.org/standards/iaasb/2020?section=MASTER_35#MASTER_35

International Auditing and Assurance Standards Board (IAASB). (2015b). *ISA 705 (Revised): Modifications to the opinion in the independent auditor's report.* Retrieved October 7, 2023, from https://eis.international-standards.org/standards/iaasb/2020?section=MASTER_37#MASTER_37

International Auditing and Assurance Standards Board (IAASB). (2015c). *ISA 706: Emphasis of matter paragraphs and other matter paragraphs in the independent auditor's report.* Retrieved October 7, 2023, from https://eis.international-standards.org/standards/iaasb/2020?section=MASTER_38#MASTER_38

International Financial Reporting Standards (IFRS). (n.d.). In *Wikipedia.* Retrieved February 12, 2024, from https://en.wikipedia.org/wiki/International_Financial_Reporting_Standards

Iqbal, A. (2012). Liquidity risk management: A comparative study between conventional and Islamic banks of Pakistan. *Global Journal of Management and Business Research, 12*(5), 54–64.

Isbil, N., Koroglu, A. G. N., & Zaif, F. (2021). Digital reporting in accounting: XBRL and integration to accounting department curriculum. *Gazi Journal of Economics and Business, 7*(3), 188–202. doi:10.30855/gjeb.2021.7.3.001

ISO. (2019). *ISO/IEC CD 15944-21*. ISO. Available at https://www.iso.org/standard/78924.html

ISO/IEC. (2015). Information Technology — Business Operational View — Part 4: Business Transaction Scenarios — Accounting and Economic Ontolog. ISO/IEC International Standard 15944-4. Second edition 2015-04-01.

Issa, H., Sun, T., & Vasarhelyi, M. A. (2016). Research ideas for artificial intelligence in auditing: The formalization of audit and workforce supplementation. *Journal of Emerging Technologies in Accounting, 13*(2), 1–20. doi:10.2308/jeta-10511

Ivanov, D., Dolgui, A., & Sokolov, B. (2019). The impact of digital technology and Industry 4.0 on the ripple effect and supply chain risk analytics. *International Journal of Production Research, 57*(3), 829–846. Advance online publication. doi:10.1080/00207543.2018.1488086

Jacquemot, P., & Raffinot, M. (2019). La mobilisation fiscale en Afrique. *Revue d'économie financière, 131*(3), 243-263. doi:10.3917/ecofi.131.0243

Järvenpää, M. (2007). Making business partners: A case study on how management accounting culture was changed. *European Accounting Review, 16*(1), 99–142. doi:10.1080/09638180701265903

Jensen, M. C. (1993). The modern industrial revolution, exit, and the failure of internal control systems. *The Journal of Finance, 48*(3), 831-880.

Jensen, M. C., & Meckling, W. H. (2019). Theory of the firm: Managerial behavior, agency costs and ownership structure. In *Corporate governance* (pp. 77–132). Gower.

Jin, Q., & Wang, K. (2024). Exploring the moderating role of digital finance in the two-way foreign direct investment and green technology innovation nexus: an empirical evidence from China. *Environmental Science and Pollution Research,* 1-10. doi:10.1007/s11356-024-31896-z

Johannesen, N., & Zucman, G. (2014). The End of Bank Secrecy? An Evaluation of the G20 Tax Haven Crackdown. *American Economic Journal. Economic Policy*, *6*(1), 66. doi:10.1257/pol.6.1.65

Johnson, J. (2020). Gartner's AI Maturity Model: How AI Can Work for You. *BMC*. Retrieved from https://www.bmc.com/blogs/ai-maturity-models/

Kamani, E. F. (2019). The effect of non-traditional banking activities on systemic risk: Does bank size matter? *Finance Research Letters*, *30*, 297–305. doi:10.1016/j.frl.2018.10.013

Karajovic, M., Kim, H., & Laskowski, M. (2019). Thinking outside the block: Projected phases of blockchain integration in the accounting industry. *Australian Accounting Review*, *29*(2), 319–330. doi:10.1111/auar.12280

Kareem, H. M., Dauwed, M., Meri, A., Jarrar, M., Al-Bsheish, M., & Aldujaili, A. A. (2021). The role of accounting information system and knowledge management to enhancing organizational performance in Iraqi SMEs. *Sustainability (Basel)*, *13*(22), 12706. Advance online publication. doi:10.3390/su132212706

Karmańska, A. (2021). Internet of Things in the accounting field–benefits and challenges. *Operations Research and Decisions*, *31*(3), 23–39. doi:10.37190/ord210302

Katua, C. M. (2019). *Digitization Of Tax Administration, Technology And Tax Compliance By Small And Medium Sized Enterprises In Nairobi Central Business District* [Doctoral Dissertation]. University of Nairobi.

Kaur, G. (2023). Application of Blockchain for Sustaining Green Finance. In *Perspectives on Blockchain Technology and Responsible Investing* (pp. 226–235). IGI Global. doi:10.4018/978-1-6684-8361-9.ch011

Kelly, C. (2023). Australians report record $3.1bn losses to scams, with real amount even higher. *The Guardian*. Retrieved from https://www.theguardian.com/australia-news/2023/apr/17/australians-report-record-31bn-losses-to-scams-with-real-amount-even-higher-accc-says

Kennedy, D. W. (1985). Functional endoscopic sinus surgery: Technique. *Archives of Otolaryngology*, *111*(10), 643–649. doi:10.1001/archotol.1985.00800120037003 PMID:4038136

Khamis, A., Li, H., Prestes, E., & Haidegger, T. (2019). AI: A key enabler of sustainable development goals, part 1. *IEEE Robotics & Automation Magazine*, *26*(3), 95–102. doi:10.1109/MRA.2019.2928738

Khelil, I., Khlif, H., & Achek, I. (2023). The economic consequences of money laundering: A review of empirical literature. *Journal of Money Laundering Control*. doi:10.1108/JMLC-09-2023-0143

Kimm, T., Cen, R., Rosdahl, J., & Sukyoung, K. Y. (2016). Formation of globular clusters in atomic-cooling halos via rapid gas condensation and fragmentation during the epoch of reionisation. *The Astrophysical Journal*, *823*(1), 52. doi:10.3847/0004-637X/823/1/52

Kingdom of Morocco. (2021). *Framework Law 69-19 on Tax Reform*. Author.

Kircher, E. E. (2008). Enforced versus voluntary tax compliance : The slippery framework. *Journal of Economic Psychology, 29*(2), 210–225. doi:10.1016/j.joep.2007.05.004

Kirchler, E. (2007). *The economic psychology of tax behaviour.* Cambridge University Press. doi:10.1017/CBO9780511628238

Kitsios, E., Jalles, J., & Vedier, G. (2020). *Tax Evasion from Cross-Border Fraud Does Digitalization Make a Difference?* International Monetary Fund.

Klai, N., & Omri, A. (2011). Corporate governance and financial reporting quality: The case of Tunisian firms. *International Business Research, 4*(1), 158–166.

Knudsen, D.-R. (2020). Elusive boundaries, power relations, and knowledge production: A systematic review of the literature on digitalization in accounting. *International Journal of Accounting Information Systems, 36*, 100441. doi:10.1016/j.accinf.2019.100441

Kogler, C., Olsen, J., Kirchler, E., Batrancea, L. M., & Nichita, A. (2023). Perceptions of trust and power are associated with tax compliance: A cross-cultural study. *Economic and Political Studies, 11*(3), 365–381. doi:10.1080/20954816.2022.2130501

Köhler, M. (2015). Which banks are more risky? The impact of business models on bank stability. *Journal of Financial Stability, 16*, 195–212. doi:10.1016/j.jfs.2014.02.005

Kokina, J., & Davenport, T. H. (2017). The emergence of artificial intelligence: How automation is changing auditing. *Journal of Emerging Technologies in Accounting, 14*(1), 115–122. doi:10.2308/jeta-51730

Kokina, J., Mancha, R., & Pachamanova, D. (2017). Blockchain: Emergent industry adoption and implications for accounting. *Journal of Emerging Technologies in Accounting, 14*(2), 91–100. doi:10.2308/jeta-51911

Kong, D., & Liu, B. (2023). Digital technology and corporate social responsibility: Evidence from China. *Emerging Markets Finance & Trade, 59*(9), 1–27. doi:10.1080/1540496X.2023.2199122

Kong, T., Sun, R., Sun, G., & Song, Y. (2022). Effects of digital finance on green innovation considering information asymmetry: An empirical study based on Chinese listed firms. *Emerging Markets Finance & Trade, 58*(15), 4399–4411. doi:10.1080/1540496X.2022.2083953

Konishi, M., & Yasuda, Y. (2004). Factors affecting bank risk taking: Evidence from Japan. *Journal of Banking & Finance, 28*(1), 215–232. doi:10.1016/S0378-4266(02)00405-3

Korhonen, T., Selos, E., Laine, T., & Suomala, P. (2021). Exploring the programmability of management accounting work for increasing automation: An interventionist case study. *Accounting, Auditing & Accountability Journal, 34*(2), 253–280. doi:10.1108/AAAJ-12-2016-2809

Korstjens, I., & Moser, A. (2018). Series: Practical guidance to qualitative research. Part 4: Trustworthiness and publishing. *The European Journal of General Practice, 24*(1), 120–124. doi:10.1080/13814788.2017.1375092 PMID:29202616

Kozlowski, S. (2018). An audit ecosystem to support blockchain-based accounting and assurance. In *Continuous Auditing* (pp. 299–313). Emerald Publishing Limited. doi:10.1108/978-1-78743-413-420181015

KPMG LLP. (2019). *KPMG forms strategic alliance with Guard time*. Available at: https://www.prnewswire.com/news-releases/kpmg-forms-strategic-alliance-with-guardtime-300798827.html

KPMG. (2016). *Leveraging data analytics and continuous auditing processes for improved audit planning, effectiveness, and efficiency*. https://assets.kpmg.com/content/dam/kpmg/pdf/2016/05/Leveraging-Data-Analytics.pdf

Krahel, J. P., & Titera, W. R. (2015). Consequences of big data and formalisation on accounting and auditing standards. *Accounting Horizons*, *29*(2), 409–422. doi:10.2308/acch-51065

Krieger, T. (2021). A model-theoretical analysis for digital tax administrations. *International Journal of Innovative Technologies in Economy*, *2*(34). Advance online publication. doi:10.31435/rsglobal_ijite/30062021/7543

Kroon, N., Alves, M. C., & Martins, I. (2021). The Impacts of Emerging Technologies on Accountants' Role and Skills: Connecting to Open Innovation—A Systematic Literature Review. *Journal of Open Innovation*, *7*(3), 163. doi:10.3390/joitmc7030163

Kyeremeh, K., Kyeremeh, B. B., & Forson, M. A. (2022). Role of Accounting Information Systems In Organizational Decision Making: Evidence From Banking Sector In Ghana. *Journal of Accounting and Taxation*, *2*(3), 123–144. doi:10.47747/jat.v2i3.912

La Porta, R., Lopez-de-Silanes, F., & Shleifer, A. (1999). Corporate ownership around the world. *The Journal of Finance*, *54*(2), 471–517. doi:10.1111/0022-1082.00115

La Porta, R., Lopez-de-Silanes, F., & Shleifer, A. (2002). Government ownership of banks. *The Journal of Finance*, *57*(1), 265–301. doi:10.1111/1540-6261.00422

La Porta, R., Lopez-de-Silanes, F., Shleifer, A., & Vishny, R. (2000). Investor protection and corporate governance. *Journal of Financial Economics*, *58*(1-2), 3–27. doi:10.1016/S0304-405X(00)00065-9

Laeven, L., & Levine, R. (2009). Bank governance, regulation and risk taking. *Journal of Financial Economics*, *93*(2), 259–275. doi:10.1016/j.jfineco.2008.09.003

Laeven, L., & Majnoni, G. (2003). Loan loss provisioning and economic slowdowns: Too much, too late? *Journal of Financial Intermediation*, *12*(2), 178–197. doi:10.1016/S1042-9573(03)00016-0

Laidroo, L. (2009). Association between ownership structure and public announcements' disclosures. *Corporate Governance*, *17*(1), 13–34. doi:10.1111/j.1467-8683.2008.00717.x

Lamboglia, R., Lavorato, D., Scornavacca, E., & Za, S. (2021). Exploring the relationship between audit and technology. A bibliometric analysis. *Meditari Accountancy Research*, *29*(5), 1233–1260. doi:10.1108/MEDAR-03-2020-0836

Lascău, A. (2022). The benefits of audit digitalisation and the effects on the work of auditors. *Annals of University of Craiova-Economic Sciences Series*, *1*(50), 68–75.

Lassoued, N., Sassi, H., & Attia, M. B. R. (2016). The impact of state and foreign ownership on banking risk: Evidence from the MENA countries. *Research in International Business and Finance*, *36*, 167–178. doi:10.1016/j.ribaf.2015.09.014

Laszlo, P. (n.d.). *KPMG Origins Bringing better transparency to global supply chain.* KPMG. https://kpmg.com/xx/en/home/insights/2021/04/kpmg-origins-transparency-global-supply-chains.html

Lawal, A., Mohamed, R., Abdalla, H., Elkelish, W. W., & Lasyoud, A. A. (2022). the Role of Accounting Information Systems in Firms' Performance During the Covid-19 Pandemic. *Journal of Governance and Regulation*, *11*(1), 45–54. doi:10.22495/jgrv11i1art5

Lei, X., Shen, Z. Y., Štreimikienė, D., Baležentis, T., Wang, G., & Mu, Y. (2024). Digitalization and sustainable development: Evidence from OECD countries. *Applied Energy*, *357*, 122480. doi:10.1016/j.apenergy.2023.122480

Levine, R. (1996). Foreign banks, financial development, and economic. *International financial markets: Harmonization versus competition, 224.*

Levin, R. C. (1982). The semiconductor industry. In R. R. Nelson (Ed.), *Government and Technical Progress: A Cross-Industry Analysis* (pp. 9–100). Pergamon Press.

L'Hours, H., Verburg, M., de Vries, J., Cepinskas, L., von Stein, I., Huber, R., . . . Mathers, B. J. (2022). *D4. 6 Report on a maturity model towards FAIR data in FAIR repositories*. Academic Press.

Lichtenthaler, U. (2020). Five maturity levels of managing AI: From isolated ignorance to integrated intelligence. *Journal of Innovation Management*, *8*(1), 39–50. doi:10.24840/2183-0606_008.001_0005

Liew, A. (2015). The use of technology-structured management controls: Changes in senior management's decision-making behaviours. *International Journal of Accounting Information Systems*, *17*, 37–64. doi:10.1016/j.accinf.2014.05.001

Li, J., Ye, S., & Zhang, Y. (2023). How digital finance promotes technological innovation: Evidence from China. *Finance Research Letters*, *58*(December), 104298. doi:10.1016/j.frl.2023.104298

Lim, J. M., Lam, T., & Wang, Z. (2020). *Using Data Analytics in a Financial Statement Audit*. IS Chartered Accountant Journal.

Li, S. (2003). Future trends and challenges of financial risk management in the digital economy. *Managerial Finance*, *29*(5/6), 111–125. doi:10.1108/03074350310768797

Li, T., & Yang, L. (2021). The effects of tax reduction and fee reduction policies on the digital economy. *Sustainability (Basel)*, *13*(14), 7611. doi:10.3390/su13147611

Liu, M., Wu, K., & Xu, J. J. (2019). How Will Blockchain Technology Impact Auditing and Accounting: Permissionless versus Permissioned Blockchain. *Current Issues in Auditing, 13*(2), A19–A29. doi:10.2308/ciia-52540

Liu, Y., & Chen, L. (2022). The impact of digital finance on green innovation: Resource effect and information effect. *Environmental Science and Pollution Research International, 29*(57), 86771–86795. doi:10.1007/s11356-022-21802-w PMID:35794335

Liu, Y., Zhao, C., Dong, K., Wang, K., & Sun, L. (2023). How does green finance achieve urban carbon unlocking? Evidence from China. *Urban Climate, 52*, 101742. doi:10.1016/j.uclim.2023.101742

Lobez, F. (2010). Too big to fail: Gouvernance et régulation des banques. *Revue d'Economie Financiere, 100*(4), 187–199. doi:10.3406/ecofi.2010.5830

Loiseau, E., Saikku, L., Antikainen, R., Droste, N., Hansjürgens, B., Pitkänen, K., Leskinen, P., Kuikman, P., & Thomsen, M. (2016). Green economy and related concepts: An overview. *Journal of Cleaner Production, 139*, 361–371. doi:10.1016/j.jclepro.2016.08.024

Lombardi, R., de Villiers, C., Moscariello, N., & Pizzo, M. (2021). The disruption of blockchain in auditing – a systematic literature review and an agenda for future research. *Accounting, Auditing & Accountability Journal*. Advance online publication. doi:10.1108/AAAJ-10-2020-4992

Luan, H., Geczy, P., Lai, H., Gobert, J., Yang, S. J., Ogata, H., Baltes, J., Guerra, R., Li, P., & Tsai, C. C. (2020). Challenges and future directions of big data and artificial intelligence in education. *Frontiers in Psychology, 11*, 580820. doi:10.3389/fpsyg.2020.580820 PMID:33192896

Lugli, E., & Bertacchini, F. (2023). Audit quality and digitalization: Some insights from the Italian context. *Meditari Accountancy Research, 31*(4), 841–860. doi:10.1108/MEDAR-08-2021-1399

Lutfi, A., Alkelani, S. N., Alqudah, H., Alshira'h, A. F., Alshirah, M. H., Almaiah, M. A., Alsyouf, A., Alrawad, M., Montash, A., & Abdelmaksoud, O. (2022). The Role of E-Accounting Adoption on Business Performance: The Moderating Role of COVID-19. *Journal of Risk and Financial Management, 15*(12), 617. Advance online publication. doi:10.3390/jrfm15120617

Lutfi, A., Al-Khasawneh, A. L., Almaiah, M. A., Alsyouf, A., & Alrawad, M. (2022). Business Sustainability of Small and Medium Enterprises during the COVID-19 Pandemic: The Role of AIS Implementation. *Sustainability (Basel), 14*(9), 5362. Advance online publication. doi:10.3390/su14095362

Lu, Y. (2019). The blockchain: State-of-the-art and research challenges. *Journal of Industrial Information Integration, 15*, 80–90. doi:10.1016/j.jii.2019.04.002

Macchiavello, E., & Siri, M. (2022). Sustainable finance and fintech: Can technology contribute to achieving environmental goals? A preliminary assessment of 'green fintech'and 'sustainable digital finance'. *European Company and Financial Law Review, 19*(1), 128–174. doi:10.1515/ecfr-2022-0005

Maechler, A., Mitra, S., & Worrell, D. (2005, October). Exploring financial risks and vulnerabilities in new and potential EU member states. In *Second Annual DG ECFIN Research Conference: "Financial Stability and the Convergence Process in Europe," October* (pp. 6-7). Academic Press.

Maheswar, R., & Kanagachidambaresan, G. (2020). Sustainable development through Internet of Things. *Wireless Networks, 26*(May), 2305–2306. doi:10.1007/s11276-020-02269-4

Ma, J. (2023). How digital finance promotes renewable energy consumption in China? *Environmental Science and Pollution Research International, 30*(46), 102490–102503. doi:10.1007/s11356-023-29504-7 PMID:37667128

Malik, S., Chadhar, M., Vatanasakdakul, S., & Chetty, M. (2021). Factors affecting the organizational adoption of blockchain technology: Extending the technology–organization–environment (TOE) framework in the Australian context. *Sustainability (Basel), 13*(16), 9404. doi:10.3390/su13169404

Manita, R., Elommal, N., Baudier, P., & Hikkerova, L. (2020). The digital transformation of external audit and its impact on corporate governance. *Technological Forecasting and Social Change, 150*, 119751. doi:10.1016/j.techfore.2019.119751

Männasoo, K., & Mayes, D. G. (2009). Explaining bank distress in Eastern European transition economies. *Journal of Banking & Finance, 33*(2), 244–253. doi:10.1016/j.jbankfin.2008.07.016

Manni, F., & Faccia, A. (2019). *Financial Accounting - Text and cases*. doi:10.1016/j.bcra.2021.100037

Manni, F., & Faccia, A. (2015). *Introduction to accounting*. Aracne Editrice.

Mardi, M., Perdana, P. N., Suparno, S., & Munandar, I. A. (2020). Effect of Accounting Information Systems, Teamwork, and Internal Control on Financial Reporting Timeliness. *Journal of Asian Finance. Economics and Business, 7*(12), 809–818. Advance online publication. doi:10.13106/jafeb.2020.vol7.no12.809

Marei, A., & Iskandar, E. D. T. B. M. (2019). The impact of Computer Assisted Auditing Techniques (CAATs) on development of audit process: An assessment of Performance Expectancy of by the auditors. *International Journal of Management and Commerce Innovations, 7*(2), 1199–1205.

Marrone, M., & Hazelton, J. (2019). The disruptive and transformative potential of new technologies for accounting, accountants and accountability: A review of current literature and call for further research. *Meditari Accountancy Research, 27*(5), 677–694. doi:10.1108/MEDAR-06-2019-0508

Marshall, B., Cardon, P., Poddar, A., & Fontenot, R. (2013). Does sample size matter in qualitative research?: A review of qualitative interviews in IS research. *Journal of Computer Information Systems, 54*(1), 11–22. doi:10.1080/08874417.2013.11645667

Marshall, T. E., & Lambert, S. L. (2018). Cloud-based intelligent accounting applications: Accounting task automation using IBM watson cognitive computing. *Journal of Emerging Technologies in Accounting, 15*(1), 199–215. doi:10.2308/jeta-52095

Mascagni, G., Mengistu, A. T., & Woldeyes, F. B. (2021). Can ICTs increase tax compliance? Evidence on taxpayer responses to technological innovation in Ethiopia. *Journal of Economic Behavior & Organization*, *189*, 172–193. doi:10.1016/j.jebo.2021.06.007

Mashuri, A. A. S. (2023). Determinants of Tax Avoidance and Audit Quality as a Moderating Variable. *Ilomata International Journal of Tax and Accounting*, *4*(1), 117–127. doi:10.52728/ijtc.v4i1.661

Mat, Z., Meiryani, S. L., & Tsudrajat, J. (2020). *Accounting information systems as a critical success factor for increased quality of accounting information* [Los sistemas de información contable como factor crítico de éxito para mejorar la calidad de la información contable]. Academic Press.

Matthews, D. (2006). *A history of auditing: the changing audit process in Britain from the nineteenth century to the present day* (Vol. 5). Routledge. doi:10.4324/9780203965634

Mavlutova, I., Spilbergs, A., Verdenhofs, A., Kuzmina, J., Arefjevs, I., & Natrins, A. (2023). The Role of Green Finance in Fostering the Sustainability of the Economy and Renewable Energy Supply: Recent Issues and Challenges. *Energies*, *16*(23), 7712. doi:10.3390/en16237712

McCarthy, W. E. (2001). *Re: Company centric view ends. Data goes to the Net.* Available at http://linas.org/mirrors/www.gldialtone.com/2001.07.14/McCarthyPost.htm

McCarthy, W. E., & Holman, G. K. (2019). *Blockchain and eBusiness. The Open-edi Distributed Business Transaction Repository.* ISO/IEC 15944-21 OeDBTR.

McCarthy, W. E. (1982). The REA Accounting Model: A Generalised Framework for Accounting Systems in a Shared Data Environment. *The Accounting Review*, *57*(3), 54–78.

McClure, C. G. (2023). How costly is tax avoidance? evidence from structural estimation. *The Accounting Review*, *98*(6), 1–28. doi:10.2308/TAR-2020-0465

Means, G. (2017). *The modern corporation and private property*. Routledge. doi:10.4324/9781315133188

Mearian, L. (2019). *Deloitte launches 'Blockchain in a Box' hands-on demonstrator.* Computerworld. https://www.computerworld.com/article/3433856/deloitte-launches-blockchain-in-a-box-hands-on-demonstrator.html

Megginson, W. L. (2005). The economics of bank privatization. *Journal of Banking & Finance*, *29*(8-9), 1931–1980. doi:10.1016/j.jbankfin.2005.03.005

Melis, A. (2007). Financial statements and positive accounting theory: The early contribution of Aldo Amaduzzi. *Accounting Business & Financial History*, *17*(1), 53–62. doi:10.1080/09585200601127640

Meraghni, O., Bekkouche, L., & Demdoum, Z. (2021). Impact of Digital Transformation on Accounting Information Systems – Evidence from Algerian Firms. *Economics and Business*, *35*(1), 249–264. doi:10.2478/eb-2021-0017

Miao, F., Holmes, W., Huang, R., & Zhang, H. (2021). *AI and education: A guidance for policymakers*. UNESCO Publishing.

Micco, A., Panizza, U., & Yanez, M. (2007). Bank ownership and performance. Does politics matter? *Journal of Banking & Finance*, *31*(1), 219–241. doi:10.1016/j.jbankfin.2006.02.007

Migliorelli, M., & Dessertine, P. (2019). *The rise of green finance in Europe* (Vol. 2). Palgrave Macmillan Cham. doi:10.1007/978-3-030-22510-0

Milliron, V. C. (1985). A behavioral study of the meaning and influence of tax complexity. *Journal of Accounting Research*, *23*(2), 794–816. doi:10.2307/2490838

Milosavljević, M., Radovanović, S., & Delibašić, B. (2023). What drives the performance of tax administrations? Evidence from selected european countries. *Economic Modelling*, *121*, 106217. doi:10.1016/j.econmod.2023.106217

Moghadasi, M., Mousavi, S. M., & Fazekas, G. (2018). Cloud computing auditing. *International Journal of Advanced Computer Science and Applications*, *9*(12). Advance online publication. doi:10.14569/IJACSA.2018.091265

Mohamad, A. A. S., Mohamad, M. T., & Samsudin, M. L. (2013). How Islamic banks of Malaysia managing liquidity? An emphasis on confronting economic cycles. *International Journal of Business and Social Science*, *4*(7), 253–263.

Mohamed, E. K. A., Oyelere, P., & Al-Busaidi, M. (2009). A survey of Internet financial reporting in Oman. *International Journal of Emerging Markets*, *4*(1), 56–71. doi:10.1108/17468800910931670

Moher, D., Liberati, A., Tetzlaff, J., & Altman, D. G. (2009). Preferred reporting items for systematic reviews and meta-analyses: The PRISMA statement. *Annals of Internal Medicine*, *151*(4), 264–269. doi:10.7326/0003-4819-151-4-200908180-00135 PMID:19622511

Mokyr, J. (2014). *Secular Stagnation? Not in Your Life. In Secular Stagnation: Facts, Causes, and Cures*. CEPR Press.

Moll, J., & Yigitbasioglu, O. (2019). The role of internet-related technologies in shaping the work of accountants: New directions for accounting research. *The British Accounting Review*, *51*(6), 100833. doi:10.1016/j.bar.2019.04.002

Mondejar, M. E., Avtar, R., Diaz, H. L. B., Dubey, R. K., Esteban, J., Gómez-Morales, A., Hallam, B., Mbungu, N. T., Okolo, C. C., Prasad, K. A., She, Q., & Garcia-Segura, S. (2021). Digitalization to achieve sustainable development goals: Steps towards a Smart Green Planet. [Reference Link]. *The Science of the Total Environment*, *794*, 148539. doi:10.1016/j.scitotenv.2021.148539 PMID:34323742

Monteiro, A. P., Vale, J., Silva, A., & Pereira, C. (2021). Impact of the internal control and accounting systems on the financial information usefulness: The role of the financial information quality. *Academy of Strategic Management Journal, 20*(3).

Montes, G. A., & Goertzel, B. (2019). Distributed, decentralized, and democratized artificial intelligence. *Technological Forecasting and Social Change*, *141*, 354–358. doi:10.1016/j.techfore.2018.11.010

Morgan, P. J. (2022). Assessing the risks associated with green digital finance and policies for coping with them. In *Green Digital Finance and Sustainable Development Goals* (pp. 51–68). Springer. doi:10.1007/978-981-19-2662-4_3

Moshirian, F., Sahgal, S., & Zhang, B. (2011, November). *Non-interest income and systemic risk: The role of concentration.* In Global Systemic Risk Conference. working paper.

Mosteanu, N. R., & Faccia, A. (2020). Digital systems and new challenges of financial management – fintech, XBRL, blockchain, and cryptocurrencies. *Quality - Access to Success*, *21*(174).

Moşteanu, N. R., Faccia, A., & Cavaliere, L. P. L. (2020, August). Digitalization and green economy-changes of business perspectives. In *Proceedings of the 2020 4th International Conference on Cloud and Big Data Computing* (pp. 108-112). 10.1145/3416921.3416929

Mo, Y., Che, Y., & Ning, W. (2023). Digital Finance Promotes Corporate ESG Performance: Evidence from China. *Sustainability (Basel)*, *15*(14), 11323. doi:10.3390/su151411323

Mulyani, S., Kasim, E., Yadiati, W., & Umar, H. (2019). Influence of accounting information systems and internal audit on fraudulent financial reporting. *Opcion*, *35*(21).

MunevarK.PatatoukasP. N. (2020). The Blockchain Evolution and Revolution of Accounting. SSRN. doi:10.2139/ssrn.3681654

Munteanu, I. (2012). Bank liquidity and its determinants in Romania. *Procedia Economics and Finance*, *3*, 993–998. doi:10.1016/S2212-5671(12)00263-8

Myers, N. (1990). The biodiversity challenge: Expanded hot-spots analysis. *The Environmentalist*, *10*(4), 243–256. doi:10.1007/BF02239720 PMID:12322583

Nambisan, S., Lyytinen, K., Majchrzak, A., & Song, M. (2017). Digital innovation management. *Management Information Systems Quarterly*, *41*(1), 223–238. doi:10.25300/MISQ/2017/41:1.03

National Institute of Standards and Technology (NIST). (n.d.). *NIST Cybersecurity Framework.* Retrieved February 12, 2024, from https://www.nist.gov/itl/smallbusinesscyber/nist-cybersecurity-framework-0

Negrini, S., Donzelli, S., Aulisa, A. G., Czaprowski, D., Schreiber, S., de Mauroy, J. C., Diers, H., Grivas, T. B., Knott, P., Kotwicki, T., Lebel, A., Marti, C., Maruyama, T., O'Brien, J., Price, N., Parent, E., Rigo, M., Romano, M., Stikeleather, L., ... Zaina, F. (2018). 2016 SOSORT guidelines: Orthopaedic and rehabilitation treatment of idiopathic scoliosis during growth. *Scoliosis and Spinal Disorders*, *13*(1), 1–48. doi:10.1186/s13013-017-0145-8 PMID:29435499

Nguyen, H. T., & Nguyen, A. H. (2020). Determinants of accounting information systems quality: Empirical evidence from Vietnam. *Accounting*, *6*(2), 185–198. Advance online publication. doi:10.5267/j.ac.2019.10.004

Ni, X. (2022). The Impact of Enterprise Digital Transformation on Innovation Performance. In *Proceedings - 2022 8th International Conference on Information Management, ICIM 2022*. Atlantis Press International BV. 10.1109/ICIM56520.2022.00046

Nielsen, S. (2018). Reflections on the applicability of business analytics for management accounting–and future perspectives for the accountant. *Journal of Accounting & Organizational Change*, *14*(2), 167–187. doi:10.1108/JAOC-11-2014-0056

Nikomaram, H., Taghavi, M., & Diman, S. (2013). The relationship between liquidity risk and credit risk in Islamic banking industry of Iran. *Management Science Letters*, *3*(4), 1223–1232. doi:10.5267/j.msl.2013.02.025

Niu, Y. (2011). Tax audit impact on voluntary compliance. *Journal of Economic and Social Measurement*, *36*(4), 237–251. doi:10.3233/JEM-2011-0346

Nofer, M., Gomber, P., Hinz, O., & Schiereck, D. (2017). Blockchain. *Business & Information Systems Engineering*, *59*(3), 183–187. doi:10.1007/s12599-017-0467-3

Norén, G., & Alldén, S. (2023). *The development of artificial intelligence (AI) within the management accounting and control profession*. Umea University.

Nouha, K., & Walid, K. (2016). Le rôle des mécanismes de gouvernance dans la prévention de la fraude managériale. *Management Accounting Research*.

O'Leary, D. E. (2003). Auditor environmental assessments. *International Journal of Accounting Information Systems*, *4*(4), 275–294. doi:10.1016/j.accinf.2003.09.001

Obert, R. (1994). *Pratique internationale de la comptabilité et de l'audit*. No Title.

Oduro, S., De Nisco, A., & Mainolfi, G. (2023). Do digital technologies pay off? A meta-analytic review of the digital technologies/firm performance nexus. *Technovation*, *128*, 102836. doi:10.1016/j.technovation.2023.102836

OECD Competition Trends 2021. (2021). doi:10.1787/308565fd-en

OECD. (2016). *Technologies for Better Tax Administration : A Practical Guide for Revenue Bodies*. OECD. doi:10.1787/9789264256439-

OECD. (2021). *Supporting the Digitalisation of Developing Country Tax Administrations*. www.oecd.org/tax/forum-on-tax-administration/publications-and-products/supporting-the-digitalisation-of-developing-country-taxadministrations.htm

Ofori, P. E., Ofori, I. K., & Asongu, S. A. (2022). Towards efforts to enhance tax revenue mobilisation in Africa : Exploring the interaction between industrialisation and digital infrastructure. *Telematics and Informatics*, *72*, 101857. doi:10.1016/j.tele.2022.101857

Okafor, O. N. (2022). Shaming of tax evaders: Empirical evidence on perceptions of retributive justice and tax Compliance intentions. *Journal of Business Ethics*, 1–19.

Okunogbe, O. (2021). *Becoming Legible to the State : The Role of Detection and Enforcement Capacity in Tax Compliance*. The World Bank. doi:10.1596/1813-9450-9852

Okunogbe, O., & Pouliquen, V. (2022). Technology, Taxation, and Corruption : Evidence from the Introduction of Electronic Tax Filing. *American Economic Journal. Economic Policy*, *14*(1), 341–372. doi:10.1257/pol.20200123

Olaoye, C. O., & Ogundipe, A. A. (2018). Application of tax audit and investigation on tax evasion control in Nigeria. *Journal of Accounting Finance and Auditing Studies*, *4*(1), 79–92.

Ølnes, S., Ubacht, J., & Janssen, M. (2017). *Blockchain in government: Benefits and implications of distributed ledger technology for information sharing*. Elsevier.

Olsen, C. (2023). Toward a Digital Sustainability Reporting Framework in Organizations in the Industry 5.0 Era: An Accounting Perspective. *Lecture Notes in Networks and Systems*, *557*, 463–473. Advance online publication. doi:10.1007/978-3-031-17746-0_37

Ostern, N. (2017). Do we really want Blockchain-based accounting? Decentralized consensus as enabler of management override of internal controls. Darmstadt Technical University.

Otto, M., & Thornton, J. (2023). The Role Of Digital Finance And Technological Innovation In The Growth Of The Green Economy. *Qo 'qon universiteti xabarnomasi, 7*(7), 19-22. doi:10.54613/ku.v7i7.771

Otto, M., & Thornton, J. (2023). The Role Of Digital Finance And Technological Innovation In The Growth Of The Green Economy. *Qo 'qon universiteti xabarnomasi, 7*, 19-22.

Ouyang, J., Liu, S., & Li, H. (2023). How does the development of digital finance affect small business tax compliance? Empirical evidence from China. *China Economic Review*, *80*, 101971. doi:10.1016/j.chieco.2023.101971

OXFAM. (2021). *Fair Tax Monitor : Analyse du système fiscal marocain*. Oxfam International. https://www.oxfam.org/fr/publications/fair-tax-monitor-analyse-du-systeme-fiscal-marocain

Ozili, P. K., Ademiju, A., & Rachid, S. (2023). Impact of financial inclusion on economic growth: Review of existing literature and directions for future research. *International Journal of Social Economics*, *50*(8), 1105–1122. doi:10.1108/IJSE-05-2022-0339

Pacio. (2018). *Pacio Technology*. Pacio Whitepaper Extract. Available at https://www.pacio.io/docs/Pacio_Technology.pdf

Paillé, P., & Mucchielli, A. (2012). L'analyse qualitative en sciences humaines et sociales (3e éd.). Paris: Armand Colin.

Paltrinieri, N., Comfort, L., & Reniers, G. (2019). Learning about Risk: Machine Learning for Risk Assessment. *Safety Science*, *118*, 475–486. doi:10.1016/j.ssci.2019.06.001

Panetta, K. (2019). The CIO's guide to Artificial Intelligence. *Gartner*.

Papagiannidis, E., Enholm, I. M., Dremel, C., Mikalef, P., & Krogstie, J. (2021). Deploying AI Governance Practices: A Revelatory Case Study. In Responsible AI and Analytics for an Ethical and Inclusive Digitized Society (pp. 208–219). Springer International Publishing. doi:10.1007/978-3-030-85447-8_19

Pashang, S., & Weber, O. (2023). AI for Sustainable Finance: Governance Mechanisms for Institutional and Societal Approaches. In *The Ethics of Artificial Intelligence for the Sustainable Development Goals* (pp. 203–229). Springer International Publishing. doi:10.1007/978-3-031-21147-8_12

Pathan, S. (2009). Strong boards, CEO power and bank risk-taking. *Journal of Banking & Finance*, *33*(7), 1340–1350. doi:10.1016/j.jbankfin.2009.02.001

Pathan, S., Skully, M., & Wickramanayake, J. (2007). Board size, independence and performance: An analysis of Thai banks. *Asia-Pacific Financial Markets*, *14*(3), 211–227. doi:10.1007/s10690-007-9060-y

Păvăloaia, V.-D., & Necula, S.-C. (2023). Artificial intelligence as a disruptive technology—A systematic literature review. *Electronics (Basel)*, *12*(5), 1102. doi:10.3390/electronics12051102

Pavlidis, G. (2021). Europe in the digital age: Regulating digital finance without suffocating innovation. *Law, Innovation and Technology*, *13*(2), 464–477. doi:10.1080/17579961.2021.1977222

Payne, R. (2014). Discussion of 'Digitisation,'Big Data'and the transformation of accounting information'by Alnoor Bhimani and Leslie Willcocks (2014). *Accounting and Business Research*, *44*(4), 491–495. doi:10.1080/00014788.2014.910053

Pazarbasioglu, C., Mora, A. G., Uttamchandani, M., Natarajan, H., Feyen, E., & Saal, M. (2020). *Digital financial services*. World Bank. Retrieved from https://pubdocs.worldbank.org/en/230281588169110691/Digital-Financial-Services.pdf

Pearce, J. A. II, & Zahra, S. A. (1992). Board composition from a strategic contingency perspective. *Journal of Management Studies*, *29*(4), 411–438. doi:10.1111/j.1467-6486.1992.tb00672.x

Pebrina, E. T., Novitasari, D., Sukriyah, S., Firmawati, Y., & Tsoraya, N. D. (2022). The Role of Accounting Information Systems in the Industrial Revolution 4.0 Era. *Edumaspul: Jurnal Pendidikan*, *6*(2), 2409–2412. doi:10.33487/edumaspul.v6i2.4571

Peters, G. W., & Panayi, E. (2016). *Understanding modern banking ledgers through blockchain technologies: Future of transaction processing and smart contracts on the internet of money*. Springer.

Petutschnig, M. (2017). Future orientation and taxes: Evidence from big data. *Journal of International Accounting, Auditing & Taxation*, *29*, 14–31. doi:10.1016/j.intaccaudtax.2017.03.003

Piazza, F. S. (2017). Bitcoin and the blockchain as possible corporate governance tools: Strengths and weaknesses. *Bocconi Legal Papers*, *9*, 125.

Pichard-Stamford, J. P. (2000). Légitimité et enracinement du dirigeant par le réseau des administrateurs. *Revue Finance Contrâle Stratãgie, 3*(4), 143-178.

Ping, W. (2021). Data mining and XBRL integration in management accounting information based on artificial intelligence. *Journal of Intelligent & Fuzzy Systems, 40*(4), 6755–6766. Advance online publication. doi:10.3233/JIFS-189509

Platov, A., Kalemulloev, M., & Zikirova, S. (2021). Management accounting in the context of digitalization. *SHS Web Conf., 106.* 10.1051/shsconf/202110601037

Prasad, A., & Green, P. (2015). Governing cloud computing services: Reconsideration of IT governance structures. *International Journal of Accounting Information Systems, 19*, 45–58. doi:10.1016/j.accinf.2015.11.004

Prentice, C. (2023). Leveraging Emotional and Artificial Intelligences for Employees and Customers. In *Leveraging Emotional and Artificial Intelligence for Organisational Performance* (pp. 157–176). Springer. doi:10.1007/978-981-99-1865-2_11

Prinz, A. (2023). Cultural tightness, trust, and power in enforcing tax compliance. *Economic and Political Studies*, 1–28. doi:10.1080/20954816.2023.2203306

Puschmann, T., & Leifer, L. (2020). *Sustainable Digital Finance: The Role of FinTech.* InsurTech & Blockchain for Shaping the World for the Better.

Pustylnick, I., Temchenko, O., & Gubarkov, S. (2017). Analysis of the use of XBRL-based accounting data in financial research. *WSEAS Transactions on Business and Economics, 14.*

Qiu, W., Li, Y., & Wu, H. (2023). The role of direct financing on regional green development: Inhibition or promotion? *Economic Change and Restructuring, 56*(5), 3665–3699. doi:10.1007/s10644-023-09546-0

Quattrone, P. (2016). Management accounting goes digital: Will the move make it wiser? *Management Accounting Research, 31*, 118–122. doi:10.1016/j.mar.2016.01.003

Raffegeau, J., Dufils, P., & De Ménonville, D. (1994). *L'audit financier.* Presses Universitaires De France.

Ramdi, I. (2021). La technologie digitale et la profession d'audit: Quel impact? *International Journal of Accounting, Finance, Auditing, Management and Economics, 2*(6-1), 126-144.

Ramos, M. G., do Rosário Lima, V. M., & Amaral-Rosa, M. P. (2018). IRaMuTeQ Software and discursive textual analysis: interpretive possibilities. *World Conference on Qualitative Research*, 58–72.

Rao, V. S. (2020). Blockchain Accounting in A Triple Entry System – Its Implications on the Firm. *Our Heritage, 68*(1), 10499–10512.

Ratinaud, P. (2009). *IRaMuTeQ: Interface de R pour les analyses multidimensionnelles de textes et de questionnaires* [IRaMuTeQ: R interface for multidimensional analysis of texts and questionnaires]. Academic Press.

Ratinaud, P. (2009). *IRaMuTeQ: Interface de R pour les Analyses Multidimensionnelles de TExtes et de Questionnaires*. http://www.iramuteq.org

Ratinaud, P., & Marchand, P. (2012). L'analyse de similitude appliquée aux corpus textuels: Les primaires socialistes pour l'élection présidentielle française (septembre-octobre 2011). In A. Dister, D. Longrée, & G. Purnelle (Éds.), *11èmes Journées internationales d'Analyse statistique des Données Textuelles*. http://lexicometrica.univ-paris3.fr/jadt/jadt2012/Communications/Marchand,%20Pascal%20et%20al.%20-%20L'analyse%20de%20similitude%20appliquee%20aux%20corpus%20textuels.pdf

Redlein, A., & Höhenberger, C. (2020). Digitalisation. *Modern Facility and Workplace Management: Processes, Implementation and Digitalisation*, 139-175.

Reis, J., Amorim, M., Melão, N., Cohen, Y., & Rodrigues, M. (2020). Digitalization: A literature review and research agenda. *Springer.*

Riahi-Belkaoui, A. (2004). Relationship between tax compliance internationally and selected determinants of tax morale. *Journal of International Accounting, Auditing & Taxation, 13*(2), 135–143. doi:10.1016/j.intaccaudtax.2004.09.001

Riaz, Z., Ray, P., & Ray, S. (2022). The impact of digitalisation on corporate governance in Australia. *Journal of Business Research, 152*, 410–424. doi:10.1016/j.jbusres.2022.07.006

Richins, G., Stapleton, A., Stratopoulos, T. C., & Wong, C. (2017). Big data analytics: Opportunity or threat for the accounting profession? *Journal of Information Systems, 31*(3), 63–79. doi:10.2308/isys-51805

Ricou, B. (2022). *Droit des procédures fiscales*. Ellipses. doi:10.14375/NP.9782340064386

RNZ. (2023). *Scams cost Kiwis almost $200m - Ministry of Business, Innovation and Employment (MBIE)*. Retrieved from https://www.nzherald.co.nz/nz/scams-cost-kiwis-almost-200m-ministry-of-business-innovation-and-employment-report/7BA6OADPBBGNLDXU765DEXUFQM/

Rogers, E. M. (1995). Diffusion of Innovations: modifications of a model for telecommunications. *Die diffusion von innovationen in der telekommunikation*, 25-38.

Rooney, H., Aiken, B., & Rooney, M. (2017). Q. Is internal audit ready for blockchain? *Technology Innovation Management Review*, 7(10), 41–44. doi:10.22215/timreview/1113

Rospigliosi, P. a. (2023). *Artificial intelligence in teaching and learning: what questions should we ask of ChatGPT?* Taylor & Francis.

Roth, J. A. (1989). Taxpayer compliance: Vol. 1. *An agenda for research*. University of Pennsylvania Press.

Rowbottom, N., Locke, J., & Troshani, I. (2021). When the tail wags the dog? Digitalisation and corporate reporting. *Accounting, Organizations and Society*, *92*, 101226. doi:10.1016/j.aos.2021.101226

Rozario, A. M., & Vasarhelyi, M. A. (2018). Auditing with Smart Contracts. *The International Journal of Digital Accounting Research*, *18*, 1–27. doi:10.4192/1577-8517-v18_1

Rückeshäuser, N. (2017). *Do we really want blockchain-based accounting? Decentralized consensus as enabler of management override of internal controls*. Academic Press.

Ryszawska, B. (2018). Sustainable finance: Paradigm shift. In *Finance and Sustainability: Proceedings from the Finance and Sustainability Conference, Wroclaw 2017* (pp. 219-231). Springer International Publishing.

Saad, M. (2023). The influence of accounting information system adoption on business performance amid COVID-19. *Computers in Human Behavior Reports*, *10*(March), 100286. doi:10.1016/j.chbr.2023.100286 PMID:37122822

Salas, V., & Saurina, J. (2002). Credit risk in two institutional regimes: Spanish commercial and savings banks. *Journal of Financial Services Research*, *22*(3), 203–224. doi:10.1023/A:1019781109676

Saleh, I., Marei, Y., Ayoush, M., & Abu Afifa, M. M. (2023). Big Data analytics and financial reporting quality: Qualitative evidence from Canada. *Journal of Financial Reporting and Accounting*, *21*(1), 83–104. doi:10.1108/JFRA-12-2021-0489

Salhi, B., & Boujelbene, Y. (2012). Effect of internal banking mechanisms of governance on the risk taking by the Tunisian banks. *International Journal of Economics, Finance and Management*, *1*(1).

Salman, F., & Siddiqui, K. (2013). Mehrangate Scandal: Corporate Governance Failure. *The IUP Journal of Corporate Governance*, *12*(4), 41–46.

Saragih, A. H., Soraya, A., & Hendrawan, A. (2021). A Decade of XBRL Research in Accounting in Indonesia: A Literature Study. *The Indonesian Journal of Accounting Research*, *24*(02). Advance online publication. doi:10.33312/ijar.522

Sarker, S., Henningsson, S., Jensen, T., & Hedman, J. (2021). The use of blockchain as a resource for combating corruption in global shipping: An interpretive case study. *Journal of Management Information Systems*, *38*(2), 338–373. doi:10.1080/07421222.2021.1912919

Sarkis, J., Zhu, Q., & Lai, K. (2011). An organizational theoretic review of green supply chain management literature. *International Journal of Production Economics*, *130*(1), 1–15. doi:10.1016/j.ijpe.2010.11.010

Saunders, A., Strock, E., & Travlos, N. G. (1990). Ownership structure, deregulation, and bank risk taking. *The Journal of Finance, 45*(2), 643-654.

Saunders, B., Sim, J., Kingstone, T., Baker, S., Waterfield, J., Bartlam, B., Burroughs, H., & Jinks, C. (2018). Saturation in qualitative research: Exploring its conceptualization and operationalization. *Quality & Quantity*, *52*(4), 1893–1907. doi:10.1007/s11135-017-0574-8 PMID:29937585

Savaş, S., & Karataş, S. (2022). Cyber governance studies in ensuring cybersecurity: An overview of cybersecurity governance. *International Cybersecurity Law Review*, *3*(1), 7–34. doi:10.1365/s43439-021-00045-4 PMID:37521508

Savignac, F. (2008). Impact of financial constraints on innovation: What can be learned from a direct measure? *Economics of Innovation and New Technology*, *17*(6), 553–569. doi:10.1080/10438590701538432

Schaede, U. (1994). The" Old Boy" network and government-business relationships in Japan (Vol. 94, No. 12). Graduate School of International Relations and Pacific Studies, University of California, San Diego.

Schallmo, D. R., Williams, C. A., Schallmo, D. R., & Williams, C. A. (2018). History of digital transformation. *Digital Transformation Now! Guiding the Successful Digitalization of Your Business Model*, 3-8.

Schildt, H. (2022). The Institutional Logic of Digitalization. In T. Gegenhuber, D. Logue, C. R. Hinings, & M. Barrett (Eds.), *Digital Transformation and Institutional Theory* (Vol. 83, pp. 235–251). Emerald Publishing Limited. doi:10.1108/S0733-558X20220000083010

Schlatt, V., Guggenberger, T., Schmid, J., & Urbach, N. (2023). Attacking the trust machine: Developing an information systems research agenda for blockchain cybersecurity. *International Journal of Information Management*, *68*, 102470. doi:10.1016/j.ijinfomgt.2022.102470

Schmitz, J., & Leoni, G. (2019). Accounting and auditing at the time of blockchain technology: A research agenda. *Australian Accounting Review*, *29*(2), 331–342. doi:10.1111/auar.12286

Schulz, K. A., Gstrein, O. J., & Zwitter, A. J. (2020). Exploring the governance and implementation of sustainable development initiatives through blockchain technology. *Futures*, *122*, 102611. doi:10.1016/j.futures.2020.102611

Schumpeter, J. A. (1934). *The Theory of Economic Development*. Harvard University Press.

Scialom, L. (2011). Stratégies et instruments d'une régulation macroprudentielle. *Revue d'Economie Financiere*, (3), 171–186.

SEC (Securities Exchange Commission). (2009). *Interactive data to improve financial reporting: Final rule SEC (2009) RIN 3235-AJ71*. https://www.sec.gov/rules/final/2009/33-9002.pdf

Secinaro, S., Calandra, D., & Biancone, P. (2021). *Blockchain, trust, and trust accounting: Can blockchain technology substitute trust created by intermediaries in trust accounting?* Retrieved from https://money.usnews.com/money/personal-finance/family-finance/articles/what-fraud-costs-consumers#:~:text=American%20consumers%20lost%20%248.8%20billion,report%20median%20of%20about%20%24650

Secinaro, S., Calandra, D., & Biancone, P. (2021). Blockchain, trust, and trust accounting: Can blockchain technology substitute trust created by intermediaries in trust accounting? A theoretical examination. *International Journal of Management Practice*, *14*(2), 129–145. doi:10.1504/IJMP.2021.113824

Secinaro, S., Dal Mas, F., Brescia, V., & Calandra, D. (2021). Blockchain in the accounting, auditing and accountability fields: A bibliometric and coding analysis. *Accounting, Auditing & Accountability Journal*, *35*(9), 168–203. doi:10.1108/AAAJ-10-2020-4987

Seethamraju, R., & Hecimovic, A. (2023). Adoption of artificial intelligence in auditing: An exploratory study. *Australian Journal of Management*, *48*(4), 780–800. doi:10.1177/03128962221108440

Shaikh, H., Jokhio, M. U., Maher, Z. A., Chandio, S., Manirajah, M., Abdullah, B., ... Shah, A. (2018). Beyond traditional audits: The implications of information technology on auditing. *International Journal of Engineering & Technology*, *7*(2.34), 5-11.

Shankaranarayana, R., Ramaswamy, S., Bagrecha, C., Hiremath, K., & Madhavi, A. (2023). Promoting Economic Sustainability Through the Adoption of Digital Payment Systems. In *The Sustainable Fintech Revolution: Building a Greener Future for Finance* (pp. 145–161). IGI Global. doi:10.4018/979-8-3693-0008-4.ch008

Shao, L., & Chen, J. (2023). Digital finance and regional green innovation: The perspective of environmental regulation. *Environmental Science and Pollution Research International*, *30*(36), 85592–85610. doi:10.1007/s11356-023-28356-5 PMID:37391561

Shapovalova, A., Kuzmenko, O., Polishchuk, O., Larikova, T., & Myronchuk, Z. (2023). Modernization of the national accounting and auditing system using digital transformation tools. *Financial and Credit Activity: Problems of Theory and Practice*, *4*(51). Advance online publication. doi:10.55643/fcaptp.4.51.2023.4102

Shehzad, C. T., De Haan, J., & Scholtens, B. (2010). The impact of bank ownership concentration on impaired loans and capital adequacy. *Journal of Banking & Finance*, *34*(2), 399–408. doi:10.1016/j.jbankfin.2009.08.007

Shen, C. H., Lin, C. Y., & Wang, Y. C. (2015). Do strong corporate governance firms still require political connection, and vice versa? *International Review of Economics & Finance*, *39*, 107–120. doi:10.1016/j.iref.2015.06.006

Shen, Y., Fu, Y., & Song, M. (2023). Digital finance promotes sustainable total factor eco-efficiency: Evidence from China. *Applied Economics*, 1–15. doi:10.1080/00036846.2023.2211337

Shleifer, A., & Vishny, R. W. (1994). Politicians and firms. *The Quarterly Journal of Economics*, *109*(4), 995–1025. doi:10.2307/2118354

Singh, R., Bhatt, V., & Bansal, R. (2023). Accounting in the demesne of big data, data analytics and artificial intelligence in industrial revolution 5.0: Applications, challenges and opportunities. Big Data: A Road-Map for Successful Digital Marketing, 49–63.

Slemrod, J., & Velayudhan, T. (2022). The VAT at 100: A retrospective survey and agenda for future research. *Public Finance Review*, *50*(1), 4–32. doi:10.1177/10911421221094595

Slemrod, J., & Yitzhaki, S. (2002). Tax avoidance, evasion, and administration. In *Handbook of public economics* (Vol. 3, pp. 1423–1470). Elsevier.

Sobb, T., Turnbull, B., & Moustafa, N. (2020). Supply chain 4.0: A survey of cyber security challenges, solutions, and future directions. *Electronics (Basel)*, *9*(11), 1864. Advance online publication. doi:10.3390/electronics9111864

Song, X., & Trimble, M. (2022). The Historical and Current Status of Global IFRS Adoption: Obstacles and Opportunities for Researchers. *The International Journal of Accounting*, *57*(2), 2250. doi:10.1142/S1094406022500019

Soudani, S. N. (2012). The Usefulness of an Accounting Information System for Effective Organizational Performance. *International Journal of Economics and Finance*, *4*(5), 136–145. doi:10.5539/ijef.v4n5p136

Spanò, R., Massaro, M., Ferri, L., Dumay, J., & Schmitz, J. (2022). Blockchain in accounting, accountability and assurance: An overview. *Accounting, Auditing & Accountability Journal*, *35*(7), 1493–1506. doi:10.1108/AAAJ-06-2022-5850

Spilnyk, I., Brukhanskyi, R., & Yaroshchuk, O. (2020). Accounting and Financial Reporting System in the Digital Economy. *2020 10th International Conference on Advanced Computer Information Technologies, ACIT 2020 - Proceedings*. 10.1109/ACIT49673.2020.9208976

Srinath & Swathi. (2022). Trends in Accounting Information System: Opportunities and Challenges in MSMEs. *Journal of Contemporary Issues in Business and Government, 28*(3).

Stalin, D., & Manayseh, M. (2023). Accounting Software Analysis of the Oman Organizations' Accounting Information System. *Shanlax International Journal of Management*, *11*(1), 11–16. doi:10.34293/management.v11i1.6377

Stein, J. C. (2002). Information production and capital allocation: Decentralized versus hierarchical firms. *The Journal of Finance*, *57*(5), 1891–1921. doi:10.1111/0022-1082.00483

Stiroh, K. J. (2004). Diversification in banking: Is noninterest income the answer? *Journal of Money, Credit and Banking*, *36*(5), 853–882. doi:10.1353/mcb.2004.0076

Strohm, L., Hehakaya, C., Ranschaert, E. R., Boon, W. P., & Moors, E. H. (2020). Implementation of artificial intelligence (AI) applications in radiology: Hindering and facilitating factors. *European Radiology*, *30*(10), 5525–5532. doi:10.1007/s00330-020-06946-y PMID:32458173

Su, L. (2023). *Tax Administration Digitization and Corporate Tax Avoidance: A Quasi-Natural Experiment Based on the Golden Tax III Project in China*. Academic Press.

Suchman, L. (2023). The uncontroversial 'thingness' of AI. *Big Data & Society*, *10*(2). doi:10.1177/20539517231206794

Suddaby, R., Saxton, G. D., & Gunz, S. (2015). Twittering change: The institutional work of domain change in accounting expertise. *Accounting, Organizations and Society*, *45*, 52–68. doi:10.1016/j.aos.2015.07.002

Sukoharsono, E. G. (2020). Industrial Revolution 4.0 and the development of accounting information system: An imaginary dialogue. *IACSIT International Journal of Engineering and Technology*, *9*(2), 474–479. www.sciencepubco.com/index.php/IJET

Su, X., Xiao, Y., & Liu, S. (2022, March). Analysis on the Impact of Blockchain Technology on the Accounting Profession. In *7th International Conference on Economy, Management, Law and Education (EMLE 2021)* (pp. 10-14). Atlantis Press. 10.2991/aebmr.k.220306.002

Syed Moudud-Ul-Huq, M. (2020). Role of cloud computing in global accounting information systems. *The Bottom Line (New York, N.Y.)*, *33*(3), 231–250. doi:10.1108/BL-01-2020-0010

Tabrizchi, H., & Kuchaki Rafsanjani, M. (2020). A survey on security challenges in cloud computing: Issues, threats, and solutions. *The Journal of Supercomputing*, *76*(12), 9493–9532. doi:10.1007/s11227-020-03213-1

Taghizadeh-Hesary, F., & Hyun, S. (Eds.). (2022). *Green Digital Finance and Sustainable Development Goals*. Springer Nature. doi:10.1007/978-981-19-2662-4

Taha, A. A. D., Ramo, W., & Alkhaffaf, H. H. K. (2021). Impact of external auditor–cloud specialist engagement on cloud auditing challenges. *Journal of Accounting & Organizational Change*, *17*(3), 309–331. doi:10.1108/JAOC-08-2020-0111

Taherdoost, H. (2023). Smart Contracts in Blockchain Technology: A Critical Review. *Information (Basel)*, *14*(2), 117. doi:10.3390/info14020117

Taipaleenmäki, J., & Ikäheimo, S. (2013). On the convergence of management accounting and financial accounting–the role of information technology in accounting change. *International Journal of Accounting Information Systems*, *14*(4), 321–348. doi:10.1016/j.accinf.2013.09.003

Talwar, S. P. (2001). Competition, consolidation and systemic stability in the Indian banking industry. *BIS Papers*, (4).

Tan, B. S., & Low, K. Y. (2017). Bitcoin–its economics for financial reporting. *Australian Accounting Review*, *27*(2), 220–227. doi:10.1111/auar.12167

Tang, D., Chen, W., Zhang, Q., & Zhang, J. (2023). Impact of Digital Finance on Green Technology Innovation: The Mediating Effect of Financial Constraints. *Sustainability (Basel)*, *15*(4), 3393. doi:10.3390/su15043393

Tapscott, D., & Tapscott, A. (2016). *Blockchain revolution: how the technology behind bitcoin is changing money, business, and the world*. Penguin.

Tapscott, D., & Tapscott, A. (2017). How blockchain will change organizations. *MIT Sloan Management Review*, *58*(2), 10.

Tawiah, V., & Borgi, H. (2022). Impact of XBRL adoption on financial reporting quality: A global evidence. *Accounting Research Journal, 35*(6), 815–833. Advance online publication. doi:10.1108/ARJ-01-2022-0002

Tax Justice Network. (2023). *The state of Tax Justice 2023.* https://taxjustice.net/wp-content/uploads/SOTJ/SOTJ23/English/State%20of%20Tax%20Justice%202023%20-%20Tax%20Justice%20Network%20-%20English.pdf

Tenny, S., Brannan, J. M., & Brannan, G. D. (2017). *Qualitative study*. Academic Press.

Teresa, M., & Matriano, D. G. (2022). *The Impact of Accounting Information on the Managerial Decision Making Process : Case of Oman Integrated Logistics Services Company, SAOG The Impact of Accounting Information on the Managerial Decision Making Process : Case of Oman Integrated Logistics*. Academic Press.

Teru, S. P., Idoku, I., & Ndeyati, J. T. (2017). A Review of the Impact of Accounting Information Systems for Effective Internal Control on Firm Performance. *Indian Journal of Finance and Banking, 1*(2), 52–59. doi:10.46281/ijfb.v1i2.89

Teszner, K. (2020). Country Note : Customs And Fiscal Control In Poland As A Radical Measure To Eliminate Tax Evasion. *Intertax, 48*(10), 922–928. doi:10.54648/TAXI2020090

The General Tax Administration. (2023). *General Tax Code*. https://www.finances.gov.ma/Publication/dgi/2023/CGI2023FR.pdf

The International Electrotechnical Commission (IEC). (n.d.). In *Wikipedia*. Retrieved February 12, 2024, from https://en.wikipedia.org/wiki/International_Electrotechnical_Commission

Tiantian, G., Hailin, C., Zhou, X., Ai, S., & Siyao, W. (2023). Does corporate digital transformation affect the level of corporate tax avoidance? Empirical evidence from Chinese listed tourism companies. *Finance Research Letters, 57*, 104271. doi:10.1016/j.frl.2023.104271

Tiron-Tudor, A., Deliu, D., Farcane, N., & Dontu, A. (2021). Managing change with and through blockchain in accountancy organizations: A systematic literature review. *Journal of Organizational Change Management, 34*(2), 477–506. doi:10.1108/JOCM-10-2020-0302

Tolzmann, M. (2022). *CGAP Funder Survey 2020*. World Bank. Retrieved from https://www.cgap.org/sites/default/files/publications/2022_01_Focus_Note_2020_Funder_Survey.pdf

Troshani, I., Locke, J., & Rowbottom, N. (2018). Transformation of accounting through digital standardization: Tracing the construction of the IFRS Taxonomy. *Accounting, Auditing & Accountability Journal*. Advance online publication. doi:10.1108/AAAJ-11-2016-2794

Tsakumis, G. T., Curatola, A. P., & Porcano, T. M. (2007). The relation between national cultural dimensions and tax evasion. *Journal of International Accounting, Auditing & Taxation, 16*(2), 131–147. doi:10.1016/j.intaccaudtax.2007.06.004

Tu, J. J., & Akhter, S. (2023). Exploring the role of entrepreneurial education, technology and teachers' creativity in excelling sustainable business competencies. *Ekonomska Istrazivanja*, *36*(1), 2119429. doi:10.1080/1331677X.2022.2119429

Tuyon, J., Onyia, O. P., Ahmi, A., & Huang, C. H. (2023). Sustainable financial services: Reflection and future perspectives. *Journal of Financial Services Marketing*, *28*(4), 664–690. doi:10.1057/s41264-022-00187-4

Uchendu, B., Nurse, J. R., Bada, M., & Furnell, S. (2021, October). Developing a cyber security culture: Current practices and future needs. *Computers & Security*, *109*, 102387. doi:10.1016/j.cose.2021.102387

Uhde, A., & Heimeshoff, U. (2009). Consolidation in banking and financial stability in Europe: Empirical evidence. *Journal of Banking & Finance*, *33*(7), 1299–1311. doi:10.1016/j.jbankfin.2009.01.006

UNEP. (2011). *Towards a Green Economy: Pathways to Sustainable Development and Poverty Eradication*. United Nations Environment Programme.

UNFCCC. (2015). *United Nations framework convention on climate change: The Paris Agreement*. Retrieved from https://unfccc.int/process-and-meetings/the-paris-agreement/the-paris-agreement

Unicorn. (2018). *Can blockchain truly disrupt the accounting industry?* https://blockchain.wtf/2018/08/industry-impacts/finance/accounting/

Ursillo, S., & Arnold, C. (2019). *Cybersecurity Is Critical for all Organizations – Large and Small*. Retrieved from https://www.ifac.org/knowledge-gateway/preparing-future-ready-professionals/discussion/cybersecurity-critical-all-organizations-large-and-small

Uyar, A., Nimer, K., Kuzey, C., Shahbaz, M., & Schneider, F. (2021). Can e-government initiatives alleviate tax evasion? The moderation effect of ICT. *Technological Forecasting and Social Change*, *166*, 120597. doi:10.1016/j.techfore.2021.120597

Üyümez, M. E., & Hacıköylü, C. (Eds.). (2023). *Current debates on public finance : Theory and practice*. Peter Lang. doi:10.3726/b20820

Valkenburg, B., & Bongiovanni, I. (2024). Unravelling the three lines model in cybersecurity: A systematic literature review. *Computers & Security*, *139*, 103708. doi:10.1016/j.cose.2024.103708

Van de Wetering, R., Milakef, P., & Dennehy, D. (2022). Artificial Intelligence Ambidexterity, Adaptive Transformation Capability, and Their Impact on Performance Under Tumultuous Times. In The Role of Digital Technologies in Shaping the Post-Pandemic World (pp. 25–37). Springer International Publishing.

Vasarhelyi, M. A., Kogan, A., & Tuttle, B. M. (2015). Big data in accounting: An overview. *Accounting Horizons*, *29*(2), 381–396. doi:10.2308/acch-51071

Vazquez, F., & Federico, P. (2015). Bank funding structures and risk: Evidence from the global financial crisis. *Journal of Banking & Finance*, *61*, 1–14. doi:10.1016/j.jbankfin.2015.08.023

Verdier, M. G., Rayner, B., Muthoora, M. P. S., Vellutini, C., Zhu, L., Koukpaizan, V. de P., Marahel, A., Harb, M., Benmohamed, I., Hebous, M. S., Okello, A., Reyes, N., Benninger, T., & Sanya, B. (2022). *Mobilisation des recettes pour une reprise résiliente et inclusive au Moyen-Orient et en Asie centrale : Executive Summary*. International Monetary Fund. doi:10.5089/9798400215346.087

Vial, G. (2019). Understanding digital transformation: A review and a research agenda. *The Journal of Strategic Information Systems*, *28*(2), 118–144. doi:10.1016/j.jsis.2019.01.003

Vigna, P., & Casey, M. J. (2019). *The truth machine: the blockchain and the future of everything*. Picador.

Vikas, N., Venegas, P., & Aiyer, S. (2022). Role of Banks and Other Financial Institutions in Enhancing Green Digital Finance. In *Green Digital Finance and Sustainable Development Goals* (pp. 329–352). Springer Nature Singapore. doi:10.1007/978-981-19-2662-4_16

Vishnevsky, V. P., & Chekina, V. D. (2018). Robot vs. tax inspector or how the fourth industrial revolution will change the tax system : A review of problems and solutions. *Journal of Tax Reform*, *4*(1), 6–26. doi:10.15826/jtr.2018.4.1.042

Vitale, G., Cupertino, S., & Riccaboni, A. (2020). Big data and management control systems change: The case of an agricultural SME. *Journal of Management Control*, *31*(1-2), 123–152. doi:10.1007/s00187-020-00298-w

Vlahovic, N. (2023). E-Accounting System as a Service (E-ASaaS): A Conceptual Overview. *2023 46th ICT and Electronics Convention, MIPRO 2023 - Proceedings*. 10.23919/MIPRO57284.2023.10159833

Vysochan, O. S., Hyk, V., Mykytyuk, N., & Vysochan, O. O. (2023). Taxonomy of Financial Reporting in the Context of Digitalization of the Economy: Domestic and International Analysis Scientific Research. *Studia Universitatis Vasile Goldis Arad. Economics Series*, *33*(2), 49–70. Advance online publication. doi:10.2478/sues-2023-0008

Wahab, R., & Bakar, A. (2021). Digital economy tax compliance model in malaysia using machine learning approach. *Sains Malaysiana*, *50*(7), 2059–2077. doi:10.17576/jsm-2021-5007-20

Wang, Q., Sun, T., & Li, R. (2024). Does artificial intelligence promote green innovation? An assessment based on direct, indirect, spillover, and heterogeneity effects. *Energy & Environment*.

Wang, J., Wei, B., Zhang, J., Yu, X., & Sharma, P. K. (2021). An optimized transaction verification method for trustworthy blockchain-enabled IIoT. *Ad Hoc Networks*, *119*, 102526. Advance online publication. doi:10.1016/j.adhoc.2021.102526

Wang, M., Song, W., & Qi, X. (2023). Digital inclusive finance, government intervention, and urban green technology innovation. *Environmental Science and Pollution Research International*, (October), 1–14. doi:10.1007/s11356-023-29395-8 PMID:37848800

Wang, Y., & Kogan, A. (2018). Designing confidentiality-preserving Blockchain-based transaction processing systems. *International Journal of Accounting Information Systems*, *30*, 1–18. doi:10.1016/j.accinf.2018.06.001

Warren, D., Peytcheva, M., & Gaspar, J. (2015). When ethical tones are at the top of conflict: Adapting priority rules to reconcile conflicting tones. *Business Ethics Quarterly*, *25*(4), 559582. doi:10.1017/beq.2015.40

Whidbee, D. A. (1997). Board composition and control of shareholder voting rights in the banking industry. *Financial Management*, *26*(4), 27–41. doi:10.2307/3666125

Wolf, M., & Dale, S. (2019). Les technologies numériques au service de l'administration de l'impôt. *ERA Forum*, *19*(3), 457-464. 10.1007/s12027-018-0540-5

Wong, C. W., Lai, K., Shang, K.-C., Lu, C.-S., & Leung, T. (2012). Green operations and the moderating role of environmental management capability of suppliers on manufacturing firm performance. *International Journal of Production Economics*, *140*(1), 283–294. doi:10.1016/j.ijpe.2011.08.031

Wulandari, S. S., & Ali, S. (2019). Incorporating XBRL topics into the accounting curriculum: Empirical evidence from Indonesia. *Accounting Education*, *28*(6), 597–620. Advance online publication. doi:10.1080/09639284.2019.1679205

XBRL. (2023). *Oman launches Bayanat data portal | XBRL*. https://www.xbrl.org/news/oman-launches-bayanat-data-portal/#

Xiao, M., & Peng, X. (2023). Decomposition of carbon emission influencing factors and research on emission reduction performance of energy consumption in China. *Frontiers in Environmental Science*, *10*, 1096650. doi:10.3389/fenvs.2022.1096650

Xuan, S., Ge, W., Yang, P., & Zhang, Y. (2024). Exploring digital finance, financial regulations and carbon emission nexus: New insight from resources efficiency, industrial structure and green innovation in China. *Resources Policy*, *88*, 104452. doi:10.1016/j.resourpol.2023.104452

Xue, L., & Zhang, X. (2022). Can digital financial inclusion promote green innovation in heavily polluting companies? *International Journal of Environmental Research and Public Health*, *19*(12), 7323. doi:10.3390/ijerph19127323 PMID:35742571

Xun, Z., Guanghua, W., Jiajia, Z., & Zongyue, H. (2020). Digital economy, financial inclusion and inclusive growth. *Chinese Economy*, *15*(3), 92–105.

Xu, R., Yao, D., & Zhou, M. (2023). Does the development of digital inclusive finance improve the enthusiasm and quality of corporate green technology innovation? *Journal of Innovation & Knowledge*, *8*(3), 100382. doi:10.1016/j.jik.2023.100382

Xu, Y., Li, S., Zhou, X., Shahzad, U., & Zhao, X. (2022). How environmental regulations affect the development of green finance: Recent evidence from polluting firms in China. *Renewable Energy*, *189*, 917–926. doi:10.1016/j.renene.2022.03.020

Yang, D. C., & Vasarhelyi, M. A. (1995). The Application of Expert Systems in Accounting. *Unpublished Working Paper*.

Yang, C., & Masron, T. A. (2022). Impact of digital finance on energy efficiency in the context of green sustainable development. *Sustainability (Basel)*, *14*(18), 11250. doi:10.3390/su141811250

Yang, G., Wang, F., Deng, F., & Xiang, X. (2023). Impact of digital transformation on enterprise carbon intensity: The Moderating Role of Digital Information Resources. *International Journal of Environmental Research and Public Health*, *20*(3), 2178. doi:10.3390/ijerph20032178 PMID:36767545

Yannakogeorgos, P. (2021). Cyber Competition and Global Stability. In C. Ankersen & W. P. S. Sidhu (Eds.), *The Future of Global Affairs*. Palgrave Macmillan. doi:10.1007/978-3-030-56470-4_10

Yan, Y., Ibrahim, R. L., Al-Faryan, M. A. S., & Oke, D. M. (2023). Embracing Eco-Digitalization and Green Finance Policies for Sustainable Environment: Do the Engagements of Multinational Corporations Make or Mar the Target for Selected MENA Countries? *Sustainability (Basel)*, *15*(15), 12046. doi:10.3390/su151512046

Yermack, D. (2017). Corporate governance and blockchains. *Review of Finance*, *21*(1), 7–31.

Yigitcanlar, T., Mehmood, R., & Corchado, J. M. (2021). Green artificial intelligence: Towards an efficient, sustainable and equitable technology for smart cities and futures. *Sustainability (Basel)*, *13*(16), 8952. doi:10.3390/su13168952

Yılmaz, F., & Coolidge, J. (2013). *Can E-Filing Reduce Tax Compliance Costs in Developing Countries?* The World Bank. doi:10.1596/1813-9450-6647

Yilmaz, N. K., & Hazar, H. B. (2019). The rise of internet of things (IoT) and its applications in finance and accounting. *Press Academia Procedia*, *10*(1), 32–35. doi:10.17261/Pressacademia.2019.1139

YooY.LyytinenK. J.BolandR. J.BerenteN. (2010). *The next wave of digital innovation: Opportunities and challenges*. doi:10.2139/ssrn.1622170

Yuan, H., Cen, W., & Du, T. (2023). Digital Finance and County Ecological Performance—New Evidence from China Counties. *Sustainability (Basel)*, *15*(24), 16691. doi:10.3390/su152416691

Yuji, I. (1982). *Triple-Entry Bookkeeping and Income Momentum*. American Accounting Association.

Yu, T., Lin, Z., & Tang, Q. (2018). Blockchain: The introduction and its application in financial accounting. *Journal of Corporate Accounting & Finance*, *29*(4), 37–47. doi:10.1002/jcaf.22365

Zemankova, A. (2019). Artificial intelligence and blockchain in audit and accounting: Literature review. *WSEAS Transactions on Business and Economics, 16*(1), 568-581.

Zemánková, A. (2019). Artificial Intelligence and Blockchain in Audit and Accounting: Literature Review. *WSEAS Transactions on Business and Economics, 16*, 568-581. https://www.wseas.org/multimedia/journals/economics/2019/b245107-089.pdf

Zhang, C. A., Cho, S., & Vasarhelyi, M. (2022). Explainable artificial intelligence (xai) in auditing. *International Journal of Accounting Information Systems*, *46*, 100572. doi:10.1016/j.accinf.2022.100572

Zhang, D. (2023a). Can digital finance empowerment reduce extreme ESG hypocrisy resistance to improve green innovation? *Energy Economics*, *125*(September), 106756. doi:10.1016/j.eneco.2023.106756

Zhang, G. (2012). Determinants of Financial Restatements in the Listed Companies in China. *Data Mining and Knowledge Discovery*, 725–730.

Zhang, J. C., Yao, W., Dong, C., Yang, C., Ren, Q., Ma, M., Han, M., & Hashimoto, K. (2015). Comparison of ketamine, 7, 8-dihydroxyflavone, and ANA-12 antidepressant effects in the social defeat stress model of depression. *Psychopharmacology*, *232*(23), 4325–4335. doi:10.1007/s00213-015-4062-3 PMID:26337614

Zhang, T., Morris, N. P., McNiel, D. E., & Binder, R. (2023). Elder Financial Exploitation in the Digital Age. *The Journal of the American Academy of Psychiatry and the Law*, *51*(2), 173–180. doi:10.29158/jaapl.220047-21 PMID:36928135

Zhang, X., Li, J., Xiang, D., & Worthington, A. C. (2023). Digitalization, financial inclusion, and small and medium-sized enterprise financing: Evidence from China. *Economic Modelling*, *126*, 106410. doi:10.1016/j.econmod.2023.106410

Zhang, Y., Xiong, F., Xie, Y., Fan, X., & Gu, H. (2020). The Impact of Artificial Intelligence and Blockchain on the Accounting Profession. *IEEE Access : Practical Innovations, Open Solutions*, *8*, 110461–110477. doi:10.1109/ACCESS.2020.3000505

Zheng, C., Moudud-Ul-Huq, S., Rahman, M. M., & Ashraf, B. N. (2017). Does the ownership structure matter for banks' capital regulation and risk-taking behavior? Empirical evidence from a developing country. *Research in International Business and Finance*, *42*, 404–421. doi:10.1016/j.ribaf.2017.07.035

Zheng, W., Lai, C. F., He, D., Kumar, N., & Chen, B. (2020). Secure storage auditing with efficient key updates for cognitive industrial IoT environment. *IEEE Transactions on Industrial Informatics*, *17*(6), 4238–4247. doi:10.1109/TII.2020.2991204

Zheng, Z., Xie, S., Dai, H., Chen, X., & Wang, H. (2017, June). *An overview of blockchain technology: Architecture, consensus, and future trends. In 2017 IEEE international congress on big data (BigData congress).* IEEE.

Zhou, G., Zhu, J., & Luo, S. (2022). The impact of fintech innovation on green growth in China: Mediating effect of green finance. *Ecological Economics*, *193*, 107308. doi:10.1016/j.ecolecon.2021.107308

Zhou, S., Zhou, P., & Ji, H. (2022). Can digital transformation alleviate corporate tax stickiness: The mediation effect of tax avoidance. *Technological Forecasting and Social Change*, *184*, 122028. doi:10.1016/j.techfore.2022.122028

Zhou, Y. (2022). The application trend of digital finance and technological innovation in the development of green economy. *Journal of Environmental and Public Health*, *2022*, 2022. doi:10.1155/2022/1064558 PMID:35865872

Zhutiaeva, S. A. (2021). *Digitalization Of Tax Control In The Russian Federation : Analysis And Trends*. doi:10.15405/epsbs.2021.03.56

About the Contributors

Ahmad Alqatan is currently an Assistant Professor at Arab Open University and former Assistant of the Dean of the Faculty of Business and Law. Dr Ahmad has published 20-refereed papers in academic journals, three chapters and one book. In addition, he organised a member of committees, a discussant, and a presenter at more than 58 international conferences. His principal research area is concerned with corporate governance, diversity earnings management, and firm performance. He has been awarded several times, such as the prestigious 2019 Best Paper Award of the honour issuer Financial Economics Meeting: Post-crisis challenge conference and the prestigious 2019, Best poster Award of the 15th Research and Innovation Conference, Most viewed paper award (2019). Also, Dr Ahmad got the title "The Pride of Kuwait" from Youth Public Authority in 2019. In addition, Alqatan got the fifth rank for the accounting research award in Kuwait (2021). Alqatan is a Co-Editor-in-Chief of eight international journals. Also, he got a Professional Internation Certificate of CertIFR, Certificate in International Financial Reporting Standards, ACCA, UK. (2021), Professional Internation Certificate of CertIA, Certificate in International Auditing, ACCA, UK (2022), Professional Internation Certificate of CertIPSAS, Certificate in International Public Sector Accounting Standards, ACCA, UK (2022) and the status of Fellow (FHEA), UK.

* * *

Dana Abeuova is an Assistant Professor of Management at KIMEP University. She received her Ph.D. in Management from ESCP Business School, as part of the École Doctorale de Management Panthéon-Sorbonne, France; M.S. in Information Systems from Kelley School of Business, Indiana University Bloomington, USA; B.S. in Informatics from School of Informatics, Indiana University Bloomington, USA. Her teaching experience includes lecturing at Kazakh-British Technical University in Kazakhstan and at ESCP Europe Business School in France. Her research interests lie in the areas of talent management, new venture development and sustainability.

Muhammad Arslan is a faculty member at the Open Polytechnic of New Zealand (Te Pukenga). He holds a Ph.D. degree from Lincoln University, New Zealand, with a focus on accounting and finance. He is a full member of CPA Australia and holds the designation of Certified Practising Accountant (CPA). Arslan is the recipient of the Dean's Award for his PhD thesis from Lincoln University, New Zealand, and has also received two Emerald Literati Awards for "Highly Commended Paper".He has completed the New Zealand Certificate in Adult and Tertiary Teaching (NZCATT) for further development of his pedagogical skills. His international reputation in research is demonstrated by 30 publications (18 Scopus-indexed publications (12 Web of Science (WoS), including three papers in Q1, five papers in Q2, and five papers in Q3), three chapters (two Scopus-indexed), and eight international conferences such as Academy of Management (AOM), International Conference of the Journal of International Accounting Research, Annual New Zealand Finance Colloquium, ICGS Conference among others. He is an academic editor at PLOS One, SCIE indexed journal. He is also serving as an Associate Editor of the International Journal of Business and Management (ISSN: 2815-9330), reviews funding applications, and research articles for leading journals in his field. His status as an internationally established expert and the cumulative impact of his work is further reflected in an overall h-index of 15 and i-index of 18 (Google Scholar). His papers have received 700+ citations (Google). He is an efficient, well-organised, and responsible scholar who knows how to make things happen. He has already supervised several master's and PhD students. He is open to research collaborations, funding opportunities, and student supervision.

El Houssan Attak holds a PhD in Business Administration from Aix-Marseille University and a Master's degree in Research from the University Paris-Panthéon-Assas. He is an academic and researcher specializing in the field of taxation. Currently a Taxation Professor at The National School of Business and Management - Cadi Ayyad University, Marrakesh, Dr. Attak's research centers around investigating the intricate interplay between taxation and economic activities. With more than a decade of experience, he conducts thorough analyses of tax policies and their potential impact on various industries and sectors.

Mohamed Ali Bejjar is a Prof at Higher business school of Sfax. PhD thesis, University of Sfax in Financial methods and Accounting. Holder of Master in "Strategy and Information System" from the Faculty of Economics and Management of Sfax. Holder of Master in "Accounting and Information System" from the Higher Institute of Management of Tunis. "Member of the Research Unit of URECA FSEG Sfax.

Rida Belahouaoui is a PhD Researcher specializing in digital taxation, tax compliance, and tax avoidance at Cadi Ayyad University. He has established himself as an expert in the field of taxation with a keen focus on compliance and avoidance strategies. His academic endeavors are directed towards unraveling the complexities of tax legislation and the mechanisms to curb tax avoidance.

Vyomkesh Bhatt is currently working as an Assistant Professor at the Department of Management Studies, G L Bajaj Institute of Technology and Management. He was prior positioned as Assistant Professor at the Faculty of Management Studies at Gurukula Kangri (Deemed to be University). He has also held position as Associate Managing Editor of the Gurukul Business Review and as Editor of the Manthan-Bi Annual Newsletter of FMS. Mr. Bhatt is a scholar at Quantum University, where he is pursuing a Ph.D. (Business Administration and Management) in the field of banking, and he holds a Master of Commerce (Finance and Marketing) degree from DAV College, Dehradun (affiliated to H.N.B. Garwhal Central University). At Uttaranchal University, he earned a Bachelor of Commerce (Honors) with a specialization in Financial Management. He has published research papers in peer-reviewed, refereed international journals and book chapters on the contemporary topics pertaining to finance, accountancy and entrepreneurship. He has also authored International Business- New Paradigms, Entrepreneurship Development- An Admeasurement, Industry Jargons - A Quick Reference into Industry Analysis for Future Analysts and co-edited book on Changing Role of Financial Markets in Indian Economy.

Alimshan Faizulayev, a Ph.D. graduate in finance from Eastern Mediterranean University, is currently working as a Research Director and Associate Professor at Bang College of Business, Kimep University in Kazakhstan. With over 12 years of teaching experience and 5 years in the finance industry, he brings a wealth of knowledge and expertise to his role. Alimshan's research interests span corporate finance, conventional and Islamic banking, energy economics, and green finance. In his capacity as Research Director, he continues to contribute significantly to both academia and the industry, fostering a dynamic environment for research and innovation at Bang College of Business.

Laksitha M. Herath earned her Master of Science in Accounting degree at New York University's Stern School of Business and plans to join PricewaterhouseCoopers (PwC). Prior to her current endeavor, she gained valuable experience as a program accountant at Enstar Group Limited, a well-known global insurance company and at Deloitte in Atlanta and New York. Laksitha holds a Bachelor of Arts degree in Accounting from Clark Atlanta University, where she and her team won the Deloitte Regional Case Study Competition and held executive positions in its Toastmasters

Club. She also published two book chapters and an article in a reputable journal. In her leisure time, she enjoys photography, cooking, and quality time with her family and friends.

Siriyama Kanthi Herath is an Associate Professor of Accounting at Clark Atlanta University's School of Business (CAU). She earned a B.Com (Hons) and an MBA from the University of Colombo in Sri Lanka, as well as a Ph.D. and an M.Com (Hons) in Accounting from the University of Wollongong in New South Wales, Australia. She was a Visiting Associate Professor at the University of Lynchburg before coming to CAU. She has worked at Georgia State University, and Georgia Institute of Technology, among other places. Dr. Herath worked in Australia at the University of Wollongong and Western Sydney University before relocating to the United States. She has also worked in Sri Lanka at the University of Ruhuna and the University of Colombo. Accounting Education, Management Control and Outsourcing, Cost Management, Corporate Governance, and Environmental Accounting are among Dr. Herath's research papers. She has been a member of the editorial boards of several academic journals and has published in a variety of journals. She was a Toastmasters Area Director in 2020-2021 and the President of the Georgia Institute of Technology Toastmasters Club (Techmasters) in 2019-2020. In 2020, she was awarded the Distinguished Toastmaster (DTM) title. In 2021, Dr. Herath got the Google Data Analytics Professional Certificate. She is a Renwick Faculty Fellow at New York University's Stern School of Business. She enjoys traveling and gardening.

Umar Kayani is currently working as an Assistant Professor at Al Ain University, United Arab Emirates. He is a versatile academic with over 10 years of teaching, administrative and regulatory experience for tertiary programs (undergraduate and postgraduate). He graduated from Lincoln University, New Zealand with a Ph.D. in Accounting and Finance. Recently, he completed his post-Doctoral fellowship from the Lincoln University, New Zealand. He was awarded Lincoln University Doctoral Scholarship and Lincoln University Summer Research Scholarship. He has published refereed articles in leading international accounting and finance journals. He is a reviewer for several international journals and served as conference chair for multiple international conferences. He has presented his research work at various international conferences; he won the outstanding paper award at 17th Global Business Research Conference, Tokyo, Japan. He has supervised a number of research students. Besides academia, he also worked as Quality Assurance and Accreditation Expert for more than 10 years at the Higher Education Commission of Pakistan (HEC). HEC is a regulatory body for the higher educational institutions of Pakistan, with core functionalities involve fundings to universities, oversee, regulate, and accredit the higher educational institutions of Pakistan.

Kaushikkumar Patel is a distinguished leader in harnessing data-driven strategies within the financial sector, boasting an extensive career that intersects finance and technology. He is pivotal at TransUnion, where he innovates through Big Data, enhancing decision-making processes and financial strategies. His profound knowledge extends to Data Analytics, Financial Technology (FinTech), and Digital Transformation, contributing significantly to advancing tech integration in finance. Based in the United States, Mr. Patel is renowned for his strategic oversight in developing solutions that navigate the complex challenges of data privacy and risk assessment, ensuring compliance and governance in dynamic financial landscapes. His insights have fortified business intelligence, utilizing machine learning and cloud computing solutions to drive organizational success. An influential thought leader, Mr. Patel has shared his expertise and vision through various high-impact publications, shedding light on the transformative power of data in finance. His commitment to excellence was internationally recognized when he was honored with the ET Leadership Excellence Award for his groundbreaking work in Data-Driven Financial Strategies. Mr. Patel's dedication transcends his immediate professional sphere, having a lasting impact on societal well-being. He actively engages in CSR initiatives, leveraging technology to enhance lives and contribute to sustainable development. His unique blend of technical prowess and strategic acumen establishes him as a visionary in his field, continually pushing the boundaries of what's possible at the intersection of finance and technology.

Manjari Sharma is an accomplished academic with over 15 years of international teaching experience. She has a profound understanding of finance, underscored by her completion of two master's degree programs and a PhD in finance. Dr. Sharma is a prolific writer and researcher, contributing extensively to her field through numerous research papers, book chapters, and books.

Ram Singh is a new-age innovative educator working at the MM Institute of Management Maharishi Markandeshwar (Deemed to be University) Mullana-Ambala, Haryana. Dr. Singh has vast teaching and research experience spanning more than 14 years in teaching, research, and administration. Being a researcher, Dr. Singh holds multifarious positions in the field of academics, for instance, he is a member of the Editorial Board of various reputed journals in the domain of accounting, finance, and general management and a reviewer in IGI Global and Inderscience journals. Besides, Dr. Singh has also been awarded the 'Excellent Reviewer Award-2020' by Bilingual Publishing Company Singapore, 'Best Doctoral Thesis Award-2022' by the International Association of Research & Developed Organisation, Ghaziabad, India, and 'National Elite Teacher Award-2022' by the International Institute of Organised Research (I2OR), Chennai. Currently, his professional affiliation includes being a member of four national and international academic organizations: a Life Member of the Indian Commerce Association (ICA), and a Life Member of the International Association of Academic plus Corporate Society (IAACS).

Vikas Tripathi is Professor and Head of Department of Management Studies, GL Bajaj Institute of Technology and Management, Greater Noida.

Jae Koo Yoo is an instructor in the Department of Decision Sciences Supply Chain Management at Clark Atlanta University. He received his MBA from Clark Atlanta University. He certified SAP Business Associated in SAP ERP 6.0 EHP5 (TERP 10), SAP Certified Business Associate – BPI with SAP S/4 HANA, and ERPSim level 2. His research interests include Business Intelligence, Data Mining, Business Warehouse, Business Objects, and Business Analysis.

Afshan Younas is an Assistant Professor in the Faculty of Business Studies at Arab Open University, Sultanate of Oman. Her research focuses on Accounting, Finance, Corporate governance, corporate social responsibility, and Economics. She has published several research papers in referred journals and is currently involved in developing a CSR Index research grant through MOHERI. Additionally, she has served as an editor, reviewer, and advisory member for various conferences and journals.

Index

A

B

C

D

E

F

G

I

L

O

R

S

T

X

www.ingramcontent.com/pod-product-compliance
Lightning Source LLC
LaVergne TN
LVHW081348300926
849161LV00008B/2099